The Soviet Pharmaceutical Business During Its First Two Decades (1917–1937)

american
university
studies

Series IX
History

Vol. 202

PETER LANG
New York • Washington, D.C./Baltimore • Bern
Frankfurt am Main • Berlin • Brussels • Vienna • Oxford

Mary Schaeffer Conroy

The Soviet Pharmaceutical Business During Its First Two Decades (1917–1937)

PETER LANG
New York • Washington, D.C./Baltimore • Bern
Frankfurt am Main • Berlin • Brussels • Vienna • Oxford

Library of Congress Cataloging-in-Publication Data

Conroy, Mary Schaeffer.
The Soviet pharmaceutical business during its first two decades
(1917–1937) / Mary Schaeffer Conroy.
p. cm. — (American university studies. Series IX, History; v. 202)
Includes bibliographical references and index.
1. Pharmaceutical industry—Soviet Union—History.
I. Title. II. Series.
HD9671.A3S68 338.4'76151'094709041—dc22 2005010681
ISBN 0-8204-7899-7
ISSN 0740-0462

Bibliographic information published by **Die Deutsche Bibliothek**.
Die Deutsche Bibliothek lists this publication in the "Deutsche
Nationalbibliografie"; detailed bibliographic data is available
on the Internet at http://dnb.ddb.de/.

The paper in this book meets the guidelines for permanence and durability
of the Committee on Production Guidelines for Book Longevity
of the Council of Library Resources.

275 Seventh Avenue, 28th Floor, New York, NY 10001
www.peterlangusa.com

Printed in the United States of America

This study is dedicated to the memory of those who lost their pharmacies, drug stores and pharmaceutical factories when the Bolsheviks took over, citizens and health-care personnel who suffered because of this, and the new managers of Soviet pharmaceutical businesses and institutes who tried to make the system work.

Table of Contents

Acknowledgements

I wish to thank the following: Ludmilla Gennad'evna Kiseleva, one of the excellent and sympathetic archivists at GARF, Berezhkovskaia naberezhnaia in Moscow; Viktor Matveevich Salo, historian of Russian/Soviet Pharmacy and former Director of the Pharmacy Museum in Moscow, whose expertise I have valued over twenty years and his wife, Lydia Petrovna, whose hospitality was so gracious during my many visits to Moscow; Dr. El'vira Yershova, dear colleague and friend, who located the material on the purge of I. I. Levinshtein in GARF, Pirovskaia ulitsa; "Sasha," the archivist-in-training at RGAE, who helped me find important documents; Dr. Rustem Khaziev, who assisted my research in the State Archive of Bashkortostan, Ufa, his wife Marina, sister-in-law Larisa, and mother-in-law Maria Sergeevna, who was not only an elegant hostess but very knowledgeable about Stolypin's peasants in Siberia; Dr. Tat'iana Robakidze, Chief of Akrikhin's Foreign Relations Department, Dr. V. K. Afanas'ev, historian at Akrikhin, and the other helpful people at the Akrikhin Pharmaceutical Company, Staria Kupavna, who generously shared the history of the company and its new, internationally competitive facilities; Dr. Michael Kaser, senior specialist on Soviet medical history, who offered enthusiastic encouragement about the topic of Soviet pharmacy and the pharmaceutical industry; IREX (The International Research and Exchanges Board), who provided some funding for my many trips to Russia; Dr. Gregory Higby, Dr. Elaine C. Stroud and other helpful individuals at the American Institute of the History of Pharmacy; Dr. Rita Benischek, historian of Pharmacy from Tulsa, who spurred me on; Dr. Geraldine Kelly; Professor George Yaney, who read the manuscript and offered suggestions—deviations and mistakes are mine alone; DiAnne Hughes at ADM (formerly Moorman Manufacturing) in Quincy Illinois, who provided helpful information about Santonin; and above all my husband Tom, without whose unflagging help and support, at the expense of his own international business, this book could not have been written.

Spelling Conventions for Pharmaceuticals Cited

The Russian names of raw materials and finished pharmaceuticals were idosyncratic. I have attempted to make them conform to Western names where possible or to cite Western and Soviet names simultaneously if the Soviet products were clones of Western trade-marked or proprietary and patented products. When referring to Soviet products or to raw materials and products where I could find no Western equivalents I have used the names found in the Russian-language documents.

Introduction

It is generally believed that, despite the trauma of collectivization, the horrors of the Gulag, and an economy that lagged behind the West and finally imploded in the 1980s, the Soviet Union could unequivocally boast of three achievements—free or relatively low cost, excellent health care for all; high level, universal education; and victory over Nazi Germany in World War II. But if health care was stellar, then the pharmaceutical industry must have been stellar also, for without medicines physicians can only diagnose, but not treat and cure; without soap and disinfectants infectious diseases run rampant; preventive medicine is impossible without sufficient vaccines.

When we traveled to the Soviet Union as exchange students and scholars from the 1960s through the early 1990s, however, we noted a dearth of basic pharmaceuticals. Public toilets were filthy and lacked soap and toilet paper. Lack of detergent apparently accounted for dishes and utensils in factory *stolovie* and even in the cafeteria of the Lenin Library being encrusted with the remnants of former meals. Soviet acquaintances asked us to bring them cardiac medications, asthma preparations, insulin, and even aspirin. *Apteki* (pharmacies) did not purvey feminine hygiene products, abortion was the normal form of birth control, and baby diapers and sometimes formula were non-existent. Soviet physicians had developed the Lazarev treatment for stretching bones and the radial keratotomy procedure for near-sightedness, but hospital equipment was outmoded and routine procedures like tonsillectomies and tooth extractions were performed without anesthesia in the 1970s. In Moscow in the 1980s pharmacists found it necessary to substitute for deficit ingredients when filling prescriptions and patients purchased medicine *po blatu* (under the table). Prominent individuals died of misguided asthma treatment.[1] As late as the second half of the 1990s, Clinic No. 1 in St. Petersburg was shabby and patients brought their own receptacles to the clinic pharmacy to receive medications. Although Russian colleagues enjoyed hydrotherapy cures at pre-revolutionary spas, they normally treated themselves with home-made nostrums and poultices.

Obviously, there was a disconnect between the trumpeted level of Soviet health care and the amount and quality of Soviet pharmaceuticals available. When I queried Soviet pharmacists as to the reasons for this situation, they invariably claimed that, first, the Soviet Union had inherited a backward pharmaceutical system and, secondly, strides made after the Great October Revolution had been dashed by the Great Patriotic War of 1941 to 1945.[2]

The latter explanation became increasingly unsatisfying as this cataclysmic event receded thirty and then forty years. Moreover, accounts of Soviet health care point to deficits of pharmaceuticals in the 1930s and on the eve of the war. During their 1932 tour of the Soviet Union, for example, Sir Arthur Newsholme and John Adams Kingsbury were impressed with urban medical facilities but criticized rural ones. And although they admired dispensing in one pharmacy in a *sovkhoz* (state farm) in Georgia they also noted that "[S]elf medication, except with herbs and the like, is likely to be exceptional in the U.S.S.R. Drugs are almost fabulously dear and scarce."[3] Four years later, Haden Guest enthused that "prescriptions [are] given as in Great Britain, and numerous chemists' shops dot the city [of Moscow] which any visitor may see for himself how busy they are."[4] But Johns Hopkins professor Henry Sigerist, in the Soviet Union to promote socialized medicine in 1936 and impressed with many medical facilities, nevertheless remarked that pharmaceutical production was "still insufficient and, as a result, drugs are relatively expensive. Patients in hospitals and those suffering from communicable diseases as malaria and syphilis receive drugs free of charge. Other patients have to pay for medicines and, as the price is high, it often happens that they do not purchase the drugs prescribed."[5]

Soviet pharmacy specialists themselves lamented the dearth and poor quality of pharmaceuticals. For example, in 1934 the journal *Chemical-Pharmaceutical Industry* referred to a chronic shortage (*golod*) of medicaments, claiming that "the most important preparations" were "absent from pharmacies."[6] The old Bolshevik Izrail I. Levinshtein lambasted the "Abnormal Situation in the Pharmacy Business" in his article published in the same year.[7] Ordinary citizens recalled periodical shortages of commonplace remedies in the 1934. This was six years before the Great Patriotic War broke out. On the very eve of the cataclysm there still were shortages of basic pharmaceuticals.[8] In 1940, one A. N. Sorokhin stated that pharmacies had to have "hidden reserves" to compensate for outmoded equipment in the factories and unsatisfactory distribution network. He warned that "the need for prepared medicines was great."[9] In January 1941, a scant six months before the onset of the Great Patriotic War, a report from the Chief Pharmacy Administration of the Russian Republic (*Glavnoe Aptechnoe Upravlenie Narkomzdrava RSFSR)* complained to higher officials about "interruptions" and sometimes complete absence of basic items like ether, cocaine, Novocaine, caffeine, Liuminal, pilocarpine, barium for x-rays, ice bags, autoclaves, x-ray machines, needles and syringes, boxes, dental wares, and eyeglass lenses.[10] After the war Soviet officials admitted the parlous state of basic pharmaceuticals. In 1945 Assistant Commissar for Health A. G. Natradze[11] acknowledged that "before the war the medical industry did not satisfy in full measure the requirements of our country for medicines. In 1940, for example, the need for aspirin was satisfied 46 percent, for sulfuric barium 30 percent, for [the antisyphilitic] Novarsenol 76 percent, for [the sulfa drug] Streptotsid 44 percent, for ephedrine 6 percent, and so on."[12] In 1947 Henry Sigerist ruefully conceded that "[I]t cannot be said…that the output of the Soviet pharmaceutical industry was producing in 1941 at what we would consider an adequate level for civilian needs."[13]

Thus it is clear that the Soviet pharmaceutical industry's under performance preceded the war and was due to other factors. Indeed, it is tempting to ask whether shortages of pharmaceuticals exacerbated health problems and were partially responsible for the approximately 25 million Soviet deaths that occurred during the war.[14] Since wartime brings abnormal stresses and wars typically stimulate production and productivity we will reserve the unraveling of that issue to another volume. In this volume we have at hand an important enough conundrum. Did shortages of pharmaceuticals—not only medicines but soap, disinfectants, hormones, vitamins, barium for x-rays and so forth—impact the system of public health that the Soviet Union was building in the 1920s and 1930s to provide for its own labor strength and, additionally, convince visitors from capitalist countries as to the merits of Soviet socialized medicine? The availability of food, of course, was a factor. Food supplies improved during the 1920s, as compared to the civil war but they declined in the late 1920s and early 1930s. Vitamins and food supplements produced by the industry would have impacted the food situation. This factor aside, did vaccination and increased immunity cancel out the shortages of pharmaceuticals, as some have suggested? Did self treatment with herbs rectify the situation? Satisfactory answers are hard to come by both in foreign and in Russian literature. For example, in 1932, while finding pluses in the Soviet medical system—progress in controlling venereal disease, alcoholism, tuberculosis; decline in other communicable diseases; and assiduous attention to pre-natal and pediatric care—Newsholme and Kingsbury noted shortages of doctors, nurses, and dentists and assessed the Soviet Union "behind" in preventive medicine as compared with "other countries which began preventive work earlier."[15] They linked the prevalence of dysentery, typhoid fever and typhus to lack of "domestic cleanliness and communal sanitation." Relapsing and typhus fevers were "important indices of intense overcrowding and of social backwardness. So also are the figures for trachoma.... The fact that there is fifteen times as much typhoid fever in Russia as in England for equal units of the population shows the need for great reforms in municipal and communal sanitation...."[16] The products needed to improve sanitation and hygiene—disinfectants, antiseptics, toilet paper—came from the pharmaceutical industry.

The starry-eyed Haden Guest gave a flat "thumbs up" to Soviet public health care as well as to the availability of pharmaceuticals. He asserted that as early as 1931 the "epidemic and general infectious and contagious diseases situation" was "normal" and in 1936 "the medical situation of the Union" was "up to the standard of any European country."[17] But Frank Lorimer, demographer for the League of Nations, cited "40 thousand cases of typhus in the European parts of the Russian Republic in 1932 and in 1935," as compared to "15 thousand reported cases" in "1929-1931," and "27 thousand cases...in the Asiatic part of the R.S.F.S.R. in 1932," the increases stemming from collectivization and industrialization.[18] In 1938, the American Embassy in Moscow reported that although there were "70 medical schools...with an enrollment of 100,000 students, and 90,682 doctors and 10,500 dentists in the Soviet Union...diseases arising from malnutrition and lack of sanitation" were "prevalent in the country...dysentery, typhoid fever and typhus were quite common and trachoma" was "widespread in the Asiatic portions of the U.S.S.R. Smallpox" existed "and malaria" was "frequent."[19] Henry Sigerist provided a nuanced picture of Soviet health care in 1936. He applauded progress in combating diseases. However, he opined that whereas Salvarsan attacked relapsing fever, there were regions where an epidemic of typhus could develop. Similarly, vaccination had vanquished cholera and helped diminish typhoid fever, but typhoid was still a problem, as was dysentery "in southern and oriental sections of the country" because of unsanitary conditions. Smallpox, diphtheria, scarlet fever and measles were no longer of concern, but malaria and tuberculosis were still serious problems.[20] Quite clearly, inadequate amounts of cleaning supplies and insecticides spawned diseases and diluted the impact of vaccination programs.

Despite the connection between the pharmaceutical industry and health care, most studies on Soviet health care that have appeared recently make only passing references to pharmaceuticals. Among English-language works on Soviet medicine before World War II, one of the most enlightening and accessible is a chapter by Christopher M. Davis. He provides detailed economic analysis of why Soviet health care foundered during the First Five-Year Plan, arguing that inflation eroded investment into the sector.[21] By implication the pharmaceutical industry was affected along with other aspects of health. However, Davis does not dwell on the industry. Chapters by Sally Ewing and Neil B. Weissman in the same compilation blame problems in Soviet health care during the 1920s less satisfyingly on turf wars, on the fact that the Soviet Union was pioneering various health schemes and on an economy in the throes of recovering from the civil war.[22] In any case, these authors do not discuss the pharmaceutical industry. J. D. Barber and R. W. Davies affirm that "medicines and medical equipment...increased far less rapidly" in the 1930s than the number of physicians and auxiliary health personnel"and the consequences were serious." They do not elaborate, however, and conclude that "the most important factor making for poor health was malnutrition."[23] Their contention deserves more scrutiny. At the very least lack of medicines and other pharmaceuticals affected citizens' comfort and well-being.

Most other English-language studies on Soviet health care that have appeared in the last few decades focus on the post-war period and mention pharmaceuticals and pharmacies only tangentially.[24] Michael Kaser amassed information on pharmaceuticals for his assessment of health care in the Soviet Union and Eastern Europe in the late 1960s and early 1970s, but his publishers included just a few references to Soviet pharmaceuticals, issuing his findings about this lynch-pin of health care only to a specialized audience.[25] The more general British version of Kaser's study was limited to discrete information about pharmaceuticals.[26] Still, from it, the reader could infer that the quality of Soviet pharmaceuticals were not on the level of foreign or Eastern European products and that there were shortages of basic pharmaceuticals, not only medicines but items like disinfectants, toilet paper, cleaning products, and also medical supplies. The American version of Kaser's work referred to "quack remedies," among them a purported cure for cancer and the shortage of vitamins due to delay in the building of a vitamin plant.[27] Two other specialists, Murray Feshbach and Fred Friendly, speaking of the 1970s, 1980s and early 1990s, confirmed that problems with Soviet pharmaceuticals lingered, asserting that "[T]he deficits [of medicines, vitamins, and medical supplies] were the sharp edges on a pyramid of failures in the Soviet economy and planning system."[28] Unfortunately, they did not explain why the industry faltered. Meanwhile, a work on the world-wide pharmaceutical industry, published in 1989, reiterated that improved diet and hygiene were important in driving down mortality between 1901 and 1935 but stressed the contributions made by chemotherapy since the 1930s. The authors pointedly noted that between 1945 and the late 1980s, no new drugs came from the Soviet bloc.[29] They did not go into detail, however, and did not discuss the period before 1945.

Russian-language accounts shed scarcely more light on the role of the pharmaceutical industry in Soviet health care. The articles of the erudite Viktor Matveevich Salo, pharmacist and director of the former pharmacy museum in Moscow, focused on dispensing and pharmacological research. Salo lauded both pre-Soviet and Soviet pharmacologists, but found fault with pre-Soviet dispensing and implied that, in addition to the Great Patriotic War, any problems in the Soviet pharmaceutical industry were a legacy from the pre-Soviet period. Two Russian-language works on individual Soviet pharmaceutical factories present a different picture. *Istoriia chimkentskogo khimiko-farmatsevticheskogo zavoda im. F. E. Dzerzhinskogo*, a work published during the Khrushchev era, described a thriving Santonin-opiate factory in Central Asia founded in the 1880s. The book glossed over the Soviet era, however. The recently published history of the Akrikhin Factory for antimalarials, established in a village near Moscow in the mid-1930s on the site of an older factory dating to the early nineteenth century, bitterly details the factory's trials and tribulations in the Soviet period. However, this book demonstrates (as does the museum on the premises of the factory) that the pre-Soviet factory was progressive.[30] Unfortunately, a thirty-five volume series on Soviet medicine during the Great Patriotic War, half of which dwell on surgery, the other half on treatment of diseases, yield virtually no information on pharmaceuticals. The volumes are parsimonious with comprehensive data on diseases, as well.[31]

My own study of pharmacy, pharmacists, and the pharmaceutical industry in late imperial, early Soviet Russia piqued my interest about what happened farther into the Soviet period. That work documented that, although dispensing was inadequate in the countryside, the pharmaceutical industry of late Imperial Russia was adequate. It was, moreover, pretty-much on a par with American and British pharmaceutical industries before World War I in that all three relied upon medicinal botanicals and imported the new chemically synthesized drugs from Swiss and German houses. The evidence I compiled indicated that dispensing deteriorated during the civil war. This study did not carry the story past the early 1920s, though, and did not investigate pharmaceutical production in the Soviet period.[32]

My subsequent article did adumbrate developments in the pharmaceutical sector up to the Great Patriotic War but did not examine the pharmaceutical industry in any depth.[33] That article was based on archival records as well as pharmaceutical journals of the period. And both these sources, while touting progress in research and development during the 1920s and 1930s, indicated ongoing problems in pharmacy, in the training of and sufficiency of pharmacists, and in the pharmaceutical industry. The archival reports, in particular, were rife with laments about the inability of the pharmaceutical industry to consistently bring sufficient amounts of pharmaceuticals downstream despite first-class research and development of prototypes. Were these complaints exaggerations designed to acquire more funds for the industry or to exonerate the industry for not reaching government-mandated goals? Or did they testify to real problems that adversely affected public health, the quality of life of Soviet citizens, perhaps even mortality rates? The present study seeks to answer those questions.

Using additional archival materials and close reading of Soviet pharmaceutical publications of the 1920s and 1930s, supplemented by English-language reports, the present work focuses mainly on the core pharmaceutical industry. Before the Second World War it comprised only a fraction of the one hundred pharmaceutical enterprises that operated under the old regime (although enterprises were added over ensuing years). Nevertheless, the core industry supplied 50 percent or more of the pharmaceuticals used in the Soviet Union. The remainder were imported or produced by the eighty or so other pre-revolutionary factories that were under local control. These second- and third-tier factories are examined to a limited extent. The work also reviews dispensing and preventive medicine, the last admittedly in only one provincial area. Yet, since the Soviet Union was still predominantly rural in the 1930s, this seems a fair, if partial, test of Soviet preventive medicine.

Investigation into the Soviet pharmaceutical industry during the first two decades might appear arcane. However, it is significant for three reasons. This study above all fits into the genre of business history. As such it opens more windows onto how a mid-level industry operated in the Soviet economic system—how it acquired basic capital and operating capital, how it sourced, how it attempted to produce, how it marketed. In other words, this is a case study of a Soviet business, one owned by the government yet expected to produce commodities which Soviet citizens needed. The work does not dwell on the subjunctive—on government and party plans and proposals, on the theories and debates of planners, bankers and other exogenous specialists, but rather looks at the production and distribution of pharmaceuticals through the eyes of those in the field—the board that managed the core industry, the directors of the core factories, pharmacologists and pharmacists—the people in the trenches. Purges did affect the industry, but the main drama in its story is how an industry, vital for the well being of the Soviet populace, was laid low and then thwarted in repeated comeback attempts by officials who were perhaps well-intentioned but unknowledgeable about and unqualified to produce and distribute pharmaceuticals. The individuals who were qualified and responsible for the business achieved what they did in spite of rather than because of the Soviet economic system, by applying traditional business methods similar to those used in market economies. As such, this work complements microeconomic studies on railroads, agriculture, banking, the metallurgical industry, and trade, which have appeared in the last decade as a result of the opening of archives in the former Soviet Union.[34]

Ipso facto this study yields information on Soviet health care in the 1920s and 1930s. Since pharmaceuticals are integral to medical practice, information from the archives and publications of the period add dimension to our knowledge of Soviet medicine.[35] The work explains why botanicals remained more important in Soviet medicine than in American,[36] and also discusses how some unusual therapies like phages or bacteria-specialized viruses became part of mainstream Soviet medicine. The work suggests a connection between the industry's performance and Soviet mortality figures. Although it is difficult to absolutely tie shortages of medicines, disinfectants, antiseptics, anesthesia and the like to 11 plus million who died during the civil war of 1918-1921, to those who perished in the famine of 1932/1933, and to the millions (past estimates ranged as high as 40) who died in the Great Patriotic War, common sense dictates that there was a connection. At the very least, since insufficiency of aspirin and hygiene products affected the quality of life of Soviet citizens for decades, a study of how and why this came about merits attention.

Finally, since pharmacists and pharmaceutical specialists not only trumpeted achievements but complained about inadequate production and distribution in industry reports and in their journals, this study expands our knowledge of how Soviet professionals thought and felt in the Soviet Union of the 1920s and 1930s.[37]

1
How Things Were: The Pharmaceutical Industry, Pharmacy and Preventive Medicine in Late Imperial Russia

Soviet publicists always claimed that health care improved after the Great October Revolution. Some foreigners and subsequent Soviet generations believed them. Was this story true? This chapter investigates the quantity, quality and product mix of pharmaceuticals in pre-Soviet Russia and Russia's international trade in pharmaceuticals, noting that vaccines and serums were produced in separate institutions. The chapter examines why, although Russia had chemical enterprises—some sizable—she, like the United States, did not develop synthetic pharmaceuticals before the First World War. The chapter also reviews how available pharmaceuticals were through pharmacies (*apteki*) and drug stores (*aptekarskie magaziny*).

Pharmaceutical Factories

In late Imperial Russia one hundred or more Russian pharmaceutical enterprises disseminated medicinal plants and produced half or more of the medicines, serums, vaccines, disinfectants, medical and surgical instruments, soaps, toilet paper, washing powders and cleaning supplies used within the Russian Empire.[1] Branches of German, Swiss and American pharmaceutical houses operated in Russia, such as Merck, Schering, and Parke-Davis. However, the vast majority of pharmaceutical firms were owned by Russians, either natives or foreigners who had taken on Russian citizenship. Many concerns were small, owned by individuals or families. Some were large, sophisticated conglomerates, organized as closed partnerships (*tovarishchestvo*) or publicly-held joint stock corporations (*aktsionernoe obshchestvo*). Additionally, the Russian army had its own pharmaceutical factory. [2]

In the United States the privately held H. K. Mulford Company produced vaccines, serums, and antitoxins from 1895, complementing production of these items by public health departments in cities and the federal government's Marine Health Service in the last decades of the nineteenth century and first decades of the twentieth.[3] In Russia, in contrast, the public sector monopolized production of vaccines, serums, and antitoxins. From the late eighteenth century the Free Economic Society had been engaged in smallpox vaccination. Medical societies, elected municipal councils (*duma*, in the singular), elected provincial and county councils (zemstvos)—after their establishment in the 1860s—and institutes in St. Petersburg and other major cities also participated in this endeavor from the 1870s.[4] In Ufa, located due east of Moscow on the western slope of the Ural Mountains, for example, a Bacteriological Institute was founded in 1905 to produce serums, vaccines and otherwise engage in preventive medicine. From 1908, under zemstvo management, the institute gained scientific status, adding a veterinary section in 1911, a chemical-hygienic production unit in 1912, and a microbiology department in 1913.[5]

Driven by the market, some of the largest Russian pharmaceutical companies made their own packaging, employed innovative advertising and marketing techniques, selling through catalogues and agents, and offered credit purchase to attract customers. Some Russian concerns got high marks for the quality of their products.[6]

Although in this regard Russian houses resembled British or American ones, they were not as free in their operations as their Anglo-Saxon counterparts. The Russian government dominated the pharmaceutical sector as it did other branches of the economy and education, culture and philanthropy. The Medical Council in the Ministry of Internal Affairs assayed medicines produced in or imported into the Empire and closely regulated the pharmacies and drug stores that sold these products. The Russian government's leading strings did not choke private enterprise. Paternalism and interference did, however, chafe pharmaceutical entrepreneurs as other business folk. By the early twentieth century some owners of pharmaceutical firms were at odds with the Russian government, as we shall see.

Pharmaceutical companies were situated throughout the Russian Empire. Most were located in the fifty Russian provinces and Russian Poland. Some provinces had clusters of pharmaceutical firms. For example, there were ten chemical-pharmaceutical and thirteen soap and perfume enterprises in Warsaw, the capital of Russian Poland.[7] Thirteen chemical-pharmaceutical firms and three soap and perfume manufacturing companies operated in Riga, the capital of today's Latvia.[8] The Joint-Stock Solve and Company, a conglomerate with branches in Ekaterinoslav, and Perm and Tomsk in Siberia, was one of the largest with annual income of ten million rubles. There were major enterprises in the Caucasus, Minsk and Grodno, Tver,' Kazan,' Kostroma, Nizhni-Novgorod, and Saratov, on the Volga, and in Olonetsk and Dvinsk.[9] Some sixteen pharmaceutical factories, producing mainly galenicals, but significant for the health of the populace nonetheless, operated in the Ukraine, including Galenika Joint-Stock Company and Sanitas in Khar'kov, IUROTAT and the Karbonik oxygen-producing factory in Kiev, Stella in Odessa, three enterprises in Kremenchug, and eight in Kherson Province.[10]

Twelve pharmaceutical companies were located in the capital of the Empire, St. Petersburg. One was the Pel' firm, founded in 1885, from which A. V. Pel' sold his famous spermine and other products. Another major house was Farmakon, founded in 1908. A third was the St. Petersburg Chemical Laboratory Stock Company, which produced toilet soap, cosmetics and perfume, and had an income of half a million rubles annually.[11]

Moscow was the hub of the pharmaceutical industry with thirty-two pharmaceutical houses. There were medium-sized to small, specialized companies, like the Bandaging Materials factory of N. Iakovlev and the Laboratory of Dr. Ia. M. Bliumental'. There also were very large companies. One of the most important for consumers was the Keler firm, which produced and aggressively advertised toiletries, soaps, and household cleaning supplies, chemicals and pharmaceuticals. The firm was self contained, making its own packaging and selling through agents throughout the empire, bringing an annual income of one and a half million rubles.[12] The Ferrein pharmaceutical firm was equally, if not more, impressive. This family-held conglomerate included a research laboratory, which designed new products and manufactured galenicals and chemicals, and a warehouse situated in the yard surrounding the home of the founder and owner, Vladimir Karlovich Ferrein. Ferrein's main pharmacy, the largest in the world at that time, was situated on Nikol'skaia Street, just off Red Square. The pharmacy, which still operates, was elegant, with polished cabinetry throughout. Corinthian columns, busts of medical figures in the high ceiling cove, and electrified globes distinguished the main waiting room. A drug store that sold sundries and prepared medicines was attached to the pharmacy, its bentwood tables and chairs making it appear like an American drugstore cum soda fountain. Three other drug stores were situated in various sectors of the city. On the outskirts of Moscow, around his wooden dacha, Ferrein had a plantation of medicinal herbs. Another of his pharmaceutical enterprises was situated in the city of Mologa, Iaroslavl' province. In 1912 the Ferrein conglomerate employed 600 chemists, pharmacologists and other specialists, and 1,000 workers. Annual turnover amounted to 7 million rubles.[13]

Ferrein, descended from Huguenots who had migrated to Russia via German states in the 1830s, was not only a talented businessman but generous to his employees. His main pharmacy was open, like other Russian pharmacies, around the clock, sometimes dispensing almost three thousand prescriptions a day. Staff pharmacists, however, worked enlightened seven-hour shifts and benefited from a profit-sharing plan, instituted in the 1880s. Laboratory specialists were protected from noxious chemicals.[14] In 1913 the Ferrein Association acquired the Veber factory, in the village of Nizhnie Kotly. In 1913 this branch began to produce various galenical preparations, soaps, tablets, and chemicals.[15]

Several factories in Russian Central Asia, conquered by Russia in the 1860s and 1870s and subsequently colonized, produced Santonin.[16] The Russian pharmaceutical industry enjoyed a world-wide monopoly on this product, the significance of which shall be discussed later. Additionally, four soap factories operated in Semipalatinsk *Oblast'* (region), now Kazakhstan, a factory in a slaughterhouse produced soap in Syr-Dar'ia *Oblast'*, today's Uzbekistan; and two factories produced soap in Fergana *Oblast'*, now Tadzhikistan.[17]

Soap was one of the major curbs of infectious diseases in the early twentieth century, before the advent of bactericides and antibiotics, and Russia produced 180,000 tons of soap for the 125 million to 144 million inhabitants of the empire.[18] Botanicals and therapies derived from them—cocaine, morphine, heroin, quinine, digitalis, iodine—also were major weapons in the medical arsenal in the nineteenth and early twentieth centuries, as were biologicals—serums, vaccines and hormones.[19] Russian pharmaceutical houses were strong in both areas, as we shall see, although they were hampered by a lack of some plant materials.

Chemically Synthesized Medicines

But the magic bullets in the war on disease and medical problems were chemically synthesized medicines. In the late nineteenth and early twentieth centuries these drugs included antiseptics and disinfectants like phenol or carbolic acid; febrifuges like antipyrine, Pyramidon, Butazolidin, Phenacetin, and acetyl salicylic acid or aspirin; anesthetics like Novocaine; and the antivenereal, Salvarsan. According to Renate Reidl of Sandoz, the quality of these drugs did not measure up to today's products. Nevertheless, patents on them, as well as on prepared medicines and galenicals based on botanicals—such as a water soluble form of guiacol, sold under the trade name Thiocol, the cough syrup Sirolin, and the heart medicine Digalen—enabled pharmaceutical firms in Basel (CIBA, Hoffman-La Roche, Sandoz, and Geigey) and in Germany (Bayer, Hoechst and Merck) to dominate the world drug market before World War I. The Russian market accounted for one fifth of Hoffman-La Roche's sales in the early twentieth century. The fact that the most successful products of that company were Sirolin (a cough syrup made from guaiacum, a tropical American shrub), Pantopon (an alkaloid of opium in the form of hydrochloric salts), and Digalen (an extract of purple foxglove) testified as much if not more than the synthetics to the research, development, and marketing skills of the Swiss and German pharmaceutical houses.[20]

By all odds, Russians should have been leaders in the production of chemicals and synthetic drugs. In 1841, seven years after the discovery of nitrobenzene at the University of Berlin, Nicholas Zinin, a Russian chemist, produced a compound from nitrobenzene which a St. Petersburg colleague, Carl Julius Fritzsche, christened "aniline."[21] Aniline became the base first for synthetic dyes and then, in the 1880s, for synthetic drugs when scientists noted that the chemical structure of synthetic dyes had medicinal properties.

Russians did develop a fairly decent chemical industry by the second half of the nineteenth century. Basic chemicals were produced in the 1840s and 1850s. Disinfectants made from imported phenol became big business in Russia in the 1860s, at about the same time Joseph Lister applied phenol to wounds and it began to be used as an antiseptic spray in the operating theater. By the mid 1880s there were five enterprises in St. Petersburg, four in Moscow, and in Odessa, Iaroslavl', Ekaterinburg, and Mogilev provinces producing significant amounts of disinfecting preparations.[22] There would be another growth spurt in chemical production in the last decades of the nineteenth century.

Still, although production of chemicals moved forward, although plenty of pharmaceuticals were produced in Russia, and although some Russian chemists were renowned, Russia, like the United States and

Great Britain, did not create a *chemical-pharmaceutical industry* to rival those in Germany and Switzerland before the First World War.[23]

There were several reasons for Russia's failure to compete. Swiss and German firms had the advantage of readily available coal-tar waste—either of local provenance or cheaply imported—which was the base for the new chemical drugs. Ample amounts of capital and the ready expertise of chemists, pharmacologists, and patent lawyers facilitated research and development; shrewd businessmen and convenient trade routes promoted sales.[24]

At first Russia lacked a ready supply of benzol, the raw material for aniline. This problem began to be resolved in the 1870s. The emergence of the coal industry in the Donbass region of southeastern Ukraine, thanks in part to the British immigrant John Hughes, and the emergence of the petroleum industry in the Caucasus, provided aromatic hydrocarbons for benzene, toluene, naphthalene, and anthracene.[25]

Unfortunately, the Russian government's tariff policies hobbled the synthetic dye industry as it did the pharmaceutical industry. Focused on advancing the textile industry, the Russian Tariff Commission of 1868 placed very low duties on imported chemical dye products, presenting foreigners an advantage against which Russian chemical producers could not compete. Only in 1882 did the government review the tariff and increase duties. Predictably this boosted the chemical industry.[26] In the 1880s aniline was produced in Iaroslavl' and Moscow provinces. In 1906, the doubling of customs duties on imported aniline spurred production again, in Riga and the capital, St. Petersburg.[27]

By 1913, some two hundred fifty to three hundred enterprises produced chemicals, dyes, kerosene and oil products, pharmaceuticals, soaps, and perfumes.[28] One hundred sixty-nine specifically manufactured dyes, lacquers, and products using the centuries-old process of dry distillation of wood and the newer process of dry distillation of coal. There were seven superphosphate factories, twenty-two factories produced nitric acid, twenty-six produced hydrochloric acid, and twenty, vinegar acid. Sixteen enterprises specifically produced aniline and benzol—four in Riga, five in Moscow, one each in Kovno, Kostroma, and Kurland provinces, the St. Petersburg Stock Company for chemical products in St. Petersburg, a factory in Iaroslavl', and one in Petrovskaia Province.[29] The German pharmaceutical house Schering established a factory in Russia in 1906 to produce turpentine by wood distillation, a key ingredient in synthetic camphor, which was a major Schering product. Schering experienced financial difficulties, one of which involved building an apartment house for workers, required by Russian law. Nevertheless, Russian turpentine, made by the process of old-fashioned dry distillation of wood, would be crucial to the company into the interwar period.[30]

Some enterprises were large partnerships or joint-stock companies, such as the Tentelevskii chemical factory in St. Petersburg and the Petersburg and South Russian Chemical Societies, which sold abroad as well as within the Russian Empire.[31] Some were small workshops—so-called *kustar'* operations. For example, in 1910, *kustar'* operations supplemented the thirty-two factories that produced sulfuric acid.[32] And many small workshops as well as three large factories, such as the Ferrein factory in Mologa, Iaroslavl' Province, made salicylic acid before World War I.[33] It should be noted that the United States also relied on many small-scale chemical and essential oil manufacturers.[34]

Chemicals that could not be produced in Russia were imported. The picture was mixed as to the level of Russia's dependency or self-sufficiency. One World War I analyst complained that while Imperial Russia produced 41,651,000 rubles' worth of chemicals, she imported 100,000, 000 rubles' worth.[35] Russia imported the bulk of the benzol she used. By 1910, 5,793 *pudy* (a *pud* being 36 pounds this amounted to 104 tons) of benzol were produced domestically although an enormous 161,000 puds were imported.[36] This posed a problem during the war. On the other hand, Russian factories produced nearly all the aniline used in the empire. In 1912, five factories produced some 105,000 puds (1,340 tons) of aniline oil and aniline salts. Only 19,000 puds were imported.[37] By World War I, production had increased to 157,400 puds with only 12,000 puds imported. [38] Thus, in sum, the foundation for production of chemical-pharmaceuticals had been laid in the early twentieth century.

Nevertheless, production of chemical-pharmaceuticals lagged. Russian pharmaceutical houses, like their British and American counterparts—Glaxo, Sharp & Dohme, Mulford, and so on, continued to rely on botanicals before World War I and imported chemical pharmaceuticals.[39] The reasons for this were several.

First, Swiss and German pharmaceutical houses held patents on crucial, high-quality synthetic medicines, which impressed Russian physicians and figured heavily in their prescribing and also attracted zemstvos—zemstvo pharmacies in aggregate ordering roughly half their medicines from foreign houses. Second, Russian pharmaceutical firms were slow to respond to the competition. Some pharmaceutical enterprises, most notably those of Vladimir Karlovich Ferrein in Moscow, employed on-site pharmaceutical chemists. But in the early twentieth century there were few specialized higher pharmacy schools and there were no chairs, courses or even specialists on pharmaceutical chemistry in the state-run higher educational institutions as late as 1916, even though some pharmacist-reformers had been calling for upgrading pharmacy education in this and other ways.

Third, the policies of the Russian government did not encourage research, development and production of synthetic pharmaceuticals. Rather, tsarist government officials blocked innovation and output of synthetic drugs, as they had aniline dyes earlier. Tsarist tariff policies were formulated for considerations of revenue and to help selected industries. They often were detrimental to other industries. The tariff of 1903 put low duties on imports of prepared medicines and high duties on raw materials the Russian pharmaceutical industry needed to import. Following on the heels of that, the Russian-German Convention of 1904 favored German pharmaceuticals. One result, according to F. A. Ferrein, probably a relative of the pharmaceutical magnate Vladimir Karlovich Ferrein, was that production of salicylic acid rose in 1909, but, insufficiently protected from foreign competition, withered in 1911 and 1912.[40] Further, the Medical Council, located in the Ministry of Internal Affairs, which assayed and approved all medicines sold in Russia, made pharmacists and pharmaceutical companies go through all manner of hoops to produce new medicines. It ought to be noted that no pharmacists or pharmaceutical industry representatives sat on the Council. Approval time took years. Worse, by the Medical Council's own admission, it was more lenient in approving sales of new foreign medicines than new Russian medicines.[41]

Finally, a very salient reason for reliance on plants in Russian medicaments was that the Empire abounded in medicinal botanicals. And so Russia was practicing good economics and dealing from her strengths—producing what she could cheaply, importing what she could not easily produce, and exporting to balance finances.

Botanicals

Five botanicals needed for crucial remedies were not available in Russia for climatic reasons or had poor quality active ingredients. The cinchona tree, source for quinine, desperately needed because malaria was Russia's main communicable disease, did not grow in Russia.[42] The same was true of the coca plant, source for cocaine. Similarly, Russia had trouble producing iodine, known to be crucial for proper thyroid function since 1895, used as an antiseptic and for water purification, and in photographic film. Iodine occurs in many places but only in very small amounts. One source was seaweed. Unfortunately, although Russia had a lot of coastline, her seaweed did not contain adequate amounts of iodine and thus, like most other countries at that time, Russia imported iodine from a German pharmaceutical syndicate which controlled and processed iodine-rich nitrate deposits in Chile. At the end of the nineteenth century, the Resettlement Administration of the Russian Ministry of Internal Affairs (the ministry that also controlled the Medical Council and Medical Department, which governed pharmacy and the pharmaceutical industry) set up a small iodine production unit in Tomsk, western Siberia, that extracted iodine from seaweed sent from the Pacific Ocean. The project was not enormously successful, however.[43] Russia also lacked opium with consistent alkaloid content. The Turkic and Iranian Moslem inhabitants of Central Asia, which Russia conquered in the 1860s and 1870s, did grow opium poppies, despite the Russian government's ban on recreational use of opium, but it was of poor quality. Analysis of opium that local authorities periodically confiscated and burned, showed it to be of little medicinal value; opium that escaped their vigilance and was sold to China brought very low prices. Thus, before World War I, Russia imported opium for medicinal uses from Persia and the Ottoman Empire.[44] Finally, Vladimir Karlovich Ferrein tried for years to grow *HydrastisCcanadensis* or goldenseal, which supplied hydrastine, an important hemostatic, on his pharmaceutical plantation outside Moscow. He finally succeeded only with the application of special fertilizers.[45] These raw plant materials that could not be gathered or cultivated in Russia and the finished preparations made from the plants were imported, as were chemically synthesized medicines and remedies protected by foreign patents.

Otherwise the Russian Empire was rich in medicinal botanicals. Some three hundred forms of plants and fungi had been used for centuries to successfully combat major ailments of the time. These included *Aconitum; Belladonna,* from which atropine was derived; the heart remedy *Digitalis; Convallaria majalis* or lily-of-the-valley, also used to treat cardiac problems; *Eucalyptus globulus* , ingredient for a salve to treat skin problems; *Romashka aptechnaia* or chamomile; the sedative *Valeriana officinalis; Solodka gladkaia* or *glycyrrhiza glabra,* commonly known as licorice, used as an expectorant, to treat constipation, and to coat pills;

and *Achillea millefolium* or "thousand leaf" as well as various types of mint, particularly *Mentha crispa et piperita,* for treatment of stomach and digestive problems.[46]

These plants were gathered and cultivated in European Russia and Ukraine, the Caucasus, Siberia, and Central Asia. In the 1840s and 1850s, the marketing of caraway seed oil, lactucarium, derived from *Lactuca virosa,* and mustard oil was big business in the Ukraine.[47] In the second half of the nineteenth and early twentieth centuries, the chief centers of pharmaceutical plant cultivation in the European part of the empire were in Voronezh Province, where cultivation of anise, coriander and *chernushka* occupied up to 3,000 desiatinas or 8,000 acres (in Biriuchenskii county); Tula Province, where cultivation of sage and chamomile occupied 100 desiatinas (in Epifanskii County); Poltava Province, where cultivation of mint occupied up to 1,000 desiatinas (in Prilukskii and Priatinskii counties); Podolia Province, where cultivation of fennel or *Foeniculum officinale,* used for medicinal purposes and in making ether oils, occupied up to 200 desiatinas; and the lower Volga River region, where cultivation of mustard occupied up to 2,000 desiatinas.[48] One of Russia's most important products, the vermifuge Santonin, was derived from *Artemesia cina,* which grew only near Chimkent in Russian Turkestan or Russian Central Asia.[49]

Russians did important research on plant alkaloids and glycosides during the nineteenth century. A. V. Pel', Master of Pharmacy in St. Petersburg, studied atropine and other alkaloids at the Military Medical Academy in St. Peterburg in the 1870s, publishing 132 scientific works. In 1896, Professor E. A. Leman of Tomsk University isolated a glycoside he called Periplotsine from the root of *Periploca graeca L.* P. V. Burzhinskii discovered that the substance was effective in treating cardiac problems.[50]

Monopoly production of Santonin, the chief treatment for roundworms in the nineteenth and early twentieth centuries, was one of the major success stories of the Russian pharmaceutical industry and highlighted the entrepreneurship of Russian pharmacists in the tsarist period. The alkaloid santonin had been discovered by a German researcher in 1830, was used in medicine from 1833, and was produced in Germany and England in the 1840s and 1850s. One of the major producers in the 1880s was the pharmaceutical powerhouse Merck in Darmstadt. The sources for santonin, the plant *Artemesia cina,* originally were found in North Africa, India, and South America. Unfortunately, the plants in North Africa were annihilated in the 1870s and those in

India and South America in the 1880s. Meanwhile, Russians had moved into Central Asia. In 1867 they conquered Tashkent, a city in the Kokand Khanate (which included also the city of Chimkent) and soon established protectorates over several other nearby small emirates in the region. The Russians noted that Kazakh or Kirghiz women in the region gathered a plant they called "Darmin" or *tsitvanaia polyn'* (wormweed, wormwood or absinthe) which produced santonin. Small amounts of the Darmin that the locals collected were exported to Germany. Fortuitously, when other sources of santonin disappeared in 1882, Central Asian Darmin became the sole remaining source of santonin in the world.[51]

Two Russian merchants, N. P. Savinkov, from Orenburg, at the southern end of the Ural Mountains, and N. I. Ivanov, from Kazalinsk, a town near the Aral Sea, determined to make the most of this situation. They sent a German pharmacist working in St. Petersburg, one V. Pfaff, to Hamburg to learn the process of making santonin, petitioned the Governor General for permission to build the factory, and formed a partnership called "Santonin." Their factory was built in Chimkent, which was already an industrial area, and began manufacturing Santonin in 1885.[52] The Russians soon faced cut-throat competition from German pharmacists, who created their own syndicate, provided financing for Pfaff and a Russian, Nikitin, built a small santonin manufactory in the city of Tashkent, and then proceeded to undersell Chimkent Santonin, forcing the Savinkov-Ivanov factory to close in the mid-1890s. Savinkov and Ivanov fought back, however. They obtained permission from the Governor General to establish a monopoly on santonin production, invited Russians to migrate to the area to help cultivate darmin, and got assistance from a noted agronomist to protect their plants. From 1897 to 1907, the Savinkov Factory enjoyed a monopoly on Santonin. During the war, in 1915, the *kustar'* manufactory of Pfaff and Nikitin in Tashkent, the Chimkent Factory of Savinkov, and others in Syr-Dar'ia, Semipalatinsk, and Fergana regions producing Santonin, formed a syndicate.[53]

Russians also contributed to the development of biologicals and hormones. Indeed they were pioneers in so-called organo therapy—extracts of organs for medicinal purposes. A. V. Pel' was the first to extract spermine in pure form and to sell it, in special ampules he invented, under his name, in the 1880s.[54] The 1918 *Dispensatory of the United States of America* recommended the use of spermine, either injected subcutaneously or taken orally, as "a nerve tonic and stimulant in all diseases due to auto-intoxication, as *typhus, syphilis,* etc."[55] Later extracted from plants and also synthesized, spermine was still a valid therapy in the last half of the twentieth century, its uses having expanded.[56] Although insulin was not developed until the 1920s when it was sold by the Eli Lilly Company in Indianapolis, in the nineteenth century, another Russian, P. P. Kravkov, isolated a hormone preparation, pancreotoxin, an "effective insulin preparation," and obtained "endocrine preparations by perfusion with blood."[57]

It also should be noted that in addition to producing medicine and household items, pharmaceutical enterprises engaged in some aspects of preventive medicine. In conjunction with city-owned laboratories, pharmaceutical companies analyzed food products to prevent adulteration and spoilage.[58]

Exports

While Russia imported pharmaceutical raw materials and prepared medicines that could not be produced domestically, she exported large amounts of medicinal botanicals and some finished products made from them, balancing out the imports. Indeed, Russia was a major player in the international drug trade.

A 1927 Russian-language publication asserted that of 30,932 tons of medicinal plants and materials collected in the Russian Empire in 1913, over 29,000 tons were exported, implying that too few plants were kept for making up at home.[59] A 1931 English-language publication completely contradicted these data, maintaining that in 1913 Russia exported 1,000 tons of "medicinal herbs," valued at 436,000 gold rubles or $220,000.[60]

The two sources agreed on what constituted key exports, however. The most important pharmaceutical export was licorice root. Also very important were Sporyn'ia (*Secale Cornutum*), made from parasites on roses and used in obstetrical practice, *Sporae likopodii* or club moss, and Santonin, the most effective treatment for roundworms.[61] Most Santonin, total production of which was estimated at 12,000 to 15,000 pounds, was sold, as noted, to Merck in Darmstadt, "which made the last refinement."[62]

Russian botanicals particularly made large, direct contributions to American health and well being. In 1913-1914 Russia was "one of the most important sources (in fact, ranking second) for imports of crude botanical drugs such as flowers, leaves, nuts, berries," to the United

States. In that fiscal year, the United States imported approximately one million dollars' worth of crude drugs from Russia—13 percent of total American imports. Licorice root "accounted for the bulk of this sum."[63] Santonin also was vital to the American hog industry as well as to humans.[64]

Pharmacies and Drug Stores

Medicines and household items produced by Russian pharmaceutical enterprises—toilet paper, soaps, and cleaning supplies—were dispensed to the masses in the first decades of the twentieth century through a network of 4,804 pharmacies and some 10,000 drug stores. The two, unlike the custom in the United States, were severely demarcated from each other and a labyrinth of laws and inspectors regulated their establishment and operation. Only pharmacies could dispense medicines and, as such, they had to be staffed by pharmacists, who numbered close to 10,000 in the first decade of the twentieth century, including about 100 women pharmacists. Pharmacies, in turn, were graded as urban (*normal'nye*) or rural (*sel'skie*). The former had to be managed by fully-trained pharmacists (*provizory*), although lesser pharmacists could assist. They were more thoroughly stocked than the latter and their numbers were ordained by population figures, which were periodically reassessed, and by the consent of nearby owners. Rural or village pharmacies, which could be managed by assistant pharmacists, contained a more basic store of medicine and supplies, and their numbers were decided by geography. By 1911, 2, 845 "normal" pharmacies operated in the Russian Empire. One thousand, eight hundred and twenty-five pharmacies were rural; 31 were homeopathic. There also were a few pharmacies in hospitals and clinics.[65]

As noted, pharmacies were required by law to be open twenty-four hours. Limitations on pharmacies meant they were expensive and difficult to purchase for pharmacists. Nevertheless, consumers in urban areas had good access to pharmacies whether they lived in European Russia, the Caucasus, or Siberia. In European Russia one pharmacy served, on average, 10,300 urbanites. In Warsaw the ratio was one pharmacy for every 13,000 inhabitants. In St. Petersburg, the capital, the ratio was 1: 16,000. The St. Petersburg pharmacy of Antonina Lesnevskaia, the Polish woman *provizor*, was staffed entirely by women, making it world famous.[66] There were not as many pharmacies per inhabitant in Moscow (the ratio was 1:22, 800) as in St. Petersburg or Warsaw. Nevertheless, along with the myriad of restaurants, stores, hotels, theaters, and retail establishments of every kind that served Muscovites in 1909,[67] there were eighty-one pharmacies.[68] In Central Asia and Siberia, one pharmacy served, on average 20,000 urban dwellers. Pharmacies in small towns were adequate, dispensing basic medicines to the populace and oxygen to hospitals and the homebound.[69]

The number of pharmacies in rural areas was, for the most part, insufficient. The ratio of pharmacies to population was particularly meager in the zemstvo provinces where one pharmacy served on average, 100,000 people. The ratio of pharmacies to rural dwellers was better in non-zemstvo provinces and very good in the Baltic provinces.[70]

Most pharmacies were owned by individuals. However, about 200 were owned by cities, zemstvos—local councils elected by taxpayers, first in thirty-four and then in more of Russia's fifty some provinces, and by charitable groups. The "public pharmacies" were grouped under the same rubric of normal or rural pharmacies as the privately owned pharmacies and had to follow the rules for each category, as did the privately owned ones. The groups that ran them, though, had socialist inclinations. They often subsidized or dispensed medicines free to the local populace and were hostile to privately owned pharmacies. The latter did dispense medicines to certified indigents without charge but otherwise they were small businesses and their owners had to make a profit. Most owners of private pharmacies were not rich and, since the government set retail prices for medicines, they had little elasticity in their prescription charges. Public pharmacies, supported by taxpayers and giving out medicines at low cost, or free, obviously posed unfair competition to owners of private pharmacies.[71]

Because pharmacies were not always conveniently located, because cost, despite government controls, may have deterred the sick from trekking to the pharmacy for medicines, and because even state-of-the-art medicine and pharmacy could do little for many diseases and medical problems in the early twentieth century, sick city dwellers probably often brewed their own teas, made their own poultices from time-honored recipes, took curative water or mud baths, or relied on other remedies, some of dubious merit.[72] Many peasants relied on wise women (*znakharki*) or male healers (*znakhari*). Although some of these individuals used incantations and spells to cure diseases, other, according to Samuel Ramer, were skilled in the use of botanicals, applied mercury to syphilis, used quinine for malaria like "real doctors", and were competent bone-setters.[73]

In sum, an infrastructure of "scientific" pharmacy existed in early twentieth century Russia. The knowledgeable pharmacist provided medical expertise as well as succor to the sick, supplementing physicians who were in short supply. The market, moreover, was correcting the dearth of pharmacies resulting from manifold restrictions on their establishment. Drug stores, which were not subject to government limitations, complemented the pharmacies very nicely. Supplying the populace with prepared medicines and hygienic and household materials, they had become twice as numerous as pharmacies by the twentieth century.

The Push for Socialized Pharmacy

Counter to the process of market principle that encouraged drug stores to fill the vacuum resulting from highly regulated pharmacies, several public groups and even some government ministers wanted to strengthen socialized dispensing or replace private dispensing altogether with socialized dispensing. In the nineteenth century, zemstvo activists attempted to buy up private pharmacies and transform them into zemstvo pharmacies. In the first decade of the twentieth century, they lobbied the government and, after the parliament was instituted in 1906, they worked to push through legislation allowing zemstvos (but not private individuals) to establish pharmacies without adhering to the regulations. Their bill passed the Duma, the lower house of the Russian parliament, in 1911 and the State Council, the upper chamber, in 1912.[74] Marxist Social-Democratic pharmacists also castigated the "pharmacy monopoly" and claimed pharmacy owners exploited their staff. They established societies and journals for staff pharmacists to counter those dominated by pharmacy owners, took over the million-ruble pharmacy pension fund instituted by V. K. Ferrein, organized pharmacy staff and fomented strikes against private pharmacies, particularly during the revolutionary upheavals of 1905. Jacob Sverdlov, arguably the most famous pharmacist in the Soviet government, actually left the field.[75] Boris Nikolaevich Saltykov exemplifies the radical pharmacists who attempted to change the system by violent means before the Great October Revolution 1917, and then after it, became managers in the Soviet pharmacy system. Saltykov received his education in the pharmaceutical department of the Medical School at Moscow University, took bacteriological training in the 1890s in the Chemical-Bacteriological Institute of Dr. Bliumental', studied "disinfecting" in the Society of Russian Physicians, worked as a chemist in the Ferrein Laboratory and then, although he did not practice pharmacy or pharmacology, organized pharmacists into unions, helped precipitate strikes, and edited left-wing pharmacy journals—*Farmatsevt, Farmatsevticheskii vestnik,* and *Farmatsevticheskii trud.*[76] Another individual, of indeterminate political orientation, one O. G. Gabrilovich, devised a practical plan to eliminate private pharmacies.[77]

Pharmacy owners presciently countered that this would transform the "private monopoly" into a "government monopoly," which, they implied, would not be receptive to the populace.[78] They did agree with Social Democratic and other socialist pharmacists, however, that pharmacy and the pharmaceutical industry should be liberated from the physician-dominated Medical Council and supervised instead by an autonomous "Pharmacy Council."[79]

Neither Marxists, zemstvo activists or Octobrists, who dominated the Third Duma, 1907-1912, nor Ministers in the Tsarist government who also were sympathetic to socialized dispensing, however, entertained the idea of doing away with private pharmaceutical firms before World War I.[80] The focus of the Duma, the government, and Social Democrats, rather, was on the benefit of factory-prepared medicines, whatever their provenance. Ironically, owners of Russian pharmaceutical firms, on the other hand, did become frustrated with the status of the pharmaceutical industry, albeit from another vantage point. They wanted less government oversight on research and development and maintained that government tariff policies resulted in unfair competition, by allowing lenient imports of chemically synthesized and patented medicines.[81]

Reliance on foreign pharmaceuticals, of course, benefited consumers, since imported medicines supplemented those made in Russia. Nor did imported medicines worry the Russian government before the war. Except for P. A. Stolypin, Minister of Internal Affairs from 1906 to 1911, most government officials took little heed of the uneven playing field on which Russian pharmaceutical firms had to compete with foreign houses. Among the many other projects Stolypin undertook before he was assassinated, was an attempt to remedy Russia's dependency on foreign medicines by encouraging domestic pharmaceutical firms to produce generic versions of trademarked remedies, with disclosures about their provenance. This precipitated outrage in the international pharmaceutical community and most of Stolypin's fellow ministers did not support his proposal.[82]

The Push for Chemical Production

The fact that some ingredients used in the dye and pharmaceutical industries—such as dinitrobenzol and nitrotoluol—were also used in explosives [83] was another matter and one that concerned the Russian government a great deal in the early twentieth century, for war between Russia and Germany loomed as an ever larger possibility, despite good trade relations between the two empires.

As a result of the need for contingency plans, the Russian government increasingly focused attention on manufacturing chemicals needed for warfare. Para-nitrotoluol, a sulfur derivative used in the defense industry, began to be produced in Moscow dye factories between 1911 and 1913. In 1911, three Russian factories began to produce nitrobenzol and nitronaphthalein, cutting imports, which still remained high. Two Moscow factories manufactured sulfuric acid fenilendiamin (phenilendiamine). A number of factories made their own equipment to produce chlorbenzol. The Baier (Bayer) Factory in Moscow produced crucial chemicals such as benzidine, dichlorbenzidine, dinitrochlorbenzol, and sulfa compounds.[84] Russia did not produce phenol but Farbwerke, Bayer, and other factories operating in Russia imported it. [85] By 1914, a network of factories in Riga, in Petrograd—particularly Tentelevskii, in Moscow—especially the foreign firms Bayer and Farbwerke, in the Donbass—Sol've and Ko, and in the Caucasus either produced chemicals needed for the defense industry as well as for the dye and pharmaceutical industries or imported crucial chemicals, providing a ready store should they be needed.

Conclusion

The Russian government thwarted the growth of the domestic pharmaceutical industry through overly solicitous supervision and tariff policies. Nevertheless, the industry expanded markedly in the second half of the nineteenth century and first decade of the twentieth. There was no absolute shortage of pharmaceuticals on the market in late Imperial Russia. Further, there was no shortage of raw materials for the hundred or so pharmaceutical enterprises that operated in Imperial

Russia. The industry was free to import what it needed. The pharmaceutical industry of late Imperial Russia supplied about half the medicines used in the empire and more of disinfectants, soaps, toiletries, and household products. The industry exported botanicals and had a monopoly on Santonin. Russian pharmaceuticals items were of high quality. The industry catered to consumers. It did not produce the dubious proprietary nostrums purveyed in the United States.[86] What was not produced domestically was imported. Industry representatives complained that Imperial tariff policies were unfair, but these policies benefited the public.

The distribution network for pharmaceuticals was poor in the countryside, where the vast majority of the population resided in late Imperial Russia. This was partially due to the infrastructure and to pharmacists' desire to work in cities rather than rural areas. Without massive social engineering, however, the latter problem would be difficult to change. In urban areas, on the other hand, the populace was fairly well served, although more affluent areas were better served than slums where the poor resided.

The one worry, as war loomed on the horizon, was that although Russia had a chemical industry, as in the United States and Great Britain, she imported the new chemically synthesized medicines and many of these came from German houses, as did medical equipment and surgical instruments. Additionally, Russia imported some key botanicals such as iodine, cocaine, opium, and quinine. Germany had a monopoly on iodine and supplied cocaine. Much opium came from the Ottoman Empire. Quinine, which was indispensable for malaria, endemic and in places epidemic in Imperial Russia, could be blocked by war.

Otherwise, the pharmaceutical industry of Imperial Russia was poised for growth on the eve of World War I. It is axiomatic that wars stimulate production and import substitution. The next chapter briefly reviews what occurred in the industry during the First World War.

2
The First World War and Revolution

World War I was a wake up call for Russia's need for a robust chemical/chemical-pharmaceutical industry and for domestic sources of iodine and opium. The chemical industry would supply fertilizers and weapons as well as medicines. There was no shortage of food during the first two years of the war, since hostilities prevented 11 million tons of grain at Black Sea ports from being shipped and the harvest in 1915, according to Peter Gatrell was "10 percent above pre-war average." However, in 1916, output of vegetables may have declined and in 1916 "grain yields fell by around four percent."[1] D. N. Prianishnikov cited statistics on the increased yields of oats, potatoes and other foodstuffs that could come from applying mineral fertilizers such as ammonium sulfate, as Germany did. Saltpeter or niter was now sequestered for weapons. But Russia had exported ammonium sulfate, a byproduct of her coal industry, to Germany. In 1916, now that the Dardanelles were closed, "3½ million puds [126 million pounds, a pud equaling 36 pounds] of ammonium sulfate lay in Russian warehouses." Prianishnikov proposed that the Zemstvo Union buy the substance at low wholesale prices and distribute it to individual zemstvos. Increased production of mineral fertilizers—ammonium nitrate, ammonium sulfate and superphosphates (phosphate rock treated with sulfuric acid)—also would boost explosives, Germany having 100 superphosphate factories which served both agriculture and her army.[2] For the pharmaceutical industry drugs, disinfectants and anesthetics were the first concern.

Government Leadership

On Saturday, August 2, 1914, immediately after Russia entered the war, the Medical Council in the Ministry of Internal Affairs, under the chairmanship of Professor G. E. Rein, met with representatives from chemical and pharmaceutical firms to discuss the status of medicines and medical instruments.[3] Representatives from leading firms, Shtol' and Schmidt, Tentelevskii, Ferrein, Keler, and Parke-Davis, attended.[4]

Typhus, carried by lice, had been largely conquered due to improved hygiene. However, health officials worried about water- and food-borne diseases and other diseases spread by parasites as well as close contact. The flare up of dysentery along the Trans-Siberian Railway in 1906, as troops returned from the war with Japan; the cholera epidemic in St. Petersburg in 1908 and 1909; research on the typhoid bacillus in 1906;[5] and the endemic nature of malaria in Russia prompted the tsarist government to issue, in August 1914, "An Instruction on the Prevention and Spread of Infectious Diseases in the Army." This directive particularly focused on preventing typhoid fever and dysentery in the army and ordained the establishment of special clinics for evacuees with infectious diseases.[6]

Vaccines had been developed for typhoid, dysentery, and cholera. These were produced in separate institutes but required items produced by the pharmaceutical industry. Additionally, very important in preventing these food- and water-borne diseases, as well as colds and respiratory diseases, were soap, phenol, Lysol, creasol, and alkaline solutions produced by the industry. Iodine was very important for use as an antiseptic and to purify water. Unfortunately, Russia did not produce enough iodine, nor did it satisfy the Pharmacopoeia.[7] Codeine, heroin, atropine, caffeine, iodine drops and camphor were needed to treat respiratory diseases. Russian opium likewise did not satisfy the Pharmacopoeia. Coal-tar salves, sulfuric salves, hydrogen peroxide, kerosene and benzine were needed for skin diseases. Venereal diseases always accompany wars. The foreign remedy Salvarsan was the best at that time. But arsenic and bismuth also were mainstays in treating venereal diseases. Quinine was needed to quell the symptoms of malaria.

Russia needed to import iodine, codeine, heroin, quinine and aspirin, on which German firms had locked up the patents. One of the main ingredients of aspirin was salicylic acid, which Russia had produced only fitfully from 1909 to 1912, as noted in the last chapter. Russia did have access to substitute febrifuges, however, produced from willow bark and other botanicals indigenous to the Empire. Belladonna and atropine, as well as hydrochloric acid, potassium bromide, and sulfuric acid magnesium were used to treat gastritis.[8] Thousand-leaf was used to treat stomach diseases. Belladonna and atropine were used to treat stomach ulcers.[9] Foxglove, from which digitalis was derived, was used to treat heart diseases. Anesthetics were needed for field hospitals, as were bandages and medical instruments. Russia imported many of the last from Germany. Russia did have a monopoly on Santonin, however, the best remedy for roundworms in humans and animals. And she also produced some key botanicals which could be traded for imports.

Diseases and Medical Problems

Although the food situation was stable at the rear until 1916, population movements were bound to spread disease. Twenty-seven recruiting points sent soldiers to the front. Meanwhile, the Russian government transported German inhabitants of Volynia eastward and Jews and other nationalities began fleeing eastward from the western provinces at the outset of the war. The number of refugees swelled as German and Austrian forces moved into Poland and the Lithuanian provinces of Kovno and Grodno by August of 1915. The population in some interior cities increased up to 30 percent, crowding housing, causing a strain on infrastructure, and causing diseases to flare up.[10]

At the front, given the status of medicine at the time, options for coping with trauma were limited. Analgesics eased pain; morphine was most commonly used. Anesthetics, bandages, surgical items, and disinfectants were crucial for operations and amputations. For the approximately 120,000 suffering from head and jaw wounds, mortality amounted to about 10 percent.[11] Spinal cord wounds, on the other hand, were 95 percent to 100 percent fatal.[12] Russian physicians developed procedures to better manage head and jaw wounds and spinal cord wounds but they were applied to only a minuscule number of those affected. In 1915, one Dr. S. S. Tigershtedt, Doctor of Dentistry (*zubnoi vrach*) in the Military Hospital in Kiev, developed a curved aluminum splint to repair jaw bones fractured by firepower. Surgeons in Kiev, Petrograd, and Moscow trained in the procedure immediately, perfecting it during the next two years.[13] Military surgeon P. K. Zavadskii reported on twenty successful operations to those with spinal cord injuries and V. L. Pokotilo also reported on the successful operation and treatment of vertebrae and spinal cord injuries, performed two weeks after the injury.[14] The majority of soldiers who died from wounds, however—according to one source up to 80 percent—died not from the trauma itself but from sepsis.[15]

Typhoid and cholera epidemics broke out during the first year of the war.[16] Between August 1914 and October 1917, typhoid fever afflicted nearly 100,000 (97,522) soldiers of some 15 million mobilized.[17] The period of greatest danger was 1915. In that year, typhoid affected 16.7

per 1,000 soldiers compared with 10.52 per 1,000 the previous year. Then the incidence of typhoid sharply contracted. In 1916, typhoid afflicted only 3.13 people per 1,000 and in 1917, only 2 per 1,000. [18] Three times more soldiers were stricken with typhoid fever than with cholera during the war. About one third of cholera victims died, however,[19] and in 1915, 44,400 cases of cholera were registered among the population at large.[20]

Dysentery fell between typhoid and cholera,[21] attacking 64,264 or 16.5 per 1,000 soldiers of the Russian army between August 1914 and October 1917. Of these only 5.7 percent died, however.[22] Dysentery was seasonal, reaching its peak in the summer months, July through September.[23] The disease engulfed the civilian population in 1918.[24] In 1892 a Russian military doctor named Grigor'ev had discovered one microbe causing dysentery; in 1898 a Japanese researcher, Shiga, had found another. Other microbes causing dysentery were discovered in the early twentieth century, motivating research on an antitoxin.[25] But in World War I, disinfecting and water purification were the major weapons against typhoid, cholera, dysentery, and other infectious intestinal, water-borne diseases, as well as insect and parasite-borne diseases. Staple disinfectants included phenol, Lysol, creasol, and alkaline solutions.[26]

Croupous inflammation of the lungs affected approximately as many soldiers as did cholera—34,619—between October 1914 and September 1917.[27] Chronic bronchitis, emphysema, and influenza, which could turn into pneumonia, were threats during the war, the great flu pandemic occurring in 1918. As noted, treatment included codeine, heroin, atropine , ephedrine—often in conjunction with caffeine, iodine drops, and camphor.[28] An epidemic of hepatitis broke out in Chita in 1915, affecting 1,937 people.[29] Soviet demographers claimed that one-half the tsarist army suffered from tuberculosis of the lungs. They admitted that conditions in foreign armies were not much better.[30] Educational campaigns and isolation of the sick were used to contain the disease in the pre-World War period,[31] because there was no cure for tuberculosis at this time.

Malaria, Russia's main communicable disease increased alarmingly during the First World War, but reached its apogee only after the war, in the civil war that followed, attaining epidemic proportions in the early 1920s.[32] Quinine was the only remedy at this time and it could only quell symptoms of the disease.

Though not life-threatening, skin diseases were widespread in all armies during the First World War, particularly for soldiers in the trenches. In one Moscow hospital, between October 3, 1914, and August 20, 1915, patients with skin diseases accounted for 5 percent of all patients.[33] Scabies or *chesotka,* caused by a parasite, and ulcerous skin diseases were especially prevalent. [34] Twice as high in the army as in the civilian population in 1913, the "itch" rose during the war among both groups.[35] Impetigo particularly attacked the lower extremities of soldiers at the front. Eczema and dermatitis accounted for about one-quarter of all skin diseases in the Russian army. Remedies included coal-tar salves, sulfuric salves, hydrogen peroxide, a 6 percent solution of hydrochloric acid, and popular remedies like kerosene and benzine applied to the affected area, as well as Peruvian balsam, "benzilbenzoate."[36]

How well did the Russian pharmaceutical industry cope?

Production of Chemicals

The most notable aspect of the industry's performance during the war was the expansion and production of chemicals and other items that had been imported, mainly from German and Swiss houses. As in the United States, Russian production of chemicals was helped by nationalization of German chemical-pharmaceutical factories, such as Schering, Farbwerke and Bayer in Moscow.[37] In addition, Russians improved their output of chemicals, sometimes alone, sometimes with the help of their allies. In 1914, Vladimir Karlovich Ferrein constructed a one-story building at his Nizhnie Kotly factory for production of Vaseline, lanolin, inorganic salts (Glaubers salts, English salts, sulfuric acid potassium), and chemicals. Production of hydrogen peroxide was transferred from the Mologa factory. In the second half of 1915 the chemical department was greatly expanded. A new building, with new boilers and other equipment, came on line at the end of 1916. Here salicylic acid, terpinhydrate, sublimate, and calomel were produced, although a fire in 1916 interrupted output of phenol or carbolic acid.[38]

In Tiflis, the large Prokhorov factory, as well as smaller enterprises, began manufacturing hygroscopic cotton, although it was not of high quality.[39] In 1915 the Tentelevskii factory in St. Petersburg, with a branch in Kiev, and the Reinbot-Morozov factory in Perm province produced chloroform. Salicylic natron, caffeine, and aspirin began to be made in Kiev.[40] In December 1915 the Keler firm had nearly completed a factory for producing salicylic acid; morphine was obtained with great difficulty.[41] Perm and Kostroma produced sulfuric acid and superphosphates.[42] Five new chemical-pharmaceutical factories were organized in Moscow during the war, in addition to Ferrein's enlargement. Four were completely new and one emerged from a beer brewery. One was built by the Union of Zemstvos, one of the most important "public organizations" that emerged during the war, since its chair, Prince George L'vov, would become the chair of the government following the abdication of Tsar Nicholas II in February 1917. At the end of 1914, the Society of the Chemical Industry, known as "Russian Dye," organized a factory, named Russian Dye, to produce both explosives and chemicals for the textile industry. The factory used confiscated German equipment and employed Polish and French engineers. Many Poles lived in Russia proper, as well as in Russian Poland, but it is not certain whether the Polish engineers cooperated voluntarily or involuntarily. In 1916, one Ensign V. M. Rodionov, who was recovering from wounds received at the front, converted the Three Mining Joint-Stock Beer Brewery into a third pharmaceutical cum defense factory to produce iodine, caustic soda, and "products for the artillery administration." In April 1916 the Stock Company (*Aktsionernoe obshchestvo*) of Russian Chemical Factories established a fourth enterprise—the Dorogomilovskii factory—on the banks of the Moscow River, across from the Novodevichii Women's Monastery. The factory was supposed to produce sulfuric and nitric acids, benzol, nitrobenzol, aniline, dimethylaniline, diphenylenediamine. Although the Joint Stock Company received a two-million-ruble subsidy from the government, production faltered due to insufficient building supplies, worker unrest, and a fire. Thus, in 1917, only picric acid was produced.[43] Although the factory, which still operates, did not fulfill its promise, it did become formidable in the Soviet period and probably produced chemical weapons in the 1930s.[44] Allen and Hansbury, the oldest pharmaceutical firm in Britain, established a fifth factory, "Allen and Ganburis," in Moscow in 1917 at the tail end of the war for Russia.[45]

Two new factories were established in the Donbass during the first years of the war. The Russian Dye Society built one, named "Russian Dye," as that in Moscow.[46] The Paramonov Factory was the second.[47] At the end of 1915, a factory built by the Perm zemstvo, in the Urals, was producing 1.2 million puds or some 21,500 tons of superphosphates. Production of sulfuric acid amounted to 693,000 puds in the fall of 1915.[48] By 1916 a factory of the Department of Agriculture was producing about 1,000 puds of superphosphates every 24 hours and a factory near Samara was producing not less than 800,000 puds per year of acidic substances.[49]

Output of phenol, toluol and benzol, needed both for aspirin and for weapons, specifically increased. The Russian Chemical Committee, established at the outset of the war, focused on phenol. In Western Europe phenol was produced from coal tar until the turn of the century when the German factory Rashig and then Hoffmann-La Roche in Switzerland began to produce phenol synthetically. In wartime Russia, phenol was first manufactured in laboratories in Moscow and Petrograd. Production was then transferred to the sequestered Farbwerke Factory in Moscow, which had the requisite equipment. By 1915 Farbwerke was manufacturing 100,000 puds of phenol from domestic raw materials. The new Russian Dye Factory in Moscow produced phenol and picric acid, as well as other chemicals. The new Paramonov and Russian Dye factories in the Donbass and the prewar R. Maier Factory in Revel produced phenol from benzol. Four large factories manufactured a total of 200,000 puds or 3,600 tons of phenol.[50] In 1915, five factories—including the V. Iu. Shumann Factory in Schlusselburg, southeast of Petrograd (as St. Petersburg was called during the war), the Ushkov Factory in Samara, and factories near Moscow and in other areas—made medicines from mononitrophenol, which they derived from picric acid.[51] Numerous small enterprises also sprang up to make phenol from benzol in 1916 and 1917, including the factory of the Kazan' Military-Industrial Committee, another important public organization—the chair of all the committees being Alexander Guchkov, who became Minister of War in the Provisional Government instituted after the fall of the Tsar in March 1917. Additionally, the Ferrein factory in Mologa and another new factory in the Donbass made phenol from coal tar in 1916 and 1917.[52]

The German company Farbwerke had produced toluidin in 1913.[53] By 1914 and 1915 Russian factories were selling toluol to the Military Department.[54] At the same time, two artillery factories, in Grozny and Ekaterinodar, produced 5,000 puds per month of mononitrotoluol.[55]

Although the poisonous character of dinitrobenzol made some factories fearful of manufacturing this chemical and the new Dorogomilovskii Factory was unable to produce it, other aniline factories did so.[56] An explosion leveled an important factory in Kazan' but small private workshops as well as the Sergeev-Samara factory produced various nitro compounds during the war.[57] Many small workshops, newly established during the war, also produced salicylic acid to supplement output by the Ferrein and other factories.[58]

Iodine Production

After war broke out it was no longer feasible to procure iodine from Germany, which controlled the world's supply, 65 percent being derived from Chilean saltpeter or niter and 35 percent from seaweed. Forty-five to almost 50 percent of wounds were to soft tissue in World War I, and in 1915 one M. V. Rostovtsev developed a special apparatus to treat such wounds with iodine steam, which he recommended in place of infusions of iodine.[59]

Thus enormous amounts of energy and money were expended on producing iodine domestically. In the decade before the war, France, Britain, and Japan had attempted to derive iodine from volcanic rock, lemons and sea weed, cutting their dependency on the German monopoly. In 1914, Professor N. D. Averkiev, later a leading Soviet scientist, deduced that Russia might derive iodine from Red Phylophora—*Phylophora rubens* or *Fillofora krasnaia* in the Russian—a plant growing in the Black Sea. Six months' research showed that the plant contained high-quality iodine. Iodine also was discovered in phylophora growing near Sevastopol in the Crimean peninsula and near Odessa on the shore of the Black Sea. Between 1915 and 1918, Averkiev directed more than one hundred expeditions to search out other sources of iodine in the Arctic White Sea, the Caspian Sea, and the Pacific Ocean.[60]

Several iodine-producing facilities were built during World War I. An iodine station using Red Phylophora was established near Odessa in 1915. Use of plants growing in the middle of the Black Sea became too dangerous in 1917, since Turkey was a belligerent. This necessitated using phylophora growing closer to the shoreline, which did not produce as high quality iodine.[61] Nevertheless, between 1915 and 1918 the Odessa iodine factory produced 4 puds or 144 pounds of iodine per month after March 1914. Total production between March 1915 and 1918 for the Odessa factory amounted to 1,000 kilograms (2,200 pounds) of metallic iodine; 2,500 kilograms of tincture of iodine, used as a topical disinfectant; 50 kilograms of various iodine preparations; and 3,000 tons of liquid disinfectants. The Tomsk factory was able to produce 3,000 puds or 36,000 pounds. Total production of iodine by mid-1916 was 2,000 puds (72,000 pounds) or 36 tons.[62] For comparison as to how Russia had coped, world wide production during the war averaged, roughly, 800 tons per year.[63] Other iodine stations were established at Beiuk Shor near Baku; on the White Sea near Arkhangel'sk; and on the shores of the Pacific Ocean. Tests were made in Murmansk. Experiments were conducted to obtain iodine from dirt in the Crimea.[64] Early in 1916 the Prokhorov factory obtained iodine from its stores of Chilean saltpeter and sulfate, tannalbin, kollargol and other disinfecting products from wood distillation.[65]

Imports of antivenereals, quinine, febrifuges, barbiturates and other important products from Japan, as well as other countries, helped fill the medicaments gap. But Russian factories also broke patents on certain crucial medicines and apparatus. For example, Russians applied for a patent on Phenacetin and began to produce it on a mass scale. (It might be noted that the British pharmaceutical industry did not produce the drug at that time.) In 1914 the Russian Dye Factory began production of Novarsolan, analagous to Neosalvarsan.[66] In 1916, I. I. Ostromyslenskii produced a variant, "Arsol," in his Moscow University clinic, although only on a small scale. Special thermometers, heretofore imported, were produced domestically.[67]

As a result of these endeavors, by the third year of the First World War, production of iodine and chemicals had expanded significantly. Indeed, Russia's production of phenol, benzol, and salicylic acid surpassed that of Britain.[68] And while Russia still lacked a sufficiency of iodine, enormous strides had been made by 1917.

Fig. 2.1 Production of Chemicals, in Tons

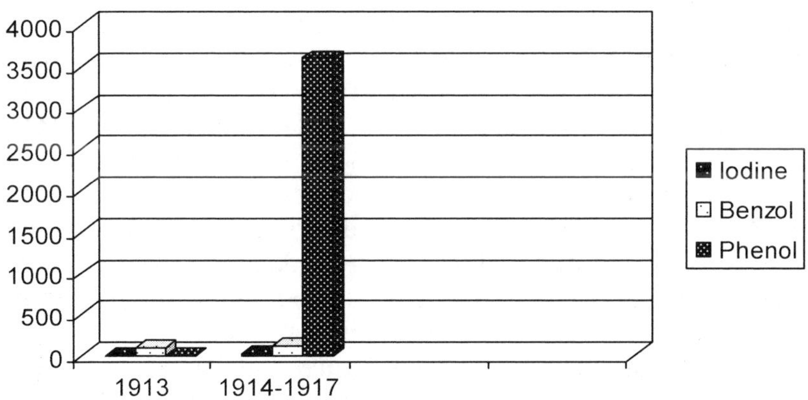

Medicinal Botanicals for Domestic Use and Export

Cultivation and collection of medicinal botanicals also increased somewhat during the war. Schoolchildren and citizens' groups, as well as specialists, set to work with a will, gathering plants and fungi. Monasteries and botanical gardens turned their grounds into plantations.[69] Much of the results were psychological rather than actual, since amateurs were ill-informed on what parts of the plants to pick and how to preserve them. Nevertheless, some strides were made. Eight thousand desiatinas or over twenty thousand acres were sown to the castor oil plant in the northern Caucasus and in the southern Ukraine in 1916. In the same year, 5,000 desiatinas were turned over to cultivation of the opium poppy in Semirech'e, Russian Turkestan, in hopes of lessening dependency on the Ottoman Empire, which now was an enemy, and on Persia, over which Britain and Russia had condominium.[70] About 1,350 puds (21,600 pounds or over 10 tons) were harvested in 1916, dropping to 900 puds in 1917.[71] In 1915, Academician K. A. Nenadkevich uncovered rich deposits of bismuth near the area of Lake Baikal, not far from the Trans-Siberian railway, although these were not exploited until 1919.[72] Over 60,000 puds of potassium were produced, however, as were sizable quantities of fish oil in Arkhangel'sk.[73]

Large amounts of Russia's best-selling medicinal plants were exported throughout the war. A whopping 652,231 puds or 11,740 tons of licorice root were exported in 1914. Exports dropped to a third of that in 1915, then to 38,000 puds or 684 tons in 1916, but climbed to 243,000 puds or 4,324 tons in 1917. Lycopodium or club moss was Russia's most lucrative export; 3,800 puds or 66 tons were exported in 1916. *Sporyn'ia* and the vermifuge, Santonin, also were exported throughout the war.[74] Sales of Santonin fell to 4.7 tons in 1914 from almost 10 tons in 1913, then rose to 6.1 tons in 1915, dropped to 5.6 tons in 1916, and leapt up to 8.7 tons in 1917.[75] During the war the main distributor of Russian Santonin was Goldberg and Company, located on the Arbat in Moscow. The firm had agencies in London, Shanghai and Kobe. The principal supply of Santonin for Europe was stored in London.[76]

The United States imported 12.3 million dollars' worth of goods from European Russia and approximately two and a quarter million dollars' worth from Asiatic Russia in 1914, about two and a half million dollars' worth of imports from European Russia in 1915, about four and a half million dollars' worth in 1916, and some 12.3 million dollars' worth in total in 1917 (with some four million dollars' worth of imports from Asiatic Russia in 1916, and two million dollars' worth in 1917).[77] Among the imports were medicinal botanicals and Santonin. American firms like Moorman Manufacturing Company, in Quincy Illinois, which sold Santonin for exterminating roundworms in hogs, had some trouble procuring the product, but not as much trouble as they were to have after the war.[78]

Fig. 2.2 Exports of Medicinal Botanicals, in Tons

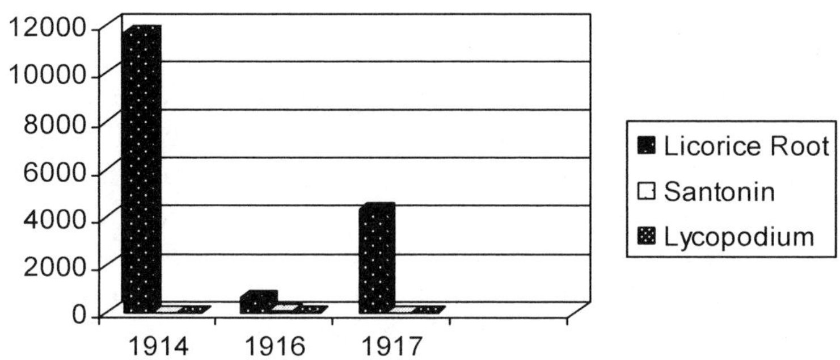

Soap, Serums and Vaccines

One of the mainstays in curbing infection was soap. Soap production varied from place to place during the war. According to *World Trade Notes on Chemicals and Allied Products,* "[B]efore the war there were in Russia some 780 soap works, with total annual output of about 180,000 tons."[79] In 1916 it was reported that in Minsk, in the vulnerable western border region of the empire, 6,000 puds of "good quality bar soap" could not be produced for 9 rubles per *pud* because of "the cost of raw material." Thus, production of soap from cottonseed oil was being investigated.[80] In the fall of 1917, David MacGowan, American Consul in Moscow related alarmingly that "[S]oap has been scarce in Russia during the last two years." Prices for "mother-of-pearl" toilet soap and "marbled soap" were high but "laundry soap" was "almost unobtainable." He attributed the shortage of soap to cost of fats, coconut oil and caustic soda, adding that "[M]easures to regulate the distribution of soap-making materials are proposed."[81]

Not of the least importance were production of vaccines and serums. In the United States, the H. K. Mulford Company became a leading purveyor of diphtheria antitoxin to the government after America entered the war in 1917.[82] In Russia, serums and vaccines were the purview of institutes like the Bacteriological Institute in Ufa, managed by the provincial zemstvo. The Ufa Institute was mainly concerned with the rise in rabies cases during the war. Numbers of those coming to its Pasteur Station for bites from wolves, as well as dogs and other domestic animals swelled to 1,377 in 1916 from 1,197 in 1915. However, under the direction of a woman physician, after the head male doctor was called to army duty, the Ufa Institute's small staff of physicians, fel'dshers and assistants also conducted bacteriological research on the White River and other water sources to prevent water-borne diseases; provided anthrax vaccine and other vaccines for the cattle, swine, and horse herds which were not only an important part of the local economy but crucial for national food, transport and leather during the war; did research on diphtheria and tuberculosis and, in conjunction with the Ferrein firm in Moscow, the Institute of Experimental Medicine in Petrograd, and the Khar'kov Bacteriological Institute, produced scarlatina, streptococcus, and antidysentery serums as well as cholera vaccine (1,101 cubic centimeters in the first 10 months of 1916), scarlatina-streptococcus, and typhus vaccines (13, 260 cubic centimeters in the first 10 months of 1916), gonococcus and smallpox vaccines (42,910 ampules or 450,000 to 500,000 doses of the latter in the first 10 months 1916). These serums and vaccines undoubtedly were distributed throughout the Empire by the All-Russian Union of Zemstvos. For example, the Institute contributed 81,443 cubic centimeters of typhus vaccine used to inoculate citizens in Kiev in August 1915.[83]

Cooperation Achieves Results

Increased output of pharmaceuticals came about through synergy between large and small pharmaceutical enterprises, the central government, local government, and private groups. The Imperial Russian government played a leading role in boosting pharmaceutical output. In addition to the conference called at the outset of the war, the government convened subsequent conferences.[84] In February 1915 the Ministry of Internal Affairs called an "Interdepartmental Committee on the Pharmaceutical Industry."[85] In March 1915 the Ministry of Agriculture called an interdepartmental meeting on increasing the output of medicinal botanicals, supplying instructions on cultivation and collection. A second conference on chemical and pharmaceutical industries, sponsored by the government, debated important medical issues from February to April 1915. Additionally, the government subsidized manufactories, particularly to increase iodine production, cultivation of medicinal botanicals, and other projects. A main figure at these conferences was F. G. (sometimes listed as F. A.) Ferrein, as noted, probably a relative of Vladimir Karlovich Ferrein.[86]

Scientific societies and public groups worked mightily to produce needed pharmaceuticals. Although sometimes their help was more superficial than real, public groups were particularly active in the fight to curb typhoid. In September 1915 the Union of Zemstvos arranged 7, 123 beds in infectious hospitals for evacuated military. In November 1915, twenty-six sanitary trains evacuated individuals at the front suffering from infectious diseases. An estimated 4, 891 typhoid patients were evacuated during the second half of 1915. In September 1915 the army ordered that a sanitary-epidemiological detachment (*otriad*) be established in each corps. In some corps these detachments were established only in the spring of 1916. Ultimately, typhoid diminished in 1916, however, due to widespread immunization against the disease beginning in that year.[87]

Although Russia experienced a *lekarstvennyi golod* (medicaments famine) in the first years of the war, by 1915, prices for bismuth and iodine fell. In 1916 prices for more items began to fall and some pharmacies enjoyed sufficient supplies of crucial medicines. [88]

Deaths from four communicable diseases fluctuated. For example, in the European part of the Russian Empire, deaths from typhus were estimated to be about 18,000 in 1914 and 15, 350 in 1915, rising to 23,600 in 1916 and then falling to a little over 19,000 in 1917. Deaths from typhoid fever ranged from over 62,000 in 1914 to almost 50,500 in 1916, with an over 10,000 drop in 1917. Deaths from dysentery were almost 23,000 in 1914 but then fell steadily reaching approximately 15,000 in 1916 and 14,800 in 1917. Deaths from cholera were very low the first year of the war, at only 510, but rose to a devastating 8,430 in 1915. They then dropped to a little over 1,000 in 1916 and fell back to their original number in 1917. These statistics do not distinguish between the military and civilian populations, but demographers theorize that the great bulk of these deaths occurred amongst the troops.[89] In general, mortality rates for Russia were not extraordinary during the First World War. Earlier estimates asserted that of the approximately fifteen million mobilized in Russia during the First World War, about one third—some five and a half million troops—died during the three years the tsarist army participated in World War I. More recent accounts have severely revised these figures downward, to 1.6 to 2 million wartime deaths.[90] S. G. Wheatcroft and R. W. Davies have concluded that abnormal deaths for civilians "did not increase substantially" during the war.[91] We can hypothesize that a stable food supply and tolerable living conditions on the home front, plus increased output of pharmaceuticals, as well as vaccines, prevented higher mortality and, concomitantly, caused mortality to decline in 1916 and 1917.

Despite a tolerable situation at the front as well as the rear, some groups were fixated on political change and on change in the pharmacy sector. F. A. Gaida has documented how prominent "liberals"—Kadets, Octobrists and Progressists in both houses of parliament, the State Duma and the State Council, the Union of Zemstvos and Cities (Zemgor) and the War Industries Committees—became increasingly dissatisfied with Tsar Nicholas' prosecution of the war and in 1915/1916 moved from insisting on greater participation in policy making to discussions on taking over the government.[92] Michael Melancon has demonstrated that some Mensheviks and Socialist Revolutionaries put revolution on hold during the war. Others, however, converted by Lenin, joined the Bolsheviks in inciting strikes and tearing down morale in the army.[93] Despite progress in the pharmaceutical sector during the war, these liberals and radicals, historically antipathetic to privately owned pharmacies and pharmaceutical factories, also became increasingly convinced that government management would benefit dispensing and pharmaceutical production

Revolution

Some opponents of the existing pharmaceutical system were pharmacist-revolutionaries. Some, in turn, were Bolsheviks. Others were Mensheviks, like B. N. Saltykov, who had advocated control over pharmacies by workers or by municipalities since the first decade of the twentieth century and had attempted to erode the pharmacy system by fomenting strikes before the war. Izrail I. Levinshtein represented another branch of socialists, who were keen to implement pharmacy education reform and disappointed with the tsarist regime's track record on this issue. Radical pharmacists called strikes during the war, viewing it as a golden opportunity to weaken private ownership of pharmacies. About a thousand strikes flared up during 1915 and 1916. Labor organizers, however, worked hard to arouse the workers' indignation to strike-level pitch. Menshevik and Bolshevik pharmacy organizers pressed for shorter work days, higher pay and increased benefits in pharmacies and pharmaceutical companies. Yet half or more ordinary pharmacists were cool to their blandishments. Pharmacy owners and pharmaceutical companies attempted to resolve disputes by partial concessions or by bringing the case to arbitration boards.[94] That pharmacy workers were not suffering unduly is borne out by the fact that refugee pharmacists eagerly accepted jobs and longer summer vacations was one of the demands of radical pharmacists in 1917.[95]

"Liberal" politicians also opposed the existing pharmacy system. Zemstvo activists had promoted "public" or zemstvo ownership of pharmacies, with subsidized or free dispensing since the 1880s. In the Second Duma, members of the Union of October or Octobrists, some of whom were landowners who had served in the zemstvos, others representing a wide spectrum of the population, had sponsored bills, which finally passed the Third Duma and the State Council in 1911 and 1912, respectively, catapulting public pharmacies ahead of private ones. During the war municipal officials became enthusiastic about city governments' orchestrating or taking over pharmaceutical production. Their justification was that pharmaceutical companies were engaging in war profiteering, a claim that does not bear up under scrutiny.[96] Kadets, Octobrists, and Progressists became more certain of the efficacy of government-managed dispensing and pharmaceutical production through their experience in Zemgor.[97] The war also thrust up recent converts to overhauling the system, like F. A. Ferrein, and Professor Karl Vladimirovich Bening, a *Magistr* of Pharmacy who, in addition to teaching chemistry in the Kazan' Dental School, wrote and taught courses on medicinal plants during the war and was involved with forensic pharmacy.

The year 1917 segued Russia into two new political systems, which impacted the economy in general and ultimately the pharmaceutical sector in particular. On February 23, crowds protesting bread shortages in Petrograd precipitated revolution. Similar riots in the United States preceded those in Russia. Between February 21 and 26, 1917, women rioted over the high price of staples in Philadelphia and New York, storming major hotels, demanding officials' attention, and screaming "We Want Bread." Significantly, the Gregorian calendar in the West was two weeks ahead of the Julian calendar used in Russia. American officials "denounced" the riots "as the work of agitators" but rushed food to the markets.[98]

In Russia, in contrast, the havoc in St. Petersburg, which shortly spread to Moscow, allowed Kadets, Octobrists, and Progressists to force Tsar Nicholas to abdicate and to form a Provisional Government. The liberals and the socialists who entered the government in the spring and summer made few major alterations to the economic system or to the pharmacy sector. Their focus on worker rights, however, made the economic environment less hospitable to business.[99]

The Bolsheviks, who seized power in October/November 1917, on the other hand, turned the economy, including the pharmacy sector, topsy-turvy. Non-Bolshevik pharmacists supported Bolshevik changes in the industry for various reasons. Saltykov and Levinshtein hoped to impose their visions on the pharmaceutical industry, pharmacy practice and pharmacy education under a Bolshevik regimen. F. A. Ferrein, an arm-chair specialist on pharmaceutical production, was receptive to a Bolshevik-managed pharmacy system, not so much because of ideological conviction as because of his annoyance with the tsarist government's policies toward the industry (particularly the government's tariff schedules), because he saw the Bolsheviks as strong, and because he saw an enhanced role for himself in a Bolshevik-run pharmacy system. The same seems true of Professor K. V. Bening who, having formed a forensic pharmacy section in the Kazan' City Laboratory in the spring of 1917, took over the laboratory in November 1918, giving himself the pompous title of Director of the Chemical-Biological Institute of the Tatar People's Commissariat of Health.[100] John Hutchinson has adumbrated other health care professionals who were "pragmatic" rather than ideological Bolsheviks.[101]

In 1918, the Bolsheviks squelched private ownership of pharmacies and drug stores, then seized pharmaceutical factories. They imposed a system more centralized and far more bureaucratic than that of the imperial government on pharmacies and the pharmaceutical industry in 1918 and 1919. Whether this benefited dispensing, the industry and the populace will be discussed in succeeding chapters.

The First Decade

3
The Civil War: Nationalization, Centralization, Bureaucratization

The civil war that engulfed the Russian Empire from 1917/1918 to 1921 wreaked far more havoc on the population than the preceding world war. While fewer soldiers died—perhaps less than 1 million as compared with perhaps 2 million during the world war—abnormal civilian deaths escalated from minimal amounts during the world war to 8 million or more during the civil war.[1] The spike in mortality that occurred during the civil war was partly the result of wanton murders perpetrated by combatants with diametrically opposed value systems.[2] Wheatcroft and Davies stress, however, that infectious diseases were the main killers between 1918 and 1920. In 1921 and 1922 famine took its toll.[3]

The flare up in infectious diseases, in turn, resulted from turbulent population movements; poor living conditions, due to chaos and deterioration of the economy; and a dearth of vaccines, soap, disinfectants, antiseptics, and medicines. Vaccines were produced in separate institutes. Their output was curtailed by economic dislocation. Soap, disinfectants, febrifuges and other medicines were the purview of some four thousand pharmacies, ten thousand drug stores and over one hundred pharmaceutical manufactories. During the civil war these enterprises were laid low because of military campaigns, because the international drug trade faltered but also because of policies forced upon them. The Bolshevik experiment in the distribution and production of pharmaceuticals during the civil war went dreadfully awry.

Civil War Diseases

During the world war, military action had been confined to the western provinces of the empire and troop and population movements had been fairly systematic. During the civil war large chunks of the population were on the move, covering large portions of the Empire. Imperial army and naval officers; Socialist Revolutionaries of various hues, Czechoslovak prisoners, Siberian Cossacks and warlords attempted to dislodge the Bolsheviks, ensconced in Moscow after March 1918, converging on them from the south, east and north/northwest, in a sort of distorted circle that stretched from the Black Sea to the Gulf of Finland and the Arctic to the Pacific and the south.[4] Anarchists and Ukrainian nationalists tried to pry the Ukraine from the Bolsheviks' grip in 1918, with German help. Contingents of French, British, Americans and Japanese got into the fray in 1918/1919, the Japanese occupying the Far East until 1922. Fighting flared in Georgia, Armenia and Central Asia. In 1920, Josef Pilsudski's Poles bested the Red Army in the Jewish Pale of Belorussia and western Ukraine.[5] Several leading Menshevik pharmacists became disenchanted with the Bolsheviks as early as January 1918, terming their action a coup rather than a popular revolution, but supported them nonetheless, in order to prevent the return of "the bourgeoisie."[6] Liberal politicians, business people and landowners resisted or fled the Bolsheviks. The Bolsheviks' erstwhile constituents, factory workers and peasants, also rose up against them, in the case of the peasants in the tens of thousands.[7]

The assorted armies and hapless civilians who crisscrossed the land on railways, particularly the eleven lines fanning out from Moscow and the Trans-Siberian, who plied the rivers, particularly the Volga, lavishly spread bacilli, parasites, spirochetes, and viruses.

Typhus, which was rare beforehand, felled half a million Red Army troops between 1918 and 1920. In 1919 typhus afflicted 130.7 per 1,000 Red Army soldiers. The population at large was less affected, but the incidence was still high—34 per 1,000 of the population were sick with typhus in 1919. Recurring fever was widespread in the Red Army. In 1920, nearly 178 of every 1,000 troops were sick with recurring fever; in 1922 recurring fever still afflicted some 171 out of 10,000 citizens at large.[8]

Typhoid, dysentery, and cholera were less prevalent.[9] Cholera was not a great threat to the Red Army during the civil war.[10] However, the water- and food-borne disease affected over forty-one thousand civilians in 1918. Although this was lower by some 3,000 than in 1915, by 1921 the number of people suffering from cholera increased four times to 179,000.[11] The influenza pandemic of 1918 is mentioned only in passing in Soviet sources. Smallpox, though, affected 32 per 10,000 people in 1919, at its apogee. The disease was most prevalent in the northwest provinces of Russia in that year, afflicting 96 per 10,000 people in Novgorod Province; 93 per 10,000 in Iaroslavl'; 81 per 10,000 in Tver';

and 78 per 10,000 in Pskov.[12]

Malaria, Russia's most widespread infectious disease, regularly affected up to three and a half million people each year. The highest concentration of malaria usually was in the Caucasus; in 1913, for example, 783 of 10,000 people were infected there. During the Civil War, malaria not only increased but became more common in the north. In 1923, malaria infected 474 per 10,000 of the population over all. The incidence of malaria was particularly high in the Volga region and in Central Asia. In 1923 in Samara province 2,779 out of 10,000 were infected; in Astrakhan, 2,554; in Simbirsk, 1,365; in Saratov, 1,942.[13]

Fig. 3.1 Infectious Diseases in the Russian/Soviet Army, per 1000

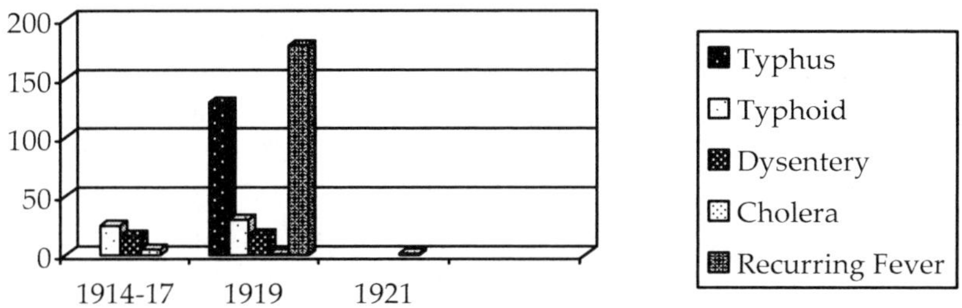

Fig. 3.2 Infectious Diseases in the General Population, per 1000

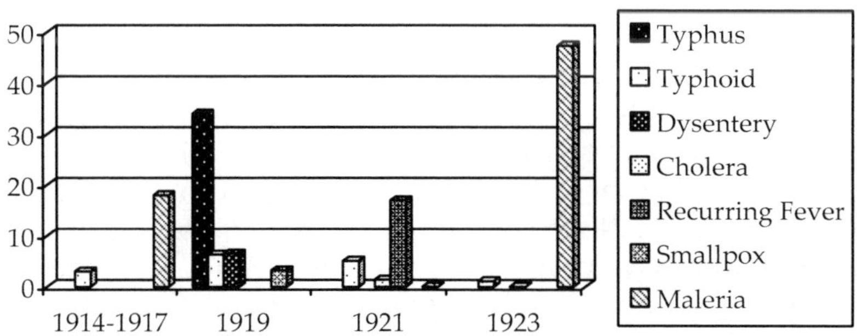

Counterproductive Bolshevik Policies

The Bolsheviks' criminalization of market activity exacerbated the public health problem. The All-Russian Extraordinary Commission or Vecheka, the Bolshevik agency charged with suppressing private enterprise, counterfeiting, counterrevolution and sabotage,[14] executed summarily but also incarcerated manufacturers, business people and traders. At the end of the civil war, in 1921, almost a quarter of a million people were crammed into prisons, labor and concentration camps managed by the Commissariat of Internal Affairs, the Commissariat of Justice, and the Vecheka. In many cases these facilities, some dating back to tsarist times, some newly requisitioned from monasteries or churches, some hastily erected, contained twice as many prisoners as there were places. They were breeding grounds for infectious diseases. Health professionals in the commissariats of Justice and Health and local physicians and health specialists lamented that sick prisoners were not separated from the healthy. They warned that inadequate medical attention, overcrowding, minimal rations, use of common bowls and utensils, filthy latrines, and lack of soap and linen could spawn epidemics in the prisons and camps that would engulf nearby towns. Health professionals urged baths, haircuts, better food, and improved hygiene and also early, even immediate release of sick prisoners to hospitals and clinics. They especially worried about minors and the mentally ill.[15]

Unfortunately, Bolshevik policies curtailed the distribution and the production of soap, disinfectants, and other pharmaceuticals. Convinced that state-run economies were, ipso facto, more efficient than those in private hands, ideologically opposed to private production and trade,[16] and desirous of channeling as many assets as possible to themselves and to the Red Army (which swelled to three then five million during the civil war), Lenin and the new Soviet officials seized businesses, bank accounts and other private property; attempted to centralize foreign trade, payrolls and distribution; attempted to militarize factory labor; demanded that factories send a certain percentage of their output to Moscow; requisitioned grain; attempted to block private trade; and printed money indiscriminately.[17] The Bolsheviks' adversaries implemented similar policies, but not to the same extent.[18]

The Bolshevik policies, known as "War Communism"—although in fact they began before the civil war erupted—were deleterious to the economy in general and to the pharmaceutical sector in particular. The contrast between Bolshevik controlled areas and the Ukraine, while the Germans and Austrians occupied it in the first years of the civil war, was striking. There the pharmaceutical sector as well as heavy industry operated fairly smoothly.[19] In the Bashkir Republic, where locals, including Bolsheviks, defied demands from Moscow, agriculture and industry worked with some semblance of normalcy and full markets lured citizens from other areas.[20] Unhappily, the pharmacy sector did not work well in the Bashkir Republic, as we shall see, and in other areas controlled by the Bolsheviks pharmacies were hard pressed to distribute and pharmaceutical factories to produce the materials needed to contain infectious diseases, succor the dying, and restore the wounded, ill and feeble to health.

Nationalization of Pharmacies

Pharmacies and drug stores were affected immediately after the Bolshevik takeover in Petrograd and Moscow and during the next two years in outlying areas. In October 1917, following the Bolshevik ascent to power, Menshevik pharmacists attempted to put cities and pharmacy workers in charge of pharmacies, a policy they called "municipalization."[21] Claiming this was "chaotic"—although in fact the procedures had been quite orderly—in December and January 1918, the Bolshevik government began to nationalize pharmacies and drug stores.

The new Soviet government's aim was to establish a more rational pharmacy system. But, although nationalization procedures were thorough and the Bolsheviks retained many imperial pharmacy rules and regulations (and issued many more), dispensing did not work as well as under the old system and, in fact, deteriorated.

The number of pharmacists declined. Some owners of pharmacies, like the energetic and creative Antonina Lesnevskaia, fled Russia when their property was expropriated. Other owners and lessees stayed on but were forced to go underground. They would surface at the end of the civil war, when the Soviet government allowed individuals to lease pharmacies, although not own them, and, for a few years, their expertise would again serve the public and the country as they managed pharmacies and led government-run unions of pharmacists.[22] Many pharmacists were conscripted into the Red Army.[23] The shortage of pharmacists was serious at the end of the civil war. Izrail Ionasovich Levinshtein, a revolutionary pharmacist in the tsarist era, had long been committed to reforming pharmacy education, as had Antonina Lesnevskaia. Unlike her, he stayed in Russia, enthusiastically helping the new Soviet government. But though he worked diligently during the civil war to produce more qualified pharmacists, he had little success.[24]

Many pharmacies were closed, partly because there were not enough pharmacists to staff them. In 1922, one Soviet pharmacy official lamented that whereas before World War I, the Russian Empire had about "4,000 pharmacies and up to 10,000 drug stores" that sold packaged medicines and sundries, at the end of the civil war the Soviet Union (admittedly shorn of the Baltic States, Poland, and parts of western provinces) "had only 900 pharmacies outside hospitals and entirely no 'drug stores' and as a result trade in medicaments" went on "in markets and bazaars, where it" was "not subject to any control and supervision," allowing "falsification by unknown firms and producers." [25]

As the number of pharmacy specialists decreased, the number of bureaucrats involved in pharmacy burgeoned. Multiple agencies were organized at every level to manage sequestered private pharmacies. At the central level there was a Pharmacy Department in the Commissariat of Health; *Farmatsentr* in the Supreme Council of the National Economy (VSNKh or the more pronounceable Vesenkha), and for a time a Pharmacy Department in the Commissariat of Internal Affairs. At the provincial and district levels there were departments (*otdely* and *podotdely*), later called pharmacy administrations (*aptekoupravleniia*). The hordes of officials staffing these agencies engaged in endless meetings and turf wars rather than constructive activities that could benefit consumers. Attempts to centralize funding, sourcing and pay made the system slow and cumbersome. Bureaucrats squelched pharmacists' initiatives to acquire medicines if they did not follow the rules. [26]

The impact of Bolshevik policies on dispensing is illustrated by developments in Ufa, capital of the Bashkir Republic. Following the February 1917 revolution the governor of the province was dismissed and replaced first by a nobleman and then by a zemstvo teacher. From December 1917 to March 1918 a pro-Bolshevik revolutionary committee ruled the city. Czechoslovak troops forced the Bolsheviks to abandon Ufa in June 1918, leaving the city duma (council) in power until the end of December of that year when the Bolsheviks regained control.[27] An ungainly report from *gubrevkom* (Provincial Revolutionary Commissar) Comrade Yel'tsin to the *Revvoensovet* (Revolutionary Military Council) of the *Vostfront* (Eastern Front) Comrade Shtemberg depicted the disease and chaos that overwhelmed the once bustling capital of the province by October 1919:[28]

> … daily on average come to Ufa about 1000 sick comrades of the red army (sic); of them die up to 100; now at the point of reception and in carts—that is wagons—are about 3000 people… they often lie on the floor and often directly on the street in the dirt without medical help from one on-duty doctor, 2 sisters of mercy and 10 *sanitarniki*. There are no blankets, no linen and baths…The situation is terrible…To my questions—why there are so few doctors and sanitary servers—I received the answer that part of the sanitary personnel are sick but the majority have scattered, do not want to serve, and the doctors entirely do not. …In the Evacuation point there is no transport for carrying the sick … the sick are not disinfected…the hospital is bad—no firewood, entirely without lighting, neither electric nor kerosene, the sick lie in darkness—there is no water supply—to my question why until now nothing has been corrected, was answered: nowhere no one gives anything and there is nowhere to make requests, there are no workers, no materials. In the provincial committee they asked for soap which, if there is, they were refused, the answer being that it was necessary to compute on the budget how much You required per month and how many people—that such things are not allowed—without a budget—but it is necessary to receive soap—also there are no good baths, so that each military section can wash and disinfect.…From October 28 I will work out a plan for struggle with the epidemic of typhus…now I turn to the Military Revolutionary Council with a request about finances… will they pay directly or will bills be transferred to *Zdravotdel* (the Health department) or another military *sanchast* (sanitary sector). It is necessary to know because we will take material for which it is necessary to pay…and expenses are colossal, such as repair of the bath, building a disinfecting chamber, building isolation points, and many other expenditures.[29]

To remedy the problems in Ufa Comrade Yel'tsin proposed administrative-command methods—orders from the Revolutionary Military Council to prevent the sanitary personnel from leaving—and planning, for "the military doctors work badly, each sanitary sector works separately by itself…not having worked out a plan…from this it appears that the military and civilian *sanchasti* (sanitary sectors) must unite—work out a general plan of struggle with epidemics."[30]

But more than demands that medical personnel obey, plan and cooperate with each other were needed to rectify the situation and indeed, regulation and bureaucracy were part of the problem. The scraps of paper emanating almost daily between authorities and pharmacists in the city of Ufa in 1919 and 1920 illustrated how bureaucracy bogged down dispensing, the growing shortages of medicines and wares, and the flight of pharmacists from the eight pharmacies, drug stores and pharmacy warehouse transferred from private and zemstvo ownership to government control. On February 15, 1919, the Ufa Sanitary Department ordered "All Managers of Soviet Pharmacies" to write "requests for materials, chemicals and galenical preparations" from the Central Pharmacy Warehouse "on the proposed blanks." Pharmacy managers were admonished "to request only the most necessary preparations, signing the *trebovanie* (requests) personally."[31] On February 25 the Head of the "Farpod" (Pharmacy subdepartment) forwarded the communique of the People's Commissar for Health of the Ufa Provincial Sanitary *otdel* (Department) to "All Managers" of pharmacies in the city stipulating that since "daily come in great amount requests from the military sector and even private people for... substances such as gum Arabic, glycerine, cotton wool and others...to me in the Commissariat for decision, I ask...that... only large military requests or requests on credit...are to be submitted for my review, requests for various substances, allowed for over-the-counter sale must be satisfied according to amounts on hand."[32] On February 21 the "Farpod" informed the managers of Soviet pharmacies that staff were to be paid every two weeks.[33] On February 21 pharmacy managers were ordered "tomorrow at 10 AM to present to the [Pharmacy] *podotdel* the cashier's books of your pharmacy for scrutiny." [34] On February 27 an "Obligatory Regulation" from the Provincial Sanitary Otdel noted that "information has come to the otdel that some private persons and also institutions have not yet presented information about the wares they have in their pharmacies—including bandaging materials and medicines. In view of this," the authorities sternly ordained, "the Otdel proposes to all not presenting information to do so in a week from the day of publication. The guilty will be taken to...the Revolutionary Tribunal with confiscation of wares found among private people."[35] A Decree of December 28, 1918 impacted drug stores, informing owners and managers to take down the sign "Aptekarskii" and put up one designating the business as "Parfumernyi." It also reminded managers that all medicinal substances were subject to control and forbade owners of drug stores from trading in medicines.[36]

Shortages were particularly noticeable in 1919. On February 17 the Ufa Farpod notified managers that in order to save paper, only dispensing according to a doctor's prescription was to be recorded; over-the-counter dispensing was to be done without this. [37] On February 21 a handwritten note from the manager of the warehouse, informing the

Administration of the Provincial Sanitary Department for pharmacy matters that "to the warehouse come requests from pharmacies and institutions ...for galenical wares," inquired whether this could be done "by Soviet pharmacies." [38] A little brown piece of paper dated February 27 bore a typed request from the Head of the Sanitary Sector of the 27th Division to the Commissar for Health for "temporary use" of "two boxes of carbolic acid and transport."[39] On March 4 a mimeographed 3"x5" piece of paper from the RSFSR People's Commissariat for Health informed "Managers of Rural Soviet Pharmacies" that the Farpod of the Provincial Sanotdel "makes known to You that in view of the insufficiency in the market of warehouse products and until there is a special decree, it is necessary to prepare"—here a dotted line was left blank for handwritten insertion of the item—"without syrup, explaining that minors who are sick, for correcting the taste, can add honey or sugar."[40] This, of course, presumed that these last items were available in the market. A 3" x 5" mimeographed piece of brown paper dated March 6 informed all managers of Soviet pharmacies in the city of Ufa that "a meeting of the Pharmacy Commission" informs "You" that "in view of the insufficiency of medicine...entirely to stop over-the-counter dispensing of Pyramidon, Phenacetin, Quinine, Castor oil, and all iodine salts."[41] In November 1919, over-the-counter dispensing of camphor was stopped.[42]

Evidence of pharmacists leaving Ufa in 1919 was conveyed by the following: a terse handwritten note of Adolf Lindts to the "Farmatsevticheskii podotdel" of the Commissariat of Health that "on March 6 by me was transferred management of Pharmacy number 8 to Provizor Ia. L. Bystrymkom"[43]; a missive written on stationery embellished with an Art Nouveau letterhead and flower proclaiming the "Aleksandrovskaia Apteka of A. P. Salazkin in Ufa" that one "L. Avirane" had "become the manager of the Aleksandrovskaia Pharmacy Salazkin" on July 8, 1919; [44] and the notice that a commission had been appointed to take inventory of the *aptekarskii magazin* or drug store of Ioffe, "who had fled to Siberia" and of Khtsanov, who likewise had "fled to Siberia." Further, this same communique noted that because of "defects in information" in "the matter of nationalizing pharmacies," the Collegium of the Provincial *Sanotdel* was "eliminating one Provizor Tarasevich" as manager of a pharmacy and head of the [Pharmacy] *podotdel* and replacing him with "a temporary assistant."[45]

Pharmacies became less accommodating to citizens and more cramped for staff. In March 1919 the Farpod of the Ufa Provincial

Sanitary Department of the Commissariat of Health informed managers of pharmacies that "as of the 15th night-time dispensing" was "stopped."[46] A somewhat contradictory "Declaration" in March informed citizens that three pharmacies would dispense at night in the city of Ufa. All others would "function from 9 AM to 9 PM."[47] In August a lengthy list of rules was issued for pharmacy staff, decreeing that pharmacies were to be open from 9 in the morning until 10 at night (presumably summer hours), that the normal shift was 8 hours, but that staff must come and go at designated hours, they could not be late without a major reason, they would receive a 2 hour break three hours after arriving, private conversations were forbidden on the job, prescriptions must be written in a special book, "to give medical help" was "not allowed" but "to give first aid" was "obligatory," and that "all conversations with the public and among themselves on political themes, having the purpose of spreading lies or discrediting Soviet power will be punished by the laws of wartime."[48]

The loss of pharmacists and shortages of staff were accompanied by loss of bookkeepers. The Bolsheviks were keen on husbanding the assets they had acquired. Indeed, deficits dictated the necessity for careful use of supplies on hand. These requirements led, at least in Ufa province, to schemes for turning out bookkeepers for pharmacies, particularly in districts or counties, and in warehouses. Individuals at least sixteen years of age, with a four-year education, were eligible for training in arithmetic, simple and commercial; accounting, auditing, and Latin. They were to interact with the *Gubzdravotdel* (Provincial Health Department) and to "work out, in a short time, a list of medicines allowed to be dispensed by the staff of pharmacies in extreme cases, in limited amounts, with the agreement of the management."[49]

It ought to be noted that although ordinary people had less access to soaps, disinfectants, and quality medicines, Lenin and high Soviet officials were insulated from the deficits. During 1920, like the sixteenth-century Romanov rulers, they were provided with medicines from a private pharmacy in the Kremlin, which stocked medicines from abroad. From the evidence on hand, Lenin ordered a lot of sedatives.[50]

Further, while regulated dispensing lessened, abuse of drugs escalated. Porous borders enabled more narcotics to enter Russia. Closure of pharmacies and drug stores allowed drugs to hemorrhage onto the streets. Use of cocaine and opiates, not common before the First World War, had become more prevalent during it as a result of increased prescriptions for war wounds, speculation in drugs, and, in Petrograd, disorder caused by the influx of refugees and transients.[51] The millions of children and adolescents made homeless by the civil war liberally sniffed cocaine, injected opiates, and smoked hemp. As early as May 1918, a half year after they had taken the helm, the Bolshevik government, Sovnarkom, asked the Cheka to "take exceptional measures" to stop illegal sales and speculation in drugs.[52] The Pharmacy Department of the Commissariat of Health selected forty-four pharmacists, among them Izrail Ionasovich Levinshtein, to help the Cheka stamp out trafficking in narcotics in 1921.[53]

Some shortages may have been due to hoarding and to utopian schemes for free (*besplatno*) dispensing of medicines, mentioned in letters from Ufa, for in 1920 and early 1921 in that region the availability of supplies in pharmacies and warehouses was mixed. For example, inspection of Pharmacy No. 1 in 1920 stated that "There are no medicaments besides camphor and green soap. There is insufficient morphine."[54] Inspection of another pharmacy March 19, 1920, noted "iodine, opium, spirits of wine 95%, cocaine, aspirin, glycerine and morphine," but no amounts were given.[55] Inspections of yet another yielded glycerine, morphine, cocoa, spirits of wine.[56] Investigation of Pharmacy No. 6 found Resorsin, oils, zinc, salol, carbolic acid, cocaine, spirits of wine, aspirin—again with no information on quantities.[57] Some reports referred to "small amounts,"[58] still others to "sufficiencies" or availability "to allow dispening."[59] As in regard to the market in goods in general,[60] Ufa may have been an anomaly. In July 1920 a missive to all "*Kanzdravotdelam*" (Cantonal or District health departments) noted that along with "requisitions of medicines" by Narkomzdrav, "galenical preparations" could "be prepared for which at present there are raw materials…infusions of valerian, iodine, opium… mint drops, and some salves."[61] In November 1920, a report noted that "at present the warehouse is replenished (*popolen*) with surgical items, bandaging materials and items of care for the sick." Valerian root meanwhile "has been received in sufficient amount and about 200 puds (7,200 pounds) of fish fat, of which until now, there was severe insufficiency." There was however, an "absence of ether" and "hydrochloric acid" but the *Gubfarpod* (the provincial pharmacy subsection) had "taken measures to procure these preparations locally."[62] And in January 1921 a Circular proclaimed that: "The extremely limited amount of medicines made it necessary" to limit "powders…or capsules to the sick" to a "two-day" supply, "to dispense drops not more than 10.0, in mixtures not more than 15.0," and "pills not more than 30 *shtuk*."[63]

The old, the young and the handicapped were ill-cared for in Ufa in 1920. They received the bare minimum of food and medical care.[64] And the availability of medicines and household items was uneven throughout Soviet Russia as a whole. Circular No. 37 from the Head of the Pharmacy Sector A. Aluf, dated February 23, 1921, to All Provincial Health Departments and Pharmacy Sub-departments decreed that: "In view of insignificant stores of camphor and the extremely important significance of it for typhus and other epidemic diseases, it is proposed to limit preparation and dispensing both with regard to doctor's prescriptions as well as over-the-counter sale of all preparations containing camphor for any kind of use. All stores are to be used exclusively for subcutaneous injections of internal usage."[65]

Shortages of Botanicals

Lack of pharmaceuticals mainly resulted from fall-off in production and to some extent from breakdown in international trade links. On the supply side there were a few points of light. Chemists in Irkutsk produced bismuth preparations in Military-Drug Store Number 14 (which heretofore had produced ether, nitric acid and bismuth nitrate) from sources discovered in 1915 and uncovered new bismuth sources farther east near the city of Blagoveshchensk.[66] The Santonin Factory in Chimkent, following seizure from its former owners, produced limited amounts of Santonin, licorice and soap and began to experiment with production of technical morphine.[67] Otherwise, output of Soviet pharmaceuticals declined.

A major factor was the withering of cultivation and collection of medicinal botanicals, from which many medicines were derived. Armies interrupted production but so did Bolshevik economic policies. Opium production in Turkestan fell to 80 puds (2,800 pounds) in 1919 from 850 puds (30,600 pounds) in 1918 and 900 puds in 1917.[68] In Ukraine officials reported that peasants who had taken over large estates "turned away from specialized production…because of the need to produce foodstuffs" and also "because of the contraction of the market."[69] They recounted that in 1914 and 1915, at the height of the world war, there had been "massive collection of medicinal plants in Poltava and Podolia provinces." In 1920, during the civil war, in contrast, *Adonis vernalis* (important in veterinary practice), *Valeriana officinalis, Delphinium consolida Z., Origanum vulgare Z., Iuniperus communis Z., Teucrium chamaedrys Z.* (used by the locals to combat malaria), mint, chamomile, lily-of-the-valley (used as a cardiac remedy) and other crucial medicinal plants were grown on some *khutory* or private farms and sold in bazaars. However, typical of the fate of producers and purveyors of medicinal plants was "an old woman in the village of Baitalakh, Kherson province," who collected pharmaceutical botanicals but then, "with insufficient labor and bread, very dear, turned to agriculture" and also an old man—a "*znakhar'* (healer) living in Anan'ev county, Kherson province, who stopped sending plants to Odessa because of difficulties and lack of orders." Some individuals continued to collect medicinal plants in Kherson Province. Many desperate inhabitants, however, were reduced to scouring schools and hospitals for old stores of dried medicinal plants. Fifty-seven puds were located in October 1920, an "insignificant amount," in the opinion of one Soviet specialist, "in view of the richness of medicinal plants in the region" and, further, the dried plants did not retain all their potency.[70] Meanwhile, the state farms or *sovkhozy* which the Soviet government established to produce commercial crops, including medicinal plants, did not fulfill their expectations.[71]

Fine chemicals, which Soviet commentators emphasized "were available on the pharmaceutical market before the revolution" for "compounding in pharmacies," likewise were scarce during the civil war.[72] In 1922, Farmapravlenie, the Administrative Board that managed nationalized pharmaceutical factories, agonized that "for preparation, even of a curtailed list [of pharmaceuticals], 250 designated raw materials" were needed whereas, "in the Pries-kurant of Ferrein in peacetime in 1914 there were more than 3,000 items."[73]

Imperial Russia had been a major exporter of botanicals, but diminished cultivation and collection of medicinal plants meant less of these items available for export and, in turn, less revenue flowed to the government for investment into the industry. Exports of Russia's best selling pharmaceutical products, such as Sporyn'ia, made from rose parasites and used in obstetrical practice and Solodokovyi koren or licorice continued to be buoyant during the First World War but plummeted during the civil war. During the world war Santonin, on which Russia had a monopoly, was stored and traded from abroad. In the course of the civil war, the Savinkov Chimkent Santonin Factory, which came under the jurisdiction of the semi-independent Turkestan Soviet Socialist Republic, "continued to produce Santonin," but did so "to a significantly lesser degree," selling the product to India and China.[74]

International politics threw a monkey wrench into the international drug trade. Both Soviet and Western firms felt the impact. However, the Soviet pharmaceutical industry probably was hurt most. The Soviet pharmaceutical industry was dealt its first blow by the Treaty of Brest-Litovsk, signed March 3, 1918.[75] The treaty ended hostilities and reestablished diplomatic relations between Soviet Russia and Imperial Germany. It also resurrected trade links between the two countries. However, the tariff provisions in the treaty were detrimental to Soviet pharmaceutical firms, for German firms were allowed to export chemical products into Russia at duties even lower than the preferential ones of 1903/1904. In fairness to the Bolsheviks, the Germans were, as yet, victors. So, perhaps the new Soviet government had no choice. Or perhaps the pharmaceutical industry was regarded as expendable. In any case, although the Brest treaty potentially increased supplies of medicaments and ancillary equipment for the Russian masses—as well as for the Red Army—it had negative implications for the pharmaceutical industry.[76]

American-Soviet pharmaceutical trade also foundered on the shoals of politics. Between 1918 and 1922 some ten prominent Americans, mostly Republicans, were keen to continue the trade, manufacturing and financial connections that had developed with Imperial Russia and to form new trade and joint venture contracts with the Soviet government. Other American business, political and labor leaders adamantly opposed renewing trade as well as diplomatic relations with the Soviet government, citing the latter's repudiation of war debts, withdrawal from the war, nationalization of private enterprises, and suppression of civil rights.[77] Soviet officials did negotiate with the United States for railway equipment during the civil war.[78]

However, the Soviet government curtailed sales of pharmaceuticals, particularly the vermifuge Santonin. Santonin was not sold directly by the Santonin Factory in Chimkent, but by the Goldberg Company, headquartered on the Arbat in Moscow. The agent had branches in London, Shanghai and Kobe and stores of Santonin still existed in them during the civil war. Nevertheless, the Soviet government blocked exports of Santonin to the United States [79] and Britain,[80] in part because of declining output in the Chimkent Factory. [81] In 1920, American firms like the Moorman Company in Quincy, Illinois, which purveyed Santonin to the local hog industry, desperately attempted to procure not only prepared Santonin but the flower-bearing seeds of *Artemesia cina*—also called *Artemesia pauciflora*[82] and sometimes "zedoary seed"—from the Baltic States, the Caucasus, Constantinople, and other venues[83] through a multitude of intermediary trade organizations, such as the "Yuoroveta Home and Foreign Trade Co" headquartered in New York City. [84] The Americans were not successful.

Although the Soviets won this round of the trade war, they lost the peace. Before the Great War, Santonin was largely sold to Merck in Darmstadt, which refined the product. Sales "were estimated…before the [First World] war…between 12,000 and 15,000 lbs."[85] Thus, the ban on sales of Santonin negatively impacted Soviet finances.

Nationalization of Pharmaceutical Factories

But it was the Bolshevik policy of nationalization that most enervated the pharmaceutical industry, particularly the largest pharmaceutical enterprises, causing shrinkage of medicines and household supplies. Some chemical-pharmaceutical factories, such as Ferrein and Dorogomilovskii, remained in the hands of their owners and managers for a few months. However, Soviet officials began to sequester them in the spring and summer of 1918.

Thomas Remington has argued convincingly that concentrating major branches of production under state management was meant to imitate German efficiency, to make the Russian economy the most rational economy in the world.[86] At one of the initial meetings of the *Pravlenie* or managing Board of State Chemical-Pharmaceutical Factories (*Gos. Khim-Farm Zavodov*) on May 30, 1918, L. Ia. Karpov, manager (*zaveduiushchii*) of the Department (*Otdel*) of Chemical Industry of Vesenkha, the Supreme Council of the National Economy, told six members of the board that the origins and purpose of the board were to coordinate production of medicaments during wartime and suggested that when peace arrived, the system would be "demobilized" and "conform to the needs of peacetime." Nevertheless, he stressed that the board had "the tasks to regularize and coordinate the activity of factories, review and approve budgets of the state factories, supply them with [financial] means, unite accounting and control, guarantee raw materials and fuel, [coordinate] technical control over production, supervise administration, review and approve the order of sales of the products."[87] The transfer of pharmaceutical enterprises from their owners and managers to the government, however, did not produce the coordination desired.

Nationalization was not uniform. Eighty of the one hundred or so pharmaceutical factories, laboratories and workshops that had operated throughout the Russian Republic and other areas of the Empire before 1918, some medium-sized, some small, came under the authority of various agencies and groups during the civil war. In areas controlled by the Bolsheviks, local pharmacy administrations *(aptekoupravleniia)* were put in charge of most manufactories that produced chiefly galenical preparations, packaging for pharmaceuticals, and some household and perfume-cosmetic wares. A few of the factories put under pharmacy administrations were fairly sizeable, such as the March 8 (former Iakovlev) Bandaging Factory in Moscow, the factory of the Leningrad Medsantorgprom, the Sibmedtorg Laboratory in Tomsk, western Siberia, and some factories in the Ukraine.

Workers in Chimkent, Central Asia, took over the Santonin Factory in November 1917. In April 1918, the Turkestan Soviet took the Chimkent Santonin Factory out of worker hands, declaring it "nationalized," along with cotton factories, slaughterhouses, banks and other concerns. The actual transfer of ownership from the "Santonin Association" to the "Commissar" of the factory, Mikhail Ivanovich Zubarov, occurred between July 1 and 14, 1918, after thorough inventories of Darmin, packaging materials, and other stock had been taken. The factory was put under the ultimate jurisdiction of the Commissariat of Health of the Turkestan Soviet Republic until 1920 when it was transferred to the jurisdiction of the Chemical Department of the Turkestan Central Soviet of Public Economy or *Sovnarkhoz*. [88]

"The Health of the Worker Factory" in Khar'kov, eastern Ukraine, and "Farmakhim," a chemical-pharmaceutical factory in Nizhni-Novgorod, also came under the jurisdiction of local councils of public economy (*sovnarkhozy),* branches of the Supreme Council of the National Economy or Vesenkha. A "cooperative" took over the pharmaceutical factory Galen in Moscow. At the end of the civil war a "union of unemployed and a collective of workers" ran the former Snapir pharmaceutical laboratory in Kremenchug, Ukraine; the former Kuchuka laboratory in Nikolaev, in the Black Sea area; and the Sopitat Chemical-Pharmaceutical Factory in Petrograd.[89]

In Petrograd the Farmakon and Tentelevskii factories were nationalized. The Pel' Factory, relocated to Nizhni-Novgorod, was nationalized.

Moscow, the capital of Soviet Russia after March 1918, had been the hub of the pharmaceutical industry, with thirty-two pharmaceutical enterprises located there. The Soviet government began to nationalize the major chemical pharmaceutical factories in the city in May 1918. These key Moscow factories became the core of the Soviet pharmaceutical industry, with factories in Petrograd, Ukraine and Central Asia added on subsequently. They were put under an Administration (*Pravlenie)* which was, in turn part of the State Chemical-Pharmaceutical Factories (*Goskhim-farm- zavodov* or *Khimfarmazav*) sector, in turn subordinate to Vesenkha, the body that was organized to orchestrate major nationalized businesses.

The Core Soviet Chemical-Pharmaceutical Factories (Goskhimfarmzavodov or Khimfarmazav)

Soviet nationalization procedures embodied the Prussian Protestant virtues Lenin so valued. Anti-bourgeois they might have been, but, like the Soviet officials in Anatole Lunacharskii's Commissariat of Education, immortalized in old photographs in their hats and gloves examining sequestered icons and art collections, the Soviet bureaucrats who nationalized pharmaceutical factories were punctilious in taking over the assets of private and publicly owned properties—the fruits of others' labors.

As noted above, five government officials, including L. Ia. Karpov and I. R. Kornblium, and two representatives from the ranks of manual and white-collar workers, established the *Pravlenie* or Administration of State Chemical-Pharmaceutical Factories on May 30, 1918, in the jurisdiction of Vesenkha. At its initial meeting the Chemical-Pharmaceutical Administration determined that it would consist of a maximum of seven individuals; set up an office and pertinent sections—Finance, Accounting, Materials, Commercial and Technical, Personnel, and Economic; appointed individuals to these sections; set their salaries; and requested a 20,000 ruble advance from Vesenkha to begin operations.[90]

The Chemical-Pharmaceutical Administration began nationalizing chemical-pharmaceutical factories in May 1918. In May and June 1918 the Administration slated the "reception" of chemical-pharmaceutical factories owned by the Red Cross, the Zemstvo Union, the Union of Cities and Zemstvos or Zemgor, and the Organization of the (Imperial) Military Department Warehouse. Detail work was done by a "Reception Commission."[91] In December, the Commission discussed the "reception" of additional factories—Schering, at first called Factory No. 3 and then

No. 4; The Russian Dye Factory, initially called Factory No. 4; the former Bliumental' and Iakovlev factories, called No. 6, and the Pel' Factory, called No. 10.[92]

The procedures for nationalizing large pharmaceutical factories were methodical and businesslike. Excruciatingly detailed inventories were made—for example, the lists of equipment and assets of one factory amounted to four pages of over one hundred items of equipment and materials.[93] Nevertheless, this also signals how one of the flaws inherent in bureaucracies—endless discussion, often about trivialities—began to bog down constructive activity. Agendas were long and committees often became mired in detail.

At the meeting of the Administration of State Chemical-Pharmaceutical Factories on June 14, to provide just one example of deliberations, S. V. Maiat, the requisite worker representative, inquired about methods for selling products of the factories. The rest of the board discussed inventories of medicinal herbs and chemicals in the factories and warehouses, the need to utilize the 3,000 puds (108, 000 pounds) of benzol available to produce medicines—"in view of the medicaments' famine" and also the need for production of phenol and atropine in the Moscow Alkaloid Factory.[94]

In December 1918 the Administration of Chemical Factories reviewed its past two and a half months' work. It had scrutinized inventories, compiled by the Reception Commission, of raw, semi-finished and finished materials, moveable and immoveable property for factories Nos. 1, 3, 4, 6, and 10. In January and February 1919 the Administration of State Chemical-Pharmaceutical Factories heard reports of surveys of factories Nos. 2, 5, and 3 by members of the Reception Commission, discussed the need to complete the "reception" of Factory No. 3 so as to move on to Factory No. 6, and worried that supplies of Sporyn'ia in Factory No. 3 were spoiled and presented a fire danger. The minutiae that occupied the Administration is reflected in the resolution to reimburse members of the Reception Commission for their tram tickets.[95]

Following review of information amassed by the Reception Commission, the Administration sent "telephonograms" to factory managers ordering them to appear before the Administration to transfer ownership. Sometimes the old management showed its mettle. For example, the representatives from the Society of Russian Dye, in whose jurisdiction Factory No. 4—the former Russian Dye Factory—was, "did not show up" at the 3 PM preliminary meeting on January 10, 1919. Nevertheless, the Reception Commission imperiously determined it would take over the factory at 10 AM on Thursday, January 30, as planned, with or without the cooperation of the expropriated management. [96] Although the commission was cavalier about getting rid of the old management, their disappearance did not benefit the industry.

Loss of former owners. One of the nationalized factories that formed the core pharmaceutical industry, Schering, had already been nationalized by the tsarist government during the war, since it was a German firm. Three enterprises had been founded during World War I by public and professional organizations. The Red Cross had established the Alkaloid Factory, the Union of Zemstvos the Salicylate Factory, and the Russian Dye Association the Russian Dye Factory. Allen and Hansbury, the venerable British company, had established a fourth factory in 1917. Five other core factories had been privately owned or structured as family corporations for decades. These were the Ferrein, Keler, Iakovlev, Bliumental', and Pel' enterprises.

Owners of some pharmaceutical production entities stayed in Russia, as did some owners and lessees of pharmacies.[97] They were barred from running their former properties, however.

Vladimir Karlovich Ferrein died in April 1918 at the age of 84, [98] in the midst of the nationalization procedures. His main factory had been located in Mologa in Iaroslavl' Province, two hours by train north of Moscow. Nevertheless, he, like Keler and Pel' , had been a hands-on owner. He had lived in Moscow (in a house originally belonging to Maliuta Skuratov, (Tsar Ivan "The Terrible's" henchman), surrounded by his laboratory, where research and development were conducted, his warehouse, and near to his main pharmacy and drug store.

Whether the former owners were old, whether they emigrated or were merely prevented from running their companies, their knowledge of production and sales, their entrepreneurial drive, their concern about the quality of the company's products and about consumer satisfaction—described in a previous chapter—evaporated when their ownership ceased. At the very least, eliminating prior owners and changing management at one fell swoop was very disruptive.

No owners at all. In some cases no individual or group took proper charge of the nationalized factories for some time. Charles Ruud has described how officials who took over publisher Ivan Sytin's enterprises wasted the paper supply and mishandled equipment.[99] The same destruction occurred in pharmaceutical enterprises. Major pharmaceutical factories in Moscow were in a state of disrepair at the end of the civil war. Factory No. 8, the former Ferrein Factory, which Soviet authorities proudly regarded as "the largest chemical-pharmaceutical factory in Russia" and newly equipped in 1912, had manufactured galenicals, chemicals—sublimate, cyanide, amido-chlorine, iodide mercury, and disinfecting products, Naftalizol and Lysol "on a large scale—50 thousand kilograms per month."[100] Production was minimal at the end of the war. The factory sorely needed remodeling. Output of disinfectants and the hormone Ovarin had been held up by lack of spirits and this ingredient, in turn, was unobtainable because of insufficient monies.[101] Distribution of one of the factory's main products, Neo-benzarsan, of "great importance for treating syphilis, recurring typhus, and malaria" had been held back by lack of ampules. Production of soap had been stopped because of the poor quality of the oil on hand. [102] The perfume department did not operate because of lack of spirits and ether oil.[103]

Factory No.12, the former Keler factory, which produced galenical medicaments, chemicals, photographic and x-ray equipment, had been sadly neglected after it was nationalized. In the spring of 1922 a leaky roof in the factory warehouse spoiled materials that needed to be kept dry. In the Lithography Department of the factory "where the former owner had worked daily with the five machines" to print labels, Soviet officials lamented that only one machine was being used and blank labels, for which the Administrative Board of the Pharmaceutical Industry had paid 606,000,000 very inflated rubles, sat unused. Distribution of medicines had faltered because the factory lacked glass flagons in which to dispense them.[104]

Too many managers. In other cases too many authorities were involved in pharmaceutical production. Ensuing turf wars choked production and distribution. Boris Vogau/ Pilnyak lampooned the government agencies that proliferated in early Soviet Russia and the reams of directives they issued, in his otherwise tragic and unsettling novel about the civil war, *The Naked Year*. The tangle of jurisdictions and thicket of regulations were certainly no laughing matter for the new managers of the pharmacy industry, who were eager to rebuild factories and produce medicines, soap, disinfectants, and toiletries not only to enhance their own careers but because the country desperately needed these items.

The clash in 1919 between the new director of the Pel' Factory, renamed No.10, located in the Volga city of Nizhni- Novgorod, and the local *sovnarkhoz* or economic council, a branch of Vesenkha, documented how nationalization resulted in neglect and misuse of the factory's assets and also how subordination of the factory to two discrete authorities made it difficult to rectify the dismal state of the factory. In August 1919, the new Director of the Pel' Factory in Nizhni-Novgorod—Pel' had invented spermine and pioneered its dispensing in ampules along with the innovations in other therapies and distribution techniques, thus marking the factory as an important component of the pharmaceutical industry—informed the Pharmaceutical Administration some hundreds of miles to the west in Moscow that the factory was a skeleton of its former self. The factory building had become a repository for "lathe-tools remaining from the workshop of the Nizhni-Novgorod Military Industrial Committee," the body forged to help tsarist efforts in the world war. "Raw materials and spirits" were lacking; the director had requested "hydrochloric acid in May" (that is, four months previously) but production facilities in "Ivano-Vosnesensk had not sent it." There were no adequate "vessels for preparing tinctures," a "vacuum apparatus" and "refrigerator were absent." Obviously dismissal of the former owners had not benefited the factory and acquiring chemical supplies from a chemical-dye factory in the textile town of Ivano-Voznesensk, now under a separate bureaucracy, was not working.

But most annoying were the wrangles between the factory director and the local economic council. According to the director, the *sovnarkhoz* regarded the factory as "an alien" enterprise. Not only did the *sovnarkhoz* "not show any support" but it had not yet "transferred to the factory the property belonging to it, preserved in the warehouse." The *sovnarkhoz* held "the key to the warehouse" and some of "the keys belonging to the factory." Meanwhile the *sovnarkhoz* arrogated to itself production of items sorely needed by the local population. Lack of soap and population movements during the Civil War had particularly caused parasite-borne diseases to flare up. When the local Military Sanitary Organization requested vaseline and anti-mite salve from the *sovnarkhoz* to cope with skin rashes, that body organized its own "primitive lab" for production of this and "other items that" the factory director fumed, "could have been more successfully prepared in Factory No. 10."

"For successful organization and development of the pharmaceutical factory in Nizhni-Novgorod," the director asked that the factory be allowed "to free its premises from the lathe tools," "to work with the technical section" of the administration to devise "a project for the pharmaceutical factory," "to develop a project for installing equipment to produce 20,000 kilos of...acid per year," to have "full use of the equipment of the former Pel' factory and also the equipment in the laboratory closed by Farmatsenter" (the body that supervised local pharmacies), "to propose to the Nizhni-Novgorod Sovnarkhoz to unite its technical-chemical laboratory with Factory No. 10," allowing the latter to organize a proper "technical-chemical department," and finally—and this is very telling—to allow Factory No. 10 "to utilize the experience and technical knowledge of Engineer Nemirovskii, inviting him" to serve "in the capacity of the factory's chief engineer."[105] In other words, the management of the Pel' Factory wanted autonomy and the expertise of trained, experienced professionals rather than meddling bureaucrats.

Multiple authorities clogged the importing of chemical and botanical materials needed by pharmaceutical enterprises. Farmapravlenie, the Administrative Board of Glavfarmzav, the Commissariat of Foreign Trade, and Vesenkha all had their fingers in importing and exporting for the core pharmaceutical industry. Further, the government, the Council of Ministers (Sovnarkom), the Council of Labor and Defense or STO, and party bodies sometimes interfered in foreign trade.

Broken affinities. Additionally, the organization set up for the pharmaceutical industry and related industries was dysfunctional. Natural affinities between the chemical and pharmaceutical industries were broken. Various components and stages in the production and sale of pharmaceuticals were splintered and housed in multiple jurisdictions.

After being nationalized, key chemical-pharmaceutical factories were put under the Administration of State Chemical-Pharmaceutical Factories.[106] These chemical-pharmaceutical factories—all of which were located in Moscow—were additionally grouped in a "*Glavk*" or Department called *Glavfarmzav* (The Glavk or Division of Pharmaceutical Factories), which was under the jurisdiction of Vesenkha. (There were, in total, forty-two *glavki* in Vesenkha.)[107]

Factories that produced mainly chemicals were also placed under the jurisdiction of Vesenkha after nationalization. However, their division or *glavk* was the Chemical Department—Glavkhim—separate from Glavfarmzav. Thus, factories like Dorogomilovskii in Moscow that produced chemicals needed for the chemical-pharmaceutical industry or medicines based on chemicals, were separated by a Chinese wall from Moscow factories like Alkaloid, Keler or Ferrein that were involved with the manufacture of medicines, soap, cosmetics, toilet and household items as well as chemicals and medicines. [108]

Enterprises that manufactured medical equipment or items ancillary to pharmacy such as glass vessels and ampules or ceramic containers were put in still another venue after being taken from their owners. These included such venerable enterprises as the Suksunskii sanitary equipment factory, founded in 1728; a medical instruments factory in St. Petersburg, that dated to 1760; a sanitary equipment factory in Penza, established in 1848, and a medical equipment factory in Nizhni-Novgorod, established in 1914.[109] Such severe compartmentalization made sourcing difficult.

Unqualified managers. Finally, in most cases, the individuals selected to run key pharmaceutical industries were no match for the former owners and managers.[110] Political and party affiliations were paramount in appointing managers to the newly nationalized factories, as they were to deciding positions on the plethora of boards that sprang up to administer pharmacies, chemical factories and pharmaceutical factories. Some of the new managers had expertise in the field of industrial chemistry, a few had been practicing pharmacists, some had held management positions in the enterprises they now directed. But while all appeared ambitious and upwardly mobile, not all were highly qualified. Additionally, the new managers did not necessarily have the same concern for the health of the factories put at their disposal or the same level of business acumen possessed by former owners of the nationalized concerns.

S. N. Khitrik was thirty years old when he became director of the Alkaloid Factory, established by the Red Cross and named Factory No. 1 in 1921. Jewish, in 1917 he had been merely a student at the Khar'kov Medical Institute. During the civil war he supplied the Red Army.[111]

A. F. Vagner, appointed director of Factory No. 2, the factory established by the Zemstvo Union during the First World War, was a better choice for his post. He not only was familiar with the factory but had management expertise, having served as director of the factory before the October Revolution.[112]

L. P. Orlov, however, who was appointed director of Factory No. 4 (an appellation which in 1922 applied to the former Schering Factory, rather than to the Russian Dye Factory) had only meager qualifications for the post. Orlov was proud of his humble social origins—he listed himself as both worker and peasant—and that from them he had risen to the level of practicing chemist. That did not mean that he was a competent manager of a pharmaceutical factory, however. At age sixteen Orlov had attended the Chemical-Bacteriological Institute in Moscow. At age eighteen he became "master of production" at the institute. "Recognizing the insufficiency of knowledge of his field" he "attended lectures at the Shoniaveskii University," a sort of people's institution, and "studied on his own." Working fourteen and sometimes sixteen hours a day, when the October Revolution occurred he was elected workers' representative. He became a member of the Communist Party in 1918, served in the Red Army from 1918 to 1921, and in 1920 worked in the Workers and Peasants' Inspectorate (Rabkrin), which Stalin ran.[113]

Artem Izrailovich Zil'berberg was fairly qualified for appointment as director of Factory No. 6, which combined the Bliumental' Bandaging Factory and the Ostromyslenskaia Laboratory. He had taught and managed the chemical and bacteriological laboratory at the Techno-Neurological Institute in Petrograd before his appointment. He also had served as director of production at the Bliumental' Factory, Factory No. 9, before it was merged with Factory No.11, forming Factory No. 6.[114]

Alexander Sergeevich Garnak, appointed director of the former Ferrein Factory, now called Factory No. 8, was one of the few appointees with high credentials. He graduated from the Geneva Institute with a specialty in organic chemistry, and after stint as an assistant there, came to Russia where he was invited to outfit the first Russian factory producing formalin. In 1911 he went to work at the Ferrein factory where he rose to position of production manager, with particular responsibility for manufacture of reagents. After nationalization of the factory in 1919 he became a member of the Collegium of Glavfarmzav (the Board that managed all the nationalized factories) and then Chair of the administrative board that ran the Ferrein Factory. Subsequently he was appointed director of the factory. He also participated in the "professional" or state-run union of chemists.[115]

In contrast, S. M. Kharzak, the new assistant director of Factory No. 8, had strong political credentials, but lightweight scientific and managerial ones. He was born in Vitebsk, the city made famous by Paul Chagall, into a large and poor Jewish family. He attended Jewish schools. He was hampered from attending the classical *gimnaziia* that offered entree to the university, however, by the education quotas placed on Jews after 1881. Smart and ambitious—early on he tutored lower-level students at his school—but finding his path to university barred, Kharzak became a pharmacy apprentice and worked his way up through apprenticeship, auditing university lectures, and passing examinations to the level of Assistant Pharmacist. Along with his pharmacy studies, Kharzak, as Sverdlov before him, became a revolutionary. Many of his comrades were members of the Bund, a Marxist Jewish workers' organization, which he joined in 1917. When that organization split into left and right factions in 1918, Kharzak joined the leftist "Communist Bund" and in 1919 became a member of the Russian Communist Party (bolshevik). He also served in the Vitebsk provincial soviet. Kharzak assisted the Red Army as a pharmacist, organizing a military hospital and pharmacy warehouses in various theaters of the war.[116]

Mark Anatol'evich Kagan, appointed director of Factory No. 12, the former Keler Factory, was a chemist who had some familiarity with the factory, having been manager of production there before nationalization.[117]

Grigory L'vivich Podviz, appointed director of Factory No. 13, the factory established by Allen and Hansbury in 1917, was a Provizor or fully-qualified pharmacist, but had never managed a pharmaceutical firm. He worked in pharmacies in Russia, then emigrated in 1912 and worked in the pharmaceutical factory "Kanon" and the factory "Luriia" in Paris, before returning to Russia. His qualification for director was that he became a member of the Communist Party in 1919 and served the Red Army in the supply administration in the Donbass, a hotly contested area during the civil war.[118]

Political correctness was as if not more important for those in the Administration of the Chemical-Pharmaceutical Factories, which set policies for the industry after nationalization. Isaac Romanovich Kornblium, Chair of the Administration, Farmapravlenie, in November 1921, had been a member of the Bolshevik party in emigration before the October revolution. Nikolai Grigor'evich Panukov, member of the Presidium of Farmapravlenie, was a mere engineering and technology teacher at the Moscow Higher Technical School. B. E. Gorbovitskii, another member of the Presidium, was a pharmacist and a member of the party.[119]

Feodor Andreevich Ferrein, who held the dual posts of manager of production in Factory No. 8, the former Ferrein factory, and manager of production for the Pharmacy Administration (Farmapravlenie),[120] may have been a relative of Vladimir Karlovich Ferrein, founder of the Ferrein pharmaceutical conglomerate. As noted in the previous chapter, during World War I, one F. G./A. Ferrein had strongly criticized the tsarist government's tariff policies. If this was the same person, Feodor Andreevich knew whereof he spoke. Additionally, Feodor Andreevich Ferrein had a *Magistr* of Pharmacy degree. He wrote many articles and two books on the pharmaceutical industry, and would take an active part in managing the industry until his death in 1940.

N. A. Krasnopevtsev, member of the Administration and a manager of the former Ferrein Wholesale Warehouse, was one of the most overtly political of the new pharmacy leaders. Born in Riga in 1894, he "came from a revolutionary family, his father having been a member of the Social Democratic Party who participated in the revolution of 1905. Krasnopevtsev himself attended the Tula *Gimnaziia* and then Moscow University where he specialized in chemistry. He became a member of the Bolshevik faction of the SD [Social Democratic] Party while a student at the university in 1916. In 1917, he participated in meetings…protests, strikes." During the civil war, as a "dutiful Communist" he "worked in responsible [albeit noncombatant] positions" provisioning the front and in 1921 joined the Commissariat of Foreign Trade where he attempted to export Russian chemical products.[121]

Political reliability was not only important for acquiring a position in the pharmaceutical industry but for maintaining it. For example, in 1922 a secret (*sekretno*) missive testified not only that Podvidz, director of Factory No.13, was "firm... and correct in the line of his work," that he had done the "maximum that he could do" and that he was "an old party member of the RKP" (the Russian Communist Party).[122]

Conclusion

In conclusion, nationalization did not improve dispensing or the Russian pharmaceutical industry the first three years the Soviet government was in power. Nationalization did not increase output and distribution of medicines, soaps, disinfectants, and other items badly needed by a war-torn and sick populace Shortage of medicinal botanicals, other raw materials, power and fuel; breakdown of railways; and severance of foreign trade hampered the industry. But that the industry's emasculation was due as much, if not more, to the Bolshevik's regimen of "War Communism" is evidenced by the fact that the prostrate pharmaceutical factories which formed the core of the Soviet pharmacy system at the outset, were all located in Moscow, which had not been a theater of war and was, moreover, the capital of the new

Soviet state and the hub of major railway lines.

Across-the-board management changes exacerbated rather than rectified these problems. Changes of management also occur in market systems, but because the core pharmaceutical industry in Russia was now so concentrated, simultaneous installation of new factory managers, with some moreover not up to the task, had wide and fundamental impact. To their credit, some of the new Soviet appointees exhibited proprietary concern. But they were throttled in properly running their factories. Many factories were in a state of ruin. It took time for most of the new managers to familiarize themselves with technical production details. Division of the chemical-pharmaceutical industry from the chemical and ancillary industries impeded sourcing. Hordes of officials and bureaucratic procedures complicated operations. Now that the war was winding down, would the new state pharmacy system enable the largest pharmaceutical enterprises, the core pharmaceutical industry, to better cope with the country's health problems? That is the subject of our following chapters.

Fig. 3.3 The Ferrein / No. 8 / Karpov Factory and Headquarters of Farmatrest/ Gosmedtorgprom from *Gosudarstvennyi khimiko-farmatsevticheskii zavod imeni L. Ia Karpova* (Moscow: Akts. O-va "Gosmedtorgprom," 1926), p. 1

4
Getting Back to Business: The First Half of the NEP

The civil war was an abnormal time in which to judge the effectiveness of the new pharmacy system the Bolsheviks had implemented. Cessation of hostilities in 1921 allowed the Soviet government to demonstrate the benefits of nationalization and centralization of health care,[1] proof of which was sorely needed because public health problems worsened rather than decreased at the end of the civil war.

Famine swept many areas of the Soviet Union in the summer of 1921.[2] Millions of children and adolescents, made homeless by the three-year civil war, lived on the streets during the 1920s, stealing, prostituting themselves, taking and selling cocaine and narcotics.[3] Venereal disease was widespread in 1922. Soviet prisons and camps were packed with more inmates at the end of the civil war than in its first years. In December 1921, there were 220,000 or more prisoners in various detention and labor camps designed for 161,700.[4] These facilities were hotbeds of typhus, recurring fever, typhoid, cholera, and venereal disease. Malaria reached epidemic proportions in the early 1920s. In 1922 there were nearly three times more cases than in 1914, with high incidence in Moscow and Voronezh provinces in the Russian Republic, in the Donbass, in Ekaterinoslav and Kherson provinces and Odessa in the Ukraine, and also in the Caucasus, especially Georgia. In 1922, 42,000 cases of malaria were reported in the Ukraine alone. Additionally, the tropical and fatal form of the disease—*Plasmodium falciparum*—had become more prevalent.[5] By the summer of 1923, ten million people in the Soviet Union were sick with malaria.[6]

Pharmaceuticals were available only in limited quantities. The situation with soap and disinfectants was dire. As noted in chapter 2, before the First World War Russian produced 180,000 tons of soap. By 1921 "the total output" had "fallen to 5,400 tons."[7] Farmatrest's 1922 survey of its factories and wares (*Ukazatel' predpriiatii i tovarnyi katalog*), partly compiled by I. Levinshtein, attempted to show how the factories in the trust had gotten back on their feet. The photographs of the Wholesale Warehouse, Packaging Department, and Bandaging laboratories, indeed replicated photographs from the French and Russian promotion booklets of the Ferrein conglomerate published in 1910! The 1922 "Catalog" also bravely alluded to "large-scale production of disinfectants *naftalizol* and *lizol* [Lysol]" by Farmzavod No. 8 (Ferrein's former factory), "widened production at the current time" of the anti-venereal Novarsol by Factory No. 6, and the potential for the production of other pharmaceuticals. However, the catalog referred as well to "the continuing medicaments famine" (*medikamentnyi golod*)—a term used at the beginning of World War I—and cautioned that the shortage "dictates the necessity of using...preparations...available in certain amounts (*v nekotorom kolichestve*) in the warehouses and stores of Farmatrest."[8]

The preparations on hand were mainly the products of foreign firms, such as CIBA, Parke-Davis, Hoechst, Roche, Riedel, and Merck; the products of foreign factories that had operated in Russia prior to 1917—Bayer, Schering, and Farbwerke; products of the Warsaw factory Spiess; and the wares of nationalized Russian enterprises— Ferrein, Saturn, and Pashkevich.[9] By June 1923, however, stores of quinine had run out.[10] Farmapravlenie, the board that administered nationalized pharmaceutical factories and warehouses, estimated that it was necessary to import 130,000 kilos of quinine, if only half the sick received a bare minimum (*golodnaia norma*) dose of 20 grams.[11] And in the fourth quarter of 1923, it was estimated that approximately 100 raw botanical and chemical materials were lacking for Factories No. 2, 4, 8, and 13,[12] the factories formerly belonging to the Union of Zemstvos, Schering, Ferrein, and Allen and Hansbury.

Characteristics of the NEP

Other industries also were foundering at the end of the civil war, agriculture languished, and basic necessities were difficult to procure, prompting Lenin to inaugurate a New Economic Policy in March 1921. The NEP, as the policy is always referred to, was an uneasy amalgam of market practices and government control. Some sectors of the economy and some regions of the former Russian empire had continued on with normal market procedures during the civil war, as related in the previous chapter. On the one hand, the NEP legalized and extended these practices. To revive food and consumer-goods production and eliminate the black market the government stopped requisitioning peasant grain and officially endorsed market sales of many agricultural products and small-scale production and trade in consumer goods, filmmaking and book printing, and services like restaurants. To encourage foreign investment the government stopped printing money and backed the ruble with gold. Paralleling comparative freedom in the arts, economists enthusiastically debated alternative models of economic development. On the other hand, the government continued to orchestrate the economy throughout the NEP as during the civil war. Soviet officials purchased a percentage of grain at fixed prices, kept control of large factories, allocated housing, and monopolized foreign trade. Large entities were subject to government plans and regulations throughout the NEP.[13]

Further, the NEP was not all of one piece. During the first half of the NEP—from 1921 to 1924—private enterprise was more acceptable, despite periodical crackdowns on entrepreneurs.

During the second half of the NEP, preparing for nation-wide, five-year plans that focused on accelerated growth of heavy industry and infrastructure, officials ratcheted up taxes to suppress private businesses, began buying up pharmacies that had been leased to private individuals, and curbed economists who questioned whether market-oriented policies should be summarily abandoned.

This chapter looks at the nationalized, centralized Soviet pharmaceutical industry during the first half of the NEP. The following chapter examines the industry during the second half. Chapter 6 zeroes in on pharmacies, chapter 7 on production of vaccines during the NEP.

The Structure of Soviet Pharmaceutical Industry at the Outset of the NEP

At the beginning of the NEP the entire pharmaceutical industry consisted of eighty-seven or so enterprises, located in Moscow, Petrograd, and other areas in Russia and in the Ukraine, which was re-attached to Russia through the civil war. The work force in these factories amounted to 15,000 in 1921.[14]

The industry was divided into three levels. The core pharmaceutical industry, the subject of our study, was on the top rung. At the outset of the NEP the core industry consisted of seven large factories, six in Moscow and one in a nearby village; the Ferrein warehouse; and three drug stores in Moscow.[15] After being nationalized during the civil war, these core enterprises had been put under the jurisdiction of *Gos-Khim-farm-zavodov* (State Chemical-Pharmaceutical Factories), which in turn was under the jurisdiction of Glavfarmzav, one of 42 *glavki* or departments of Vesenkha, the Supreme Council of the National Economy.

The second level of the pharmaceutical industry included the remaining eighty or so pre-revolutionary enterprises, some small, others fairly sizable. During the NEP these second-tier enterprises remained under the jurisdictions of local pharmacy administrations, regional departments of Vesenkha (*sovnarkhozy*), and employed or unemployed workers who had taken them over during the civil war. A few individuals also were allowed to manufacture pharmaceuticals during the NEP. Some of these so-called *kustar'* operations became quite successful and played an important part in the output of pharmaceuticals by larger enterprises. The government allowed the second-tier enterprises and the small-scale manufactories quite of bit of latitude in their operations. However, the government's hand—through the agencies of Vesenkha, government commissariats, and the political police (OGPU)— lay heavy on the core pharmaceutical industry.[16]

Indeed, the core industry was an ungainly hybrid—part legal person, part extension of the government. In December 1921 the seven factories and three warehouses (two more had been attached) in the core pharmaceutical industry were formed into a joint-stock company— or more accurately a trust—called Farmatrest.[17] Although the core industry thus appeared analogous to a corporation in a market economy, since it was considered a key sector of the national economy, an element of the so-called "Commanding Heights," in actuality it was subject to direct government control. And, although the Imperial government had dominated the pharmaceutical industry, the Soviet government did so to a far greater extent.

Government agencies micromanaged core pharmaceutical factories. The first layer to which core pharmaceutical enterprises answered was Farmapravlenie, formed at the end of the civil war to administer them. By the end of 1921, Farmapravlenie consisted of 228 people—57 administrative personnel, 162 administrative technical staff, and 109 white collar workers. Its chair during the early 1920s was L. I. Nisenman.[18] Farmapravlenie held meetings twice a week, on Tuesday and Saturday at 3:00 PM, mainly not to make policy decisions but to scrutinize the most minute aspects of factory operations. For example, on December 1, 1923, S.O. Khozak, Assistant Director of Factory No. 8, the former Ferrein Factory; M. A. Borob'ev, Manager of Factory No. 4; A. F. Vagner, Manager of Factory No. 2; B. E. Gorbovitskii, Manager of

Factory No. 13; S. N. Khitrik, Manager of Factory No. 1; G. L. Podviz, manager of Factory No. 12; and A. S. Pavlovskii, Manager of the Wholesale Warehouse reported on expenditures, profits, production, and problems for the month of October.[19] The board assiduously surveyed these reports, reviewed the performance of factory managers (sometimes hiring and firing them), approved firewood and oil fuel deliveries, and supervised sales— to the point of scrutinizing prices and demanding daily cashier reports from factories. Detailed agenda items sometimes had larger import, such as the investigation of adulteration in opium and morphia packets received at the Chemical-Pharmaceutical Office of Gostorg, spoilage in factories, trade-marks, and other such matters.[20] At other times the agenda disintegrated into trivia, with Farmapravlenie specifying amounts for New Year's trees for workers' children.[21]

Farmapravlenie, in turn, was subject to higher government agencies. American pharmaceutical firms in the 1920s received little assistance from the United States government, particularly in forging international deals. They had to badger officials in the Commerce Department—who at times were distracted by upcoming Princeton and Yale football games—for help in importing quinine, *Artemesia* flowers (the basis for the vermifuge Santonin), and other raw materials, and in exporting their products.[22] In the Soviet Union, by contrast, Vesenkha, the Supreme Council of the National Economy, under the chairmanship of the fiscally conservative Feliks Dzerzhinskii—who also was the director of the political police, the OGPU—issued monthly, quarterly, annual, and five-year production and financial plans for Farmatrest and the individual factories comprising it.[23] Vesenkha also devised plans for some medium-sized factories under regional pharmacy administrations, like the March 8 Bandaging Factory in Moscow, a Leningrad laboratory, a factory in Tomsk, and some manufactories in the Ukraine.[24]

Vesenkha's plans specified raw material inputs and the amount and kinds of products to be manufactured and marketed.[25] Workers had their own productivity quotas to fulfill.[26] Farmapravlenie reviewed the production, work and finances in the factories of Farmatrest, sending detailed reports to Vesenkha.[27] Thus, almost a decade before central planning, before the "Command-Administrative" system became a feature of the Soviet economy as a whole, the core Soviet pharmaceutical industry had to toe the line.

The plans imposed upon the pharmaceutical industry were very ambitious. The "Commercial Program for Farmatrest," issued in the first quarter of 1924, directed enterprises to produce some 150 chemical items, over 200 galenical items, and about 35 "patented," that is, prepared, items that pharmacies could dispense in ready form. These prepared items included suppositories and chocolate laxatives; Pertussin, for coughs; hormone preparations—Ovarin, Thyroidin, and Mammin; the febrifuge Phenacetin, and medicinal soap.[28] The 1924 plan for chemically-pure reagents listed about 100 items that Farmatrest was to produce.[29]

Quite obviously, the Soviet government was interested in, nay demanded, increased amounts of pharmaceuticals. Farmapravlenie, the Board that managed the core industry, and enterprise directors were equally committed to providing medicines, soap and disinfectants, hormones, and other items necessary to maintaining public health. Yet, despite apparent synergy, government and industry goals were basically divergent. Industry leaders were idealistic. In 1923, for example, L. I. Nisenman, the chair of Farmapravlenie, averred that "The Trust cannot be only a merchant (*kuptsom*), but must also be [a] state [entity]; if the population needs this or that product, not considering commercial feasibility or infeasibility, it requires that the needs of the population be satisfied."[30] Government officials, meanwhile, were above all concerned about maintaining state coffers. Government policies often thwarted pharmaceutical production by impeding the industry's ability to respond to the difficult environment in which it operated during the early years of the NEP. The core pharmaceutical industry, thus, navigated between the Scylla of the government and the Charybdis of the market in a fragile craft.

Industry Problems

Financial Difficulties

Farmatrest suffered from a lack of basic and operating capital. As was its organization, the trust's financial setup was hybrid. Its basic capital included the assets of the ten Moscow enterprises that comprised it—about 7 million rubles. The Trust also received 1 milliard [no doubt very inflated] rubles, when it was separated from Glavkhim and some materials and fuel in the enterprises of Glavkhim, which amounted to over 4 and one-half million rubles.[31] Farmatrest received credit from the State Bank, Gosbank, which charged 8 percent interest, and had a line of credit with the Banking Department of Vesenkha. The credit from Gosbank amounted to 20 milliard rubles in December 1921, rising to 60 milliard rubles in March 1922, the large figures reflecting the worthlessness of the ruble at the outset of the NEP. The line of credit with the Banking Department of Vesenkha amounted to 20 milliard rubles for one and a half to two months at 24 percent interest per month and 1 percent commission. In 1923 Farmatrest received, by order of the Party Commission of the bank, a long-term loan of 9 million gold rubles.[32] Farmatrest also was empowered to raise operating capital from sales, basing the valuation of products and their prices on the 1914 *Preiskurant* or sales catalogue of the Ferrein firm.[33] This aspect of its operations will be considered later in the chapter.

The trust was perennially short of cash. Investment in the pharmaceutical industry was minuscule when compared with the defense industry. Pharmaceutical industry budgets in the early 1920s were in the low millions[34] as compared to military budgets of 329.2 million rubles in 1923-1924 and 410 million rubles in 1925-1925. Admittedly these supported 600,000 to 700,000 troops as well as production, but military enterprises also received an additional 17 million rubles for imports, sums that ungrateful officials in that industry considered low.[35] The number of those employed in core pharmaceutical enterprises was, of course, much smaller, only a couple thousand. Moreover, the ratio of administrative personnel, technical personnel, and white collar workers (*sluzhashchie*) to ordinary workers in pharmaceutical enterprises was fairly high—153 administrators, 149 administrative technical staff, and 277 white collar workers to 1,506 workers, excluding administrators—although this spoke to the specialized nature of the pharmaceutical industry.[36]

Because Soviet officials were keen about— indeed obsessed with—husbanding state resources in order to rebuild sectors of the economy they deemed especially important, even when monies were allocated, they were not always disbursed. But, the hierarchical system in which the core industry operated hampered initiative in finding alternatives. When enterprise directors circumvented central authorities and went out to find resources on their own, they were reprimanded, as illustrated by the difficulties encountered by the directors of Factory No. 8 (the former Ferrein Factory) in getting monies to build a railway spur. Farmapravlenie approved monies for the railroad and the factory contracted with a workers' artel to build it. The money was not disbursed, however. The workers, failing to receive their pay, left the construction site, and the cost of building the railroad escalated. So "Factory No. 8, without the sanction of Farmapravlenie," decided to build the railroad on its own. The factory directors had trouble acquiring materials from private persons and were forced to barter, but they finally succeeded. Irritatingly, the government responded not with appreciation but criticism. The factory management, however, was not so easily cowed. They not only were unrepentant but defiantly questioned whether they should be subordinated to Farmatrest at all, asserting that "If the Trust" was "not in a position to manage Factory No. 8 in the regular order, than the factory must receive a certain autonomy ...unfettered use of advances under its responsibility."[37]

Profiteering, of course, was absolutely forbidden. Gosmedtorg, the sales arm of the Trust, allowed factories to sell only specified items on the free market.[38] In July 1922, I. A. Pakovich, Director of Factory No. 4 (the former Russian Dye Factory) and Assistant Director Malkin were caught secretly selling on the free market, wares manufactured by the factory, that were not in the approved list, at prices lower than those set by Farmatrest. A worker in the Wholesale Warehouse blew the whistle on the culprits. One Bogdanov, a Vesenkha official, had sternly warned that citizens must "struggle...against...speculative...trade and methods of work that encouraged speculation." In August 1922, the two "speculators" were fired and brought before the Court of the Moscow Military Tribunal, a venue that anticipated severe punishment.[39]

Sourcing Problems

Shortages of medicinal botanicals. In addition to organizational cumbersomeness and financial inadequacies, the trust suffered from a dearth of raw materials. A major obstacle to revival of the pharmaceutical industry was lack of medicinal plants. During the first years of the NEP agriculture and then industry recovered far faster from the civil war than Soviet economists anticipated.[40] Production of medicinal plants is specialized, however. To encourage production of medicinal botanicals the government retracted the punitive measures enforced under "War Communism" and concomitantly encouraged private enterprise, particularly in cultivation of mint, chamomile, sage and opium poppies. [41] In 1921 the Soviet government, Sovnarkom or the Council of People's Commissars, decreed that every citizen had the right to collect and cultivate medicinal plants. A proviso warned that no one could hire labor and make a profit from this endeavor, but the caveat about making a profit was, under dint of necessity, ignored. Although officials hoped that cooperatives and the government would play a leading role in the collection and cultivation of plants, by 1923 Vesenkha planned to liquidate the *sovkhozy* or state farms that had been erected for specialized cultivation during the civil war.[42] As a further inducement to individuals or cooperatives, the government exempted those occupied with the cultivation of medicinal botanicals from the "natural tax."[43] The pharmaceutical administration hoped these measures would not only spur domestic production but increase exports.[44]

Unfortunately, while food production revived quickly in the nascent Soviet Union, throwing the balance between industrial and agricultural prices out of kilter in the so-called "scissors crisis" of 1923,[45] it was not so easy to produce certain medicinal plants not native to the country. In imperial times four or five plants that produced important medicines were not available because of climatic and geological reasons. In 1924, Feodor Andreevich Ferrein, most probably nephew of the former pharmaceutical magnate Vladimir Karlovich Ferrein, erstwhile founder of what was now Factory No. 8, himself an advisor to the tsarist government on pharmaceutical production during the Great War, and during the NEP member of Farmapravlenie, listed a number of products for which he believed there was little or no hope of domestic production. Among these were cocaine, strychnine, pilocarpine, and quinine.[46] These would have to be imported for the foreseeable future.

Production of iodine, crucial as an antiseptic and disinfectant, and in the prevention of goiter, had begun to show results during the First World War but had fallen off during the Civil War. Only minimal amounts of iodine were being derived from the ashes of White Sea seaweed at the facility near Arkhangel'sk that had been erected in 1916. Since production was unprofitable it was shut down for a time, then reopened in 1923. Fifty kilograms of iodine were extracted in 1923 and 90 kilograms in 1924. However, this amount did not nearly satisfy need. The facility was located in an inhospitable area and to get one pud (16.6 kilograms) of iodine, 8,000 puds of seaweed were required.[47]

Russian opium did not meet the standards of the pharmacopoeia. Central Asia had been planted to the opium poppy during World War I and some amount of technical morphine was being produced in the Chimkent Santonin Factory in 1922 and 1923.[48] However, the alkaloid content of Russian opium continued to fluctuate from 4.5 to 18 percent, reaching an average of 7 to 14.5 percent in the early 1920s.[49] In 1924,

Acospo, a stock company for collection and working up of opium, was established to improve the caliber of the drug. The shareholders were the Commissariat of Internal Trade, the State Medical Industry (Gosmedprom), the "Santonin Trust," and the Administration of Raw Materials of the Turkestan Republic.[50]

Additionally, the industry had to contend with obstreperous tillers of the soil. For example, in 1923 peasants in Poltava turned from production of mint to producing more lucrative *makhorka* tobacco.[51]

Difficulty in acquiring other inputs. The Chinese Wall dividing the pharmaceutical industry from the chemical, glass, and medical equipment industries blocked acquisition of chemicals and ancillary items. The Tentelevskii chemical factory in Petrograd, Russian Dye, Three Mining, Dorogomilovskii in Moscow, and some other factories produced medicines composed of chemicals, as well as chemicals for other industries. These factories, like the key pharmaceutical factories, were under the jurisdiction of Vesenkha. However, they were grouped in their own trust— Aniltrest— the Aniline Trust. Farmatrest officials maintained that Aniltrest received preferential treatment from the government, since Aniltrest controlled more chemical factories than Farmatrest and was better funded.

At times, this severe compartmentalization compromised public health. For example, in 1922 antivenereals were sorely needed in Russia to cope with the flare-up in sexually transmitted diseases. Farmatrest imported 100,000 dozen ampules of Neosal'varsan from Germany[52]—a huge and expensive amount. Meanwhile, the main product of Factory No. 6, one of the factories run by Farmatrest was Novarsol, a substitute for the German Neosal'varsan. Factory No. 6 had difficulty in producing Novarsol, however, because the sodium chloride it was able to obtain did not have the requisite purity and the factory was forced to purify it by cooking the salt. Farmapravlenie fumed that Lenin lauded the quality of Aniltrest's Novarsolan—when this product was two and a half times more expensive than Farmatrest's Novarsol and another Farmatrest antivenereal, Benzarsan. A third Farmatrest antivenereal, Neobenzarsan was produced by Factory No. 8, the former Ferrein Factory.[53] The product had been tested on typhus patients with excellent results and was also said to be effective in quelling the symptoms of malaria, anthrax (called in Russia "Siberian plague") and other dread diseases.[54] But large-scale production of Neobenzarsan was held up by Aniltrest's domination of the market, despite the fact that Iauzkaia

Hospital in Moscow begged Farmatrest and Factory No. 8 to distribute it.

Lack of legal leverage compounded supply problems. For example, in the fall of 1923 Khozak, Assistant Director of Factory No. 8, complained that "insufficiency of raw materials," their "poor quality," and "untimely deliveries" held back the chemical department. Vorob'ev, Director of Factory No. 4, lamented the high cost of raw materials, particularly iodine. Vagner, head of Factory No. 2, informed Farmapravlenie that his "factory was little supplied" in October, thus "production of salol and metallic ether was cut short," and the "aspirin [department] worked only one day." [55]

Unfortunately, the mechanism for enforcing contracts was weak. In 1922, for example, Factory No.12, the former Keler Factory, placed an order for glass flagons with Farmapravlenie. The order arrived late. It was incomplete and the factory finally rejected the materials because of their poor quality.[56]

Feodor Andreevich Ferrein lamented sourcing problems in the third quarter of 1923. Factories in Farmatrest had not met their production targets, either in absolute terms or in percentages, because of "insufficient supplies" of "raw materials and equipment."[57] Thus, although mercury preparations were fulfilled 103 percent during the third quarter, iodine preparations were fulfilled only 31 percent and inorganic preparations only 21 percent. These last failures, in turn, were explained by factories "entirely not receiving sulfuric acid, ammonia, and working only with chemically cleaned ammonium chloride." "Nitrous acid bismuth fell short of the goal because bismuth was not sent from the Lake Baikal region"; boric acid was not manufactured because of "the absence of boratsita," sulfuric acid magnesium was produced to a significantly less degree because of "insufficient equipment," as was also the case with Glaubers' salts; hydrogen peroxide was not produced because of "the absence of barium." This influenced "also the supply of chemicals for Factory No. 8." Salicylic preparations were off their mark because of defects in the apparatus. Only salt and metallic salicylate were manufactured and those "not in full volume." [58] Finally, workers' summer vacations also disrupted production in 1923.[59]

Import constraints. Shortages of medicinal botanicals, minerals and chemicals within the USSR necessitated imports. In 1922 Farmatrest imported 4,500 kilograms of iodine, in 1923, 1,675 and requested sizable amounts of sulfur, caffeine, opiate alkaloids, paraffin, rubber goods, thermometers, syringes, ampules, and pharmacy dishes. Purchases in Riga and Berlin from August 1922 to May 1923 equaled 717,000 gold rubles.[60] In 1923 Farmatrest informed the Department of Foreign Trade in Vesenkha that seventy-five "Basic Imported Raw Materials" were "Necessary for" its factories "to Expand Production." The items, indeed, ranged from basic raw materials to sophisticated synthesized medicines. In addition to antipyrine, Neosal'varsan, quinine, and Protargol, Farmatrest imported sizable amounts of prosaic items, as the table illustrates. The soaps included soap "residue" as well as olive-oil soap.[61]

Table 4.1 Compiled from RGAE, f. 871, op. 3, d. 17, ll. 73, 75, 78

Imports in Kilograms, 1923	Quantity
Iodine, England	30,000
Barium, England, Germany	50,000
Cocoa Oil, England, USA	15,000
Hydrastis Root, England, USA	6,000
Ipecacuanha, England, Germany	2,000
Nut Gall, England, Germany	240,000
Soap, France, Italy	21,000
Bismuth, Germany, England	8,000
Castor Oil, England, France	50
Menthol, England	200
Gum Arabic, Germany, England	5,000
Cocaine, Germany	100
Potassium Sulfo-gauiacol, Germany	5,000
Theobromine, Germany, England	2,000

The cost of these imports also was sizable: 1, 632,254 gold-backed rubles.[62] In addition, 65 boilers and other pieces of equipment "from abroad" were "necessary for production" of codeine, aspirin and other items "in the factories of Gosmedtorgprom" in 1923 and 1924.[63]

It was estimated that thirty-five imports would be needed for the pharmaceutical industry to fulfill the projected production plan for 1924-1929. The imports required included sublimate; ten metals, such as lead, bismuth, zinc, nickel; seven partially manufactured items, such as aniline, p-nitrophenol, Dimetilamin; and eighteen raw materials, including bromine, sulfuric acid ammonia, and French or American turpentine. How far domestic production declined during the civil war is illustrated by the fact that in the early twentieth century Russian turpentine had formed the basis for one of Schering's main products, synthetic camphor, inducing the German house to build a plant in Moscow to more easily obtain it. As were annual imports, those projected were large—for example, 16, 000 kilograms of sublimate for the fourth year and 32,000 kilograms for the fifth; 1,000 kilograms of aniline for the first year of the 1924-1929 plan and 6,000 kilograms in the fifth year.[64]

By May 1924 sizable amounts had been imported: 200 kilograms of amidopirin and 200 kilograms of antipyrine from Germany; the 100,000 dozen ampules of German Neosal'varsan mentioned above; 1,000 kilograms of the disinfectant Protargol from Germany; 5,000 kilograms of quinine from Holland and Germany; and so on, for a total of 604,000 rubles.[65] Subsequently 70,000 more kilos of quinine were imported.

Soviet trade representatives bargained hard, like capable businessmen in capitalistic states, for the best prices and terms. Trade and diplomatic links with Germany did not make them more disposed to trade with German firms than with those of other countries. Both the trade representative of Vesenkha and Gosmedtorg looked for the best quality goods at the lowest prices. For example, in January 1924 the Trade Representative *(Torgovyi predstavitel'* or *Torgpredstvo*) of the RSFSR attempted to buy iodine in London. The German firm Schering claimed that it had the monopoly rights to receive raw iodine for Russia, because the firm had owned a factory in Russia before the October Revolution. The Russian Trade Representative countered that Schering no longer owned its former factory in Russia, since the Soviet government had nationalized it and therefore the firm could claim no monopoly. London suppliers also demanded that Russia promise not to rework the iodine and resell it outside of Russia and, further, that they pay sterling cash for the iodine. The Trade Representative informed Farmatrest that, in his opinion, after the first payment, Russia would be able to get wares on credit.[66]

Similarly, in May 1924 the Berlin branch of Gosmedtorg reported that Farmapravlenie could probably purchase quinine, cocoa butter, theobromine and caffeine more cheaply in Holland than in Germany—because of the financial crisis in Germany and also because of temporarily poor relations between Germany and the USSR at the time. Gosmedtorg advised Farmapravlenie, that Russia could purchase other pharmaceutical items it needed more cheaply in England and France. Medical and surgical items could be obtained from other countries but at prices higher than in Germany. Microscopes, for example, could be purchased favorably in Austria.[67] In May 1924 Vesenkha administrators, representatives from the chemical industry, and Farmatrest administrators averred that contracts with Italy, locking Russia into orders for industrial and agricultural products at 7 million rubles a year, were throwing the Soviet export plan out of kilter and perhaps should be discontinued.[68]

Soviet pharmaceutical imports were not inordinate. In 1937, the United States estimated that it needed to import 1,000 pounds (about 450 kilograms) of Santonin, 260,000 pounds (about 118,316 kilograms) of Belladonna leaves and roots, approximately the same amount of ergot of rye (partly from Russia), and so forth.[69] Nevertheless the Soviet government was concerned about the cost of pharmaceutical imports. And so, just as the government kept a tight rein on imports of consumer goods,[70] although medicines and disinfectants would seem to fall into the category of basic necessities, Vesenkha strictly controlled import credits for Farmatrest, as much because of the worthlessness of Soviet currency in the early NEP as to conserve gold.[71]

The core pharmaceutical industry also was dismayed by imports—not because of cost to the national treasury but because of the damage that might accrue to the domestic industry. In the spring of 1922, Vesenkha gave Feodor Andreevich Ferrein, Manager of Production at Factory No. 8 as well as a member of Farmapravlenie, permission to travel to Germany to procure clay, glass and porcelain pharmacy vessels. In April 1922 Russia was in the process of forging military exchanges and trade agreements with Germany at Rapallo while other major European nations participated in an economic conference at nearby Genoa. However, although Ferrein had been allotted 40,000 gold rubles, he did not place the order and was not given the money. Ferrein, nonetheless, received a dressing down from his peers. His colleagues in Farmapravlenie strongly criticized his attempts to source abroad because it deprived Soviet glass and porcelain factories of orders.[72]

Still, the Soviet pharmaceutical industry had little choice but to import. But concentration of the industry, as well as bureaucracy, complicated rather than ameliorated the situation. There is no indication that the core industry received a discount for massive import orders. Had one company done the importing that company would have had to defer the cost of the imports through sales. In the Soviet system, consolidating import orders magnified their weight.

A further complication (which also impacted exports and domestic sales) was that during the first half of the NEP Farmatrest was designated the main producer of the Soviet Union's pharmaceuticals but imports of raw materials and marketing of botanicals and Farmatrest's finished products were entrusted to a separate agency, Gosmedtorg (The State Medical Trade Agency). The inefficiency of this arrangement was increased by the fact that whereas Farmatrest was under the jurisdiction of Vesenkha, Gosmedtorg was housed in the Commissariat of Health. On the foreign side, Gosmedtorg had branches in Berlin, London and Paris in 1924.[73] The London and Paris branches were closed in May 1927.[74]

Additionally, even though Gosmedtorg was under the jurisdiction of the Commissariat of Health, Vesenkha meddled in its purchasing activities abroad. Importing was done chiefly through the Trade Representative of Vesenkha in Berlin, although Gosmedtorg also imported on the free market.[75] For example, in September 1923 the Vesenkha Trade Representative purchased wares for the pharmaceutical industry in Germany worth 500,000 gold rubles. Both the representative of Vesenkha and the Berlin representative of Gosmedtorg, the commercial arm of the pharmaceutical industry, signed the contract.[76] Financing similarly was splintered. One hundred thousand gold rubles were available to Farmapravlenie for purchases in 1924, part through a loan from Vesenkha and part from Farmapravlenie's own resources. Gosmedtorg also purchased raw materials and finished items for Farmapravlenie on credit.[77] Interestingly, as late as 1924 advances for trips abroad and payment for imports were sometimes made in American dollars.[78]

The plethora of government agencies involved in imports and their penchant for thoroughly discussing each and every order and permit to go abroad held up decision-making and the acquisition of raw materials. For example, in the fall of 1923 one Rotenburg, a buyer for Farmapravlenie had to delay his buying trip to Germany because he had not received the requisite papers.[79] An additional frustration for pharmaceutical factories was that, as in cases of their internal purchasing and remodeling, monies allocated in the budget for foreign purchases were not always disbursed on time or fully. For example, in one case, 80,000 American dollars had not been disbursed to pay for wares.[80] Excessive bureaucracy also annoyed higher officials. In 1924 Vesenkha fumed that sharing foreign trade activities with the Commissariat of Foreign Trade was annoying and that multiple authorities in charge of imports slowed up orders badly needed by pharmaceutical factories. [81]

And, finally, just as public health had been sacrificed in the competition between Aniltrest and Farmatrest, so too, public health was sacrificed to prevent too large a trade imbalance. For example, in September 1923 a representative of the Epidemiological Section of the Commissariat of Health urged that 130,000 kilos of quinine be imported to cope with the ten million sick with malaria. A representative of Gosmedtorg, however, countered that "the purchasing power of the population" must be taken into account and "from the commercial side" there could not "be imported a greater amount of quinine than" could "be sold and preserved in the warehouses of Gosmedtorg." The final decision was to import 75,000 kilos of quinine—only about half the amount health authorities believed was needed.[82]

Competition from kustari. The cumbersomeness of the core Soviet pharmaceutical industry was magnified by the success of small-scale operators or *kustari.* The raison d'etre of nationalizing large pharmaceutical factories had been to put a key sector of the economy at the government's disposal and to realize economies of scale. However, shortages of raw materials and equipment forced large pharmaceutical factories in Farmatrest and their parent Farmapravlenie to outsource with very small-scale *kustar'* producers.

Large manufacturers in Western countries also "relied on a sprawling network of small-scale suppliers to support their centralized operations."[83] In the United States, essential oils from peppermint, spearmint, wormwood, tansy and other plants, were distilled in Michigan, Indiana and Illinois; "Oil of Wormseed" [a roundworm expellant for hogs akin to santonin] was produced "in Carroll Country, Maryland"; and from "New Hampshire to the Carolinas," oils were distilled from "non-cultivated raw materials…wintergreen leaves, birch bark, pennyroyal herb, hemlock, spruce, white cedar boughs, and the like." The oils were produced for supplementary income "chiefly by small farmer distillers," working "independently with home-made apparatus"[84] In addition, many small chemical enterprises worked alongside large companies to supply ingredients for American pharmaceuticals.[85] And there were numerous smallish companies making prepared medicines and toiletries.[86] Small-scale producers, thus, contributed in a major way to output of American pharmaceuticals

In the Soviet Union, however, small-scale, primitive producers sometimes held up the giants for ransom. Exchanges between Farmapravlenie and its factories with the small-scale producers were made partly in barter but also in cash payments. Although the amounts appeared larger than they were, since they were computed in inflated paper rubles rather than the new gold- backed *chervonets*, their outlay, nevertheless, kept the large factories in thralldom.

In 1922, for example, Factory No. 8 contracted with a *kustar'* for ampules, although of the 25,000 ampules needed the factory received only 1,750.[87] Factories No. 3, 8, and 12 purchased oil from "private persons," although when it turned out to be of poor quality they refused to pay.[88] Farmatrest concluded seven contracts during the spring of 1922. The Trust procured fuel from Moskvotop using monies on hand and barter. Farmapravlenie concluded a contract with citizen Kantsel'son who was to make 5,000 kilograms of aspirin in his laboratory, Farmapravlenie receiving part of the product free in exchange for supplying Kantsel'son with salicylic acid from Factory No. 2 and acquiring the rest of his output at a 15 percent discount. Why Factory No.2 could not produce the aspirin itself was unclear but Kantsel'son himself was delayed in the production because his laboratory was not equipped on time. Farmapravlenie concluded a contract with the Saratov State Amalgamated Chemical Factories (OKhAZE) to produce 100 kilos of ichtyol—unfortunately also delayed. Engineer Moshkin, meanwhile, contracted with Farmatrest to make [synthetic] camphor using a secret recipe. This emphasized how small-scale producers had outpaced Farmatrest for before World War I synthetic camphor was a Schering exclusive, important for celluloid as well as a medical item, and Russia had merely supplied a key ingredient, turpentine. Moshkin received an advance of 50 million rubles. K. Iu. Spade received a 4.2 billion ruble advance to purchase both cocoa oil and lamb abroad. Farmapravlenie sent 34 milliard rubles worth of medicaments from its factories to Sibzdrav, the Siberian Health Department, in exchange for camphor, cookies, and 19 milliard rubles cash. The Stekol'no-Farfornaia Manufactory, which was part of the Glass-Porcelain Trust, agreed to supply Farmapravlenie pharmacy vessels to the sum of 3,000 rubles in exchange for medicaments of the same value, based on the 1914 Ferrein *Preis-kurant* or catalogue.[89]

Strategies to Solve the Problems

Hamstrung by systemic flaws in the macro economy and fetters on their operations, managers of enterprises and Farmapravlenie nonetheless were determined to modernize the core Soviet pharmaceutical industry and increase revenue. They hoped to jump-start production by acquiring capital, technological know-how and finished products through foreign concessions and joint ventures, and then to increase operating revenue through foreign and domestic trade. To their advantage was a plethora of potential international investors and traders. Unfortunately, Soviet executives and officials made some bad judgment calls, dismissing several candidates with apparently strong credentials and signing on with dubious ones, mainly, it would seem because they let politics and emotions cloud their reasoning.

Concessions and Joint Ventures

By 1923 many would-be concessionaires were eager to develop the Soviet Union's native plant and mineral resources. Soviet officials, however, although desirous of foreign capital were suspicious of foreigners' intents. Whether this was because the tsarist government had approved a few dubious pharmaceutical ventures before the war or because Lenin's fear of foreigners' surveillance was contagious is hard to assess.[90] Additionally, Soviet officials, including Lenin and Stalin,[91] were very concerned about Soviet finances. Therefore, pharmaceutical industry representatives were required to bargain hard for the best financial deal, putting this above the upstream needs of the industry or the downstream results for the populace. As a result, a number of proposals to the pharmaceutical industry from foreign venture capitalists were rejected.

Firms from Japan, which had taken over a portion of far eastern Siberia during the civil war, relinquishing the territory only in 1922, were some of those most eager to do business in Russia. In July 1923 the Union of Japanese Businessmen for Developing Trade with Russia, located in Harbin, Manchuria, informed the Plenipotentiary of the Far East Industrial Bureau of Vesenkha that the Japanese Stock Company, Hoshi Pharmaceuticals Company, Ltd., wanted to build a factory in Chita, near Lake Baikal. The Japanese Union assured the representative of Vesenkha that "the company was one of the largest in their field with a capital of 50,000,000 yen." Its headquarters were in Tokyo with branches in other cities in Japan, New York, and South America. Hoshi was a conglomerate that produced and traded pharmaceutical products and perfumes, and also food, paper, and cartons. A letter from November 1923 cited chemicals that the company produced—Codeine Phosphate, Morphine Hydrochloride, Atropine Sulfate, Scopolamine Hydromide, and Heroin Hydrochloride. However, in a "secret" missive Farmapravlenie rejected the offer , considering it "undesirable since the need for these preparations can be filled by existing [Soviet] State factories" although they "are still not fully supplied." [92] This was a foolish decision, for Hoshi Pharmaceuticals was very favorably reviewed in the Soviet journal *Khimiko-farmatsevticheskaia promyshlennost'* in 1935. [93]

In October 1923 Feodor Andreevich Ferrein brought to the attention of Farmapravlenie another Japanese proposal for concessions, from the firm Ronzo Iod "about permitting the production of alkaloids of opium—morphine, heroine, and codeine—in Vladivostok." Farmapravlenie also rejected this proposal, it would seem because of excessive national pride. The board explained that there were "large areas, sown with poppy seed in Turkestan and the Far East" and thus it was "inappropriate to import opium from abroad." Further the technical base for morphia had been established in the Santonin Factory in Chimkent, Central Asia. Additionally, negotiations were already being finalized with Soviet Citizens Levitskii and Kukushkin in Vladivostok to produce technically-based morphia to be marketed to the Second Moscow State University.[94]

In January 1924 Farmapravlenie discussed more proposals—forwarded secretly—from "representatives of Japanese firms" to the Concession Committee of Vesenkha for permission to produce alkaloids of opium in the Russian Far East, along with iodine, and to export the opiates. The companies planned "to import necessary raw materials from abroad and to export the prepared products, and sometimes ... to produce exclusively for the external market." The Far Eastern Industrial Bureau of Vesenkha had recommended approval, considering the proposals "desirable since there" would "be corresponding monetary profit with each pound of imported and exported opium."[95]

Farmapravlenie, however, also opposed this project, for slightly more sensible reasons. In a "secret" reply to the Concession Commission of Vesenkha, it boasted that "production of alkaloids of opium to a sufficient degree has grown in the factories of Farmatrest and at present the manufacture of alkaloids—morphia hydrochloric acid, codeine, dionin, heroin, etc.—fully satisfies the requirements of the country." Additionally—and more significantly—Farmapravlenie warned the Concession Commission that "the production of alkaloids in the Far East ...has the purpose of disguising illegal trade in opium with China. For this purpose entrepreneurs attempt to get permission to import opium from abroad, as necessary for the production of morphia, and in the future they propose to export it to Japan, where it is reexported to China." Farmapravlenie was willing to allow "production of alkaloids in the Far East only in those cases where collection of opium is done locally" and there was thorough "supervision and control over production so that the entrepreneurs" did "not make opium available to local workers—Chinese and Koreans."[96]

One might have assumed that Farmapravlenie had a bias against the Japanese, who were on-again, off-again antagonists of Russia. Russia had lost a war to Japan in 1905, although Russia and Japan had made territorial agreements in the years prior to the outbreak of the First World War and Japan had secured medicines and other pharmaceutical products for Russia during that war.

However, in the spring of 1923 and during 1924, Farmapravlenie also dismissed German propositions. These included a proposal from Schering for a concession to produce iodine in Russia; a prospectus from a German firm, Leo, to produce lead and tin tubes for cosmetics and some pharmaceutical preparations; and a proposal from the Khemishe Industryi Konstern [sic] "to organize a factory in Leningrad or Moscow to produce aromatic substances for perfume... soaps, oils,"[97] as well as proposals from other firms. Despite strong import-export links with Germany through the Berlin office of Gosmedtorg, Farmapravlenie reacted negatively to these offers because they did not appear to advance the Soviet pharmaceutical industry.

In the Schering case, Farmapravlenie was dealing with a syndicate to produce iodine in a lake in the Aspheron Peninsula of the Caucasus, which supposedly had great potential, and also in Beiuk-Shor near Baku which reputedly contained 20,000 puds of iodine. This deal appeared more lucrative than Schering's.[98] As for the lead and tin tubes, Farmapravlenie researched pre-war production and discovered that although some tubes of this sort had been imported, a firm called Fol'ga, in Libau and the Butyrskaia factory in Moscow both made the tubes. Farmapravlenie was convinced that the Butyrskaia factory could fully supply the one million tubes that Farmatrest needed annually.[99]

But whereas Japanese and German initiatives sometimes got short shrift, Soviet executives were enthusiastic about American proposals despite lack of diplomatic relations between the two states.[100] Some deals, of course, like those with Armand and Julius Hammer's Allied Drug and Chemical Company and the Moness Chemical Company, were shields for channeling funds from Moscow to the American Communist Party.[101] The joint venture between Farmapravlenie and E. Virgil Neal's firms, Tokalon and International Consolidated Chemical Corp., signed in January 1924, on the other hand, reflected the Soviets' awe of "Americanism" as well as Neal's charisma and his superior negotiating and entrepreneurial skills.

From modest beginnings in Benton County Missouri,[102] by 1932 Ewing Virgil or (E. Virgil as he was always called) would be a millionaire. In 1923 he was en route. His residence and business headquarters at 11 East 36th Street, New York City, duly noted in the letterhead of his Cyrillic letter of introduction to Farmatrest, shared a block with Tiffany's, the J. P. Morgan Museum of Art, and B. Altman's Department Store. Nevertheless, by his own admission, Neal's finances had their ups and downs. Thus, the potential of the Soviet market lured him. One is tempted to see Neal as the epitome of a freewheeling, can-do economic system (but one that led to spurious pharmaceuticals) and the Soviet pharmaceutical executives as symbolic of a hidebound system that nevertheless preserved pharmaceutical integrity. However, this would be an oversimplification, for Neal was but one type of American businessman and the Farmatrest executives represented but one Soviet sector engaged in one deal. Still, the wily American and his staff mesmerized their neophyte Soviet counterparts.

Both legitimate and unorthodox businesses had fueled Neal's success. The former included his enrollment, then stint as teacher at a business college in Sedalia Missouri; an even briefer stint as teacher at the still extant Peirce College of Business in Philadelphia; and in 1902 co-authorship of a popular textbook, *Modern Illustrative Banking*. Neal hit the jackpot when the American Book Company bought the rights to the concise ninety-page text, netting him one-third of a million dollars.[103] By 1903 and 1904 he was a banker, hob-nobbed with the society elites, lived on Riverside Drive in New York City—and was being sued for fifty thousand dollars for alienating one man's wife's affections—the first documented casualty of Neal's relentless womanizing.[104] In 1905 and 1906 he founded the Neal Biscuit Company in Syracuse, New York, which produced biscuits targeted to relieve indigestion or "dyspepsia." This modest endeavor was superseded by another legitimate but far more lucrative business, the establishment of the Tokalon Perfume and Cosmetics Company.[105] Like the concerns of Richard Hudnut and Estee Lauder, Tokalon proved to be a gold mine for Neal. The company had branches in Paris, London, Berlin and Moscow by 1911.

But Neal also had a shadier side. In the 1890s, he became a noted hypnotist. He lectured and authored works on hypnotism, under the pseudonym X. Lamotte Sage as well as his own name, one of his books being translated into Russian in 1931.[106] Neal was not interested in spiritualism in and of itself—all the rage in late nineteenth-century America, as well as in late Imperial Russia[107]—but for its application to business negotiations and marketing. His ability to convince people led to the establishment in 1902 of "The Force of Life Chemical Company," which sold proprietary medicines to over one million "patients," mainly through the mails. Wall Street tycoons and celebrated civil war hero General James Rowan O'Beirne helped capitalize the company at one million dollars and served as officers and on the executive board.

Unfortunately the company ran afoul of the law in 1906. The winter and spring of that year was the zenith of the "Pure Food and Drug Movement" and zealous journalists, legislators and physicians, outraged that President Teddy Roosevelt had ignored their campaign against proprietary medicines and adulterated meat products, targeted Neal's company as their cause celebre. Evidence that the blood of one "Miss Lucille Hoffman," which had been analyzed and prescribed a Force of Life remedy, was in fact that of a horse and claims by the company doctor that his lecithin-based products could prolong life indefinitely finally spurred federal authorities to shut down the company, charging that it had used the mails to sell fraudulent medicines. Some officers were tried in court but Neal escaped the dragnet.[108]

In truth, he had been pilloried somewhat unfairly. American newspapers of that time and later were rife with medicine advertisements that were as, if not more, egregious in their claims.[109] Indeed, when Neal resurfaced, he asserted with his usual bravado that the publicity had been invaluable to his Biscuit Company, which he brazenly advertised through 1906.[110] However, Neal was no sacrificial lamb. A few years later he was sued for conning an elderly widow out of almost thirty thousand dollars.[111] He sported false academic titles and continued to market spurious health and beauty products, earning the censure of the American Medical Association until 1918.[112]

Neal's joint venture with Farmatrest had the hallmarks of both sides of his game. The 1924 introductory letter explained that although Tokalon was "an American firm" headquartered in New York, with branches in London and Paris, the "founder and chief owner being E. V. Neal, an American citizen . . . the General Director for Europe was a Dutch citizen living in Paris," one J. Oppenheim. "[I]n America, France and other countries" the letter cautioned, "Tokalon did not sell its pharmaceutical products under the firm name" partly because it originally was a purveyor of toilet and perfume products, and also "because of customs legislation, regularizing the production and sale of pharmaceutical products." Rather, in the United States, pharmaceutical products were produced by the International Consolidated Chemical Corporation, located in Manhattan, and by the Dae Laboratories in Detroit.[113] These legal distinctions should have been a red flag to Farmatrest.

Neal claimed that he "desired to organize a factory of pharmaceutical production in Moscow for production and sale of the most necessary pharmaceutical products" that would "use our capital, experience and American principles of organization in the USSR." Amongst Tokalon's chief products were salicylic acid, "Nuxated iron—a strengthening substance sold in the territory of the United States in the quantity of 600,000 flagons per month," and "Bisurated Magnesium—well known in England and other countries on the continent as a practical substance against stomach pain." A postscript in English cited a "Mrs. Neal at the Russian Commercial Bank [sic] in Moscow" as a reference.[114]

Tokalon was a legitimate company. Its sleek perfume bottles were designed by the Depiniox firm and by Lalique; they and Tokalon's stylish powder boxes command high sums today.[115] But "Nuxated Iron," which had been introduced in 1917, was no better than ordinary iron and, furthermore, Neal got into trouble a year after the Soviet joint venture was signed by paying Jack Dempsey ten thousand dollars to promote the product before the pugilist had used it.[116]

Nevertheless, the contract of March 1924 merged Farmatrest and Tokalon into a joint stock company (*Aktsionernoe obshchestvo*) to produce and sell "practical necessary items for the struggle with frequently recurring illnesses such as malaria, dysentery, infections of the digestive tract or stomach, fevers, anemia, and so forth." The preparations were to be prepared and sold under the trademark Tokalon, which the Soviet Government promised to protect from forgery. Production was to be on a large scale, based "on the principles of americanization," that would "allow the possibility to give the population cheap products and guarantee of quality" and "sales' management of these medicaments also" was to be "American." If the activity of the stock company were liquidated, Tokalon had the right to take back formulas and trademarks. The new company had the right to import and export raw materials. Interestingly, the foreigners enjoyed a dominant position in the new company. Farmatrest received 45 percent of the shares; Tokalon, 55 percent. The Administrative Board of the new company was to be located in Moscow and to consist of five members, three from Tokalon and two from the Soviet Government. The contract, which was to extend for ten years, subject to renewal at any time, specified distribution of profits, general meetings, and gave the Soviet Government—with two members to Tokalon's one—preponderance in the "Revision" or Investigation Commission.[117]

Although salicylic acid was needed at the outset of the NEP and Neal's biscuits might have soothed Soviet digestive systems, the Soviet Union needed no more perfume and cosmetics and, in the main, the Soviet venture appears to have been another of E. Virgil Neal's scams. The contract with Farmatrest did not close the book on his notoriety, as a future biography will detail. Thus, while earnest Soviet pharmaceutical executives had signed other joint ventures of dubious value, such as that with one Dr. Stoltzenberg of Hamburg,[118] they undoubtedly were especially relieved when the Tokalon venture fizzled out.

Domestic Sales

Like businesses in capitalist countries, thus, Farmatrest was supposed to raise capital through investment and joint ventures and to cover expenditures through internal sales (*prodazha*) and exports as well as through handouts from the state budget and bank. The "Production Report" of Factory "No. 8" (the former Ferrein Factory) for 1922 balanced *Prodazhnaia stoimost'* (sales' value) with *Stoimost' proizvodstva* (value of production). Amounts were quoted in terms of both "pre-Revolutionary" rubles and gold rubles. The factory's cost of production suitably was below revenue from sales, in terms of prerevolutionary rubles. In terms of the new chervonets gold-backed rubles, unfortunately, the factory's production costs outstripped income from sales.[119]

Farmatrest as a whole reported uneven sales figures for 1922. Whereas 215,839 kilos of chemical preparations were manufactured only 161,760 kilos were sold. Similarly, lower quantities of mercury preparations, inorganic compounds, salicylic preparations, Novarsol, extracts, solutions, and oils were sold than manufactured. This was a pity, considering consumers' dire need of these items. On the other hand, the 1922 report catalogued a higher quantity of preparations of silver, bromine, iodine, and alkaloids sold than produced. Obviously,

Farmatrest was dipping into stores on hand. Similarly, according to the report, the trust sold more salves, vaseline, and plasters than were manufactured. The number of infusions sold was almost equal to the number produced. More disinfecting substances and soaps were sold than produced during the year but fewer "dosed preparations."[120] Again, presumably, items sold in excess of production came from stock still in warehouses, for imports were negligible.

Disappointing sales figures reflected the low level of production in pharmaceutical factories and also the sorry state of transport. They also indicated abysmal marketing techniques.

Terms of sales for medicaments and products from the core Soviet pharmaceutical industry were both harsh and vague during the NEP. Certainly they were far less attractive than in the imperial period. Before 1917 Russian pharmaceutical houses competed with each other and foreign houses for customers. In an 1898 brochure, for example, the Keler Company in Moscow contended that the prices for its medicines and products listed in its *Preis-kurant* or catalogue were lower than those of the Ferrein Association in Moscow and also foreign firms, particularly Merck. R. R. Keler's tract was aimed mainly at zemstvos or local councils, most of which subsidized prescriptions and some of which dispensed medicines free. He stressed that they were obligated to save their taxpayers money, which they could do if they purchased locally. Local purchasing also was more convenient. Finally, Russians in general were obligated to nurture the domestic pharmaceutical industry in case war should come.[121] Part of the convenience lay in Keler's credit terms. In his July 1914 *Preis-kurant,* Keler noted that purchasers could get credit with "solid references." Payment for credit purchases was due within one month. Purchasers were charged 8 percent more for delayed payment. The Keler Association was not responsible for spoilage en route. Insurance for transport was arranged in each case. Some products were not distributed in cold weather. Flammable liquids were sent in special railway cars. Returns could be made within forty days, upon the approval of the Keler Association.[122]

In 1922, in contrast, Farmatrest's "Terms of Sale" made no effort to convince purchasers that prices for its wares were lower than other producers. It merely noted that "Wares" were "distributed according to prices stated in the Bulletin periodically issued by Farmatrest. The prices" referred "to goods from the wholesale warehouse in Moscow *without packaging*." [Italics mine] "Wares," the terms of sale continued, were "distributed to institutions and individuals for ready cash with full or partial payment beforehand with the approximate cost of the order," or "with payment for the order upon the appearance of the bill," and also "on credit with a promissory note." Gosmedtorg gave discounts of 2 percent or so for each order and also extended credit to the local pharmacy administrations, but they were penalized if they deviated from the contract. The administrations forfeited their right to independently trade abroad.[123]

Exports

Soviet officials particularly hoped that exports of botanicals, lucrative before the war, would again bring in needed revenue during the NEP. At first, however, exports were not very successful. In 1923 and 1924, Russia sold only 3,860 tons of plant materials in contrast to the more than thirty thousand tons exported in 1913.[124]

Mercantilism threw a monkey wrench into the international pharmaceutical trade in general in the 1920s. For example, the United States had trouble obtaining quinine throughout the 1920s because the best cinchona bark came from the Dutch colony of Java and the Dutch had a monopoly on the product. The cultivators organized a combine, the N. V. Bandoengsche Kininefabriek. Auctions were "held periodically," but they were "restricted only to quinine producers who" were "members of the quinine convention," with "prices fixed by the convention." The Dutch Quinine Bureau controlled 90 percent of the quinine trade, "guarding…information" on it "with the avidity of a Prime Minister."[125] Many chemicals also were difficult to come by. The "unsettled condition" in Germany in the early 1920s made it difficult for the United States to obtain liquid sulfur dioxide,[126] and other chemicals.[127] French occupation of the Ruhr in 1922 further derailed production and trade in German pharmaceuticals.[128]

Additionally, cash-flow problems on the part of foreign buyers, particularly Germany, impeded Soviet exports. In 1924 the Berlin office of Gosmedtorg glumly reported that "the severe money crisis in the country" did "not give a favorable perspective for the established activity…in medicinal plants."[129]

As was the case with imports, the plethora of agencies involved also complicated and slowed Soviet exports. The Commissariat of Foreign Trade, along with Vesenkha, supervised exports.[130] The Russian Republic People's Commissariat of Agriculture was involved when medicinal plants were exported, and so was the Russian Republic Commissariat of Health.[131]

A major impediment on the Soviet side was lack of plant products. To obtain suitable materials, Gosmedtorg was compelled to source from very small-scale producers. On July 9, 1923, Gosmedtorg contracted with the Administration of the Tersk Central Agricultural Industrial and Credit Cooperative to "prepare for Gosmedtorg in 1923, 50,000 puds of *solodkovyi koren'* (licorice root)...clean...to the standards of the foreign market." A pud being 36 pounds, this was an enormous amount. According to a similar agreement (*Soglashenie*) of March 29, 1924, and executed on behalf of Gosmedtorg by Vladimir Nikolaevich Cherniatsev, Ivan Petrovich Karelin, an inhabitant of the small Volga mercantile town of Myshkin in Tver' Province, promised "preparation of buckthorn (*Krushiny lomkoi*)... to the amount of three wagons [about 800 puds] for the price of one ruble, 25 kopeks per pud." The material was to "be gathered in the spring...well-dried, cleaned...without any kind of mixture, fully answering the requirements of the foreign market...."[132]

Export of Santonin, potentially one of the Soviet Union's most lucrative pharmaceutical products, was fraught with specific problems. The leading treatment for roundworms in humans, Santonin also was a major veterinary product, used to treat ascarid or worm diseases in livestock. In the 1920s, the Soviet Union concluded trade treaties with England and Germany giving the U.S.S.R. exclusive rights to use the name "Santonin," analogous with the trade name "Aspirin" by the Bayer firm in Germany at the turn of the nineteenth, early twentieth centuries.[133] But during the NEP as during the civil war, Soviet authorities refused to sell Santonin to American firms.

The Americans fought back. In 1923 and 1924, in order to "find another source of santonin besides Russia," the United States assayed seeds of "*Artemesia Maritima*" acquired from Calcutta, "to determine" their "content of santonin." [134] American companies experimented with cultivation of various species of *Artemesia* from which santonin could be derived. The McLaughlin Gormly King Company was amongst those attempting to cultivate "Levant wormseed" obtained from Constantinople.[135] W. A. Konantz, "a graduate of the Iowa State College of Pharmacy" and from 1920 to 1924 "first director of research," at Moorman, the Quincy, Illinois company that purveyed to stockmen, went to Carroll County, Maryland, got worm seeds and persuaded local farmers to grow and distill them, thereby successfully developing a Santonin substitute, Moorman's CleanSweep Worm Expeller for Hogs, by early 1924.

Konantz published his experiments in growing the plants and distilling the product, which became "the foremost treatment for large roundworms" in the *Journal of the American Pharmaceutical Association* in March, 1924. [136] In the mid-1920s, additionally, Soviet officials alleged that the American pharmaceutical firm, Parke-Davis, was flooding the market with "surrogate Santonin." [137] Thus, the Soviet trade embargo on Santonin backfired.

The Results

The core pharmaceutical industry did progress to a certain extent during the first half of the NEP. In his report to Farmapravlenie, Podviz, Director of Factory No. 12, admitted that the factory's deliveries in October 1923 only partially fulfilled its "norms": "culinary" items ranked highest at 81.5 percent, then perfumes and chemicals, each at 45 percent. Household items, however, were produced only at 27 percent of the plan target, photographic supplies at 19 percent, and galenicals at 19 percent.[138] Nevertheless, in November 1923, the wholesale *Preis-kurant* of the Semasko Factory (the former Keler Factory, until then factory No.12) again offered consumers a modicum of creature comforts, advertising medicines, soap, dish-washing powder, "Metamorfoza" cold cream, perfume, face powder, toothpaste and powder, shampoo, "Komfort" toilet paper, Russian vaseline, egg dye and fruit essence. The eleven pages of wares in the catalogue were meager, however, when compared with the over one hundred pages of wares—domestically produced and imported—that had been offered in the Keler wholesale *Preis-kurant* of July 1914.[139]

Soviet production of crude borates and hence borax and boric acid was very low. As a result, these key items, as before the first war, had to be imported. In 1923-1924 imports of crude borax were nine times less—and in 1924-1925, one half the amount—imported in 1913. However, imports of refined borax were triple and double pre-war amounts, respectively, in those years, and imports of refined boric acid were five times the pre-war amount in 1923-1924 although only a little more than double the pre-war amount in 1924-1925.[140]

On the other hand, in 1924, one L. Gartsshtein exulted that a large range of items was produced in the Soviet Union—antifebrin, mercury, Phytin, Digalen, heroin, Dionon, Pantopon, Novosal'varsan, nitric acid, barium for x-rays, amygdalin, tannin, Ovarin, salol, aspirin, narcotic chloroform, terpinhydrate, sulfuric ether, and codeine. These, Gartsshtein claimed, supplied about 60 percent of need.[141] Ferrein more soberly estimated that 70 percent of the Soviet Union's needs for salicylic acid was being met by domestic production. The milk powder Mal'ton, a food supplement aimed at children and highly advertised in 1924, was admitted to be inferior to similar foreign products.[142] However, the former "Russian Dye Factory," under Aniltrest, developed a new, superior antivenereal combining Neosalvarsan and silver, Neosilbersal'varsan,[143] which excited foreigners.

A report produced by the Chemical Division of the United States Department of Commerce confirmed an upswing in Soviet pharmaceutical production as the following table indicates:

Table 4.2: Correspondence, February 28 and March 3, 1925, NAUSA, File 231, BFDC.[144]

	1922-23	**1923-24**
	Thousands of poods [sic]	**Thousands of poods [sic]**
Basic Chemicals	11,941.2	20,387.5
Dyes	146.7	185.5
Paints	558.6	688.9
Soap	2,342.2	4,236.7
Cosmetics, dozen	638,000.0	1,081,000.0

The American report did not itemize the chemicals being produced, though, nor did it specify which Soviet trust was producing the categories cited. In other words, Farmatrest was not necessarily moving forward, despite increased output of pharmaceuticals. Aniltrest—the Chemical Trust—and not Farmatrest—had developed "silver salvarsan" (neosilbersal'varsan), a fact which an American report of September 1924 enthusiastically noted.[145] That product, as well as the saccharin and crystal violet which the report attributed to the Aniline Trust, emphasized the stronger position of Aniltrest compared with Farmatrest.

Conclusion

In sum, by the middle of the NEP, output of some basic pharmaceuticals increased although production was uneven. But the core industry accomplished these gains by applying traditional business practices used by autonomous pharmaceutical houses in market economies rather than because key factories had been consolidated and put under state management. Indeed, Farmapravlenie and enterprise directors had to buck government officials at every turn. Farmapravlenie also was buffeted by international market fluctuations and made some misguided decisions on its own. But additionally, bureaucratic intervention hampered the trust's decision-making and initiative and that of subordinate factory directors. Government funds fueled production to some extent, but government limits on imports curtailed production and hurt final consumers. Severe vertical organization of the macro economy, resulting in the separation of the pharmaceutical from the chemical pharmaceutical industry impeded sourcing. Separation of the production arm of the industry made exports and sales cumbersome, thwarting revenue-raising. The core industry had little leverage over its suppliers. The industry, in turn, did not treat intermediary consumers as well as they had been treated in the pre-Soviet period. The fact that bigger is not always better, that independent management allows for more innovation and quicker decision-making than layers of bureaucracy is underscored by the success of *kustar'* pharmaceutical production. It remained to be seen whether the state-run pharmacy system would perform better during the second half of the NEP.

5
Expanding Research, Production and Sales during the Second Half of the NEP

In 1924, government officials merged Farmatrest, the production arm of the core pharmaceutical industry, and Gosmedtorg, its sales arm, creating an entity called Gosmedtorgprom. This eliminated the dysfunction of production being under the jurisdiction of Vesenkha, the Supreme Council of the National Economy, and the sales arm being under the Health Commissariat (Narkomzdrav) of the Russian Republic. Moreover, with its basic capital "of 7,000,000 rubles," the new conglomerate, its management crowed, became "the largest organization in the Soviet Union for production and trade in medicines, surgical instruments, and other forms of health products."[1]

Was this the recipe for success? The core pharmaceutical industry had increased output during the first three years of the NEP. The merger had removed a major structural impediment and provided economic potential. Soviet capital goods industries made remarkable progress by 1926/1927. Consumer goods industries did not do as well but food increased spectacularly.[2] The pharmaceutical trust fell between these sectors. Which pattern would it follow? Put another way, following the merger, would the industry now be able to demonstrate the superiority of a state-owned pharmaceutical conglomerate over pharmaceutical companies operating in a market system—the reason the factories that comprised Gosmedtorgprom had been nationalized? Pharmaceutical weapons against diseases were limited to basics in the 1920s.[3] Would the core industry, now be better able to produce soap, disinfectants, antiseptics, anesthetics, medicines and hormones in sufficiency, supplemented by lesser manufactories and a modicum of imports?

The Visible Hand and Other Constraints

Gosmedtorgprom became larger and financially stronger on paper in 1924. However, making it a successful business was scarcely less easy for the management than in the preceding years. The first liability was the trust's very subordination to government bureaucrats.

The procedures of the merger were similar to those for companies in market economies, for example that of Mulford and Sharp & Dohme in 1929, but government officials made the decision to merge, rather than the management of Farmatrest and Gosmedtorg.[4] On February 28, 1924, the Supreme Council of the National Economy (*Vesenkha*) and, on the following day, the Commissar (*Narkom*) of the Commissariat of Health, Nikolai Aleksandrovich Semashko (indicating the subordination of the latter to the former) resolved to combine Farmatrest, under the jurisdiction of Vesenkha, and Gosmedtorg, housed in the Commissariat of Health, into a new joint-stock company called Gosmedtorgprom. The rationale for the merger was to "[I]ncrease turnover monies" (revenue from sales) and "intensify production of the most import chemical-pharmaceutical preparations" through "large-scale capital reconstruction of equipment and new construction," "improving conditions and methods of work," "free access to the foreign market" and "intensified preparation of raw materials."[5]

Due diligence was thorough—as thorough as in any capitalistic business environment. The *Pravleniia* or administrations of Farmatrest and Gosmedtorg hammered out details of the merger in meetings held each Friday during the month of March. They decided upon a new joint administration or *Pravlenie,* with A. P. Golubkov as chair. L. I. Nisenman, chair of the *Pravlenie* of the now defunct Farmatrest, was downgraded to Assistant Chair. Vladimir Karlovich Ferrein's old premises on Krivokolennyi pereulok, from which he had run his pharmaceutical factories, gigantic pharmacy, and four drug stores and which, after nationalization of his properties, had become the headquarters of Farmatrest, were kept as the headquarters of Gosmedtorgprom. F. A. Ferrein, possibly a relative of the deceased old patriarch, continued to play a major role in the *Pravlenie* of Gosmedtorgprom, as he had in the Administration of Farmatrest. A "Revision" or Supervisory Commission and a "Liquidation" Commission were formed to phase out the old trusts.[6] It was decided that orders for pharmaceutical products were to be received at a central location, distribution was to be done from the warehouses of both institutions, and there was to be reciprocal accounting. The property of Farmatrest and Gosmedtorg were transferred to Gosmedtorgprom "not with [paper] balances but in actuality."[7]

Officially, the new conglomerate was a joint-stock corporation, as Farmatrest had been. However, as was the case with its predecessor, Gosmedtorgprom's shares were not publicly held. Rather, all shareholders were government entities. Most of the founding (*ustavnyi*) capital for Gosmedtorgprom came jointly from Vesenkha and the Commissariat of Health, the former contributing some 3.5 million rubles and the latter 2.5 million, with 31,000 rubles supplied by provincial sales organizations or Gubmedtorgs.[8] In 1926, in addition to Vesenkha, shareholders included the Russian Republic (RSFSR) Commissariat of Health; Ukrmedtorg—the Ukrainian Medical Trading Company; Bashmedtorg—the Bashkir Medical Trading Company; Krymgosmedtorg—the Crimean State Trading Company; the Novgorodskii and Saratovskii Gubmedtorgs—the trading companies in Novgorod and Saratov Provinces; and, finally, the Stalingradskoe, Uzbekskoe and Penzenskoe Pharmacy Administrations, who managed and purchased for pharmacies in the city of Stalingrad, the Uzbek Republic, and the city of Penza.[9]

Gosmedtorgprom itself became a stockholder in at least one other government corporation. In one mid-March meeting, Gosmedtorg and Farmatrest discussed the possibility of their participation as shareholders (*paishchikov*) in the food organization "Narpit." The parent organization of the two, the Commissariat of Health, was to purchase 20 shares amounting to 200 gold rubles each for the new entity Gosmedtorgprom and, with this wedge into Narpit, discussions would commence on the latter establishing cafeterias for Gosmedtorgprom.[10]

Intra- and Inter-Industry Competition

Being subordinate to the government meant that experimental theories were imposed upon Gosmedtorgprom, such as Nikolai Bukharin's insistence that government entities should compete with each other.[11] Eight pharmaceutical-related entities competed with Gosmedtorgprom. These included Khimfarmtorg, Uk(raine)medtorg, Russavstorg, Belo(russian)torg, Zakrostorg (the Caucasian Botanicals Association), Sel'skosouiz (the Agricultural Union), and Rusot. A booklet describing the mission of Khimfarmtorg explained that, according to Bukharin, monopolies were destructive and that competition amongst the entities would result in lower prices and better pharmaceuticals.[12] Unfortunately, the parameters of these entities were not entirely clear. Further, bureaucratic interference, often arbitrary, periodically altered the rules and sometimes skewed the entire competition.

For example, Gosmedtorgprom's charter stated that it would have "the right of free entry into the foreign market" and "use of intensified preparation of raw materials."[13] The mandate of Khimfarmtorg, Gosmedtorgprom's rival, was to import chemicals and sell these to large-scale factories. Yet, the government also allowed Khimfarmtorg to sell to smaller entities from its warehouses, as a temporary expedient. Further, Khimfarmtorg was to encourage the cultivation of medicinal botanicals and to export them.[14]

Governmental Reorganization

What the government had given the government could take away and officials periodically tampered with Gosmedtorgprom's internal organization. Following the merger, the government reduced the number of factories that comprised Gosmedtorgprom to five, instead of the seven that had made up Farmatrest—Moscow Salicylate (formerly the factory of the Zemstvo Union, then No. 2); Factory No. 4 (formerly Schering); the Karpov Factory (formerly Ferrein and known for the past three years as Factory No. 8); the Semashko Factory (formerly Keler, later Factory No. 12), with its soap-making department; and Factory No. 13 (formerly Allen and Hansbury or as the Russians called it, "Allen i Ganburis"). Factory No. 6, which had combined the Bliumental' Factory and Ostromyslenskaia Laboratory, was no longer part of the pharmaceutical trust.[15]

In 1926, the government increased the number of factories under Gosmedtorgprom to six. The Schering Factory was excised from the core pharmaceutical industry, but four of the Moscow factories remained—Salicylate, Karpov, Semashko, and Allen and Hansbury (now called the Alkaloid Factory—in place of the former Alkaloid Factory, Factory No. 1, which had been founded by the Red Cross during the First World War). Tangentially connected with Gosmedtorgprom was the Dzerzhinskii Santonin Factory in Chimkent, once part of Russian Turkestan or Russian Central Asia, but now part of the Kazakh Republic. The Experimental Iodine Factory in Baku also was added to the system. The number of warehouses climbed back up to three and there were ten "Sanitary and Hygiene Stores" analogous to the drug stores of Tsarist times, one pharmacy, and a wholesale-retail store.[16] Gosmedtorgprom also had eight field representatives, stationed in various parts of the USSR, who dealt with trade in the Caucasus, iodine production, and medicinal plants.[17] Although Gosmedtorgprom's managing board might have welcomed the acquisitions, there is no evidence that they had any input into them or into the divestitures and, at the least, the somewhat capricious reorganizations must have been destabilizing.

Cash Flow Problems

Bureaucratic decisions were not only annoying. They caused cash flow problems. Gosmedtorgpom depended heavily upon the government for revenues, receiving about half of its operating capital from the state budget and state bank credit. The other half came from normal business operations—about one-fourth from sales, the remaining from local entities' payments and banking operations.[18] Unfortunately, government subsidies and loans did not arrive any more regularly during the second half of the NEP than when the Soviet Union was first emerging from the civil war. For example, in the 1925/1926 operating year Gosmedtorgprom was allocated one million rubles from the State Budget, one-half million rubles from the Industrial Fund of Vesenkha, and a 225,000-ruble long-term loan from the Central Commercial Bank for workers' housing. In place of the promised monies the trust actually received 650,000 rubles from the State Budget (to be repaid in five years) and only one-fourth—125,000 rubles—of the promised loan from the Industrial Fund of Vesenkha (to be repaid in three years.)[19] The monies for workers' housing fell through the cracks.

Nevertheless, for the same operating year, Vesenkha imposed an ambitious production plan on Gosmedtorgprom, requiring it to increase output and to produce "new medicines heretofore imported, such as urotropin, cocaine, the febrifuge phenacetin, and guaiacol," an expectorant and local anesthetic.[20] Although this implied increased costs, simultaneously Vesenkha slashed Gosmedtorgprom's import credits for that year by more than 45 percent.[21]

Further, being partially a state dependency meant that the trust had obligations that an entirely free-standing business did not have. Gosmedtorgprom received about one-fourth of its income from "imposed payments," as well as from in-city and out-of-city trade enterprises, and from promissory notes and undefined "other sources." But the trade-off of being part of the state system was that a portion of Gosmedtorgprom's expenditures was beyond its control as mandated transfers to its own factories or other state entities.[22] Additionally, the turnover tax—8.2 percent in the last quarter of 1924-1925—was not computed on the basis of profits but as a percentage of gross income.[23]

Gosmedtorgprom's finances were particularly hit by the government's decision to move to the First Five-Year Plan. In the mid 1920s Gosplan (the State Planning Agency), the Commissariat of Finance, and the Workers and Peasants Inspectorate began to draft a comprehensive plan for the economy with concentration on rapid development of heavy industry and infrastructure.[24] In 1926, selected pharmacists participated in preparing the plan.[25] In December 1926 and February 1927, Party Politburo and planners obsessed with "overcoming the market "[26] and fearing another "scissors crisis," such as had occurred in 1923, cut prices.[27] Wholesale prices for pharmaceuticals, such as Novosal'varsan, quinine, salicylates, alkaloids, iodine, salts, all galenicals, tannin, soap and "other items" were cut 6.1 percent in comparison with 1925/1926.[28] This, coupled with a "regimen of economy" in preparation for the First Five Year Plan, that "caused many local pharmacy administrations to lower their orders, often below their normal needs," Gosmedtorgprom management complained, torpedoed revenues.[29] Bureaucrats were mostly to blame but since Gosmedtorgprom also was hybrid, market difficulties, principally loss of the Ukrainian market, discussed momentarily, contributed to financial embarrassment.

In 1925 and 1926 Gosmedtorgprom reported "financial tension" (*finansovoe napriazhenie*). Income in the 1924/1925 operating year amounted to 22,568,000 rubles. Expenditures were 120,000 rubles higher, for a total of 22,688,000 rubles.[30] Gosmedtorgprom Director A. I. Finn and Chief Accountant P. P. Lisitsyn lamented that "in view of the contraction of financial and construction plans it was difficult to state with certainty that the complete production plan would be realized."[31] At the close of the 1925/1926 fiscal year, executives at Gosmedtorgprom asserted that "notwithstanding a host of unfavorable factors, such as difficulty in receiving bank credit, in particular import credits, lower realization [of production and sales] in the second half of the year, harsher conditions of credit imposed by suppliers… finances were fully stable." But, since capital remodeling for 1926/1927 was estimated at nearly 1.3 million rubles and as net profit was only a little over one million rubles, they admitted that it would be necessary to get additional budget allocations of 390,000 rubles.[32]

Old Equipment

By the second half of the NEP factories and equipment were in need of retooling. However, Vesenkha blocked the Trust's modernization efforts. At a Production Conference held in September 1925, representatives of the board lamented that the pharmaceutical factories under its jurisdiction had fulfilled their plan only 34 percent—to a great extent because of inadequate buildings and equipment. Gosmedtorgprom was not able to remodel because of its "strained financial condition" (*napriazhenie finansovogo sostoianiia*) and also because in 1925/1926 "foreign equipment" that had been ordered "was not received" because of a "delay in getting [import] licenses" from Vesenkha.[33]

Frustratingly, Vesenkha encouraged well-heeled foreign businessmen to lease Soviet pharmaceutical factories and install modern equipment, thereby enabling them to out-produce Gosmedtorgprom. Such was the case with "Citizen Briuk."

In April 1924 the Concession Commission in Vesenkha informed Gosmedtorgprom in a "secret missive" that "German citizen G. F. Briuk" wanted the use of Chemical-Pharmaceutical Factory No. 5, the former "Standart" in Moscow, which had been leased to a private individual during the first half of the NEP and now was "in the jurisdiction of the Lease Administration of MSNKh [Moscow Council of the National Economy, a department of Vesenkha]." Vesenkha saw much that was positive in the would-be concessionaire's proposal, emphasizing that there appeared to be no "competition with the state [pharmaceutical] industry." The would-be concessionaire proposed to spend about 180,000 gold rubles to produce patented preparations and reagents, work-up medicinal herbs for export, and distribute some of these items to "the borderlands, where there" were "limited staff to serve the sick." Specific items to be produced included phenol, benzol, toluol, vinegar acid, and sulfuric acid. Citizen Briuk was to bring in equipment such as a refrigerator, steam boilers, and drying chambers.[34]

Briuk's proposal might have benefited Soviet consumers but Gosmedtorgprom viewed it as a threat which would not easily be offset. Thus the conglomerate temporized. Vesenkha had stipulated that Gosmedtorgprom was to respond in thirty days. But only eight months later, on December 30, 1924, did the Trust inform the Concession Commission that it did "not consider the proposal of Briuk solid and interesting for the USSR." Most of the products were to be made on a small scale. More valuable would be production, "on a factory scale," of "chemical preparations," such as aspirin, Pyramidon, chloral hydrate, iodoform, Sul'fonol, Veronal (trademark for barbital), phenacetin, and camphor. Still, in the end, Gosmedtorgprom was forced to capitulate to the higher authorities, agreeing that Briuk could be given "some concessions" to work up "organic reagents" and "in extreme cases some inorganic reagents not prepared by us" according to "the production program established by Vesenkha…."[35] Meanwhile, Gosmedtorgprom was constrained by the macroeconomic environment in the Soviet Union.

The Macroeconomic Environment

During the second half of the NEP, as during the first half, the severe vertical organization of heavy industry and separation of the pharmaceutical industry from the chemical industry impeded Gosmedtorgprom. In 1926 many chemicals still were in short supply, or at least in short supply insofar as the pharmaceutical industry was concerned and government-mandated import controls compounded the problem. The Amalgamated Moscow State Factories of Basic Chemical Production, under the jurisdiction of MSNKh, informed Gosmedtorgprom in early 1926 that "until receiving potassium from abroad, dispensing of nitrous acid" would "not be done." Additionally, the chair of the MSNKh reported to Vesenkha and the Presidium of the Moscow Soviet that, although production of sulfuric acid would continue fully according to the basic program of 1925-1926, production of nitrite was to be contracted 50 percent and production of lead salt, 60 percent. Gosmedtorgprom was going to be able to deliver only 50 percent of the contracted amount of nitrous acid to the Electric Trust and 7 percent of the contracted amount of this substance to a second purchaser "VTS"; the Trust was going to stop all deliveries of nitrous acid to the Moscow Trade Agency, Mostorg, for the time being. "When supplies of potassium" were "received production would continue as normal according to the contracts."[36] To put this problem in context, it must be remembered that Russia produced 75,000 puds of potassium during World War I, when the chemical industry was freer.[37] During the production year 1926/1927, Gosmedtorgprom's reports continued to complain that shortfalls in manufacture were caused by "interrupted supplies of raw materials" and "foreign apparatus [that] was not received." Production of silver and mercury preparations was lower than the previous year.[38] Thus, importation of raw materials and equipment not available in the Soviet Union was a necessity.

Imports

The issue of imports, however, was a two-edged sword. On the one hand, Gosmedtorgprom depended upon certain foreign inputs in order to produce key pharmaceuticals. On the other hand, importation of finished pharmaceuticals, not produced or not produced in sufficiency by Gosmedtorgprom, posed strong competition to the Soviet pharmaceutical trust. However, imports of such items were necessary in the short run for the health of the Soviet people. More complex was the issue of price. Should the industry contest imports of pharmaceuticals that duplicated items produced in the Soviet Union if the imports were cheaper? Lively debates on these issues peppered the pages of Soviet pharmaceutical journals in the mid-1920s.

Some ideologues[39] in the pharmaceutical sector argued that large wholesale firms made fantastic profits importing items from abroad that were made domestically and, thus, that the Foreign Trade Commissariat needed to raise tariffs to support domestic industry. More practical industry executives, such as A. Aluf , S. Mar, and F. A. Ferrein, debated the new tariff schedules of 1924 with a good deal of common sense. For example, Aluf and Mar emphasized that while Farmatrest and Aniltrest indeed produced Antifebrin, sulfuric barium, lanolin, tannin, narcotic chloroform, salol, arsenic, and artificial Peruvian balsam, these were produced more cheaply abroad. Additionally, some substances—such as quinine—were not produced and would not be produced in Russia in the foreseeable future. Further, they admitted that small *kustar'* industries produced some substances—most notably iodine—more cheaply than did Gosmedtorgprom or Aniltrest. In this situation, high tariffs for items produced abroad more cheaply or not produced in Russia would constitute a tax on the sick. In particular, tariffs should be lowered for quinine. When factory production became cheaper *kustar'* industries should be phased out, but in the meantime, small scale production had to be supported.[40]

Ferrein was bullish about the industry's production of caffeine and Diuretin (theobromine with sodium salicylate); alkaloids of opium (codeine, dionin, heroin and morphine)—the formulae for which "the best chemists in Russia" were working; substitutes for atropine; hydrastine, aconitine, Digalen and Digapuratum; Adonilen and some other products. He advocated that the 1924 tariff should stop imports for ichtyol. He averred that the tariff properly protected many items, including sulfur preparations, boric preparations, bromine preparations, ammonium chloride, salicylic preparations, iodide salts, chloroform and chloral hydrate, and alkaloids of opium. On the other hand, he complained that the tariff insufficiently protected other items such as bismuth, codeine, lanolin, camphor, strichnine, theobromine, cocaine, novocaine, antipyrine, pyramidon, anestezin, creosote, and pure milk acid. Finally, he admitted some items were in an "indefinite position" according to the 1924 tariff. These included hydrogen peroxide, benzoic acid, veronal, phenacetin, terpinhydrate, lecithin, antifebrin, and quinine products. In sum, Ferrein opined that "a significant part of the chemical-pharmaceutical industry was protected by the new tariff and could organize production" of important items. Yet, "from the other side, there was a significant list of important and necessary products about which organization and production could not be dreamed." For these the industry could only "work out methods and prepare materials."[41]

Large-scale production of pharmaceutical prototypes required a healthy economy. The Soviet economy remained dysfunctional during the second half of the NEP, however. Therefore, government-mandated import cuts, in conjunction with preparation for a Union-wide economic plan to quickly build up heavy industry, resulted in shortages of pharmaceuticals and medical items.

Economic historians have remarked that lowering prices for industrial goods in 1927 "resulted in substantial goods shortages."[42] In the pharmaceutical sector, prices for basic items like tannin, quinine and soap, were cut in 1926/1927. But although 30,000 kilograms had been produced, tannin was in short supply the year prior to the price cuts. The "severe insufficiencies of quinine, surgical instruments, and medical equipment" in 1926/1927 were due to lower imports, not to lower internal prices, which progressive pharmaceutical executives like Aluf, Mar and Ferrein endorsed, as noted above. To cope with the deficit of equipment, the industry established repair workshops.[43] In opposition to the suggestions of Aluf, Mar and Ferrein, however, in 1927 the Soviet government not only placed prohibitive tariffs on luxury items like perfume, eau de cologne, pomade, and cosmetic soap but on crucial medicinal items. Tariffs on cocaine were raised from 6 rubles, 30 kopeks per kilogram in 1924 to 30 rubles per kilogram in 1927. Tariffs on bromine and iodine were doubled. Duties on medical instruments were raised from 74 kopeks per kilogram in 1924 to 1 ruble, 50 kopeks per kilogram in 1927. Only quinine and its salts were entirely exempted from customs duties, indicating ongoing eruptions of malaria, hence desperate need for these items [44]

Soviet customs duties, thus, had an opposite effect from those in Tsarist era. Tsarist customs duties focused on swelling government coffers. They often hurt the pharmaceutical industry but benefited consumers. Now the pendulum swung in the opposite direction. The Soviet government's tariff hikes on iodine, cocaine, and medical instruments might have been intended to protect nascent Soviet production of these items but they hurt citizens because domestic production did not cover need. "Cocaine is produced inside the country," a leading Soviet pharmaceutical journal noted in 1928, "but in insufficient amounts and it is not certain whether it needs to be imported from abroad."[45] The same was true of iodine and medical instruments. By1927-1928 most medical instruments were produced in fairly large-scale state enterprises. To supplement the five medical-dental instrument and equipment factories existing from Tsarist times, the Lenin-Borema Factory was established in the Gor'kii region in 1926 and the Technological Factory on Gorokhovskaia street in Moscow was established in 1927 to produce medical instruments and medical equipment, respectively.[46] Total output of medical instruments, however, satisfied only 60 to 70 percent of need. Additionally, according to one Soviet commentator, most medical instruments made in the Soviet Union were of the "simpler variety" and the quality of x-ray, electrical, and complex laboratory equipment did not come up to the standards required "for improving medical help, for the progress of scientific thought in medicine."[47] Making imports more expensive, therefore, was bound to impact public health adversely and cause hardships for the Soviet people.

Gosmedtorgprom's Business Strategies

What did Gosmedtorgprom do to overcome these hurdles? Like the management of enterprises and conglomerates in market economies, Farmapravlenie, the Board that managed Gosmedtorgprom, tried to make the pharmaceutical trust successful and profitable by using business practices traditional in market economies. They were similar to those implemented during the first half of the NEP but they were more varied, more aggressive—and in some cases underhanded and devious.

Cost-cutting and Marketing

At the beginning of the fiscal year, October 1, 1925, the share capital of Gosmedtorgprom amounted to a little over 6 million rubles (as opposed to the 7 million required in its statute). During the 1925/1926 operating year the trust increased its share capital by about half a million rubles.[48] The trust doubled its banking and credit operations in comparison with the previous year,[49] selling three times more promissory notes than the year before.[50]

The trust vigorously attempted to reduce sourcing costs. In the spring of 1924 it cancelled the contract made in 1922 with Engineer Moshkin to prepare [synthetic] camphor. Though a feat, since camphor had been a Schering exclusive in Imperial times, the venture was no longer profitable for the pharmaceutical industry. Moshkin's camphor, produced on a small-scale, cost 7 rubles, 60 kopeks per kilo whereas foreign camphor cost 5 rubles, 85 kopeks per kilo, with the addition of 120 rubles per 100 kilos import duties.[51] In 1925/1926 "in order to guarantee uninterrupted fulfillment of the budget," Gosmedtorgprom "concluded advance contracts with suppliers for dates ranging from one-half to one year for all basic raw materials, fuel, and ancillary materials."[52] Although fuel costs, which were outside the control of Gosmedtorgprom, took a larger share of the trust's budget, raw materials declined from 72.3 to 70 percent of expenditures during the 1925-1926 operating year.[53] Payroll costs went up in 1925/1926 compared with the previous year although they declined as a percentage of total costs compared with the previous year, as did costs for amortization and "preservation of wares."[54] The Semashko Factory (originally Keler and then No. 12), in particular, achieved economies in 1925-1926 by reorganizing warehousing and transport operations. This enabled the factory to lay off 38 ordinary workers and 71 white collar workers.[55] Thus, workers in the workers' state were sacrificed in the interests of profitability.

During the second half of the NEP, the industry's marketing strategies became more robust. It "paid special attention to strengthening the role of general contracts (*dogovory*) with local health agencies."[56] These contracts, locking purchasers into the core pharmaceutical industry's products, paid off at first. In 1924, Gosmedtorgprom concluded 23 contracts for 3,508,000 rubles. In 1925, the conglomerate concluded 34 contracts for 6,357,000 rubles' worth of wares. In 1926, Gosmedtorgprom concluded 43 contracts worth 14,676,000 rubles. The contracts were signed with "Medtorgs" in the republics of Georgia, Azerbaijan, and Belorussia. Overall sales for Gosmedtorgprom increased from some 27 million rubles in 1924/1925 to almost 32.5 million rubles in 1925/1926. Additionally, the Commissariat of Health sold medicaments and surgical instruments worth 427,580 rubles.[57] Average duration of credit was 94 days.[58] Unfortunately, Gosmedtorgprom met resistance when it tried to lock in the Ukrainian market.

Ukrainian nationalism. The Ukrainian Republic possessed a wealth of medicinal plants—70 forms out of 95 in the entire USSR and 100 in all of Europe.[59] Over thirty-two pharmaceutical production units operated in the Ukraine, including two major, reputable pre-revolutionary factories, Iurotat and Snapir. Most Ukrainian factories produced high-quality galenicals and basic products like turpentine and vinegar, which had a strong market. One factory produced salicylic acid.[60] A Chemistry-Pharmacy Institute and three pharmaceutical technicums also operated in the Ukraine, although, despite ambitious curricula, Ukrainian pharmacists as well as the Commissariat of Enlightenment admitted that the schools were not sufficient to supply needed cadres.[61]

The Ukraine had lost political independence with the victory of the Red Army in 1920/1921 and formation of the Soviet Union in 1921-1924. Nevertheless, the Ukrainian pharmaceutical industry was independent and Gosmedtorgprom viewed it as a competitor. Farmapravlenie had planned to tie Ukrainian trading organizations (*gubmedtorgi*) more closely to Moscow as early as the fall of 1923. Matters heated up after the merger of Farmatrest and Gosmedtorg into Gosmedtorgprom in 1924. Farmapravlenie cloaked its reason for dominating the Ukrainian market in pious rhetoric, opining that "competition between the Russian or RSFSR Gosmedtorg, operating in the Ukraine, and Ukrmedtorg, the Ukrainian Trading Agency," was "an unhealthy deviation, leading to anarchy in the market and trade losses—expenditures not productive for state interests."[62]

In March 1924, officials of Farmatrest and Gosmedtorg announced that having agreed "to unite the commercial activity of both [their] institutions," it was "desirable that the Kiev Gubmedtorg—the Kiev provincial trading organization—work in the capacity of a branch of [the soon to be merged] Gosmedtorg and Farmatrest." Although "representatives of the provincial trading organization" were to be summoned "to Moscow for discussions about the stated business," it was clear that Moscow had already made the decisions, for the administrations of Farmatrest and Gosmedtorg opined that "the Kiev and Odessa trade organizations should be considered branches (*filii*) of Farmatrest, with immediate subordination to the central apparatus." Further, although these points were to be "reviewed by a commission" and the Khar'kov Gubmedtorg was to remain independent, it was to be more firmly linked to Moscow—indeed one "Comrade Kremer" was to be appointed as assistant manager of the Khar'kov Department (*otdelenie*).[63]

The new Ukrainian "regional office" was to be called "Iuvkhimtorg," under the jurisdiction of an intermediate-level authority, "Kraitorg Prombiuro." Iuvkhimtorg was to be on "*khozraschet*," that is, it was "to conduct state trade in wares and materials on its own account and on a commission basis in the internal and foreign market with state, cooperative, and private enterprises and persons." Legally it was to be "an independent economic entity with rights of a judicial person." Its administration or *pravlenie*, which was to consist of three people, was to have the right to hire and fire workers and pay workers according to contracts established with the unions. But, tellingly, at the same time, it was stressed that Iuvkhimtorg was "a part of Kraitorg" and had to work "within the limits of the funds disbursed to it by Kraitorg." Additionally, the "extent of judicial and property rights of the Office of Iuvkhimtorg" could "be changed only by special resolution of the Administration of Kraitorg." Futher, "[M]onies for the Iuvkhimtorg administration" and "dispersal of profits were to be set by Kraitorg." [64]

If the administrators of the pharmaceutical industry in Moscow thought subordinating the Ukrainians would go smoothly, they were in for a rude awakening. Although Ukrainian pharmacists were no longer politically independent, they wanted to maintain professional independence. Thus, during March and April 1924, representatives from the Ukrainian Commissariat of Health and from Ukrmedtorg (the Ukrainian Trading Agency)—one Kagan and one Landis—railed against "the subordination of the Kiev and Odessa branches of…Farmatrest…to the central apparatus, through the Khar'kov Department."[65]

The Ukrainians did agree to market 100,000 rubles' worth of products from Farmatrest in the Ukraine. They did not agree to the rest of the deal, however, and minced no words in assailing their Muscovite colleagues. Landis, the representative from the collegium of the Ukrainian Commissariat of Health, stated that as "a responsible worker in health care" he appreciated "the all-union nature of health care." He also asserted, however, that "the work done by Gosmedtorg damaged the Ukraine for the benefit of the interests of the RSFSR" and reported that at an initial meeting in the Ukraine, Ukrainian pharmacists had labeled Moscow a colonial exploiter: " [N]ot considering the fullness of health care in the stated region nor the scope of the market, Gosmedtorg, having conquered the Ukrainian market by means of unhealthy competition, now wants 'to chuck' [the expression in the protocol] Ukrmedtorg, so that, having established hegemony over the Ukrainian market, to dictate to the organs of health care in the Ukraine its conditions and 'to take' from them with excess...."[66] Labeling the "union of Ukrmedtorg with Gosmedtorg" "formation of a monopoly syndicate," Landis declared that "the latter would dictate economic issues which would be harmful." He insisted that Ukrmedtorg "must have full responsibility to buy independently on internal and foreign markets." Ukrmedtorg should be required to buy from Farmatrest [in Moscow] only "in cases when Farmatrest" could "guarantee cheaper and better quality wares to Ukrainian health agencies...." The attempt of Gosmedtorg-Moscow "to take over Ukrmedtorg markets and imports," Landis asserted darkly, was "a desire [on the part of Moscow] to become rich."[67]

At the outset of the squabble, the other Ukrainian representative, Kagan, appeared to support Moscow's dominance.[68] Two months later, however, he swung over to Landis' contention that the Ukraine must maintain independence in marketing pharmaceuticals—"in the area of preparing medicinal botanicals Ukrmedtorg must be given the right to set prices," to "export medical raw materials," "to buy in foreign markets and import wares for the Ukraine," which would "resurrect the local manufacture of galenical preparations in Kiev."[69]

The Ukrainian pharmacists fought stubbornly. Kagan successfully argued that "preparations of Ukrainian galenical manufacturing concerns" were "cheaper than [Farmatrest's] since spirits for production of galenical preparations" came "from the Ukraine." A compromise resolution was finally adopted. Acknowledging that "in the Ukraine two organizations occupied with the market of the same pharmaceutical wares was undesirable," nevertheless, for the time being, it was conceded that Ukrmedtorg was to enjoy supremacy in the internal market of the Ukraine. Ukrmedtorg was "to present... not later than the 25th of the month two copies of...a concrete proposal to Farmatrest about conditions for transferring representation [of the pharmaceutical industry] in the Ukraine to Ukrmedtorg." In return, Ukrmedtorg was to "guarantee the amount of market in the Ukraine to pharmaceutical and galenical preparations of Farmatrest with a lower percentage of *nakladnykh* expenditures (expenditures to support the administration) to Farmatrest." It was stipulated that "the independent movement of Ukrmedtorg into [buying in] the foreign market parallel with Farmatrest was undesirable, if Farmatrest" could deliver "wares for prices not higher than those that Ukrmedtorg" could "purchase independently."[70]

The resoluteness of the Ukrainian pharmacists brought them autonomy in the pharmacy sector for the duration of the NEP. The Ukrainian Department of Gosmedtorgprom was "liquidated" in Khar'kov, Odessa, and Kiev. The Ukrainian Trading Agency, Ukrmedtorg, became the trade representative in the Ukraine for sales of the wares of Gosmedtorgprom.[71] In 1926 Ukrmedtorg, the Ukrainian Stock Company for the sale of Medicines and Medicinal Plants prepared and sold a host of items on "credit and easy terms" and exported medicinal botanicals.[72]

For Gosmedtorgprom, Ukrainian pharmaceutical independence contributed to a decline in revenues.[73] Thus, Gosmedtorgprom now had to implement other strategies to compensate.

At a September 1925 production conference, Gosmedtorgprom heard a laundry list of suggestions on how to improve its financial situation—"forge stronger links with the chemical industry"; better train its work force and build better housing for them; improve apparatus and increase supplies in pharmaceutical factories, thus strengthening links with them; cultivate more botanicals; improve the quality of it goods—particularly those for export that needed to be standardized; and increase domestic sales by making the public more aware of its products, by better distribution of products to the hinterlands, and by lowering prices that were "still very high, notwithstanding lower wholesale prices."[74]

Gosmedtorgprom could not realize the first point, but tried to implement the others. The push for contracts accelerated. Despite failure in the Ukraine, by the second half of the 1920s, Gosmedtorgprom monopolized the wholesale drug market. Already in 1924, Gosmedtorgprom constituted 80 percent of the pharmaceutical industry.[75] In 1925/1926, in turn, over 99 percent of pharmaceuticals put out by the six factories belonging to Gosmedtorgprom were purchased by state bodies (*gosorgany*). Pharmacy Administrations purchased almost 90 percent of pharmaceuticals for pharmacies. Most drugs came from Gosmedtorgprom, although some came from second-tier pharmaceutical factories also under the administrations' jurisdictions. Cooperatives and private persons, together, purchased less than 1 percent of pharmaceuticals directly, although they purchased almost two- thirds of cosmetics, perfumes, and household items produced by the Semashko (former Keler) Factory. Cooperatives purchased almost half of these items—47.1 percent; private persons, 18 percent; and state organs, 34.9 percent. [76]

Fig. 5.1 Purchasers of Gosmedtorgprom Products, in Percentages 1925-26

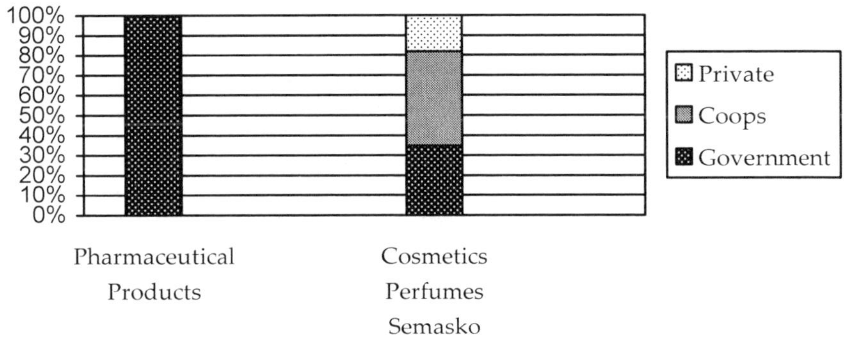

These statistics did not mean that Gosmedtorgprom *actually supplied* 80 percent of pharmaceuticals needed in the Soviet Union. Output of aspirin, salicylate preparations, salol, sulfuric ether, sodium iodide, ferratin, tanal'bin, and terpinhydrate rose in 1924. But Gosmedtorgprom supplied only about 60 percent of these basic items in general and in the case of salicylate and iodide preparations, less so.[77] Therefore the Trust still had hurdles to surmount.

Exports of Medicinal Botanicals

Botanicals had always been Russia's strong suit. Gosmedtorgprom thus concentrated on increasing the collection and cultivation of them so that "in case of war or blockade…there would be no risk…of insufficient medicaments" and strove to increase exports of botanicals to help the Soviet Union to achieve a favorable trade balance and conserve its "gold supply."[78] Export measures were more strenuous and more sophisticated during the second half of the NEP than during the first half. Hopes were pinned on Santonin but in 1924 the Soviet Union's main plant exports actually were *likopodii* (Lycopodium) or club moss, Spanish fly, licorice root, and lime-blossoms.[79] German and Italian, as well as Soviet ships that carried the products sailed from Hamburg to Shanghai, docking not only in Leningrad and Murmansk but also in Riga and Revel, ports in Latvia and Estonia, former provinces of Imperial Russia that gained independence after World War I.[80]

Fig. 5.2 Exports of Medicinal Plants, Percentages

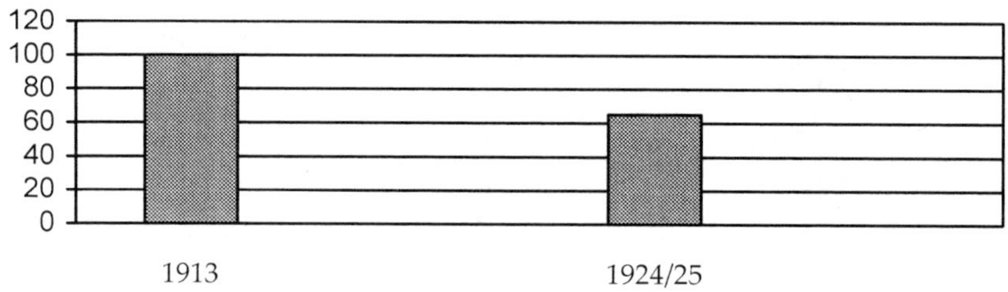

As during the early NEP, export goals were not easy to achieve, however. As before, a major hindrance was the plethora of agencies involved in foreign trade. They had now multiplied. In addition to Gosmedtorgprom, Khimfarmtorg, Ukr[aine]medtorg, Sel'skosoiuz and four other agencies exported botanicals.[81] Industry analysts opined that eight exporters resulted in "disorganization" and "disorder."[82] Also, they disparaged the quality, consistency and packaging of Soviet exports, which were not, as yet, up to international standards.[83] Further, some foreigners indulged in dishonest practices, as did Parke-Davis with Santonin, described in the previous chapter. Because of these problems, during the 1924/1925 operating year Russia exported less than two-thirds—65 percent—of the botanicals exported in 1913.[84]

Interestingly, although Khimfarmtorg prepared a third more botanicals than Gosmedtorgprom, Gosmedtorgprom exported and sold twice the tonnage of botanicals that Khimfarmprom did.[85] Why this was so is not clear.

In 1924/1925, Soviet Russia's main customers for medicinal botanicals were Germany, which bought about 43 percent of Gosmedtorgprom's exports; England, which purchased about 21 percent; and the United States, which bought about 28 percent. Trade with France, Austria and Estonia was negligible, at 3.5 percent, 1 percent, and 0.1 percent, respectively.[86]

Fig. 5.3 Purchasers of Soviet Medicinal Botanicals

In 1925/1926 the United States, Germany and France took the lion's share of Gosmedtorgprom's wares at 43.4 percent, 33.1 percent and 18.5 percent respectively. England's share of Russia's trade dropped to 4.3 percent. Trade with Latvia amounted to only 0.2 percent and that with Austria and Estonia was non-existent.[87]

Nevertheless, in 1925/1926 botanical exports did not meet government-mandated targets. The chief botanical exports remained licorice root, cleaned and uncleaned lime blossom, club moss, buckthorn, and Spanish fly. But only about 40 percent of the Foreign Trade Commissariat export target of 612,000 rubles was realized. Lack of success, as before, was attributed to problems in the international market—"low orders and low prices" and "competition from other countries which themselves collected and cultivated medicinal plants" and, on the Soviet side, too much bureaucracy. Pharmaceutical executives lamented that "disagreements on the part of a whole range of organizations, both in the preparation of medicinal plants in the internal market and in selling them abroad" complicated exporting.[88]

During the operating half-year, October 1926 to June 1927, the pharmaceutical export plan, mainly for licorice, club moss, and buckthorn was fulfilled only 45 percent. Only 358,483 rubles were realized instead of the 790,000 rubles projected in the plan. The failure to reach targets, yet again, was ascribed to "insignificant" orders, due to competition from foreign exporters, and continued confusion on the Soviet side, due to the multiplicity of agencies involved in exporting.[89]

Gosmedtorgprom was not deterred by these setbacks. To increase export revenues, the Trust decided, first, to take over the Santonin Factory in Chimkent and a licorice factory in the Urals, for Santonin and licorice were valuable export commodities. Secondly, Gosmedtorgprom resolved to improve the quality of botanical exports.

Acquisition of the Santonin Factory. Acquisition of the Santonin Factory was reminiscent of the attempt to take over Ukrainian sales offices, for it involved an autonomous political entity, the Kazakh Republic. But Gosmedtorgprom was more successful in this endeavor than in the Ukrainian one.

Russian officials originally decided to transfer the Chimkent Santonin Factory, which had been taken over by workers and then nationalized by the government of Turkestan, from the jurisdiction of the Turkestan Council of the National Economy (*sovnarkhoz)* to the Russian Republic Council of the National Economy, Vesenkha, in 1921. The actual transfer took place in 1923 when the enterprise was proclaimed a corporation called the Santonin Trust, although the trust included only the Santonin Factory.[90] In 1924 part of Syr-Dar'ia and Semipalatinsk Oblasts were transferred to the Kazakh Republic and with the territory came the Santonin Factory-Trust. The Santonin Trust was liquidated in 1925 and its property shifted back from the Russian Republic Vesenkha to the Kazakh Vesenkha. This measure once again decentralized production but marketing and sales of Santonin were kept firmly in Moscow's grip. The USSR Commissariat of Foreign Trade had a monopoly on foreign trade during the NEP and in 1925 acquired exclusive rights to sell Santonin and the *Artemesia cina* seeds whence it was derived on the world market. Although the Kazakh Autonomous Soviet Socialist Republic did receive 60 percent of the profits while only 40 percent were sent to the coffers of the central USSR Treasury, the Chimkent Factory was named in honor of "Felix Edmundovich Dzerzhinskii," the Pole who had run the Cheka in the early Soviet period and subsequently headed the Supreme Council of the National Economy, Vesenkha, indicating that more centralization was to come.[91]

The Ural Licorice Factory worked seasonally[92] but licorice, like Santonin, was an important Soviet commodity. The factory was located in the Ural Mountains. However, much licorice root came from Turkestan, or Khoresm, as this part of Soviet Central Asia was sometimes called in the 1920s, an appellation reminiscent of the kingdom that Chingis Khan encountered in his advance westward in the thirteenth-century. In 1932, in his *National Geographic* article, "Khoresm—Parts of Asiatic Russia Which Have Been Closed to Western Travelers Since the World War," Lyman D. Wilber, an American engineer brought to the Soviet Union to consult on improving irrigation and transport on the Amu Dar'ia River, described "the native craft...loaded with loose piles of licorice root, a commodity which Khoresm sometimes exports to the United States."[93] Actually, Soviet licorice root was not only a "sometime" export to the United States but constituted one of America's main pharmaceutical imports, because by this time the Soviet industry had managed to ensure consistent high quality.[94]

Sharing Santonin and licorice production between Moscow and the Kazakh Autonomous Republic was only a temporary measure. The Chimkent Derzhinskii factory became even more important at the end of the twenties, when it began to manufacture tannin, part of which was used in the leather industry; nicotine from *makhorka*, a strong native tobacco; and Anabazin, with the purpose of reducing imports of these items.[95] The Kazakh Chemical Trust dominated the Dzerzhinskii Factory for a time, a saltpeter factory in the Turkestan section of Syr-Dar'ia (indicating the close connection between pharmaceutical chemicals and military chemicals), and the "Ural Licorice Factory." But, by 1927-1928, Gosmedtorgprom had complete control over the Dzerzhinskii Factory.[96] And the independent Kazakh Chemical Trust was liquidated in 1931.[97]

Quality and standardization. A second action plan to increase export revenues was to guarantee the quality of botanicals.[98] Gosmedtorgprom employed six plenipotentiaries to supervise the cultivation and collection of medicinal plants. They were located in Leningrad, Voronezh and Rostov-on-Don in the Russian Republic, in Kiev and Odessa in the Ukraine, and in the Caucasus.[99] Additionally, the industry standardized the plant products it exported. This was crucial, for lack of standardization, particularly in cardiac remedies could be fatal, as an article on proper production of Digitalis and other products made from foxglove (Digitoxin, Digitalein, Gitalin, etc.) translated from the German and reproduced in a Ukrainian trade journal, reminded pharmacists in 1926.[100] At least two Soviet standardization commissions applied themselves to the task. The first worked during 1925 and 1926 to standardize forty-four of the most saleable plants.

The Standardization Commission in the USSR Commissariat of

Foreign Trade (Narkomtorg), which published an 86-page account of its work, included S. Ia. Shiutte, Director of the Chemical Division of the Administration of Foreign Operations of Narkomtorg, as chair; nine professors and plant specialists; the chair of the Bureau of Standardization in the USSR Commissariat of Trade; and two other officials—chairs of the Russian Republic commissariats of agriculture and health.[101] The commission standardized 71 plants organized into three groups—most marketable, less marketable, and barely marketable.[102] The thirteen most marketable plants included anise, mustard, coriander, lycopodium, lime blossom, licorice root, and sporyn'ia.[103] Twenty-five less marketable plants included valerian root, *Adonis vernalis*, stramonium (Durman or *Folia stramonii)*, lily of the valley (*Flores convallariae majalis* or *Tsvet landysha*), another parasite, several types of berries, including juniper berries, chamomile (*romashka*), myrtle, Spanish fly (*Cantharides* or *Shpanskie mushki*), and Kefir fungus (*Kefir siccum* or *Kefirnye gribki*)—a bacterium, used either wild or cultured in milk. *Belladonna, Artemesia ansinthium*, and thousand-leaf were used widely in the Soviet Union but apparently not popular for export. The book described less known leaves, blossoms, roots, berries, pine needles, and spores, gave instructions for obtaining and packaging them, and warnings about methods used to falsify them.[104]

Other books appeared in 1927 to encourage individuals and groups to cultivate and collect botanicals. The encyclopedic *Lekarstvennye i lekarstvenno-tekhnicheskie rasteniia SSSR: Sbor, kul'tura, pererabotka i eksport (Medicinal and Medical-Technical Plants of the USSR: Collection, Cultivation, Work Up, and Export)* pictured and described a hundred or more plants, their useful parts, geographical location, applications, importance, the amounts used domestically and for export, and average prices. This 236-page book included 64 illustrations, a history of the collection and cultivation of medicinal plants, a chart displaying key points about the plants with a "yes" or "no" check list as to whether they should be collected or not, and an extensive bibliography.[105]

A group of botanists from Leningrad put out a third small, specialized guidebook, *Lekarstvennoe promyshlennoe syr'e (Rukovodstvo po standartizatsii) (The Pharmaceutical Raw-Materials' Industry: A Handbook on Standardization)*. Two authors were appropriately named Monteverde. The first—N. A.—was Chief Botanist at the Botanical Garden in Leningrad, established by Peter the Great and still in existence. Another author, Dr. I. A. Obergard, was a professor at Leningrad University. In 1937 he would be chair of a Pharmaceutical Committee that undertook the purge of the old pharmacist educator, Izrail I. Levinshtein.[106]

The even more specialized, *Orientirovochnaia kal'kulatsiia nakladnykh raskhodov na eksportnoe leksyr'e po severo-zapadnoi oblasti (Preliminary Calculation of Overhead Expenditures on the Export of Pharmaceutical Raw Materials for the Northwestern Region),* self-published by E. Iu. Shass, offered accounting help to cultivators and collectors. Shass discussed the balance between "manufacturing prices (*zagotovitel'nye tseny*)" and "overhead (*nakladnye*) expenditures," counseling that the former would be "correct and, consequently, normal, if overhead expenses would be lower...the more would be guaranteed success of manufacture and most of all export." The book cited percentages of sales costs for twenty botanical materials, including valerian, chamomile, clover, buckthorn, lycopodium or club moss, lily-of-the-valley, sporyn'ia, billberries (*chernika*), stressing that local costs included packaging, storage, rail rates, local railroad taxes, and insurance and that costs "from the base to the ship," included customs duties, insurance, packaging for ocean transport, and "other."[107]

Synthetics and Biologicals: Training Abroad, Industrial Espionage, Reverse Engineering

Although the cultivation and export of botanicals capitalized on Russia's strengths, chemically-synthesized pharmaceuticals and biologicals were considered more advanced. Unfortunately, most were produced by West European houses and were, moreover, patented or trade-marked. In 1927 an industry publication averred that the "[T]wo basic tasks...confronting Gosmedtorgprom" were "fully supplying treatment and medical-sanitary institutions of the Union with all types of medical wares and the implementation and growth of the production of medical substances in its own factories, with the purpose of establishing independence from foreign markets."[108] To produce state-of-the-art foreign remedies, Gosmedtorgprom had the option of licensing them, as British firms did in the interwar period.[109] But this would not have achieved the independence the trust sought. Therefore, the only option was to decipher their codes.

In fact, to expand production of chemicals and biologicals, Gosmedtorgprom employed both fair means and foul. On the legitimate side, factory personnel were sent abroad for training. On the other side, the Soviet pharmaceutical industry engaged in industrial espionage and put out proprietary and patented products, apparently without licensing, through reverse engineering.

Training abroad provided information about products as well as methods. In 1928, Farmapravlenie reviewed V. A. Ioffe's file, prior to his being sent to Merck in Germany for "improvement and training" particularly for "study of the installation of the making of chemical reagents and the apparatus relating to this production." Ioffe was recommended by the Dean at the Chemical-Pharmaceutical Institute at the Second Moscow State University and by the Karpov (former Ferrein) Factory where he had worked in the chemical section for about two years. "Secret" missives assured Farmapravlenie, that he was "a very good, thoughtful worker... oriented to theoretical issues...well-versed in foreign literature," imbued with "love in his heart for his work," "one of the ablest young chemists in the factory," and that he had worked on many of the 120 specific preparations manufactured by the factory, including magnesium chloride, sulfuric acid magnesium, and sulfuric acid potassium."[110] Ia. G. Mazover of the State Salicylate Factory was sent to Berlin to study the methods of producing salicylic acid and "looking over chemical-pharmaceutical factories." He stayed abroad 59 days at a cost of 554.40 American dollars. L. I. Nisenman, former Chair of Farmapravlenie, was scheduled to be sent to Germany from one and a half to three months, at a cost of 1,500 rubles, "to become familiar with chemical pharmaceutical production." E. T. Evseev, manager of the Dzerzhinskii Factory in Central Asia, was to be sent to Germany for the same length of time, but at a cost of only 700 rubles, "to become familiar with production of tannin and the technique of guaiacol production." One Ia. M. Nadelman, Director of the Factory of Medical Instruments and Medical Equipment, was to be sent to Germany for one and one half to three months at a cost of 800 rubles to gain familiarity with production of medical instruments and medical equipment. L. A. Shimanovich, manager of production at the Semashko Factory was to be sent to Germany for work in chemical-pharmaceutical production for one and a half to three months at a cost of 1,000 rubles.[111]

Another method of obtaining information was industrial espionage. Soviet representatives abroad, mainly in Germany, and sometimes the Red Army, funneled drawings and technical information back to Moscow in "top secret" correspondence. For example, in June 1924 the Secret Organ of the Commissariat of Health forwarded to Gosmedtorgprom materials gathered by the Soviet representative of the Commissariat of Health in Germany, which described the Villi (Willi)

Zalge (Salge) firm's method for obtaining iodine, one of the items which the USSR desperately needed. Detailed drawings of apparatus were included.[112] In 1925 the Red Army sent Gosmedtorgprom "secret" information on methods and apparatus used to produce aspirin in the Bayer Factory in El'berfel'd [sic]. Included in the packet of materials was a handmade pencil sketch of the apparatus.[113] [See Figure 5.4] In 1928 Nisenman, Chair of the Administration (*Pravlenie*) of Gosmedtorgprom, sent two drawings and thirty-six pages of German text describing production of synthetic ether oils to a Comrade Fel'dman at the State Scientific Chemical-Pharmaceutical Institute. Comrade Fel'dman, however, opined that the material had "little value since it" consisted "nearly exclusively of excerpts from works or articles in journals... the drawing also" was "taken from a popular book."[114]

In some cases, German specialists *offered* their expertise to the Russians. For example, on August 10, 1926, German Doctor Hans Gzell wrote Vesenkha that he was a "specialist on producing a whole range of chemical-pharmaceutical apparatus" and wished "to work in the USSR." His file contained a letter from the representative of Gosmedtorg in Paris, Comrade Tinkhasiko, asking for information about the applicant.[115]

Interestingly, in 1924, one Butkevich noted the antibacterial properties of penicillium, used from 1893 by A. Wehmer to produce citric acid. This did not lead to the production of Soviet penicillin, however.[116] But in the second half of the NEP the Soviet pharmaceutical industry did produce items ambiguously listed under the rubric of "new production of formerly imported items." Some of these were said to be "patented."

During the 1925/1926 operating year, for example, the Karpov Factory began "new production" of cocaine, Urotropin (an internal disinfectant trademarked by Schering from 1913 through the 1930s), Antifebrin, iodoform, and a few other medicines "heretofore imported."[117]

Advertising amounted to only 0.84 percent of the industry's budget in 1926, but the industry tooted its horn.[118] And among the nineteen alkaloid, salicylic, iodide, mercury, alkaline, organic, and chemical preparations touted in 1927 were Pantopon(a Roche and, in 1922, a Poehl product); Dionin and Stypticin; the hormone products Adrenalin,

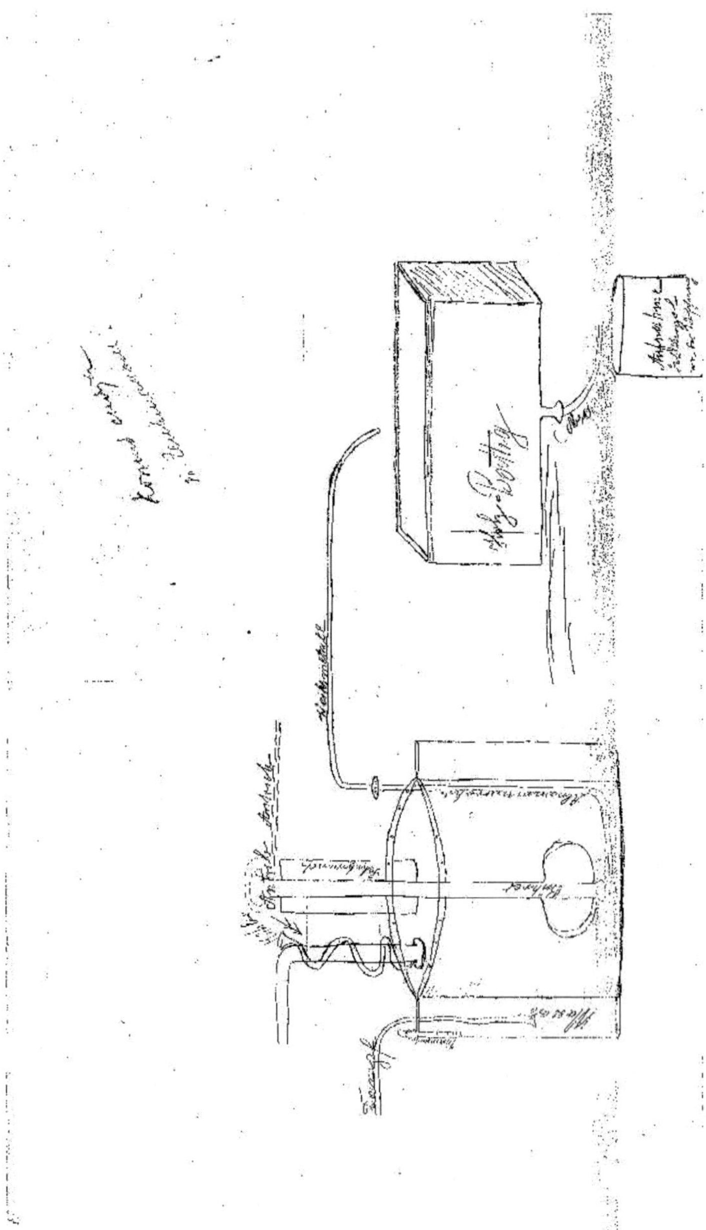

Figure 5.4 Industrial Espionage: Drawing of Apparatus in the Bayer Factory in El'berfel'd [sic]. (Source: RGAE, f. 871, op. 3, d. 56)

Mammin, Ovarin and Tyreoidin (in 1922 a Poehl product for skin diseases) ; and Novosal'varsan, Ferratin, Osarsol, Pepsin, Tannalbin, and "Theobromin natro-salicylic (Diuretin)."[119] These had been developed at the Scientific Chemical-Pharmaceutical Institute in Moscow[120]—the institute Boris Nikolaevich Saltykov, left-wing pharmacist from Tsarist times, created in 1922 from the research laboratory at the former Ferrein Factory where he began working in 1892—[121] and then produced on a factory scale. Exactly *how* these "new preparations...heretofore imported from abroad"[122] were developed was not disclosed. Undoubtedly it was through reverse engineering.

In 1927 Gosmedtorgprom advertised five new preparations. They had been developed to compete with foreign products. Three were "standardized cardiac preparations"—Adonilcn, Diginorm "R", and Gitalen. Diginorm "R" was the Soviet equivalent of Digipurat, and Gitalen was the Soviet equivalent of Digalen; both were made from the leaves of foxglove. Adonilen was made from *Adonis vernalis*. Biokhinol' (exported under the spelling "Bijochinol") and Bismutogvi "were two new antisyphilitic preparations made partly from heavy metal bismuth" that supplemented Novosal'varsan. These also had been developed at the Scientific Chemical-Pharmaceutical Institute in 1926. Additionally, in 1926, the Institute was in the last stages of developing a standardized preparation of Sporyn'ia. Natural sporyn'ia consisted of parasites collected from roses. The standardized product was going to be transferred to factory-scale production under the name "Sekakornin," but was not yet advertised.[123]

In 1927, the industry also produced ten "patented substances." They included the "strengthening substance Phytin, the cough syrups Sirolin and Pertussin, a children's food supplement Mal'ton, and so on."[124]

There are no records of Soviet patents for these products or products similar to other foreign products produced by Gosmedtorgprom in the interwar period. Therefore, the question arises as to whether the imitations were legal or illegal.

Some of the "patented" products may actually have been ethical or proprietary medicines. Soviet pharmaceutical journals did assiduously publish formulae for "New Medical Substances."[125] So perhaps these items were in the public domain. A further consideration is that Schering sold santonin, which had been a Russian exclusive before World War I and, in the mid-1920s, some "eight to ten" enterprises in various countries, including two in the Soviet Union (one the *kustar'* operation of Engineer Moshkin and the other apparently the Karpov—formerly

Ferrein, then No. 8 —Factory) produced camphor, which had been a Schering exclusive before World War I.[126]

Russian production of hormone preparations particularly reflected pioneering in this area. Medical researchers had begun investigating the use of sex hormones for rejuvenation in the 1880s. In the 1890s they realized the importance of the thyroid gland and the problems iodine deficiency could cause.[127] A. V. Pel' and P. P. Kravkov in the nineteenth century and Liubov' Nikolaevna Lavrova, a graduate of the Women's Pharmacy School founded by one of the first women pharmacists in Russia, Antonina Boleslavna Lesnevskaia, all did cutting-edge research on hormones.[128] Thus, when the Eli Lilly Company in Indianapolis, Indiana, began to produce insulin in cooperation with researchers in Toronto in 1922,[129] the Russians had a track record and kept abreast of developments in the field. In 1926, for example, the Ukrainian pharmacy journal, *Chemical-Pharmaceutical News* (*Khimiko-farmatsevticheskii vestnik)*, reviewed a text published in Dorpat, newly independent Estonia, about new hormone preparations, including ovarian preparations.[130] The Soviet industry was on par with and even in advance of houses like CIBA which only concentrated on hormone research—progesterone, the ovarian hormone Estradiol, and testosterone in the 1930s.[131]

The Results

At the outset of this chapter we posed two questions. One was whether the core pharmaceutical industry produced more pharmaceuticals during the second half of the NEP. It did, although their distribution was problematic, a topic discussed in the following chapter. But the second question, whether state management facilitated production, would have to be answered in the negative. The industry's advances appear to have been made in spite of rather than because of state management and the Soviet economic structure.

In 1926 the Karpov (former Ferrein) Factory alone produced 89 inorganic preparations, 14 mercury preparations, 71 reagents, 116 galenical preparations—extracts, infusions, oils, salves—two kinds of soap, including medicinal green soap and 10 "dosed preparations."[132] An experimental iodine station was being built near Baku.[133] The production of pharmaceuticals, soaps, and household items increased in general as the following table shows:

Table 5.1 Production in Kilograms for Chemical-Pharmaceuticals, in Dozens for Non-Pharmaceuticals

	1924/1925	**1925/1926**
Iodine	45,797	73,177
Other organic preparations	832,368	1,228,663
Alkaloids	1,754	2,997
Salicylic preparations	80,296	143,162
Novosal'varsan	192	826
Other organic preparations	365,577	444,484
Disinfecting substances	111,804	159,653
Galenical preparations	1,206,719	1,292,554
Perfumes, cosmetics, soap	686,592	1,258,655
Technical-household items	2,257,757	2,543,845

Source: *Kratkii otchet o rabote Gosmedtorgproma za 1925/26 operats. god* (Moscow, 1927) p. 6

The near doubling of salicylic preparations, iodine and the anti-syphilitic, Novosal'varsan was heartening, but 1927 statistics were less so. They are very contradictory. One source trumpeted that by 1927, the five factories of Gosmedtorgprom (their pre-revolutionary names, Schering, Ferrein, Keler, and so on were supplied along with their new Soviet names) produced 95 percent of the chemical-pharmaceutical products and 50 percent of the galenical preparations used in the Soviet Union. But production figures here use the term "up to" (*do*) and are far more optimistic than those given for first nine months of the 1926/1927 operating year cited below. The output of alkaloids (morphine, codeine, dionin, heroin, Pantopon, stiptitsin, papaverin, and cocaine) at "up to 4,000 kilograms a year" almost doubled compared with 1926 in the chart above. The output of disinfecting substances at "up to 220,000 kilograms a year" was higher by almost 40 percent. The "up to18,000 kilograms a year"of sulfuric acid barium for x-rays produced amounted to about one-third of the 50,000 kilograms imported from Germany and England in the industry's barren year of 1923. The "1.2 millions kilograms a year" of mineral (inorganic) salts produced included sulfuric and chloride salts of caustic soda, calcium, copper, and zinc, as well potassium. Absence of the last had accounted for 5,000 kilograms of imports in the dark days of 1923. Iodine salts of potassium and soda were said to be "up to" an amazing "100,000 kilograms a year". Novosal'varsan production was "up to 1,000 kilograms a year," mercury preparations —"up to 40,000 kilograms a year" and salicylic preparations (aspirin, etc)—"up to 2,000 kilograms a year"—a great leap from 1926 production figures. Medicinal tannin production was "up to 30,000 kilograms a year," narcotic ether—"up to 30,000 kilograms a year," narcotic chloroform—"up to 30,000 kilograms a year" and so on. The decline in galenical preparations to 1.2 million kilograms, a decrease in comparison with the previous year, indicated the industry's emphasis on chemicals and hormones. Dosed substances—ampules, pills, and capsules—amounted to a respectable 50,000 kilograms[134].

Meanwhile, another source showed production for the first nine months of the 1926/1927 production year of alkaloid preparations at 2,342 kilograms; disinfecting substances at a mere 57,691 kilograms (about half the previous year's production); iodine preparations at only 42,530 kilograms —lower than the previous year; Novosal'varsan at only 502 kilograms, also lower than the previous year. Only salicylic preparations at 117,675 kilograms came close to the figure quoted in the source above.[135]

The first nitrogen factory in Russia was constructed and a new superphosphate plant was being planned in 1927.[136] Production of iodine, however, increased unevenly. In 1926 the Experimental Factory established by Gosmedtorgprom at Beiuk- Shor near Baku, on the Caspian Sea, produced 16 kilograms of crystallized iodine from water rising from drilled wells (*burovykh vod neftianykh skvazhin*) every twenty-four hours.[137] Because a lot of rain fell during the second quarter of the production year and construction occurred during the third quarter, only 333 kilograms of iodine were produced during 1926.[138] The facility near Arkhangel'sk produced 225 kilograms in 1925 but in 1926, only 180 kilograms of iodine. The drop in production was due to poor weather conditions—"the summer was rainy and windy, but without storms, tearing out the seaweed and scattering it on shore."[139] In 1928, Feodor A. Ferrein averred that iodine obtained from drilled waters at Beiuk-Shor was "insufficient for constructing a large factory" and that "[E]xperiments on the Black Sea do not give a clearer picture." He was hopeful, though, that all the efforts put forth would "sooner or later free the [Soviet] Union from imports of iodine."[140] At the very end of the NEP, some price cuts, as in a market economy, signaled increased output and did not result in shortages. In 1927 prices were low for salicylate preparations, Novosal'varsan, papaverine, and Pantopon,[141] because of "improved production" and "increased availability," a claim that coincided with the 200,000 kilograms produced in 1926. In June 1927 tablets of Atofan (Schering's anti-rheumatic, Atophan, produced from

1913[142]) and Bromural, heretofore imported, were available in sufficiency so prices for them were lowered. In 1928 F. A. Ferrein averred that although valerian root, bilberries, sage, chamomile, and some other important botanicals were in short supply and that fish-oil production was down because the plan for the Fishing Trust cut production, nevertheless, domestic production of pure benzol and toluol met the needs of the Soviet Union.[143]

Salicylate preparations increased in 1928 because improved equipment increased worker productivity. The Salicylate Factory in Moscow increased production of sodium salicylate 50 percent by replacing antiquated aluminum equipment with copper. This, in turn, enabled the factory to double production of salicylic acid. In the shop that produced aspirin, installation of foreign equipment in December 1927 raised production from 25 to 30 percent. With better equipment, two workers were able to produce and package 14,000 kilograms of pure preparations per month, compared with the 3,000 to 4,000 kilograms produced by six to eight workers in 1924.[144]

As important as increased output, the *quality* of Soviet products began to improve during the second half of the NEP. Analytical laboratories in factories and in the central warehouse checked wares to see whether they adhered to standards established by the Pharmacopoeia, which lessened *brak* or rejection of medicines at the wholesale stage. The cases of rejection (*reklamatsiia*) of defective wares by purchasers were slightly less—25.8 percent in 1925/1926 versus 26.6 percent in the previous year—although that may have been the result of shortages of some items.[145]

Research and development had moved forward. British firms imported or licensed and reprocessed proprietary drugs in the interwar period. American firms, in contrast, spent large amounts on research and development in order to compete with German firms. As a result, whereas American, as well as British, companies had been behind German ones, now American houses began to catch up, while British firms continued to lag and be dependent on German imports.[146] The validity of cloning aside, Gosmedtorgprom did have an active research and development program that paralleled the American pattern. Nevertheless, the core Soviet pharmaceutical industry still relied heavily on imitating foreign medicines rather than focusing on breakthroughs of its own.

Efficiencies—"rationalization" in Soviet parlance—of production did occur, particularly in the 1926-1927 operating year. Packaging was shifted from the Semashko Factory, new buildings were erected at some of the six Moscow factories, some new machinery was installed. Dwellings had been constructed for workers at some of the factories, although allotted space was quite small.[147] A great achievement was that, in the operating period October 1926 to June 1927, the Central Surgical Warehouse succeeded in producing some items of medical furniture and quartz lamps, heretofore imported, as well as "dental chairs and drills, prepared earlier by *kustari.*"[148]

Gosmedtorgprom's financial situation was still somewhat shaky in 1926/1927, despite directors' insistence, again, that finances were "fully stable." On the plus side, the number of shareholders increased, payroll costs fell because the number of workers declined 16 percent due to "liquidation of independent commercial activity at the Semashko Factory," and "*nakladnye*" (overhead costs) were less. On the other hand, costs for raw materials and fuel rose, exports were lower than hoped, due to insufficient orders and competition from other countries, and revenue from domestic sales fell.[149]

Conclusion

The Soviet pharmaceutical industry made impressive gains during the NEP. But, excluding perhaps the initial 1924 merger of Farmatrest and Gosmedtorg, these were mainly due to industry executives bucking the economic and political environment in which the industry operated, rather than because of it. Further, while the extreme concentration of the industry enabled it to dominate the domestic market, defaults and under- production of key items could render the concentrated nature of the industry dangerous, for there were few alternatives. For example, despite the turnaround in the core Soviet pharmaceutical industry,[150] iodine production during the second half of the NEP was still far below production during World War I and some other basic items still were not produced in sufficiency. Distribution systems also needed improvement. Thus, it is instructive to compare Gosmedtorgprom with Schering, as representative of the German pharmaceutical industry.

Schering suffered vicissitudes during the 1920s just as Gosmedtorgprom did. The German pharmaceutical company had to grapple with inflation, sequestration of plant and intellectual property in Russia and the United States, competition from foreign houses, competition within

Germany from the IG Farben conglomerate (which included Bayer, Hoechst and other chemical giants), and the financial slump which affected Germany in 1925-1926 even before the Great Depression hit worldwide in 1929. Schering's merger with Kokswerke, the coal-mining and coke conglomerate with operations in Silesia, was a mixed blessing. Schering contributed more financially to Kokswerke than it appeared to get in return. Schering's management also made policy mistakes—costly increases in office and sales staff, poor acquisitions, and so forth. Nevertheless, return of 80 percent of its American property and some good decisions by its management helped the company. Schering developed new products, did hormonal research, built branches and affiliates around the world, entered a camphor cartel and an iodine cartel. In the 1920s it held 50 percent of the market in the United States (the major market in the world at the time) for synthetic camphor and was an important player in photography as well as pharmaceuticals. Although Christopher Kobrak admits that Schering's financial records were less than transparent, he considers it profitable and financially solid through 1930.[151]

But as if not more important was the fact that due to the organization of the German pharmaceutical industry in the 1920s, Schering's fate did not adversely impact consumers. Because the German pharmaceutical industry was "fragmented" (Kobrak's term), consumers were not unduly affected by the ups and downs of any one company or conglomerate. "Though one of the largest producers in Germany," Kobrak notes, "Schering's sales were only a tiny fraction of the world and German production, and even German exports." Schering's total sales were "less than one half of 1 percent of worldwide production and only 4 percent of Germany's."[152] This meant that consumers had choices and alternatives to Schering's products. In the Soviet Union, the situation was different.

A. Aluf, old pharmacist and former Menshevik Internationalist, lamented that the Soviet pharmaceutical industry he had helped to nationalize had not lived up to its expectations by the end of the NEP. Although "chemical and pharmaceutical production" was "in the hands of the government, for the most part working according to a fixed plan," he opined, "rational [that is 'dosed' or packaged] medicines" were "distributed to an insignificant degree in Russia."[153] The following chapter details the hardships consumers faced because of the extreme concentration of the Soviet pharmaceutical industry.

In sum, the benefits of the Soviet consolidated, state-run pharmaceutical industry as opposed to an industry composed of many discrete, more autonomous enterprises—the system that had obtained in Imperial Russia and still obtained in the rest of Europe and the United States in the 1920s—were by no means proven at the end of the NEP. And, as we shall see after looking at the pharmaceutical industry from the vantage point of consumers and preventive medicine, concentration of the pharmaceutical industry and its domination by exogenous officials would become even more disadvantageous during the next stage of Soviet economic development, the "Five-Year-Plan/Command-Administrative" period, which began in 1928.

6
At the Apteka During the NEP

Iuri Zheliabushkii's 1924 film, *The Cigarette Girl of Mosselprom,* and Abram Room's 1927 production, *Third Meshchanskaia Street* or *Bed and Sofa* as it was known in the United States, portrayed a Soviet Russia similar to the United States and Western Europe in the 1920s. Pretty girls wore chic "flapper" dresses and cloches; autos plied city streets along with horse-drawn vehicles; people listened to wireless sets, went to the movies[1] and, in the Room film, for airplane rides above Moscow; and although living space was tight, ample meals were served with linen tablecloths and napkins, soup tureens, china and silver and bed linens were attractive. The format or mix of pharmaceuticals produced in the Soviet Union during the 1920s also was similar to that produced in the United States and in Great Britain.[2] But what was the retail side of the pharmaceutical sector like? Were medicines and vitamins, disinfectants, toiletries, and cleaning products as available in the Soviet Union as in the United States and Great Britain? The Room film provides a hint that there were differences. Although the film is silent, we see women in the abortion clinic that the heroine Liudmila visits before she decides to keep her baby, shrieking and fainting—probably because they received no anesthetic or pain medication.

Numbers of Pharmacies and Drug Stores at the Outset of the NEP

In the first chapter we saw that in late Imperial Russia, although there were not enough pharmacies in rural areas—where most people lived—citizens in urban areas, whether in European Russia or Siberia had fairly good access to pharmacies. But the government strictly regulated pharmacies as well as pharmaceutical factories. Medicines could be made up only in a pharmacy (*apteka*) and these, in turn, were designated "*normal'naia*"—fully stocked, located in cities and managed by a trained pharmacist (*provizor*)—and rural "*sel'skaia,*" which could be managed even by paramedics. Drug Stores (*Aptekarskie magaziny*) sold ready-made packaged medicines but their staff was not allowed to prepare medicines. Russia did not have as much of a market system as the United States and Great Britain. But, since regulations made it difficult to establish pharmacies, particularly "normal" ones, drug stores sprang up to fill the vacuum. By World War I there were about 10,000 drug stores compared to some 4,800 pharmacies.

The Soviet Union maintained the practice of dividing pharmacies and drug stores and many of the rules for dispensing as well. During the civil war both types of establishments were confiscated from their owners. The number of pharmacies, drug stores and pharmacists plummeted. As a result, in the early part of the NEP both urban dwellers and peasants had much less access to proper dispensing, whether of medicines made up on the spot or pre-packaged, than they had enjoyed in the pre-revolutionary period. Pharmacy specialists lamented, as noted in Chapter 3, that only about 900 pharmacies operated in the Republic—approximately one-fifth of the pharmacies that had operated in the pre-Soviet Russian Empire. According to another statistic, compared to the 1,431 *normal'nye* or urban pharmacies that had operated in the Russian Republic before the First World War, only 600 pharmacies functioned in the early 1920s. In rural areas the number of pharmacies dwindled from some 1,080 existing before the war to virtually none.[3] Pharmacy specialists agonized over the "sad" and "severe" situation of pharmacy in rural areas in 1924.[4]

By the midpoint of the NEP in 1924-1925, there were still 39 percent fewer pharmacies in the Russian Republic than before the October Revolution. In Kostroma province, for example, 34 or 35 pharmacies—zemstvo, factory, military, and private—operated before 1917; eleven were in the city of Kostroma, three of them privately owned. In 1924 only seven pharmacies operated under the provincial medical association and the city of Kostroma had only three pharmacies.[5]

In the Ukraine in 1924 there were far fewer pharmacies in cities than there had been in 1913. In 1913, 353 pharmacies operated in Ukrainian cities. All privately owned, they were supplemented with drug stores. In Ukrainian villages, 714 private pharmacies operated. They were less well stocked and competently managed than urban pharmacies. Given the fact that there were only some 200 zemstvo pharmacies in 1916, not many "public" pharmacies or drug stores had operated in Ukrainian villages. In 1924, the number of pharmacies in Ukrainian cities had plummeted. There were only 246—100 fewer than before the war. Only 345 pharmacies existed in the Ukrainian countryside—half the number that had been there in 1913. Admittedly, Ukraine had lost her westernmost territories to Poland. Additionally, 144 "Sanitary and Hygiene Stores" (equivalent to pre-revolutionary Drug Stores) supplemented the pharmacies. One hundred thirteen of these were privately owned.[6]

Some areas did fare better than others. In 1923-1924 almost the same number of pharmacies and retail establishments operated in the city of Ufa, now part of the Bashkir Autonomous Republic, a subdivision of the RSFSR, as before the revolution. Then there had been eight pharmacies. In 1923-1924 there were "2 *apteki* with paid dispensation of medicine and 5 *aptek* with free dispensation (*besplatnym otpuskom*) of medicine," supplemented by "2 stores of 'Sanitation and Hygiene' (*magaziny sanitarii i gigieny*)." In outlying areas of Ufa Province there were three pharmacies in the town of Iglino and one each in the Blagoveshchensk and Arkhangel'sk factories; a pharmacy in the town of Davlekanovo, and a pharmacy in the town of Strelitamake.[7]

Private and State Pharmacies, Quantity and Quality in the NEP

Private pharmacies made a comeback in the early NEP. Some pharmacies that had been nationalized were leased back to individuals. Some new private pharmacies were opened as well. A number of lessees had been owners and managers of pharmacies during the Imperial period. [8] In 1923, 463 private pharmacies were operating in the Russian Republic, about a quarter of all pharmacies.[9] Probably these pharmacies were attentive to their customers. Additionally, Soviet authorities were keen that all pharmacies serve the public properly. Thus government not only supervised pharmacy operations, as the Tsarist government had done, but held competitions and awarded prizes for pharmacies that offered good service.[10]

How well did Soviet pharmacies fulfill citizens' needs? How well did the amount of pharmaceuticals in the *apteka* keep pace with increased amounts of food and other consumer goods available in stores, stalls and markets?[11] How convenient were the pharmacy hours? Availability and service varied according to locality and the items in question. In 1921, the pharmaceutical warehouse in Ufa had some amounts of acetic, tannic and tartaric acids, silver nitrate, aspirin, balsam, bismuth, calcium carbonate, calomel, chloroform.[12] One pharmacy was deemed to be in generally good condition, with supplies of aspirin, boric acid and senega.[13] Cosmetics were abundant without qualification. Dermatological items and food supplements could be procured in the

Ukraine. An Ukrainian pharmacy journal, published in Odessa, for example, advertised *kustar'*-produced lipstick, nail polish, eyebrow pencils, face powder, perfume and toilet soaps. Among the foreign medicines advertised were Sirolin, Pertussin, and Cheesebrough Vaseline. Cosmetics appeared to be of domestic provenance. They included "Damil" powder and lip gloss, "Poru" nail polish, lipstick, brow pencils; and face powders by the name of "Antik," "Kri de Pari," "Mimoza," "Diviniia," and "Kapriz mody." The journal advertised hormone products such as "Testikulin," Ovarin, and "Pankreatin," made by the Odessa Chimical-Pharmaceutical Institute.[14] The Ukrainian edition of *Farmatsevticheskii zhurnal* advertised medicines like Osarsol (a "prophylactic and treatment for syphilis, analogous to the French Stovarsol and the German Spirotsid"), Sul'folan—a sulfur-zinc salve to treat "the itch" or scabbies, Spermin, and Mal'ton, the milk drink for children.[15] The journal also advertised a Soviet razor blade, "Lora—cheaper and better than Foreign"[16] and "Kreme Metamorfoza." The Joint-Stock Association (Akts. Obshchestvo) "Kazimi" in Moscow produced this face cream—which "was the best tested substance against...redness, yellowness, burns...and other insufficiencies of the face." However, perhaps for greater cachet its label also bore the title "Metamorphosa" and the pronouncement, in French," that it had been approved by a committee on inventions."[17]

Supplies of medicines were problematical, however, especially in the early to mid-NEP. Local pharmacy administrations bought drugs for the pharmacies in their jurisdictions. In the fiscal year 1925/1926, because of "severe contraction of the import plan, there was severe deficit of imported wares." Additionally, local health organs faced "financial difficulties in connection with the using up of allocations from the budget for the first half of the year" and "spring floods in the Volga region, resulting in regional depression," as well as "a whole range of other problems caused lower orders for medicaments during the second half of the reporting year."[18]

By the end of the NEP more cough syrups, medicines, salves, hormone products, medicinal botanicals, and optical-medical-surgical instruments—of Soviet as well as foreign provenance—were available. It was estimated in 1928 that 70 percent of pharmaceuticals were produced domestically and only 30 percent imported. Neosal'varsan was 100 percent produced in the Soviet Union; 69 percent of disinfecting substances were said to be produced domestically; 88.5 percent of mercury preparations and 95.5 percent of iodine and bromine preparations were said to be produced domestically. Quinine was totally imported, of course.[19] The impressive ratio of domestic production to imports did not necessarily mean that domestic production satisfied need, for imports were kept artificially low.

Indeed, at the end of the NEP not all pharmacies were adequately stocked. In early 1927, one commentator exulted that some items heretofore in short supply were now produced in abundance by the factories of Gosmedtorgprom. But, he noted more somberly, "this did not mean that the population of our [Soviet] Union were satisfied with medicaments in full measure." Supply problems in the hinterlands, were "documented by letters, even from individuals, from various regions of the [Soviet] Union, requesting that they be sent the most basic and necessary medicines, which had not arrived in their regions."[20] In 1928, at the close of the NEP, Ukrainian pharmacists complained that "for whole months" pharmacies "cannot receive sufficient amounts of preparations such as sodium chloride, naturium benzoicum, chloroform, phytin...and many others...because production of the enumerated items is concentrated exclusively in Gosmedtorgprom...which...is not in a position to fully supply all the republics of the union."[21] Over-centralization was the problem. Gosmedtorgprom had ordered one factory to produce chloroform and salicylic preparations; it could not adequately do so and "interruption" (*pereboi*) of chloroform resulted. The Ukrainian pharmacists urged decentralization of production.[22] They also were frustrated by inadequate budget allocations to pharmacy administrations that supplied pharmacies.[23]

Despite problems, ideology superseded common sense. The experiment in private pharmacy management lasted only two years. Pharmacists in the field admitted that most of the leased pharmacies were in rural areas where pharmacies were greatly needed[24] and that private, leased pharmacies had stimulated the growth of the pharmaceutical industry. Although they acknowledged that public pharmacies were ideal, they conceded that these could not spring up immediately.[25] But rigid bureaucrats won. In June, 1924, Semashko, head of the Health Commissariat issued a circular prohibiting further leasing of pharmacies to private persons. Ironically, one of the reasons for the change was that "particularly undesirable were private pharmacies in rural localities, where it was difficult to control their activity." [!][26] State authorities did not seize existing leased pharmacies outright, but as in the case of small-scale producers and traders of consumer items, the government brought lessees to their knees by imposing punitive financial requirements.[27] For example, in 1925, pharmacies were ordered to serve all insured.[28]

The changeover happened quickly in Moscow. When the Moscow Pharmacy Administration (*aptekoupravlenie*), the government agency for pharmacies, was organized in 1922, it included only 10 pharmacies in its jurisdiction. "The remaining pharmacies"—there had been 81 under the old regime—were managed by other institutions. The majority of these were leased to private persons. By October 1, 1924, the Moscow Pharmacy Administration owned "27 pharmacies and three sanitary and hygiene stores.…During 1924 and 1925 the Moscow Pharmacy Administration took over the majority of private pharmacies," so that, "on October 1, 1925, the state agency owned 61 pharmacies" and "eight stores."[29] By 1927, the Moscow Pharmacy Administration owned almost all the pharmacies in the city. Only "six pharmacies remained leased to private persons" and six "were exploited by other state organs."[30] By January 1927 only twelve private pharmacies remained in the entire Russian Republic, eight of them in Moscow province.[31] They were supplemented by fourteen sanitary and hygiene stores. Most were drug stores that had operated under the old regime; four had belonged to the former Ferrein pharmaceutical conglomerate.[32]

By the end of the NEP, in the late 1920s, the number of pharmacies in the entire Soviet Union was about the same as in pre-revolutionary times. In general cities lost out. But some rural areas also were bereft. For example, in the city of Khar'kov there were 27 pharmacies before the Great October Revolution and 28 in 1928.[33] In Kherson province in 1918, there were 10 independent (*khozraschet*) city pharmacies plus 17 in hospitals and clinics (for a total of 27), while there were 26 rural pharmacies and 56 in rural hospitals and clinics (for a total of 82 pharmacies in rural areas.) In 1927, there were only 7 free-standing urban pharmacies plus 23 pharmacies connected with city hospitals (for a total of 30 urban pharmacies) and 32 free-standing rural pharmacies plus 35 in village hospitals and clinics in the province (for a total of 67 rural pharmacies)—far fewer than before the revolution![34] In Kremenchug pharmacies virtually disappeared during the civil war. A 1927 commentator blamed "Germans, Petliura [the Ukrainian nationalist-socialist], Denikin [the White general] and Makhno [the anarchist], and other bands." There were no rural pharmacies at all in 1920. After "nationalization, the former 10 pharmacies in Kremenchug itself, were cut to 4" with "1 worker pharmacy." By the end of 1925, the Pharmacy Administration "counted" four pharmacies in Kremenchug and 17 in the region. In 1928, there were 32 free-standing pharmacies in medical districts (*meduchastok*) and 7 pharmacies in the district center, supplemented by 8 "sanitary and hygiene" stores. The dearth of pharmacies led to seven "private perfume stores" and eight stalls selling items "in the bazaar...preparing prescriptions, selling spirits, opium and cocaine, supplying privately practicing fel'dshers with medicines." Such "underground sales" were abolished—but only in 1928! By this time, authentic pharmacies were in bad shape, so a massive effort to remodel them was underway[35] In Zinov'evsk, on the other hand, A. Shass reported that in 1928 three fewer pharmacies operated in the town (seven versus ten) than in pre-revolutionary times but the number of rural pharmacies was the same as before the revolution—thirty.[36]

Some rural areas sported more pharmacies at the end of the NEP than before the revolution but, in general, the quality of state pharmacies, particularly urban ones did not match that of the privately owned pharmacies of pre-revolutionary times. In the Ukraine in 1927 there were 339 pharmacies in cities—fourteen fewer than the 353 that had operated in 1913. The number of village pharmacies had increased, however. In 1927, there were 757 in villages versus the 714 that existed in pre-revolutionary times. They were supplemented by 242 sanitary and hygiene stores. Now, at the end of the NEP, only 7 were privately owned.[37] There also were pharmacies in hospitals and clinics but these were for patients. The quality of some state pharmacies was poor. In 1928, in Kiev six pharmacies and three *sanmagy* or sanitary stores served the public. Three pharmacies were deemed "pitiful," one "very weak," and only one well-outfitted.[38] The hours of rural pharmacies in the Ukraine, at least, focused on consumers. The majority stayed open around the clock prompting managers to complain that they had no rest time.[39] Additionally, Ukrainian pharmacies seem to have been better staffed than many in Russia. In 1928 free-standing pharmacies employed 3,462 "qualified" personnel and only 405 *praktikanty* or only semi-qualified pharmacy personnel. Pharmacies in clinics and hospitals employed more *praktikanty* (1,575) than qualified pharmacists (1,099). In total, in the Ukraine, however, only 1,980 *praktikanty* served in pharmacies versus 4,824 qualified pharmacists.[40] On the Southern and Donetsk railways, in 1928, the average cost of prescriptions was only 8 kopeks in district pharmacies, about 12 kopeks in polyclinics, and 28 to 31 kopeks in hospitals.[41]

In Ufa in the fall of 1927 Bashnarkomzdrav (the Bashkir

Commissariat of Public Health) took inventory of pharmacies Nos. 1, 2, 5, 6 and 7, in the city of Ufa, as well as regional pharmacies, apparently preparatory to assuming direct state control. The questionnaires or *ankety* listed supplies, dispensing practices, and, particularly, revenue and expenditures. [42] The local authorities berated Pharmacy No. 1 for not sending in information.[43] The questionnaires revealed that Pharmacy No. 2 stayed open around the clock and on holidays and Sundays.[44]

In general Ufa and regional pharmacies mainly served insured workers. Peasants were not insured.[45] The market obviously was at work during the NEP as far as pharmaceuticals were concerned, for the average cost of a prescription in the city of Ufa was 8 kopeks, whereas on average, prescriptions cost 23 kopeks in one outlying area and as much as 35 kopeks in another.[46]

In other parts of the Bashkir Republic, however, pharmacy facilities were non-existent in 1927. "Apteka No. 17 of the Bashkir Pharmacy Administration in the city of Belebee had been without a manager since November 21"and "in the villages and the countryside in the Tatar Republic there was trade in medicaments by hawkers." Distressed by this "abnormal situation" the authorities demanded that the locals "for their part undertake...measures" to stop the practice and "to open rural pharmacies and stores in the periphery of the Bashkir republic in the near instance."[47]

Shortages of Pharmacists

The shortage of pharmacies was due to a dearth of pharmacists. Leaving pharmacies in private hands might have generated more pharmacists if this would have resulted in profits and upward mobility. On the other hand, working for the state offered convenient hours and a steady salary. But this did not appear to be enough of an inducement for would-be pharmacists during the NEP. Pharmacists were particularly in short supply in the early years of the period. More pharmacists were produced, but, given the time lag in training, they emerged just as the chance of leasing a pharmacy declined, thus diverting candidates into the chemical industry which was going to be favored in the First Five-Year plan as discussions about the plan in 1925 signaled.

One of the advocates of the need for more pharmacists and well-trained pharmacists was Izrail I. Levinshtein. Before the revolutions of 1917, like Antonina Lesnevskaia, he had decried the fact that little formal training was available for those on the first rung of the pharmacy profession. The St. Petersburg Pharmacy Society ran a pharmacy school in the nineteenth century. Antonina Lesnevskaia's pharmacy school for women in St. Petersburg, established in 1901, graduated some 300 by World War I. Pharmacy societies in four other cities, including Moscow, established pharmacy schools by 1906 and two or three other private schools functioned in the early twentieth century. At the entry level, however, pharmacists mainly learned compounding, distilling, mixing, dispensing and so on through apprenticeship. To pass the exams for Assistant, pharmacists generally studied on their own, although a few preparatory courses were available here and there. Only fully qualified *Provizory* had routinely taken two years of university courses to prepare for their examinations. A few higher pharmacy courses were established during World War I. Lesnevskaia's school, however, ended with her departure. During the civil war, short courses to train pharmacists were the order of the day. By 1920, there were thirty seven operating.[48]

In 1921 and 1922, pharmacy schools on all levels were crucial, not only for greater professionalization but to offset "the severe need of qualified personnel."[49] Levinshtein, in particular, worked hard to create a network of elementary, middle and higher pharmacy schools. The lower schools were to accept youths of "at least 16" with "not less than 2 years of 2-class education." The hordes of homeless children or *besprizorniki* that still roamed in the 1920s and the disintegration of elementary as well as secondary education during the civil war was going to make that stipulation problematical. And, indeed, the short courses were kept on. But in addition, Levinshtein formulated a basic curriculum for a two-year course of three trimesters. The program was well-balanced, including anatomy, botany, pharmacognosy and pharmacology, chemisty, accounting, "pharmacy techniques," Russian as well as Latin, and mathematics. There was a small political component—three hours of "History of the Workers' Movement" in the second year. Unfortunately "difficult material conditions" required the central government to devolve responsibility for funding the schools "by local means." Schools were to be paid for by a "1 percent turnover tax on pharmacy preparations."[50]

Interestingly, the Bashkir Commissariat of Health, showed independence in the curriculum it devised for its local pharmacy school. The three-year curriculum was to include courses in anatomy, botany, zoology, physics, and Russian. There were no courses in history, and more sensibly, in history of "the workers' movement," but neither were there courses in "the growth of the pharmacy business."[51]

Higher pharmacy schools did emerge in Moscow, Leningrad, Khar'kov, Odessa, and some other cities. The program at the Pharmacy Institute in Odessa was a full four-year one, consisting of "twelve trimesters." Three hundred forty students were enrolled in March, 1928.[52]

Nevertheless, apprenticeship, which Menshevik pharmacists had castigated before the October Revolution, continued out of necessity, despite a Commissariat of Health "Circular" ordering that it be phased out.[53] Indeed, coming to grips with reality led to courses for semi-trained *praktikanty* being offered in the Kiev "*Farmtekhnikum*," or higher pharmacy school, where 63 men and 70 women were enrolled in 1928.[54] And, during the push for industrialization, which began in 1928, as we shall see, pharmacy practice was less attractive than industrial work.

Conclusions

Thus, although the supply side of the Soviet pharmacy sector moved on a parallel track with houses in the United States during the 1920s, dispensing lagged. American pharmacies were committed to providing good service for their customers as had been the case in the pharmacies of Imperial Russia.[55] In the Soviet Union, on the contrary, a decade after the Great October Revolution the number of pharmacies was no greater and in some areas less than before the revolution. Despite achievements in R&D, Soviet citizens had no better access to medicines, soap, disinfectants and cleaning supplies, household items and toiletries than in Imperial Russia. There were deficits of some items on pharmacy shelves at the end of the 1920s. There were shortages of pharmacists. Observers could well ask: "Why then the revolution in medicine and pharmacy following the Great October Revolution? Who had benefited from the changes?"

7
Preventive Medicine in the Periphery during the NEP

Perhaps preventive medicine canceled out deficiencies in dispensing, particularly in rural areas, during the 1920s. To test that theory this chapter examines production and distribution of vaccines and serums and sanitation measures in Ufa, located some 1,500 kilometers east of Moscow.

In the Soviet Union of the 1920s the vastness of the Soviet empire—with villages and nomadic enclaves far from railways and reachable by rivers, dirt roads or wagon tracks only at certain times of the year and at other times inaccessible because of ice, snow and the infamous *rasputitsa* or spring thaws—bedeviled the best laid schemes for vaccination and education programs as well as for dispensing. Additionally, shortages of soap and disinfectants coupled with housing shortages prevented better hygiene. Further, the health infrastructure had to be rebuilt after the civil war. Venues had to be repaired; equipment and apparatus had to be updated; calves, horses and small laboratory animals had to be replenished; biologists and ancillary health specialists had to be retrained to replace those who had died, retired or left the Soviet Union. All this required funds. The experiences of the Ufa Bacteriological Institute in the 1920s illustrate the difficulties of preventive medicine in the provinces. Comparison of conditions in Ufa with those in Denver, Colorado, gives additional perspective to the public health challenges.

Health Problems in the Hinterlands

Ufa *Guberniia* (Province) was in a more northerly latitude, its soil was richer, its climate was moister and more severely continental, and the Ural mountains on the eastern edge of the province were lower than the snowcapped Rockies which bifurcate Colorado. Nevertheless, through the first decades of the twentieth century the economy, ethnic diversity, and remoteness of Ufa province and the Rocky Mountain state were similar. Before its oil industry was developed in the 1930s, the rolling hills of Ufa province supported pastures for semi-nomadic Bashkir herdsmen as the plains of Colorado supported ranches (some based on old Spanish land grants). Both areas contained mines and metallurgical factories by the 1920s. Though at the level of northern Canada, long summer days, wide rivers and the fertile black earth of Ufa province supported agriculture as well as the clay soil and arid weather of the Colorado plains east of the Rockies. Indeed, agriculture had superseded mining as the key element of the Colorado economy by the 1920s. At least three different national and linguistic groups populated both the Bashkir Republic and Colorado. Orthodox Russian and Ukrainian peasants had been moving to Ufa since the seventeenth and eighteenth centuries paralleling the Germans from Russia, Ukrainians and other Slavs, and Mexicans who came to Colorado from the late nineteenth century to grow beets, vegetables and maize. The city of Ufa was the gubernatorial seat of the province as Denver was the capital of the new state of Colorado from the 1870s. Most buildings in both cities were wooden or log. Russian dwellings had charming carved and painted window surrounds, but nevertheless lacked indoor plumbing. More important buildings in both cities were made of stone or brick. Both Denver and Ufa had a cosmopolitan feel in the 1920s, despite being thousands of miles from major urban centers. Mining barons had brought opera stars and the latest fashions to Colorado. Thanks to the entrepreneurial spirit of sophisticated Sunni Moslem Tatars, who mingled with Slavs, a few Jews and assorted others in Ufa, the city underwent an economic revival in the 1920s with stores, restaurants, live and movie theaters, and amusement parks providing, as before the revolution, a vibrant cultural milieu and physical amenities.[1] However, civilization was pretty much confined to a few four or five urban hubs.

Similar conditions made health complexities similar, to some extent, in the 1920s, despite different political and economic systems. Although, by 1928, Coloradans had a quarter of a million automobiles, many areas of the state were inaccessible. According to physician and historian, Robert Shikes, "Colorado's death rate was slightly higher than the national rate" and "infectious disease continued to be the leading cause of death (twenty-five percent)." Tuberculosis was a major killer and, in the opinion of Shikes, "many 'nineteenth century' causes of death were still very much present." In 1928 people in Colorado died from syphilis, whooping cough, puerperal fever, and there still were "outbreaks of smallpox and diphtheria," although "vaccination and anti-diphtheria immunization had reduced the mortality of these two diseases drastically." Moreover "there were forty deaths due to typhoid in 1928" because "[D]enver water" according to a source quoted by Shikes, did "'not meet the [accepted] standard of bacteriological purity.'" Apparently "Denver and other cities were still dumping their raw sewerage into rivers which served as the sources of drinking water for communities downstream." Thus, the "'incidence of intestinal disease in Denver'" was "'still higher than that of many other cities in the United States'" and "Denver's infant mortality was the highest of any city in the country."[2]

Aside from malaria and cholera, health care issues in Ufa province in the 1920s were not too different from those in Colorado. But they were more vexing, for the area had been torn asunder during the civil war and private pharmacies and other businesses and institutions had been nationalized during the war. In 1922 a cholera epidemic hit Ufa. It was made all the more serious by "severe insufficiency of 'med personnel'" and "insufficient supplies of medical substances."[3] In 1924 the Ufa Bacteriological Institute estimated that 40 percent of the mosquitoes in Ufa were malarial, this problem being aggravated by standing water.[4] Rabies was a major problem, including an epidemic of epizootic rabies. In 1926, 998 potential victims turned to the Pasteur Station for help. [5]

The Ufa Bacteriological Institute

The Ufa Bacteriological Institute, which had operated under zemstvo control from its founding in 1908 until its transfer to local government control in 1919, valiantly attempted to grapple with these problems. As in the imperial period, the Institute produced serums and vaccines and undertook measures to combat malaria and rabies, and to improve hygiene and sanitation. The main components of preventive medicine, of course, were production of vaccines—composed of killed or weakened bacteria or viruses which enable the body to generate antibodies to ward off the bacteria, toxins and viruses that cause, variously, smallpox, cholera, diphtheria, typhoid and paratyphoid;[6] measures to improve sanitation; and insect and rodent control to ward off malaria and typhus. Serums, containing antibodies from diseased individuals, were mainly applied after disease hit, although some serums also were used to prevent disease, most notably whooping cough.[7] The Institute realized some success in these endeavors, but it also was impeded by problems, some of those endemic to the region, and others resulting from the Soviet economy and political decisions.

In 1926, the staff of the Institute included pre-revolutionary Russian scientists and newly minted, partially-trained minority peoples. Some in both categories appear to have received degrees from spurious institutions. The Director of the Institute was Dr. Vladimir Nikolaevich Kryzhanovskii, a 1897 graduate of the Medical Faculty at Minsk University (which actually did not exist), who had worked at the Institute since 1906. The Head of the Serum-Vaccine Section was Ekaterina Ivanovna Spesivtseva, a 1914 graduate of the University of Geneva, who came to the Institute in 1920. Other old-timers included two pharmacists in the Forensic Medical Department, "Qualified Pharmacist" Katsel'enbogen, who had received his [*Provizor*] certificate from Kazan' University in 1875, joining the Institute in 1922 and "Qualified Pharmacist" Gol'dshtein, who had received his [*Provizor*] certificate from Moscow University in 1907, joining the Institute in 1924. Newcomers included the head of the Diagnostic Department, one Sophia Dmitrievna Stolypina, who was said to have received a Doctor of Biology degree from Voronezh University in 1917, another apparent anomaly, since a university did not exist in that city at the time; a chemist who had received a degree from Tomsk University in 1925; laborants (laboratory technicians) including two minority people named Talova from Ufa; a doctor who had received a degree from Leningrad University in 1920; a fel'dsher who had graduated from a "Zemstvo Medical School," a "doctor" in the Malaria Station who had attended Khar'kov University in 1908; a doctor who had graduated from Perm University in 1922; and assorted technical people with lower and middle educations.[8]

Lack of Funds, Staff and Equipment

A major problem for the Institute in the 1920s was lack of money. The basic source of funding was the State Budget of the Bashkir Autonomous Republic. The Institute also received additional funds from the state budget of the Russian Republic (RSFSR) and had access to special funds.[9] As was the case with core pharmaceutical enterprises, monies allocated were not always fully disbursed. For example, in 1926, 29, 232 rubles had been allocated for staff salaries but only 20, 271 rubles were disbursed, "thanks to which the institute had to cover expenditures from special funds." The institute "asked for 16,968 rubles to build stables and an ice house" but there was "disbursed from the reserve fund of Bashsovnarkom 7,000 rubles—therefore the institute only succeeded in building the ice house, making some repairs on the buildings and equipping premises for calves and horses."[10] Meanwhile, the Institute had the same, if not greater, problems as core pharmaceutical enterprises with regard to bringing in revenue. Toward the end of the twenties, the Institute sold preparations to local pharmacies. However, as the pharmaceutical enterprises found, many institutions themselves were short of funds and could not pay. Additionally, the investigative and injection work of the Institute was done *besplatno* (for free).[11]

Lack of funds affected the staff, which the Institute considered inadequate. The staff of 49 in November 1925 was cut to 30 although personnel climbed to 41 in 1926. But in 1927, insufficient staff "entirely deprived [the Institute] of the possibility of scientific work on scarlatina…TB…others…."[12] Lack of funds also meant that the Institute could not electrify and remodel the old buildings in which it was housed nor properly equip the new buildings it was given. For example, since the premises for calves had not been remodeled they could only be injected in the old buildings. Similarly, the Institute relied on kerosene-powered equipment and much of it was inadequate, as were vessels, dyes and reagents. Indeed, in the mid twenties the Institute still "relied on prewar stores and supplies of these items dating to the time of the organization of the ARA" [the American Relief Association, which had come to assist in the famine of the summer of 1921!][13] The staff lost a lot of time because of "primitive equipment…doing centrifuge work by hand" and having to stop work "to wash the vessels." In 1926 the ventilation did not work properly. One motor "entirely did not work, the other blew air not only in the lab but all over the Institute." The institute lacked equipment for drawing blood from horses, did not have enough small laboratory animals like rabbits and white mice, and lacked ice to preserve the food of those it did have.[14] In the opinion of the individual who had drafted the 1926 report, the Institute library and training programs were in less favorable condition than before the revolution. "In the prewar period the Institute subscribed to all journals of microbiology and hygiene in the Russian language, 10 journals in German, 3 in French, and 2 in English…and acquired a range of monographs and the Handbuch of…Wasserman and Krauz. In the reporting year, equally as in the previous year," the writer of the report indignantly noted, "because of insufficient funds literature was not systematically acquired and in the reporting year the institute had the possibility to subscribe to only part of journals only in the Russian language." Similarly "with absence of funds and staff of necessary high qualifications the institute could not organize courses on bacteriology for doctors and assisting medical personnel, which in prewar times it did two or three times a year." The reporter further lamented inadequate accounting in the materials' warehouse where estimates of serums and vaccines were "left not to a separate person but to a laborant who was occupied with other duties."[15] Another defect was that the Institute did not have its own immunization point. Further, it did not receive systemic information on smallpox vaccination and revaccination,[16] nor on injections against rabies.[17]

At the end of the NEP the Institute was in debt to Bashmedtorg and the electric-water supply system. But cash flow problems prevented settling up for "the serums and vaccines left by the institute in Bashmedtorg for commission sale...were not fully realized."[18]

Achievements in Preventive Medicine

Despite these problems the Institute performed creditably. Russia had a good track record of smallpox vaccination. Unfortunately, perhaps to beef up its reporting, the Institute intermixed statistics on the amounts of human smallpox *detrit* (scab or pustule) harvested with that resulting from injections into calves and other animals, and the use of *detrit* versus lymph.[19] For example, in 1924 the Institute, despite its comparatively small staff, claimed it put out 941,880 units of *detrit*. At the beginning of 1925 the Institute had available 39,050 doses of *detrit* from humans who had died; by January 1, 1926, 25, 420 doses were on hand.[20] The Institute also discussed its development of "a strain of lymph...prepared by means of injecting *detrit* into asses and rabbits."[21]

During 1924, the Institute also put out 194, 475 units of *divaccine* (typhoid and paratyphoid B—analogous to Salmonella), 10, 825 units of scarlatina vaccine, 10, 182 units of antidiphtheria serum or diphtheria antitoxin, 25,220 units of streptococcus serum, 6, 880 units of dysentery serum, and 126,750 units of serum against typhoid.[22] Facilities for those bitten by rabid animals included a thirty-bed dormitory in the Institute. To improve control of rabies the Institute opened Pasteur stations in nine branch locations—in other towns, in a factory, a railway station, and the hospital of water transport. An emulsion of 5 percent vaccine was sent to these points in two wooden boxes by post. Additionally, the Institute engaged in educative work on the need to register domestic dogs.[23] The Institute also conducted research (some 1,043 in 1926) on foodstuffs and water, on tooth fillings using an amalgam of mercury, and studied the air in nearby leather and brick factories and in workers' quarters connected with them.[24] In 1927 the Institute was involved in "massive production of divaccines [and also] cholera, typhus, gonococcus [vaccines]," staphylococcus, streptococcus, and pneumonococcus filtrations and strains of typhoid "prepared in the form of liquid solution by Merezhkovskii."[25]

Goals Not Achieved

Nevertheless, in 1926 the Institute received a poor review from a commission which came to audit it. Some points highlighted defects the Institute itself had lamented, such as small staff. This resulted, in the opinion of the commission, in a lack of physician oversight in the departments and inappropriate use of inadequately trained lower-level personnel. The "Epidemiological department," according to the commission, was "three months without a permanent director. In all there are [only] four doctors together with the director." The commission considered unacceptable the appointment of one of the Talovas and two others to the position of laborant without their being qualified, but their main point of contention was that "before 1 April they were paid with other laborants."[26]

Indeed, admitting that because there were no "bacteriological specialists" on the commission, it was difficult to evaluate the scientific work of the Institute, the team manifested its bureaucratic mind-set in attacking the Institute for failure to draw up an annual plan and engaging in financial practices that the commission deemed to be irregular. With regard to the latter complaint, the commission's assertion that preservation of materials in the warehouse was sloppy seemed valid: "valuable chemical vessels lay on the floor," "Hygroscopic cotton" was in "an unused box," and packing materials from items received "two days ago" were still scattered about. However, other criticisms about finances mixed the important with the petty. "Firm calculation of the cost of production" was "lacking," dispensing of preparations from the warehouse was done by a laborant on an ad hoc basis, without "special accounting," notes in the books were made "with pencil—this is not allowed. Various articles having various sizes and volume are put under one rubric, for example, syringes Rekord of 1, 2, and 5 grams are noted only as syringes."[27]

The commission was annoyed that "verification of the inventory has not been done for some years." A handwritten insertion—perhaps from the Director or some later reader, noted "*Byla*" [it was done]. But the commission went on to reprove the Institute claiming that "[T]o the question of the commission as to what kind of inventory is found in the apartment of the Director of the Institute, the *zavkhoz* (individual in charge of finances) answered: 1 table, 1 little table, 1... stool...1 screen, 1 wall clock and [reminiscent of satirist Mikhail Zoshchenko's spoof on the *kocherga*] 1 poker," but the *zavkhoz* could not explain what the one table and so forth were for. When asked about inventory the director [himself] replied that he had "only a screen and a samovar."[28]

The commission was further irritated that staff were paid in kind—with apartments and such, because the Institute claimed to be short of money and, thus, used "*besplatno* [free of charge] heat, lighting, water supply and sewerage." The commission contended that "the apartments" given to laborants and laboratory service people were "not called for by any necessity, since these people do not work in the evening...during the time of immunizing animals they cannot help. Night analyses are few. Expenditures for firewood and water are not limited." Additionally, the commission decried the fact that "animal feed" in 1926 was "recorded according to norms, according to the number of head, but these norms are high," for "[A]t the time of immunizing, animals—horses—when their temperature rises, do not eat for three or four days...."[29]

Meanwhile, the commission asserted that the premises, equipment, and tables used in the labs were "satisfactory." However, their report alleged overpayments to the furniture maker, one Vlasov, as well as overpayments to the "electric repairer" one Marichev.[30]

The Institute stoutly defended itself in a rebuttal approximately thirty pages long. To the accusation that the Institute had no plan, the Director sensibly insisted that "a plan is impossible since the Institute cannot evaluate future requirements in its production, because of the impossibility to evaluate what kind of epidemics can break out and to what degree."[31] The Institute defended the use of individuals trained on the job but derided the fact that the premises and equipment were satisfactory. "To equip fully satisfactorily the laboratory and ancillary institutions, the staff of the Institute has had to work very hard, very hard, which is entirely out of the range of vision of the comrade investigators....Work connected with outfitting the Institute took a great deal of time...." [32] The Director emphasized the difficulties of "exact" and "firm" calculation versus "estimation" of costs.[33]

In his rebuttal, the Director focused on the contributions the Institute had made during the past few years. Eighteen strains of streptococcus had been identified for developing an antiscarlatina serum; the Institute had undertaken a "massive immunization" program "of horses with anatoxins for developing antidiphtheria, scarlatina, and dysentery serums"; the institute had worked to improve food stuffs; had increased the number of filtrates during the past year; and had undertaken biological analyses to uncover "diphtheria in doubtful cases."[34] Disavowing the assertion that the Institute had "done nothing to raise the scientific qualifications" of the staff and "for the whole time had not read one report of scientific character," the Institute listed its activities in this realm and further noted that raising qualifications was difficult, given the limited staff. [35] The Institute admitted that exact accounting of laboratory materials had not been done but defiantly stated that "What is the significance of daily notation…severe accounting of expenses to eliminate the possibility of abuse, this significance is—nothing."[36] The Institute report ridiculed the suggestion that the norm for horses feed was high and that they could have less during the immunization period.[37] The Institute decried the low salaries it paid out—one individual came to work with his own instruments, [38] defended the payments to Vlasov for the furniture he made and Marichev for his repairwork,[39] emphasized the poor funding of the Institute,[40] and finally, questioned the likelihood of the ability of the "comrade inspectors" to assess "an area little known to them."[41]

Conclusions

It was obvious that the Institute's staff was dedicated. Nevertheless, the new Soviet system did not improve the work of the Ufa Bacteriological Institute, in comparison with the Imperial period, when it was under zemstvo management and subject to supervision by the Tsarist government. On the contrary, in some respects, conditions in the Ufa Bacteriological Institute were worse in the 1920s than in the Imperial period. Finances were shakier. A greater degree of interference by bureaucrats in the Soviet period did not help the Institute's work and may have impeded it. Hopefully matters would improve during the next decade.

The Second Decade: "The Second Soviet Revolution"— The Five-Year Plans

The First Five-Year Plan, the beginning of an ambitious attempt to orchestrate the entire Soviet economy in order to accelerate heavy industrial output, expand the infrastructure and put agriculture on a scientific footing—a process sometimes referred to as the second Soviet revolution—was officially launched in 1928 and declared completed ahead of schedule in 1932. The pharmaceutical press lauded this new economic stage. After all, it was no surprise. Pricing and tax policies had signaled a move in this direction from 1926 and industry executives had participated in the planning process at that time.[1] Pharmacy journals enthused about the "great task of socialist reconstruction"[2] and also praised collectivization of agriculture, urging "pharmacy workers" (*aptekorabotniki*), particularly those working in the villages, to take an active part in "the reconstruction of the countryside on a new, socialistic foundation." In terminology reminiscent of nineteenth-century intellectuals, the press deplored the peasants' "lack of literacy"and "meager education," and the "persistence of darkness" in the countryside which were "holding back transformation of the economy."[3]

But the First Five-Year Plan involved massive population upheavals reminiscent of the civil war period. Tens of thousands of volunteers flocked to the Ukrainian Donbass and the Siberian Kuzbass to repair and expand existing industrial complexes and to Magnitogorsk to erect a gigantic metallurgical complex. [4] Three hundred thousand unfortunates were impressed to enlarge the Mariinskii canal system linking Moscow and Leningrad in 1932 and 1933 and to toil in mines, timber-felling and construction projects.[5] Millions of children again took to the streets as their families fragmented.[6] Collectivization—the abrupt transfer of peasants from their semi-socialistic, semi-capitalistic communes onto large-scale farms—resulted in peasant resistance and the exile of 1.5 million peasants in 1930 and 1931.[7]

People on the move spread infectious microbes and living conditions in the new industrial areas and on the collectivized farms were rudimentary.[8] As a result, as during the civil war, infectious diseases flared. In 1930 pharmacy journals discussed the need to contain typhus and typhoid epidemics,[9] leprosy,[10] dysentery, cholera, recurring fever, plague and Siberian ulcers (or anthrax), small-pox, scarlatina, diphtheria, scabbies, coughs and colds, "grippe" or flu, tetanus, rabies, and malaria.[11] Advertisements for antivenereals indicated the presence of syphilis and gonorrhea. Crop failures in the Ukraine had caused food shortages there in 1928 and 1929 and possibly spurred collectivization.[12]

The targets of the Second Five-Year Plan were saner and some heavy industry sectors made noticeable gains.[13] More consumer goods were available in the state-run retail stores and incongruous neoclassical facades of new buildings testified to the attempt to tackle the shortage of dwellings and eliminate the communal flats which housed many urbanites in major cities.[14] On the other hand, arrests, purges and war scares marred the political calm and serious public health problems remained and even intensified during the Second Five-Year Plan. The disruption of the collectivization process, the displacement of some of the most efficient farmers, excessive grain requisitioning, peasants' slaughter of their animals and destruction of their crops, capped by weather problems, "reached the proportions of famine in some southern European districts in the spring of 1933," Frank Lorimer, League of Nations demographer noted, and "reversed for a time the progress toward lower mortality."[15] Historians now estimate that perhaps four to five million peasants perished in that famine.[16] A "related program for the settlement of the nomads," Lorimer added, "produced a crisis in the Asiatic steppe region (Kazakhstan)" where "depletion of livestock reached . . . staggering proportions." He estimated that this resulted in "the number of Kazakhs" being "less by one million or more" than "normally expected in 1939."[17] For city dwellers, agricultural upheavals meant that food was rationed until 1935 and when rationing was removed the government raised prices. Some workers found it difficult to feed their families.[18] Added to this, as we saw in the Introduction, Lorimer, Sir Arthur Newsholme, John Kingsbury and Henry Sigerist all emphasized that, partly due to the heterogeneity of the Soviet population and the primitive life styles and poor hygiene of some ethnic groups, typhus, typhoid fever, dysentery, malaria, tuberculosis and venereal diseases still were endemic and periodically epidemic.

Thus, both the pharmaceutical industry and special institutes had their work cut out during the First and Second Five-Year Plans. Smallpox and diphtheria called for "isolation of the sick" and "attention of medical personnel." The vaccines to combat small-pox and the "special serums" for prevention of diphtheria, tetanus and the onset of rabies as well as vaccines and serums for typhoid fever, typhus, grippe, dysentery, and cholera were produced in the separate bacteriological institutes. But since these diseases also were spread by "lack of personal cleanliness and unclean dwellings," contaminated food and water, flies, lice, fleas, bedbugs, cockroaches, mice, and rats, "prophylactic measures"—the use of soap, bleaches, carbolic acid, sublimate, sulfur, Lysol, and other disinfectants were needed to "preclude epidemics" of them. These items were produced by the pharmaceutical industry. Similarly, the use of screens and oil were important to control the mosquitoes that spread malaria; poisons were needed against mice and rats. Insulin was crucial for diabetics. Medicines were needed to quell the symptoms of malaria and grippe, if not cure them.[19] Even before the famine, in 1930, the Soviet Pharmaceutical Association was informed that ample amounts of protein, carbohydrates, and fats were "needed by the young organism,"[20] but "[T]oday…food" has "been found to be insufficient."[21] Food shortages and deficiencies called for food supplements, vitamins and hormones. All these products were produced by the pharmaceutical industry.

The following four chapters will investigate how the Ufa Bacteriological Institute, pharmacies, and the pharmaceutical industry tried to cope with health problems, to maintain labor strength, to make life better for the populace during the second decade of the Soviet Union's existence.

8

Preventive Medicine in the Periphery: The First Two Five-Year Plans

By the early 1930s the Soviet Union was making headway in the prevention of communicable diseases through inoculation. For example, one of the most serious scourges was dysentery. In the late 1920s and 1930s vaccines given orally lowered the incidence of the disease in garrisons and hospitals in selected areas.[1] Even so, in the 1930s, the Moscow Bacteriological Institute reported that, tragically, children younger than three years of age accounted for 40 to 45 percent of those with chronic dysentery and 85 percent of those died from this disease. Thus, the All Union Institute of Experimental Medicine, the Tashkent, Rostov, and Khar'kov institutes, the Mechnikov Institute in Moscow, The Pasteur Institute in Leningrad, the Sverdlovsk Institute, among others feverishly worked to develop more effective vaccines and phages—viruses that attacked bacteria—between 1935 and 1939.[2] To gauge the effectiveness of preventive medicine in the hinterlands, where most Soviet citizens lived in the 1930s, we turn again to Ufa.

Ufa, like a number of other towns surrounded by vast rural areas, was undergoing massive changes in the 1930s. The industrialization and collectivization of agriculture that occurred during the First and Second Five-Year plans did not bypass Ufa. *Kolkhozy* (collective farms) and grain, milk and meat *sovkhozy* (state farms) were organized in the vicinity. Factories sprang up, enlarging the population in villages. The Bacteriological Institute also served the new metallurgical complex of Magnitogrosk in the Urals. The diseases in Ufa *Guberniia,* which was organized into the Soviet divisions of *oblast'* and *raion* , like other areas in 1932, also probably reflected those in other provincial areas. Malaria, rabies, dysentery, diphtheria caused concern. Smallpox sometimes flared up. Trachoma was chronic and syphilis was strong in two villages.[3] Typhoid was "endemic" in some raions of Ufa oblast and "typhus appeared there." In 1933, typhus reached epidemic proportions.[4]

The Ufa Bacteriological Institute needed products put out by the pharmaceutical industry. For example, the Institute used a 1 percent solution of calcium chloride as the immunization activator for dysentery serum. Anti scarlatina serum was prepared by immunizing horses with toxin of scarlatina streptococcus and living bacteria culture. The toxin was prepared in "Gotinger bullion with 0.5 percent defibrinated blood of horses."[5] And, like the pharmaceutical industry, the institute's staff and resources were perennially strained.

The staff was stretched. Specialists were insufficient and those at the Institute periodically departed or were sent on investigative and other trips. Some laboratory animals and equipment were inadequate or lacking altogether. "At the beginning of 1931" the Institute's report recounted, five major scientists left. These were Dr. Kryzhanovskii the director of the Institute and head of the Smallpox Department; Dr. Spesivtseva, head of the Serum-Vaccine Department; the chemist Kisnemskii, head of the Chemical-Hygiene Department; head of the Parasitology department biologist Oleinikov; and Desiatkin, the senior *laborant* (lab technician) from the Serum-Vaccine Department. The head of the Epidemiological Department was sent on an expedition in the summer, as was the head of the Clinical-Diagnostic Department. Some staff became ill during the year. There were insufficient horses for immunization, which became an ongoing problem.[6]

Financial strains were manifested in odd materials on which the reports from individual departments were written—on little brown rectangles; in the case of the new Parasite Department—on the reverse of a piece of blue, white and gold flowered wallpaper; and in the case of the Malaria Department— on the reverse of three order blanks. "In 1931 the smallpox *otdel*," the report from one of the most successful departments lamented, " operated under abnormal conditions." The director left 20 January and practically all the work was borne by a laborant until 1 July...."[7]

The Smallpox Department was crippled. Without a director "[I]t was impossible to establish control" of the vaccine. Therefore, "notwithstanding the store of dry matter, *detrit* was given out only partially." The 5,690 grams of vaccine put out in 1930 were "insufficient." Because of "insufficiency of live vaccine, the Institute used *detrit*...about 200 children were vaccinated...fewer than in 1930." To fill the breach additional vaccine was sent from Moscow, but apparently that amount also was insufficient. [8]

The Medical Department also was weakened in 1931. Its staff was "cut by 50 percent." "There was no director" and of two "worker assistants, one was sent on an expedition for 15 months, therefore in the department there remained "only one which weakened the work...." Nevertheless, the department made 8,901 analyses.[9] In 1931, 9,093 people (out of some 70,000) were sick with malaria. Institute staff treated workers in three factories—Motor, Sewing and March 8—and construction workers with quinine and also subcutaneous injections of a "preparation of arsenic" mixed with quinine—perhaps to stretch the latter. [10] As in the twenties, rabies was of great concern and 1,736 individuals were given thirteen injections throughout the year.[11] Despite the handicaps the Institute produced over 400 liters of vaccines—tetravaccine, scarlatina, and gonococcus; over 33 thousand units of antidiphtheria serum; 300 liters of typhoid serum—given out "according to request"; and conducted 8,901 analyses—approximately 5,000 bacteriological, 1,790 serological, and so forth.[12]

1932 and 1933: In the Second Five-Year Plan

In 1932 and 1933 the fortunes of the Smallpox Department improved. In 1932 The Bashkir Commissariat of Health ordered five and one-half million doses of smallpox vaccine and the Institute prepared 500,000 more to round out the number to 6 million.[13] But macroeconomic inefficiencies continued to hinder the Institute. In the third quarter of the year it was not able to inject calves, because of delay in supplies of glycerine [for the lymph] "received only in the second quarter" and inadequate amounts of ampules. Additionally, the operating table for calves was in poor condition. A new one had been ordered from Kiev but had not yet arrived. The Institute further complained that the motor on a crucial machine was old; although most vessels were sufficient this was not the case with Petri dishes. Further, insufficient linen "caused poor conditions for the work staff" and the *teliatka* or quarters for calves needed remodeling. Still, smallpox vaccinations increased impressively each year. In 1929 there were 53,000; in 1930, 70,000; in 1931, 61,000; and in 1932, 80,000.[14]

In its other activities the Institute was less successful. Deficits of crucial items held up production. A major problem in preparing antidiphtheria serum or diphtheria "anatoxin" was lack of healthy horses. This also affected scarlatina serum (prepared from the hearts of children who had died from scarlatina) and streptococcus serum. The methods for preparing these serums were Western ones—those of Ramona, Dik, Dishe.[15] But "active immunization through the skin against diphtheria was not done in 1932 because of absence in the market of lanolin." Further, the Institute lacked "Berksfel'd" and "Shamberlan" ("Chamberlain") lamps, did not have enough cylinders, lacked an isolator for small infected animals, and lacked foreign literature.[16]

In 1932, 1,320 people came to the Pasteur Institute for help. Most were from the city of Ufa. The Institute supplied all the Pasteur points with vaccine, according to previous contracts or current orders. Unfortunately, however, the Institute was able to instruct only five doctors during the year on the treatment for rabies.[17]

Typhoid fever continued to be a problem. The main cause was dirty water, but the institute also blamed dirty eating facilities and "the insufficient culture of the population." The remedies proposed indicated the close connection between preventive medicine and the pharmaceutical industry, for the Institute called for better control over the water supply; tests of those working in food preparation and better hygiene in food producing organizations; "disinfecting with bleach"; and more "baths and laundries."[18] Thus, the pharmaceutical industry had to put out or distribute more disinfectants, detergents and soap.

Malaria was an ongoing scourge. Physicians were affected as well as ordinary citizens. But, here, as elsewhere, the macro economy in the thirties caused complications. "Guarantees of quinine were very weak. To all of Bashkiriia there has been sent only 179.2 kilos. If each [person] sick [with malaria]," the Institute opined, received "20 grams, 1,300 kilos would be needed." Further, there were not enough beds in the clinic to treat those sick with malaria. Therefore, the Institute recommended palliatives: "preparations of mercury" (apparently to stretch the quinine); courses in entomology; more study of anopheles mosquitoes and malaria victims; oil—to spread on standing water and marshes: and educative work. Application of oil, however, was only a wishful solution, "since there were no stores of oil" and, in any case, "absence of transport" would make "bringing the oil difficult." The Institute suggested "a *diktat* about improving help to *maliarkov* (malaria victims)," "hydrologic work to clean rivers and ponds," and the usual fall-back—educative work. In this venue it had prepared two and one-half thousand brochures, conducted "conversations" (*besedy*) with the sick, and had made a contract with the major Moscow film studio Rosfilm to produce a documentary entitled *Malariia.* The 1000 rubles which the Institute was required to pay for the film did allow *besplatno* or free showing at twenty-four points. But the Institute admitted that, because of lack of workers, it had researched only one locality. Therefore, it also pleaded for "more workers."[19]

Expeditions to hamlets in the Bashkir Republic illustrated the difficulties in combating infectious diseases in the hinterlands and also the need for ample pharmaceuticals—disinfecting products, toilet paper and soap—as well as vaccines and serums.

Hygiene was abysmal in these outlying areas because of primitive living conditions and inadequate amenities. In June, 1932, a team comprised of a bacteriologist, chemist, entomologist and technical worker visited the Baimak region. The population was 40,783. There were eleven medical points in the area, four on wheat sovkhozes, a hospital and six outpatient clinics. The main "industry" in the area consisted of a meat sovkhoz, a grain sovkhoz and a horse-breeding sovkhoz. The population was three-fourths Bashkir, about 19 percent Russian, and slightly more than 6 percent Tatar. Sixty percent of the agricultural land had been collectivized. "Topographically" the area was "hill-steppe with severe continental climate." The township seat, the settlement of Baimak itself, had 10,000 inhabitants. In the northern part of the area was a river, "exploited chiefly by a copper factory...near the factory" were "one-story houses and a network of barracks, part of which" appeared to be "a well-constructed two-story, eight-apartment home" [perhaps the former owner's home]. There were three canteens, a bread bakery and four public wells. "The central part of the settlement" was "thickly populated...the severe dwelling crisis" with "a large influx of worker force from the outside—at the end of 1932 this rose to 6,406 in place of [the previous] 1,633—has resulted in the building of *zemlianki* [earthen dugouts] also close together."[20]

The sanitary conditions in Baimak were reminiscent of Engels' *The Working Class in England* published in 1844 to expose the evils of capitalism: "The sanitary condition of the settlement is unsatisfactory: there are no green spaces, the yards and streets are filled with offal, the public wells are not sanitary, the toilets are dirty—part of them do not have doors and are near to the canteens and other food establishments—they appear to be sources of infection; the bathhouses are insufficient—there is no isolation point and disinfecting chamber. The public canteens number eight, the bakery, kvas factory and milk farm 12 kilometers from the settlement also do not satisfy sanitary requirements."[21]

The inspection team found the hospital unsatisfactory. It had eighty beds, including 60 gynecological. The fifteen-bed infectious system for smallpox and typhus patients, though, located on the ground floor, had "a terrible smell from the toilet, which could be eliminated by an electric ventilator...there" was "one x-ray cabinet and in the lab one microscope." There was also a first aid point and a "*sanorganization*" but "the state of the vaccination campaign in Baimak district" was "fully unsatisfactory—against typhoid only 44.5 percent had been vaccinated and against smallpox—52.9 percent. Disinfecting substances" were "used incorrectly—they" were "applied indiscriminately instead of according to the disease."[22]

The team also visited a *Detskii sad* (kindergarten). The teachers had been trained in special courses, but seventy children were crammed into two rooms, which were "insufficiently light" and there were "no medical personnel." Further there were only twenty-eight beds, and sometimes two to three children in a bed.[23]

Inspection of the Beloretsk region in the fall of 1932, revealed equally disgusting sanitary conditions. The benefits of vaccination were illustrated but also underscored was the fact that not enough people received the vaccine.

In mid-October a brigade of twenty, including a physician and doctor of biology, hastened to several settlements in the raion or township, which was suffering from an outbreak of typhoid and lesser cases of typhus. The chief employer of the 2,100 inhabitants was a metallurgical plant. The specialists found the main settlement "in fully unsanitary condition: all the streets and canals...were dirty with human waste. An especially great amount was on the left bank of the River Nura near the area of water supply. Toilets," the report continued, consisted "of small wooden boxes; these boxes were so dirty that in many of them there was not the possibility of adding—liquid of human waste dripped through the cracks." As for the homes—"nearly all were investigated—in all 85 were sick." Three of these had typhus; they "were quickly sent to the infectious hospital." The rest had typhoid. The dormitories had a common kitchen, toilet, and bath but, interestingly, although "here" was "the possibility for contact of infection, notwithstanding this in the dorms there were fewer sick than in the homes." The brigade proceeded to inspect workers and food products—cabbage, bread and milk—in the canteen. They found "bacterial colonies...but not the typhoid bacillus." It appeared the outbreak of typhoid had been caused by contamination of the local water source from the River Nura. Autumn rains had caused a latrine pit (*iama*), "dirty with old and fresh human waste," to fall "into the river...at one and a half to two meters above the place for getting water." Most of the sick were women and children, the men having received "divaccine [against typhoid, paratyphoid B—analogous to Salmonella]." The brigade undertook "shock" measures. They mobilized a "mass of komsomol youth[!]" to help dig 116 new toilet pits, sink six new wells, and organize fifty-one beds in the hospital for isolating the sick. A physician and practical nurses (*dezhurnye sestry*) instructed the people "about typhoid and the necessity temporarily to drink only boiled water." Illustrating the need for a strong pharmaceutical industry to complement and implement preventive medicine practices, the medical sisters were to instruct in handwashing and "supply the sick with disinfecting substances—sublimate and chloride of lime (bleaching powder) for disinfecting toilets." By the end of November the epidemic had been quashed but the investigative team also recommended "serious improvement in the water supply and sewerage, strengthening sanitary supervision over the settlement, and opening a bacteriological laboratory in the industrial regions," the materialization of the last being doubtful, since the Institute itself had staffing and funding problems.[24]

Despite the depressingly low level of hygiene, the Institute insisted that "there was in general a lessening of infectious diseases in 1932 as compared with 1931 except for diphtheria and smallpox." There had been 12 cases of the former in 1931 and that number alone in one month in 1932. The rise in small pox cases in 1932 over the 213 cases in 1931 had occurred almost exclusively among "uninoculated Bashkirs." Typhoid resulted mainly from dirty water—it had not affected settlements away from the contaminated area—and also from "nearness to Magnitogorsk, where in 1931 there was an epidemic of typhoid."[25]

In 1933, however, the preventive medicine program of the Ufa Bacteriological Institute faltered because of macroeconomic problems. The plan for the Institute called for anti-dysentery serum "but in the absence of horses the Institute could not make it."[26] Production of filtrates and autofiltrates were held up by insufficient sterilizers, microscopes, the same Chamberlain lamps needed in the previous year, and lack of separate quarters for infected animals.[27] The "low quality of the calves which came to the [Smallpox] department" in 1933 retarded output of smallpox *detrit*. Fortunately, "comparatively small demand for vaccine in this period" and stores remaining from the previous year averted problems. The Smallpox department had received enough linen and chemical vessels, but lamented the poor quality of the machines needed to test the vaccines and particularly that "the table for injecting animals is of old construction, it does not allow work with large animals and requires great physical strength. Notwithstanding frequent requests for a more advanced table for injecting calves, this did not happen and in the near future there is not much hope that it will," the Institute report rather audaciously concluded.[28] Rabies continued to be a major problem. The Pasteur Section saw over 960 individuals for this problem and supplied vaccine "in ampules of 1.0 percent glycerine emulsion" to all branch locations. This plus remodeling had made the work of this section more convenient, but one room was still separated from the other two, only two doctors had received instruction, and the fact that the section was looking into injections "according to a Moscow scheme in place of the Berlin method practiced until this time [to give] significant economy of injection material," indicated financial curbs.[29]

An epidemic of typhoid and outbreaks of typhus stimulated an expedition to several raions of Ufa oblast in May of 1933. Only sixty-four people were sick with typhoid, but between April and June 244 people were sick with typhus.[30] The team also wanted to gather medical statistics. This required interviewing the population. Unfortunately the staff of two physicians, eleven army (*rotnye*) fel'dshers, five nurses or *medsestry*, and some sanitary workers was insufficient to interview the 85,200 plus inhabitants and, thus, party organizations, the Komsomol and even school children were called on to help.[31] Hopefully, these lay people had been vaccinated against the diseases in question.

Macroeconomic constraints curbed some of the specialists' efforts. The Institute team outlined measures "for the struggle with the epidemic." These included transport to the hospital for those seriously ill, guarantees of food, linen, soap, open baths, and two to three de-lousing chambers (*vosheboiki*). The presidium of the Party *Raikom* or raion executive committee acceded to all their demands. However "money and manufactures" were "absent," necessitating the head of the expedition and the Raion Health Organization (*Raizdrav*) to "telegraph a request about sending money and manufactures."[32]

The low level of "culture" also impeded the team. They were dismayed at the lack of laundries and de-lousing chambers. Only one village, Bakalakh, had electric lighting. That village also had one club and one movie theater. The general cultural activities in the villages revolved around celebrations for religious holidays. "Drunkenness and hooliganism" were on the rise.[33]

But the team went to work with a will. Linen and clothing were disinfected in the "sulfur chamber of the veterinary clinic, which had been built for…horses."[34] The team also investigated water and food and vaccinated 700 people against smallpox and 2,000 with divaccine.[35] They discovered that over half of those sick with typhoid were peasants—56 percent on collective farms and another 12½ percent independents (*edinolichnie*). Over half were Tatars and Bashkirs, while only a little over a third were Russians. The vast majority were young—between one and thirty.[36] The team met resistance from "conservative members of the population, including Old Believers, who hid the sick"[37] and were also frustrated that the local "teachers and their *profsovet* (Professional Council) did not participate in the struggle with the epidemics." Further the local raion government "did not fulfill...[its] obligation, guaranteeing neither soap nor food products, nor linen or manufactures."[38]

The team recommended rectifying the lack of amenities including more convenient wells and a new hospital. They dutifully noted that their forty-eight day expedition cost 1, 746 rubles and 66 kopeks in salaries and 576 rubles, 54 kopeks in other expenditures. This was a very small sum.

Nearing the End of the Second Five-Year Plan: 1936

By 1936 the Ufa Bacteriological Institute presented a mixed report of achievements. Planned output for diphtheria, scarlatina and anti-dysentery serums had not been reached but the Institute claimed shortfall for the first item was purposeful. Stores of diphtheria serum transferred to the Institute from Narkomzdrav, the RSFSR Commissariat of Health, more than covered planned need. Additionally, the Institute asserted that if a different measure were used, the amount of anti-dysentery serum actually met planned output. But, although scarlatina serum also was transferred from central stores—140 liters transferred to supplement the 30 the Institute produced—the amount of this prophylactic did not achieve the output targets of 600 liters that it was estimated Ufa needed. The whooping cough (*korevoi*) serum produced by the Institute, on the other hand, was supplemented by production from "peripheral laboratories."

Production of dysentery and scarlatina vaccines, however, increased in 1936 as compared with 1935 (1,000 liters versus 600 liters of the first and 180 liters versus 120 of the second) and production of diphtheria vaccine doubled in the same period. The Institute intended to replace the divaccine in use with a "trivaccine— typhoid plus paratyphoid A plus paratyphoid B" and also was working on "bacteriophage" preparations [viruses that kill bacteria] and other bacteriological preparations, "not having antiepidemic significance." The Institute stopped producing gonococcus vaccine because according to the Institute, the preparation did not have antiepidemic significance, there were sufficient supplies on hand, and production was being transferred to the Venerological Institute.[39]

Conclusion

This study samples only one region in Soviet Russia in the 1930s. It indicates that preventive medicine—output of serums and vaccines and their application—supplemented pharmaceuticals to some extent. Smallpox vaccination was particularly successful and vaccination against typhoid prevented this disease in those inoculated. However, preventive medicine was not fully up and running in outlying areas in the 1930s. Primitive conditions in the provinces—in new industrial regions as well as traditional agricultural and animal husbandry areas—limited the effectiveness of prophylactic measures. A weak macroeconomy negatively impacted the work of bacteriological institutes. Preventive medicine could not alone ensure the health and well being of the Soviet people. A network of well-stocked pharmacies and a robust pharmaceutical industry also were crucial. We will see how these sectors performed during the tumultuous period of the first two Five-Year Plans.

9
Pharmacies During the First and Second Five-Year Plans

G. Tsander, who gave glowing reviews to the American pharmaceutical industry in 1933, also admired American "retail establishments" (*roznichnaia torgovlaia*) which were a combination of both the Russian pharmacy and the *aptekarskie magaziny* of the Imperial period that sold sundries as well as prepared medicines. He noted that in the "retail trade in medicines," there were more than sixty thousand pharmacies and drug stores in the United States. That translated into one retail establishment for every two thousand inhabitants.[1] Although the cabinetry and accouterments of most American drugstores were not as glamorous as those in European pharmacies or pharmacies in Russian cities of the Imperial period, American druggists went out of their way to provide amenities for their customers, such as soda fountains and home deliveries.[2]

Soviet pharmacies compared neither as to number or service. In his report to the Central Bureau of the Pharmacy Sector in 1930, one Khaimovich observed that although " [I]ndustrialization of the country and reconstruction [sic] of the rural economy on socialistic lines" has "put before the organs of health care the task of maximum growth of medical and pharmaceutical service to the insured and the collectivized sector of the rural economy," nevertheless "[I]n industrial regions the insured still do not receive full free pharmaceutical care" and "medical care in the village, both as to quantity and quality, is extremely insufficient." The plenum vowed to rectify this situation.[3]

Ratios between pharmacies and the populace, particularly urban dwellers, were worse during the First Five-Year-Plan period than in pre-revolutionary times due to changing demographics. Ratios were particularly bad in Leningrad, Moscow, and new industrial centers. In pre-revolutionary times there had been 83 pharmacies in Moscow. In 1930 there still were 83, but they served a much larger population. In 1931 there were 86 pharmacies but only 11 pharmacy stores, analogous to the drug stores which had supplemented pharmacies in the pre-revolutionary period. Thus, whereas in pre-revolutionary times one pharmacy in Moscow served 22,800 people, in 1930, one pharmacy served 34,000 and in 1931, 36,000.[4] In Leningrad in 1931 one pharmacy served 24,000 people compared to 16,600 before 1917. In the industrial sections of Leningrad, during the First Five-Year Plan, one pharmacy served 54,000 people.[5] Urbanites fared better in the North Caucasus where, in the fall of 1930, one pharmacy served 16,000 (and 22, 600 in rural areas).[6] New industrial areas were almost bereft of pharmacies, however. In 1929 and 1930 the Central Committee of the Communist Party acknowledged that the "sanitary situation" in "the Donbass, the Kuzbass and the Urals" was "difficult."[7] At the end of the First Five-Year Plan the numbers of free-standing pharmacies were still insufficient. In 1932, in the Russian Republic, 1,270 pharmacies operated in cities, 1, 499 in rural areas, 250 in national minority regions (*natsraionakh*), and 56 in new industrial regions, for a total of 3,075. It was estimated that each pharmacy served, on average, 33,000 inhabitants in national minority regions, 17,000 people in new industrial regions, and 39,000 rural dwellers.[8]

The quality of some pharmacies was abysmal. In 1930 a Plenum of the Pharmacy Sector debated failures in the system, asserting that dispensing (*lekpomoshch'*) "significantly" dragged "behind the needs of workers and peasants." Not only were there too few pharmacies, they were meagerly stocked and lacked appropriate apparatus.[9] Shortages of pharmaceutical vessels were so acute in June 1928 that the Commissariat of Health published a regulation that "in hospitals where there are no infectious wards, vessels could be reused after simple washing...with a wire brush...." On the other hand, "in hospitals with infectious wards, all pharmaceutical vessels...after sorting them in the pharmacy...must be boiled in a soda solution 15 minutes."[10]

In 1929, discussions percolated about closing some pharmacies because of deficits of stock.[11] In 1930, a "book famine" was reported. "Soviet pharmacies still" had "not received one serious...handbook."[12] In 1930, pharmacists complained of a "severe crisis of supply in Moscow pharmacies." There were "defects (*defektury*)" of the most basic items: "pure caffeine, paraffin oil, ammonia, anise drops, turpentine, 'burning' (*zhozhenaia*) magnesia, *chernogorka* herbs, glycerin, camphor preparations, and many others." This was because the "factory often interrupts production of such things as corn liquid and boromenthol, and the pharmacies have to acquire them from private firms." Additionally, "on account of compulsory assortments...the pharmacies sit for months without soap." Besides "deficit medicines" and "interruptions of supplies," the "reorganization of [small-scale] *kustar'* production," was significant because it "cut short...the normal supply to pharmacies ...of household products." Pharmacists also bemoaned the long time it took to receive orders: "central supply centers…held up planned orders for 2-3 weeks and emergency orders for 7, 10 and more days."[13]

Rural pharmacies were primitive. Party leaders lambasted "the severely inadequate medical help in rural areas."[14] Pharmacists in the field provided documentation. One, from Kursk emphasized the distance peasants had to travel to pharmacies, noting that "[I]n connection with the formation of state farms, collective farms, larger village soviets, and so forth, in connection with the formation of large rural centers, it is necessary to increase the number of rural pharmacies …the radius of [pharmacies] at 30-40 kilometers at present is too big."[15]

In 1930, opining that "the distribution of medicaments…to the collectivized village…is entirely insufficient at present," one Mironovich from Kherson emphasized that "[T]here is no planned…distribution of deficit wares…[whereas] the supplying of village pharmacies ought to be uninterrupted." [16] Pharmacist Efe, from Kursk, echoed him, claiming that "in the medical districts" and "fel'dsher points," there ought to be "standardized weights, distillation apparatus, infusion apparatus," "light, dry rooms" with "one experienced pharmacist," "items to care for the sick, popular literature, and rational cosmetics."[17]

In 1932 pharmacists lamented "the *defitsit* of fats," which was "severely felt." This not only resulted in "insufficient supplies of soap, but also ingredients used in the pharmacy to prepare substances" that were "the most widespread, cheapest, and most effective against lice." Lack of ordinary disinfectants and cleaning supplies in the pharmacies imperiled the health of the populace in two ways. On the one hand, struggle with germs and vectors that spread disease was made more complicated. On the other hand, in the absence of milder disinfectants, pharmacists dispensed strong items such as sulfuric acid, formalin, and carbolic acid, even to children, violating the "general rule in pharmacy practice not to sell strong-acting substances in 'Group B' because they were poisonous and dangerous."[18]

Shortages of Pharmacists During the First Five-Year Plan

As during the NEP, the dearth of pharmacies and their poor quality were bound up with the lack of properly trained pharmacists. In 1930, 4,000 pharmacy posts were being held by barely trained individuals—

praktikanty, "more than half of whom had worked in a pharmacy two years or less. In the medical districts...often," another individual commented, there were "3-5 people 'preparing' medicines...who are military (*rotnye*) fel'dshers, midwives, and even white collar workers, with not a pharmacist among them."[19]

The shortage of pharmacists was due to various reasons: the lack of prestige accorded the profession; attempts to raise pharmacists' qualifications; low pay; and "unsatisfying conditions of work." Higher educational requirements, proposed in 1930, frightened the ill-qualified who had been working in the field for some time. The stalwart Izrail I. Levinshtein, who had devoted his career to improving pharmacists' qualifications, and other pharmacists reported a host of "troublesome news" about the upgrade. There was talk about closing one Siberian technicum, there was mass exodus of pharmacists from pharmacies, in the Chemical-Pharmaceutical faculty in Leningrad there remained only two students, uproars occurred in Moscow. Pharmacists acknowledged that the profession had little respect: "in Soviet medicine, there is no place for the pharmacy as a self-standing unit, its productive function is being transferred to chemists in factories, to pharmacist-therapists, to doctors...and pharmacists could be replaced with sisters of mercy. ..."[20] Pharmacists' pay in 1930 amounted to only 60 percent of pharmacists' pre-World War I pay.[21]

Conditions for training were often shockingly bad. For example, in Moscow, in 1931, those taking a short course of training in the use of medical instruments had to lodge in railway stations for lack of dorms. Classrooms not only lacked equipment but chairs; students sat on boxes.[22]

In 1930 the shortage of dispensing pharmacists in the Ukraine was said to be "catastrophic."[23] The situation continued to be poor in 1931.[24] In 1930, 150 students finished the Moscow Pharmaceutical Technicum. One hundred twenty refused to work as dispensing pharmacists. The newly minted pharmacists particularly dismissed village and factory pharmacies. The salary in village pharmacies was only 90 rubles per month, plus "unpaid communal labor was required."[25]

Pharmacies in new industrial areas advertised high salaries to attract pharmacists. For example, in 1931 the Karakalpak Pharmacy in Amu Dar'ia advertised for three administrators for its regional (*raion*) pharmacy at 300 rubles per month, two dispensers (*retseptary*) at 180-200 rubles per month, and two assistants at 150 rubles per month.[26]

But during the Second Five-Year Plan pharmacists continued to be in short supply. During the First Five-Year-Plan pharmacists warned authorities that appropriations of 3.5 million rubles for professional training was inadequate. The result was a feminization of the profession and reliance on *praktikanty*. In 1933, 67 percent of "pharmacy personnel" were women.[27] In 1935, 60 percent were.[28] In 1939, some managers of pharmacies were *praktikanty*. [29]

Bureaucratic Follies During the First Five-Year Plan

New Purchasing Methods

Abrupt changes that Soviet bureaucrats imposed on pharmacy administrations (*aptekoupravleniia*), which supervised and ordered wholesale for pharmacies, led to further deterioration of dispensing. The pharmacy changes paralleled the shift from private shops to state stores in the retail sector that Sheila Ftitzpatrick has termed improperly thought-out.[30]

First came changes in the infrastructure. In the late 1920s and early 1930s the Soviet Union discarded the counties (*uezdy)* and provinces (*gubernii)* that had characterized local administration since the mid-1770s, in the reign of Catherine the Great, and moved to a system of regions (*oblasti*) and districts (*raiony)* that were smaller. The system of specific republics—SSRs, ASSRs , oblasts or AOs, and regions (*krai*)— for nationalities remained. Along with the administrative redrawing, came more decentralization in pharmaceutical supply. *Oblast'* pharmacy administrations (*aptekoupravleniia,*) were established but pharmacy specialists noted that "in the districts (*raiony*) there was minimal apparatus" and during 1929 and 1930 "the number of pharmaceutical supply bases was severely cut."[31]

The Soviet postal system did not operate properly, causing supply problems. Particularly for "peripheral pharmacies in new areas... distribution by post gave deplorable results...only 20 to 40 percent of orders were received from the central warehouses." Still, capable managers could surmount the obstacles. Where managers showed "wide initiative" pharmacies were "satisfactorily supplied," although this "took a lot of time...means...and trips to the center...On average in the Moscow region there" were "fewer than 3-4 self-financed pharmacies, 2-3 hospitals and clinics, and the 3-4 managers of pharmacies travel to the center," the specialists complained, "wasting time, means, and energy to supply their pharmacies." Pharmacists queried whether "it would not be better to have a *raion* or regional base [that is a closer base] to supply pharmacies?"[32]

Pharmacy Administrations Shoulder More Costs

Simultaneously, the government devolved much of the responsibility for paying for health care onto local budgets. This affected pharmacies negatively, as Christopher Davis has shown for doctors and clinics, in his discussion of Soviet health care during the First Five-Year Plan.[33]

Under the slogan, "mobilizing internal resources" for industrialization of the Soviet Union, between 1928 and 1930, pharmacy administrations and pharmacies were made "self-financing" or put on *khozraschet*, that is, they were considered autonomous financial and legal entities with increased responsibility for their own sourcing. Their operations were supposed to turn a profit.[34]

However, the pharmacy administrations and pharmacies were limited in exercising their new rights and responsibilities. Their funding was limited, they had little control over prices, and they had to operate within the plan.[35] To complicate matters, during 1930, Gosbank issued new rules which tightened payment for wares distributed by Gosmedtorgprom to local pharmacy administrations. Credit and open accounts for purchasers were eliminated and Gosmedtorgprom's accounts in banks other than the State Bank were closed. Henceforth all payments were to go through the Moscow office of Gosbank.[36] Credit periods for purchases were shortened for pharmacy administrations from 100 days in the 1927/28 operating year to 95 days in 1928/29 and 86 days in 1929/1930.

The switchover to "self-financing" did not occur overnight. In the Russian Republic in 1929 only 121 pharmacies were self-financed, out of a total of 2,372 pharmacies, although the number of *khozraschet* pharmacies was slated to grow during 1930 to 10,217. "'Sum accounting' (*summovoi otchet)* had been introduced in nearly all the *khozraschet* pharmacies." Pharmacy executives and pharmacists complained about the new experiment. They emphasized that "the funds held by pharmacy administrations "were "extremely insufficient." They asserted that inadequate funds limited the building of new pharmacies and that to get more funds pharmacy administrations would have to "rationalize" their operations.

The actual balance sheet for the *khozraschet* pharmacy administrations in the Russian Republic appeared less gloomy. The pharmacy administrations realized slight increases in profits in the 1928/1929 and 1939/1930 operating years as compared with 1927/1928 as a result of "rationalization" measures. Payments to health organs and taxes to the Commissariat of Finance also increased, but funds on hand were slightly higher in 1929 than in 1928. Reserve capital also decreased during this period.[37]

One analyst of Ukrainian pharmacy administrations in 1930 praised some aspects of the *khozraschet* system but pointed to problems which would result for the public weal if pharmacy administrations were made fiscally responsible while their financial options were limited. The author admitted that there was little "factual information" about the new system but initial information indicated that the "budget situation" of pharmacy administrations "depended less upon their financial condition than upon their management." The change to *khozraschet* had obvious negatives for it led to "extreme contraction of stores of wares, exits... from additional long-term credits, and disorientation of pharmacy masses, especially proprietors." True, "the balances of the 27 [Ukrainian] pharmacy administrations" on *khozraschet* were "good"—"only two suffered losses," but the new system carried with it extraordinary accounting burdens: "In the *khozraschet* system each enterprise, in particular pharmacy administrations, had to calculate not only balances between property means and loans...but it" was "necessary to estimate the condition, that is the coordination, between short-term obligations and proposed expenditures. This must be done each quarter." Pharmacy administrations had to economize: "financial tautness...when finances... are used to their fullest, must be considered in our condition [of industrialization] normal and positive, for there is not yet in the country one pharmacy administration...which has a fully sufficient network of pharmacies," equipment which is "the last word in technique," and "offers pharmaceutical help to the populace at 100 percent." However, pharmacy administrations could not be relegated to the level of retail establishments in the Five-Year Plan, particularly with regard to long-term credits needed to build pharmacies. Rather, each pharmacy administration had to be given the latitude to decide whether it needed long credits. Otherwise, expansion of the pharmacy network would be held up.[38]

Pharmacists frequently expressed bitterness about the system of *khozraschet*, particularly how little it corresponded with reality for those at the lower tiers. For example, one N. Mirlin candidly asked "... about *khozraschet*....What is the meaning of this term for our pharmacies? I do not know," he acknowledged "whether precise understanding of the term exists. It is connected with self purchasing and the right of independently going to the market for acquiring raw materials and marketing production." But, Mirlin emphasized, "Self purchasing...in the majority of cases has relevance only in cities and rarely in the village. Many rural pharmacy administrations are unprofitable. The prices for prescriptions—12-15 kopeks—obviously does not cover costs." Rural pharmacy administrations needed advances from other operations. "Let's be truthful," he admitted, "the right to use profits is little realized." He scoffed at "the right of pharmacies...to acquire raw materials," pointing out the constraints that hemmed in pharmacies. "Basic raw materials...medicaments are acquired by warehouses at prices established by the pharmacy administrations... not by their clients...the amount of wares also does not depend upon the pharmacy." He questioned the validity of the "independence" recently accorded to the pharmacy administrations and pharmacies, noting that if this were actually so they could "refrain from preliminary approval of budgetary expenditures." In reality, independence meant following "fulfillment of the plan." Rather shockingly, he averred that "the good quality of medicine" dispensed in the pharmacy is "a joke," one reason being that "in the majority of cases the manager has a minimum of scientific preparation."[39]

Utopian Remedies

Somewhat utopian remedies were devised to compensate for the inadequate number of pharmacists and pharmacies. One article proposed creating "pharmaceutical factories, like that operating in Rostov-on-Don in 1931, all over the USSR." The Rostov factory filled prescriptions on an assembly line basis and supplied pharmacies in the city within a couple of hours. By 1933, two pharmaceutical factories were established in Moscow. Charts illustrated how one filled 6,000 prescriptions per day, the other 3,000. A photograph of one Moscow factory depicted long tables bearing scientific apparatus at which women, wearing white gowns and hats—and supervised by men—filled containers with medicine. There were two pharmaceutical factories in Leningrad, one in Khar'kov (filling 1,500 prescriptions per day), one in

Kiev, and one in Dnepropetrovsk.[40] A competition was inaugurated for the "best work on rationalizing a pharmacy warehouse."[41]

In rural areas "mobile pharmacies" were touted. These were pharmacies fitted out in a horse-drawn, wheeled wagon and staffed by a paramedic, nurse, and pharmacy "workers" (probably partially trained *praktikanty*) that could serve several collective farms between May and October.[42]

Fig. 9.1 Prescription Section 1 of the Moscow Factory of Medicine (Source: *Sovetskaia farmatsiia*, vol. 4, no. 6, 1933, p. 9)

Fig. 9.2 Apteka on Wheels, Collective Farm, Mineralovodskogo Raion (Source: Ibid., vol. 3, no. 5, 1932, p. 39)

The Second Five-Year Plan

Numbers of pharmacies increased in Central Asia and in the Caucasus during the Five-Year-Plan period.[43] But in the Russian Republic in 1935 pharmacy administrators lamented that "the general growth of the [pharmacy] network is entirely insufficient...400 raion centers had no pharmacies."[44] In 1937 more pharmacies and other types of dispensing centers opened in cities and rural areas in Moscow, Voronezh, Saratov, and Leningrad oblasts of the Russian Republic. Nevertheless, the quotas ordained by the Commissariat of Health had not been fulfilled and, in 1938, the first year of the Third Five-Year-Plan, there were no pharmacies in 223 raions of the RSFSR and none in 260 raion centers, organized in 1937 as a result of the growth of new industrial areas in the hinterlands.[45] An official report from 1937 agonized that "in a range of cities with significant population the number of pharmacies open at night [is] entirely insufficient...in a majority of large cities people prepare medicine at home, especially where the region [is]far from a pharmacy." [46] On the eve of the great Patriotic War numbers still were insufficient.[47]

The pharmacy situation was critical in the Ukrainian SSR during the Second Five-Year Plan, according to M. L. Siatinia, author of a new history of Ukrainian pharmacy. He puts the onus squarely on the shoulders of Moscow officials. Whereas Ukrainian pharmacists retained some autonomy in the 1920s NEP, Siatinia depicts the Ukraine as a pharmaceutical colony of the *Russian* Republic by the Second Five-Year Plan, with disastrous consequences. Siatina's claim that tsarist pharmaceutical industry was backward is based on secondary sources and does not square with the primary sources I have studied.[48] However, his portrayal of the trials and tribulations of the Ukrainian pharmacy sector during the Second Five-Year Plan is buttressed by copies of official documents from Ukrainian archives. With the exception of one error (the assertion that the Dzerzhinskii Factory was located in Moscow) the archival materials appear to be authentic. They present a depressing picture.

According to Siatinia and the documents, the network of pharmacies was completely inadequate. For example, in 1936 "in Kiev there were 36 pharmacies in place of the 45 existing before the revolution"; in the region of Lipok and some other areas there were no pharmacies; "of the 48 pharmacies in Odessa before the revolution, there remained only 35"; in Dnepropetrovsk in place of 18 pre-revolutionary pharmacies there were 12. Matters were worse in the countryside. "In 10 regions (*raiony*) of the Ukraine there were entirely no pharmacies." Further, many pharmacies needed severe restoration[49] In 1935 Ukrainian pharmacists blamed Moscow for the fact that there were only 385 pharmacies in Ukrainian cities and 975 in rural areas, government demands for profitability and insufficient capital on the part of pharmacy administrations having slowed expansion. (Ukrainian pharmacy administrations did establish 63 laboratories to analyze food products, 52 of them in rural areas in that year, however.)[50]

Deficits were endemic in the Ukraine. Although the Ukrainian Communist Party and government was encouraged to establish a chemical-pharmaceutical industry in 1932, because the republic was rich in natural resources including coal by-products,[51] lack of funding, cuts in imports of equipment, and ill-thought out reorganizations of the pharmacy sector impeded the process. The Ukrainian pharmaceutical industry did produce some eight new items.[52] Still, in 1936, in the words of archival documents, the Ukraine received "up to 80 percent of medicines and equipment from all-union contingents. The chemical-pharmaceutical and instruments industry in Ukraine grew" during the 1930s but "[D]ispersal of instruments, medicines, and equipment was done by enterprises of the RSFSR" and there were "huge interruptions," leaving Ukrainian pharmacies short of narcotics for operations, febrifuges like aspirin, pyramidon, and phenacetin, anti-syphilitics like sal'varsan, and anti-malarials. Cuts in imports further left pharmacies bereft of strichnine, cocaine, cocoa oil, and microscopes for Dr. Bogomolets' and other research institutes and a new large hospital in Khar'kov. Ukrainian officials demanded foreign literature, 200 tons of soap, and flour and bread for medical personnel who had not been paid for "2-3 months."[53] The Ukrainians implied that Moscow officials deliberately caused their plight.

Yet Russian pharmacies also were ill-stocked and the causes were manifold. Shortages of medicine, of course, resulted from inadequate production. However, *brak* or rejection of medicaments because of dirt or poor color also contributed. *Brak* affected some 5 percent of the value of production for factories comprising Vokhimfarm in 1933.[54] Poor information and lack of advertising exacerbated the situation. In 1933, Izrail I. Levinshtein admitted that shortages in the pharmacies of Neosalvarsan, ether, atropine, digitalis, codeine, and other items resulted from insufficient production but he noted that some remedies also lay unused in warehouses because physicians and medical personnel did not know supplies were available or had not received information about the products.[55] In 1934 he and Iu. Kuperman lamented pharmacies refusing the public "the most elementary products—castor oil, vaseline, fish oil, soda," claiming that "[T]he sick run from pharmacy to pharmacy and many are left without any medical help."[56]

Lack of funding harmed Russian pharmacy associations and pharmacies as much as Ukrainian ones. In 1934, pharmacy officials asserted that the State Bank and Commissariat of Finance gave "credit to all, but not to pharmacy administrations." As a result glassware and other elementary equipment were lacking in pharmacies and certified pharmacists had gone into other work. The financial situation in the North Caucasus was said to be especially bad in 1934. [57] Levinshtein emphasized in the pharmaceutical press that pharmacy associations (which purchased for pharmacies), were "living through serious financial difficulties" and consequently that pharmacies were "in extremely chaotic conditions, the quality of work had declined and that medicines in some places are dispensed without tests, in glasses and drinking bottles."[58] As did Ukrainian pharmacists, Russian pharmacy administrations ranted that monies allocated were not disbursed. For example, in 1935, more than half of the three million rubles allocated for new construction had not been distributed.[59]

Although the central government did not properly assist local pharmacy administrations, it did curtail them. Just as production exhibited signs of recovery in 1934 and 1935, the Soviet government's obsession with controlling the market, expanding state revenues, achieving balances, and fear of inflation upset finances all along the production-supply chain and limited medicines and supplies for the populace. In 1934, new preparations developed by the industry "with great difficulty" were "not distributed to local pharmacy administrations and pharmacies for fear of overstocking[!]" As a result, "medicines needed by the sick" lay unused "in the warehouses of factories."[60] But the most egregious ill-thought-out bureaucratic policy was an abrupt rise in pharmacy prices in 1935.

Price Rises in 1935

In April 1935, central authorities precipitously raised prices for prescriptions. Prices for prescriptions were regulated in Soviet Russia by the Pharmacy Tax (*Aptekarskaia taksa*). The Pharmacy Tax had set prices for prescriptions in Imperial Russia as well, but the logic underlying the tax was that prices, which fluctuated according to the international market, ought not be detrimental to the populace. An abrupt hike in prescription prices in 1935 by Soviet officials predictably kept people away from pharmacies. The report of the Chief Pharmacy Administration underscored for the bureaucrats in Moscow how the "[S]evere raising of prices lowered requests." In 1934, prescriptions dispensed in out-patient clinics had amounted to 86.7 million, the number dispensed in stationary facilities had amounted to 11.2 million, and the number of paid prescriptions dispensed had amounted to 26.6 million. During the first quarter of 1935, the number of prescriptions dispensed in out-patient clinics was 24.2 million. During the second quarter the number dispensed was 23.6 million. In the third quarter, however, the number of prescriptions dispensed dipped to 19.6 million. The number of prescriptions dispensed in stationary facilities also dipped in the third quarter, from 3.0 million to 2.6 million. The number of paid prescriptions was low in the first part of 1935, amounting to 6.7 million in the first quarter, 5.3 million in the second, and 7.5 million in the third. The number of paid prescriptions dispensed rose to 21.7 million in the fourth quarter, however, when the government discounted prescriptions to bring people back to the pharmacies.[61]

The financial distress of the local pharmacy administrations and pharmacies not only hurt the populace but negatively impacted the core pharmaceutical industry. In 1933 Vokhimfarm reported financial problems due to "weakness of the market." Local pharmacy associations, because of their "financial difficulties," "held back" their orders. The strain was compounded by the fact that central authorities had not disbursed monies for capital construction, which retarded production of many reagents.[62]

The drop in sales resulting from the price hikes of 1935 seriously undermined Vokhimfarm's financial position. Higher prices, Vokhimfarm informed authorities, "resulted in financial difficulties among basic users." Local pharmacy administrations, which supplied pharmacies, were "unable to place new orders" and also "were deprived of the possibility of purchasing supplies sent to their addresses." The local administrations "sometimes needed to refuse not only the wares sent above contract—in connection with over-fulfillment of the production plan" by pharmaceutical factories—"but even had to refuse wares that were part of the contract." "As a result of contraction of orders, in some cases there occurred a glut (*zatovarivaniia*) of preparations, even those formerly deficit—veronal, liuminal (Luminal), iodide salts, and others, and output of potassium iodide was cut in the fourth quarter." Realizing the "difficulties" it had caused, Sovnarkom reduced the prices in September.[63] But the damage had already been done.

Rural areas were particularly poorly served at the end of the Second Five-Year Plan. In 1937, one G. Smolkin lamented the inadequate numbers of pharmacies, the need to prepare more pharmacists, poor quality of medicines and even claimed that "pharmacy at present has a very weak scientific research base." The editor appended a rebuke that the author did not examine the VUZy or institutes with the "deficiencies of their teaching personnel."[64] In 1938 Smolkin asserted that "trade from village shops of the most simple medicines" was "not only small" but "sold by people technically illiterate in the field of health care." More pharmacy points, which began to be organized in 1936 in the Ukraine and in 1937 in the RSFSR, could supplement pharmacies but they needed to be located 15 to 20 kilometers from the nearest pharmacy. "Drug stores" were not the answer as they were "very poorly organized," their "assortment was very small," and "dispensers of medicines were technically illiterate in the area of pharmacy…the existing network [of pharmacies] does not serve the village adequately." "Pharmacies in clinics" were not the answer, because "as a rule they do not have a separate space, elementary equipment, and…free cadres …." They did not follow "proper procedure."[65]

Conclusions

In the Introduction, we noted that foreign observers observed shortages in the pharmacies and Soviet pharmacists complained about the deficits. In this chapter we have seen that inadequate numbers of pharmacies and pharmacists and ill-thought-out policies by government officials were partly responsible for the fact that not even insured workers were being served properly two decades after the Great October Revolution. In our last two chapters we will investigate what the pharmaceutical industry was doing to rectify this situation.

10
Medicines for the Masses: The Pharmaceutical Industry during the First Five-Year Plan

What was occurring in the pharmaceutical industry during the First Five-Year Plan? First, in contrast to pharmacies and other retail establishments, the organization of the industry and its reporting procedures did not undergo seismic change as the Soviet Union implemented a centrally planned, centrally directed macro economy.[1] Core pharmaceutical factories had been owned by the state since 1918 and had been subject to production and financial plans throughout the twenties, even though the board that managed them and some enterprise directors had a certain amount of autonomy in sourcing and marketing. This structure remained. Eighty or so other large and medium-sized pharmaceutical factories also continued to be owned by regional pharmacy administrations, workers' cooperatives, and other groups. They had not been subject to plans and directives from Vesenkha during the NEP. *Kustar'* manufacturers of medicines and purveyors of raw medicinal materials, from whom large pharmaceutical factories often sourced,[2] likewise retained their status and remained outside the orbit of the central government during the First Five-Year Plan, unlike lessees of pharmacies, small-scale producers and traders of consumer items, and peasant agriculturalists.

As during the preceding NEP, the core pharmaceutical industry was organized as a joint-stock trust, comprised of ten or so enterprises. For most of the First Five-Year Plan this conglomerate was known as Gosmedtorgprom.[3] There were fifteen shareholders. Vesenkha, the Supreme Council of the National Economy, held over half the shares. Narkomzdrav, the Commissariat of Health, held 40 percent worth of the shares. Thirteen local "medtorgs" or medical agencies and local pharmacy administrations (*aptekoupravleniia*) held less than 4 percent of shares remaining. Ukrmedtorg, the Ukrainian medical agency, held just over two percent and the Siberian, Northern Caucasus, Belorussian, and Samara medical agencies—Sibmedtorg, Sevkaztorg, Belmedtorg, and Samarskii "gubmedtorgs," respectively, as well as the Bashkir, Crimean,

Leningrad, Stalingrad, Saratov, Penza, and northern Dvina pharmacy organizations each held minute percentages of shares.[4]

Nor did the purges that rocked other industries during the First Five-Year Plan dramatically affect the core pharmaceutical industry. In contrast to the railroads, the coal mining industry, and agriculture and food-processing, where purges decimated managers, who, scapegoated for the inability of their enterprises to meet outlandish goals, were executed or sentenced to hard labor, only minor shakeups occurred in the pharmaceutical industry. In 1928, following orders from Vesenkha, Farmapravlenie—the board that ran Gosmedtorgprom—made a few personnel changes. A committee headed by V. Iu. Levita, "Chair of the Stock Company Gosmedtorgprom," reported secretly (*secretno*) to Vesenkha that the director of the Karpov factory (formerly the Ferrein factory, then Factory No. 8) needed to be replaced because "he did not have a correct relationship with the factory organization." In particular this change was needed to "establish firm discipline." The assistant director of the factory, on the other hand, was judged to be capable. It was recommended, however, that the assistant director of the Semashko Factory (formerly the Keler Factory, then factory No. 12) be replaced because "he could not work with the Director." The directors and assistant directors of other factories in the system were deemed to be adequate.[5]

Were pharmaceuticals sacrificed to steel mills, coal mines, dams, and railroads as were consumer goods and housing during the First Five-year Plan by their investments being slashed to the bone?[6] J. D. Barber and R. W. Davies have emphasized that medicines and medical equipment lagged behind the number of physicians and other health personnel churned out during the plan period, implying that lack of investment was to blame.[7] Christopher Davis postulated that inflation diluted the budget of the Commissariat of Health (Narkomzdrav), as cited in the Introduction.[8] Yet, the core industry was only indirectly affected by the commissariat's budget woes because it did not come under the jurisdiction of Narkomzdrav until 1936.[9] Admittedly, the commissariat was a shareholder in the trust and Narkomzdrav's financial status affected the industry because pharmacy administrations, which purchased medicaments mainly from the core industry, were subordinate to the health commissariat and squeezing their budgets limited their purchasing power. Even so, aside from the fact that pharmacists, like other citizens, were expected to help shoulder the costs of industrial growth by purchasing not less than one month's salary worth of bonds or "*obligatsii*," thus providing the government with 3,310 million rubles or 19 percent of the Soviet budget,[10] subsidies from the government, a main means of the industry's support, were not entirely niggardly.

In 1930, for example, the industry received a capital infusion of 22 million rubles, "of which 4 million was to go to the construction of new factories." Industry officials considered this "a large sum."[11] But two years later, in 1932, investments were cut for all economic sectors, even for the Commissariat of Heavy Industry, because of disappointing revenues. Allocations for capital construction in the pharmaceutical industry were reduced 6 million rubles compared with 1931 appropriations. Pharmacy executives complained that the 60 million rubles allocated for capital construction in 1932 was "minimal" and inadequate for building new factories or modernizing the old pre-revolutionary facilities. They also expressed frustration over their lack of control over funds, criticizing planners for not having proper data and making faulty extrapolations based on past orders rather than future needs.[12]

Planners, on the other hand, countered that the cut was justified because core pharmaceutical factories employed too many workers and tolerated absenteeism and poor work discipline, which resulted in low productivity.[13] In all fairness, 60 million rubles was much higher than earlier allocations. Inflation, though, might well have neutralized the increase, as Davis has pointed out. Further, the capriciousness of government allocations made it difficult for pharmaceutical industry executives to plan.

Financial Disabilities Imposed by Exogenous Bureaucrats

Indeed, more significant than investments were other government decisions that negatively impacted industry finances. For example, industry costs increased during the First Five-Year Plan. Manufacture of new, more complex medicines drove up production costs 20 percent. Remodeling and re-outfitting the old, pre-1917 factories in Gosmedtorgprom was expensive in the short run. Additionally, the Administration of Gosmedtorgprom spent considerable time preparing the factories in its jurisdiction to move to a self-financing status October 1, 1928, as ordained by Vesenkha.[14] Notwithstanding the trust's difficulties, the government allowed purchasers of the products from Gosmedtorgprom's factories—mainly other state entities—more lenient terms of purchase, specifically longer periods of credit. This caused consternation on the part of the trust's administrative board. Furthermore, despite the credit extension, local pharmacy administrations, which purchased pharmaceutical products for pharmacies, cut their orders, because they themselves were in financial straits. Predictably Gosmedtorgprom's revenue from sales plunged during the 1927/1928 operating year.[15] Next, government officials lopped off several integral sourcing and money-making operations.

Loss of Soap Production

The decision which theorists running the Soviet government made in 1918 to parcel out production of key pharmaceuticals like soap, iodine, botanicals, and reagents among the pharmaceutical industry and other industries caused ongoing sourcing difficulties for the pharmaceutical trust. A decade later government authorities exacerbated the trust's sourcing problems and cut its revenues by divesting it of production of the first three items.

Whereas the American pharmaceutical company Sharp & Dohme, "essentially a manufacturer and distributor of ethical drugs" with "a very small research and development organization" but "an extremely effective distribution network" purchased the H. K. Mulford Company, "as a convenient means of moving into biologicals to extend its product line and to develop new capabilities" in 1929,[16] the Soviet government summarily deprived the core pharmaceutical industry of its money-making arms by fiat.

Loss of soap production was a major blow to the industry. Soap was one of the most basic "prophylactics," and one of the easiest and cheapest to produce. Before the advent of sulfa drugs in the mid-1930s, soap was credited with limiting the spread of many diseases, particularly tuberculosis.[17] In the late nineteenth and early twentieth century, the Keler Factory had produced soap, disinfectants, and cleaning supplies and sold them throughout the length and breadth of the Russian Empire. After being nationalized, the Keler Factory, now called Semashko, became part of the core pharmaceutical industry. It continued to make and sell soap.[18] The core industry, in other words, had a good track record in production of this important commodity.

Nevertheless, "[I]n order to eliminate competition and parallelism" and to allow the core pharmaceutical industry to "concentrate on production of medicines, particularly chemically-synthesized medicines that would replace foreign imports,"in the 1927/1928 operating year, officials transferred production of perfume, cosmetics, and galenicals from Semashko and the pharmaceuticals trust to TEZhE, the Soap Trust. TEZhE was situated in Glavkhim (the Chemical Glavk) and completely separate from the Pharmaceuticals Trust, Gosmedtorgprom.[19]

Removal of the Soap Trust did result in the Semashko Factory producing a colloidal sulfur-zinc salve called Sul'folan for treating scabbies and "ulcerous infectious typhus." Intended to compete with a salve put out by the German house Reidel, Sul'folan was deemed to be "fully equal to [the] foreign [product]"[20] and was exported.[21] Semashko's new production of chloroform also was successful, at least in the Russian Republic.[22] However, since cosmetics and perfumes had amounted to over 35 percent of Gosmedtorgprom's production and were profitable, divestiture of soap-making and "galenicals" also decreased Gosmedtorgprom's cash flow.[23] Nor did excising soap production from the pharmaceutical industry increase output of this key commodity. The Soap Trust simply could not produce enough soap. The trust included ten factories and a central laboratory. Only five factories, however, including one slaughterhouse, produced soap—toilet soap, liquid soap, washing powder, glycerine—and bleach. These factories also put out perfumes and ether oils, olive and machine oils, and cartons and tubes. Factory No. 6 produced glue; Factory No. 10, gelatin; factories No. 7 and No. 8, flagons and tiles; and Factory No. 9 stainless steel machines.[24] The physical plants of the majority of these factories were old and their equipment outmoded. Two had been built in the 1870s, two in the 1880s, one in the 1890s, one during World War I, and a seventh at some indefinite point in the nineteenth century.[25]

Small-scale producers—*kustari*—supplemented the factories in the Soap Trust and, in contrast to the fate of Semashko, continued to do so during the First Five-Year Plan. However, they produced only 10 percent of the soap used in the country.[26]

The factories in the Soap Trust had been perennially short of inputs, even before the First Five-Year Plan began, resulting in failures to meet quotas, which presumably were based on the country's estimated need. For example, in 1926/1927 the Soap Trust was slated to produce 18,000 tons of household soap, 1,350 tons of liquid soap, and 11,000 "thousand dozens" of toilet soap. Liquid soap came near its target, but about 4,000 tons less of household soap than required were produced and about 3,000 "thousand dozens'" less of toilet soap. TEZhE explained that it had "not fulfilled the program" for toilet and liquid soap "because of insufficient fats." Other factories in the Soap Trust blamed their failure to meet the program on other problems. Local producers blocked imports of vegetable seeds to Moscow, resulting in a shortage of vegetable oil. "Higher organs" limited imports of cocoa for cocoa oil and bleach, and the bleach that was imported was diverted to production of face powder. Construction of new facilities held up output of gelatin. *Brak,* or spoilage, cut output in another factory.[27]

The First Five-Year-Plan aggravated shortages of raw materials for soap making. Slaughtering of animals and destruction of crops by peasants protesting collectivization coupled with turmoil in the fishing and cotton industries resulting from the crash production quotas of the First Five-Year Plan led to a "dangerous deficit in fats," predominantly vegetable fats—sunflower and cottonseed oils. The soap industry also used about "6,000 tons of fat" from fish, but in 1928 "the entirety of this quantity" was "absorbed by the leather industry."[28] In 1928/1929 the Soap Trust reported that the "severe lowering of the tempo of growth" was "explained by the...cutting of contingents of fatty raw materials and imported ether oils." The 31,200 tons of fat available in 1927/1928 declined by 2,000 tons in 1928/1929. "Under-deliveries" (*nedogruz*) of fats for household soap amounted to 30 percent and 40 percent for toilet soap.[29] By the fall of 1930, pharmacy journals publicly admitted the "[S]evere crisis in fatty materials in the soap-making industry."[30] The trust also faced shortages of other materials and, compounding its problems, monies for reconstruction were cut by "56 percent" in October 1928 and January, 1929, propelling the Presidium of the Moscow Sovnarkhoz or Economic Council to protest to the Moscow Soviet and Vesenkha.

The Soap Trust attempted to "mobilize internal resources" but soap production plummeted, worsening the financial health of the Trust[31] and threatening public health. Figures on soap production during the First Five-Year Plan vary, but the general impression is of steep decline. According to one set of data in American files, the Soviet Union produced 240,000 tons of "household soap (in 'glue soap equivalents')" in 1927-1928 and 257,000 tons in 1928-1929, but only 234,000 tons in 1929-1930.[32] Another set of "official" Soviet statistics cites the "Siberian Union of Consumers' Societies" soap plant in Siberia, production of which "constituted 8 percent of total soap production in the U.S.S.R.," as putting out "5,758 tons of laundry soap and 285,000 dozens of toilet soap" in 1926-1927 with production projected to increase one and a half times in 1927-1928.[33] In October 1928, Frank Messenger, American Assistant Trade Commissioner, reported from London, that "[T]he

Moscow Government Trading Department has submitted its requirements in household soap for...the 1928-1929 working year," asking for 22,000 tons of soap. Factoring in "industry, hospital" and other "special soaps," Messenger estimated that requirements for Moscow and "neighboring governments" were actually closer to "27,000 tons" but, he noted, "[T]he quantity of soap produced in Moscow in 1927-1928 was just 20,500 tons."[34]

Some pharmacists claimed that the shortfall in soap production was exacerbated at the retail level by cash-strapped pharmacy administrations supplying the pharmacies and stores in their jurisdictions with "cosmetics and eau de cologne" instead of soap because these items "were more profitable."[35] The Soap Trust did increase output of these items, using "aromatic materials of Russian production," in lieu of slashed imports of foreign ether oils, in a desperate attempt to salvage its own finances, but the 1928/1929 report admitted that while this saved the trust, the "deliveries of perfume and cosmetics...to the countryside...were of cheaper sorts...because of absence of imported ether oils" and "significantly lessened profits." In any case, this strategy was not the product of a sinister plot on the part of the Soap Trust or local pharmacy administrations but was necessitated by "worsening of general conditions...for deficit materials—fats, chemicals, cartons, papers, and others."[36]

Lack of soap was detrimental to public health. In 1929 per capita use of soap in the Soviet Union was one half that of Denmark, a fourth that of Norway, one fifth that of Belgium, one eighth that of France, one ninth that of Germany, and almost a tenth less than the amount of soap used in the United States.[37] In 1930, "according to statistical data" of the U.S.S.R. an appalling "almost 60 percent of schoolchildren did not use soap" and "the adult population was not much better."[38] Further, the soap and hygiene situation was due to get worse before it got better because in the Second Five-Year Plan projections, bureaucrats slashed the retail target for soap, as for books, clothes and household goods.[39]

In desperation, soap producers experimented with all manner of new ingredients. To offset the shortage of fats, in the fall of 1930, the Azerbaijan Chemical trust—Azkhimtrest—investigated the use of acids connected with the oil industry and also a special clay—"*giliaba.*"[40] By the summer of 1931, according to an English-language account, "[D]uring the civil war and intervention, a number of Russian factories used washing clays in the preparation of soap" but this "was regarded as a necessary evil...only of a temporary nature....Now however, the

Soviet government has ordered that 'mineral filler' be used in the manufacture of soap" and there were "already positive results in the use of clay for this purpose."[41] In December 1930 "a factory for the manufacture of resin soap directly from pine tar was opened at the Plesetzkaya Station in the Archangelsk [sic] region." The factory was slated to produce 1,700 tons of resin soap and turpentine. The following month, in a further attempt to alleviate the desperate soap situation, a "petroleum soap factory was opened in Tuapse in the Black Sea," which "was scheduled to produce 1,000 tons of soap" in 1931.[42]

Loss of Iodine Production Facilities

Loss of the trust's capacity to produce iodine, meager to begin with, caused further sourcing headaches. Iodine was an important disinfectant and antiseptic and also crucial to preventing goiter and mental deterioration.[43] As noted in earlier chapters, the Soviet Union had no ready supply of iodine because the alkaloid content of seaweed in the Union's oceans and lakes was too low to satisfy the national pharmacopoeia. Gosmedtorgprom was fortunate to have a small iodine production facility in Baku. But in the 1927-1928 operating year, the Caucasian Office of Gosmedtorgprom in Baku was "liquidated." The industry's "Experimental Iodine Factory" was transformed into an "Experimental Iodine Station, having exclusively experimental-research tasks."[44] Putting iodine production entirely under the chemical industry, Glavkhim, in the jurisdiction of Vesenkha at the highest level but more immediately under a separate *glavk*, complicated sourcing for the pharmaceutical industry but did not increase output of iodine.

Glavkhim did make strenuous attempts to obtain iodine during the First Five-Year Plan. Feasibility studies were conducted in several areas. Estimating that there were 600,000 tons of seaweed near Vladivostok, it was determined that a facility would be built there to produce 22,000 tons of iodine per year.[45] Attempts to derive iodine from seaweed near Arkhangel'sk, in the White Sea, were renewed.[46] The Iodine Commission of the Chemical Industry "[R]equested 2 million rubles from government coffers to develop both facilities."[47]

Iodine production foundered, however. This was one item the Soviet Union simply could not produce. In the 1920s worldwide use of iodine, annually, amounted to about 900 tons. The United States used 30 percent or 270 to 300 tons. Imperial Russia had used 100 to 120 tons per year before World War I. Soviet pharmaceutical executives estimated that Soviet Russia would need 200 tons in the First Five Year Plan and up to 360 tons in the Second Five Year Plan.[48]

In 1930 a "Committee on the 'Chemicalization' of the Country," "familiar with the results of the Experimental Iodine Manufactory" in Baku, recognized the "necessity to go forward without delay with a proposed iodine factory using industrial installation." It was hoped that the factory, which had been planned by two young chemists, Kortin and Popov, would be operational in 1931. Industry specialists were proud that "some foreign firms, who offered their patents for extracting iodine to the U.S.S.R., now want the Soviet patent for extracting iodine from oil drilling waters (*burovykh vod*)."[49] Iodine was extracted from the oily waters near Baku, but it also was suggested in 1930 that an operation in the Crimean Peninsula that had produced Borax, boric acid and tiny amounts of iodine be reopened. This manufactory had been developed during the First World War and continued until 1926. Since this was a small-scale *kustar'* operation, it had been considered unprofitable and, thus, had been closed in 1926.[50]

At the beginning of 1931 an iodine facility was begun on the Surakhansko-Ramaninskaia ditch three kilometers from the village of Surakhana in Azerbaijan. A second facility was established at Nefte-Chal in the Baku region, using the "method of absorption of iodine with activated coal." A third was built on the island of Cheleken in Turkmenestan, a fourth in Berikaia in Dagestan, and a fifth in the Arkhangel'sk region. The last also extracted iodine from oily waters.[51]

Nevertheless, during the First Five-Year Plan total production of iodine was only about 60 metric tons or less than one-third of the amount needed. In 1929/1930 the White Sea Iodine artel produced only 5,000 kilograms or about 5 metric tons of iodine.[52] In 1930 in the north and far east only 450 kilograms of iodine were obtained from seaweed. In 1931, 4,603 kilograms were produced and in the first eight months of 1932, 6,411 kilograms. Attempts to obtain iodine from oil drilling waters were more successful. In 1931 this method produced 17,341 kilograms or about 18 metric tons. In the first eight months of 1932, it resulted in 26,797 kilograms or about 27 metric tons being produced. Other methods were being investigated. In the Food Institute in Moscow the use of sea cabbage was being considered. In the Ukraine the use of Black Sea "Red Phylophora" was being studied, as during World War I. The use of seaweed in the White Sea also continued to be investigated.[53] But, in

1932, at the close of the First Five-Year Plan, there still was an "extreme deficit" (*sil'noi defitsitnosti*) of iodine.[54]

Other Divestitures

The government's decision to transfer the preparation and export of medicinal botanicals from Gosmedtorgprom to Gostorg, the State Trading Agency, in 1927-1928, further increased the pharmaceutical industry's sourcing woes, since many medicaments were based on botanicals. This decision also further diminished the trust's revenue. At the same time, some retail operations—"drug stores" (or sanitary-hygiene stores, in Soviet parlance)—were transferred from Gosmedtorgprom to one of the main state department stores or "Univermags," GUM, and other retailers.[55] In sum, divestitures were intended to render Gosmedtorgprom leaner functionally but they contributed to the trust's financial tautness.

Reagents

Access to reagents, indispensable to production of pharmaceuticals, was absolutely inadequate. In contrast to production of soap, iodine and botanicals, this problem resulted not from entrusting production to a monopoly, but from the multiplicity of agencies involved and from periodic but ineffective reorganization of the sector. In 1928 twenty-seven enterprises produced chemical reagents. Distribution of reagents was mainly done by Gosmedtorgprom and the Moscow Pharmacy Association. Ukrainian pharmacy officials complained that this caused "severe interruptions of deliveries, lasting for months, of basic materials like sodium chloride, benzoic acid, chloroform, kollargol (a disinfectant), and cocaine" and advocated localized production. Gosmedtorgprom executives insisted, instead, that Ukrainian factories take over production for the entire Soviet Union. They also proposed that they be given charge of reagents. In 1930, countering both these proposals, Vesenkha stipulated that Goslaborsnab (State Laboratory Supply) in its Chemical Sector, Glavkhimprom, produce reagents and laboratory equipment. Ukrainian pharmacists complained that this made the reagent situation worse, but to no avail.[56] Reorganization, indeed, did accentuate the shortages of reagents. In 1930, there were approximately 2,000 unfilled orders for chemical reagents. In desperation, Gosmedtorgprom devolved responsibility for supplying reagents to *oblast'* pharmacy administrations, creating twenty-one representatives with twenty-seven warehouses. However, the hapless local administrations could not give enough attention to reagents and some administrations refused to even try to supply them. Thus reagents were *defitsinye* and the quality and quantity of reagents remained unsatisfactory in 1931[57]

Shortages of Ancillary Items

Shortage of medical, surgical, and pharmaceutical instruments and equipment further hampered pharmaceutical production. This was partly a legacy from the NEP and in fact from Imperial Russia, but as in the case of reagents, splintering production compounded the problem. It was not that effort and monies were not expended. In March, 1928, *Izvestiia* announced that the "Droozhnaya Gorka" [sic] plant in Moscow had "succeeded in producing glass for thermometers" and laboratory supplies. "Fourteen foreign specialists" had "been engaged to organize the new production and teach the Russian workmen." Fifty thousand thermometers were to be put on the market in 1928.[58] On the heels of this the paper asserted that "in order to satisfy the Russian demand for thermometers" a factory had been opened in Leningrad. The Leningrad factory had manufactured its "first lot of thermometers, which had been tested and judged fit for use." The thermometers of the Moscow factory were in the process of being "tested in the Bureau of Weights and Measures." It now was claimed that the two factories were to produce "100,000 thermometers up to Jan. 1, 1929."[59]

Nevertheless, production of medical and surgical instruments remained inefficient, divided as it was among six different entities and authorities. The Department of Medical Equipment in Gosmedtorgprom sold 13 million rubles' worth in 1929; the Trust, State Laboratory Supply (Goslaborsnabzhenie), sold 18 million rubles' worth; the Trust REMA produced 1.5 million rubles' worth of x-ray equipment and electromedical apparatus; the factory Metron in the Moscow Trust of Exact Mechanics produced medical furniture and lab equipment amounting to 2.5 million rubles in sales; the factory of medical preparations in Leningrad produced surgical equipment worth 7 million rubles; and two factories in the Pavlov-Murom Metal Trust produced surgical instruments worth 1.5 million rubles. Soviet industry analysts admitted that because production was splintered, there was "no overall plan" and "prices were high."[60] But no changes were made to rectify the situation.

In 1930 two-thirds of specialized surgical equipment used in the Soviet Union, almost all thermometers, one-third of dental equipment, two-thirds of disinfecting apparatus, two-thirds of laboratory equipment excluding microscopes, two-thirds of x-ray equipment, and about one-half of electrical physical-therapy equipment were imported. However, Soviet authorities disguised this fact by trotting out data on declining imports of medical equipment, as discussed below. They implied that most general surgical equipment and instruments, operating room furniture, general medical equipment with the exclusion of thermometers, eyeglasses, items of general care for the sick such as glass, prostheses, and almost all microscopes used in the Soviet Union, were produced domestically.[61]

Finally, shortages in the glass and cardboard packaging industries held up distribution of pharmaceuticals that were produced in adequate amounts. Whether these deficits were due to cuts in investment, cuts in imports, excessive importing, or economic dysfunction is hard to tell. For example, complex, standardized tablets of codeine and terpin hydrate, codeine with sugar, and salol were rolling off the assembly line in 1931. But these products could not be distributed because of shortages of glass ampules.[62]

Limits on Imports and Excessive Exports

Thus it is clear that an inefficient macro economy and counterproductive decisions by high officials hampered the pharmaceutical industry more than insufficient investment. And among those inhospitable decisions were continued limits on imports and aggressive exporting. Import limits were no more severe than in preceding decades. But during the First Five-Year Plan, a new problem was *exports* of vast quantities of botanicals and chemicals that the industry (and the populace) needed. Excessive exports especially throttled production of pharmaceuticals.

Import reductions were justified financially. From 1921 to 1928 imports far exceeded exports, amounting to some 5 million rubles whereas exports brought in only about 900,000 rubles. Additionally, during the 1927/28 operating year, 86,000 rubles' worth of foreign equipment, purchased in 1926/1927 was installed in the Salicylate Factory and 8,000 rubles' worth was installed in the Karpov—the former Ferrein—Factory.[63]

Moreover, the amounts of imports climbed and cost more in 1927/1928 than in 1926/1927. Raw materials accounted for about one-fourth of pharmaceutical imports—some one and a quarter million rubles' worth in the operating year 1927/1928—twice as much as in the previous year. The same was true for medical instruments. Iodine accounted for over 36 percent of imports—over one million, eight hundred thousand rubles' worth—about half a million rubles more than in the previous year. Quinine at 24 percent of imports cost over seven hundred thousand rubles—almost double the cost of the previous year. Packaged medicines amounted to only about 12 percent of imports and were the only category that went down in cost compared to the previous year. But medical instruments and equipment, although they amounted to only a fraction over 2 percent, were a quarter again as costly in 1927/1928 as in the previous year.[64]

Added to the cost was that some of the imported items were found to be defective upon arrival, necessitating contracts with other foreign firms. Nevertheless, imported equipment remained crucial to the Soviet pharmaceutical industry, for enameling apparatus, Frederking apparatus, aluminum and ebonite centrifuges, vacuum-drying and tablet machines were not produced domestically.[65]

So, although import cuts made sense from a financial viewpoint, they made no sense from a medical viewpoint. Without adequate raw materials and equipment, pharmaceutical production would be impeded. And some imported raw materials, which were the mainstay of therapies at that time, were unlikely ever to be produced in the Soviet Union or could only be produced in small amounts, because of climatic and geological reasons. With upgraded equipment and improved research and development there was a possibility that the industry could, in due time, synthesize some of these products and also manufacture other medicines and medical equipment heretofore imported. However, these developments could not take place immediately. Thus, for the time being, the pharmaceutical industry had no alternative but to source abroad.

Indeed, some American manufacturers assumed the Soviet Union was a likely market for foreign pharmaceuticals as well as equipment and were eager to get a piece of the action. James Somerville, an official in the United States Department of Commerce, had his doubts, though.

He cautioned Frank Messenger, the American Assistant Trade Commissioner in London, for example, to verify Russian sources before assuming that the Soviet government would be importing "25,000 tons of soap."[66]

His intuition was correct, for despite the need for pharmaceutical imports, in order to conserve national capital for the expansion of heavy industry, many pharmaceutical imports were eliminated, including drastically needed items, such as quinine, iodine and bismuth. Imports of quinine were cut in 1928, leading to prohibitions on over-the-counter dispensing of quinine.[67] In 1931, imports of iodine, on which it was asserted that 1.5 to 2 million gold rubles had heretofore been spent, were stopped, as were imports of bismuth and some other products.[68] Bismuth was among the crucial raw materials in short supply in 1930. In 1929, a government Circular, no. 246/64, "About Discontinuing Procurement of Some Imported Preparations" listed thirty-six items which could no longer be imported, necessitating the Commissariat of Health of the Russian Republic to suggest replacements for some. None of the items appeared to be as critical as quinine, iodine, or bismuth. Nevertheless, fifteen of them simply were no longer imported.[69]

Stores on hand prevented completely empty pharmacy shelves. For example, in January 1928, a leading industry journal noted that "In Gosmedtorgprom there was a large store of foreign tablets of Pantopon (La Roche) imported long ago...Our tablets would be cheaper. But the large stores on hand...guarantee wide distribution...[at a] lowered price." On the other hand, the small amounts of Novocaine and the barbiturate, Liuminal, received from abroad "long ago" had been sent out to local pharmacy administrations. New shipments of gelatin capsules for Phytin had not arrived from abroad, although Phytin was being dispensed in tablet form.[70] Similarly, in the Ukraine, the warehouses of the—as yet—autonomous Ukrainian Medical Sales Agency (Ukrmedtorg) still contained insulin from Merck and dental wares from abroad, which were distributed without limitations. Some thirty to fifty items, though, which had arrived in Ukrainian warehouses in November 1927, were "being distributed to local Pharmacy Administrations by 'coefficients' [i.e. rationing] devised by the Ukrainian Commissariat of Health." All quinine was being distributed—directly [i. e., rationed]—by the Sanitary Epidemic Department of the Commissariat of Health. Cocaine was produced inside the USSR but insufficiently and thus, "although it was uncertain" might have to be "brought in from abroad."[71]

Imports of medical instruments as a percentage of all pharmaceutical imports declined during the NEP and continued to decline during the First Five Year Plan. Amounting to 61 percent of pharmaceutical imports in 1924/1925, medical instruments fell to 24 percent in 1926-1927, to 21 percent in 1927-1928, and to 15 percent in 1928-1929.[72] But domestic production did not compensate, as noted above.

The Soviet government's import policies were, thus, antithetical to those of the Tsarist government, which, according to Paul Gregory, encouraged imports for revenue,[73] helping consumers but providing unwelcome competition for the pharmaceutical industry. For example in 1904 German pharmaceuticals were imported at low customs rates.[74] The Soviet practice of *limiting* imports hurt both the core pharmaceutical industry and consumers.

Aggressive exporting. Just as grain exports worsened food supply during the First Five-Year Plan, zealous exporting of botanicals and chemicals affected output of pharmaceuticals. In theory, exporting medicinal botanicals was dealing from Russia's strength. Russia had been a major exporter of botanicals in the Imperial period and the industry looked upon exports as a means of acquiring revenue during the NEP, in fact, going to all lengths to improve the quality of Russian exports.[75] But during the First Five-Year Plan excessive exporting threw domestic production out of kilter.

Aggressive exporting began sensibly enough, as a response to the volatility of the international drug market. The escalating cost of imports combined with decreasing orders and declining prices for Russian pharmaceutical exports were eroding national finances.[76] In 1927/1928 pharmaceutical industry reports lamented that whereas imports totaled over five million rubles, exports of botanicals amounted to only a little more than a half million rubles and exports of finished products amounted to a paltry 124,000 rubles. Further, trading partners had shifted. Germany, the United States, England and France had been the main buyers of medicinal plant products during the second half of the NEP. Now, exports to the West had "met a whole range of difficulties, import duties, prices, and various formalities for importing products to other countries." The fact that "eastern countries, chiefly Persia" were the main buyers of Soviet prepared pharmaceuticals testified to the fact that the USSR could not compete on the world market. [77]

To compensate, Soviet officials pushed exports more vigorously, particularly the most lucrative botanicals. In 1928, following efforts at standardization, they hired one "Dr. P. J. O'Connor...a graduate of the

University of London," who had "pursued graduate work in German universities, and for the past five years been engaged in an exhaustive research in the growing of *Artemesia cina* (Berger), the manufacture of santonin, and its application as a vermifuge," as "scientific administrator." Meanwhile, Amtorg, the Soviet trade agency (and conduit for monies to the American Communist Party) appointed Gane and Ingram, Inc. of New York, "sole sales agent for santonin within the United States."[78]

In 1929-1930, the Soviet Union claimed to have exported a little over 16,000 tons of medicinal botanicals, bringing in some 5.5 million rubles.[79] Licorice root or *Solodkovyi koren'*, an export staple in the Tsarist period, amounted to well over half—slightly more than 10,000 tons—of the total. Although revenues from exports appeared to be about equal to expenditures for imports, industry executives were not entirely satisfied with these results. The plan for exports of licorice were said to have been fulfilled only 69 percent; a dry and prolonged winter hurt the crop and also affected mint, mint oil, and some other plant materials. Exports of another staple, *sporyn' ia* , were stymied because of surplus stores of this item abroad. As for lycopodium or club moss, "[I]n conjunction with industrialization and growth of the steel and copper industry, demand for *likopodii* had strongly risen in the USSR so that the amount for export diminished." Of course the Great Depression was on in 1930 and Soviet pharmaceutical managers bemoaned "lower international prices." The poor quality of Soviet medicinal plant exports, incomplete and late shipments due to steamship schedules, a lack of specialists, and foreign competition also contributed to poor export performance.[80]

This stimulated a lavish advertising campaign with hyperbole every bit equal to American advertising agencies. A brochure in English, German and French, from the early 1930s, gushed that "[T]he vast territory of the USSR, extending from the Arctic regions all the way down to the subtropic south has an immensely rich and diversified flora. Some of the most valuable of these plants are the medicinal and technical herbs, both wild and cultivated," including those yielding "essential oils," which "are gathered in large quantities." The brochure stressed both the gigantic and the scientific aspect of the preparation of raw botanical materials, the products made from them and the biologicals that the Soviet Union exported. "[T]wenty-two state farms or sovkhozes…in different parts of the Union…with "an aggregate cultivated area of 23,875 hectares" grew the plants. "Factories" then transformed them into pharmaceuticals. "Factories" in "Uralsk and Ujar, the latter in the Transcaucasus" prepared licorice root. Factories "in the towns of Priluki and Zhuravka" manufactured "peppermint oil." Factories "in Batum, Chavka, and Khoni" manufactured "geranium oil." "Muscat-sage, lavender and other essential oils" were manufactured "in Simferopol, Zuja, and Gurzuf." "Urgut, Central Asia," worked up "various raw materials." "Port warehouses for reworking, grading and packing raw materials" existed in Leningrad, Odessa, Novorossiisk, Batum, Poti, Vladivostok, and Baku. "Several Scientific Research Institutes and Stations for Experimental Agronomy" solved "problems connected with perfecting the cultivation, storage and preparation of all products, and the testing of new varieties which might be added to the list." The "USSR LEKTECHSYRIO CORPORATION" supervised all these activities.[81]

Ninety-one botanicals were touted for export. Among them were not only traditional Russian staples like Santonin, santonica seeds and Lycopodium seeds (despite need of the latter in the USSR) but also items which had not been big sellers during the NEP, such as the leaves of Belladonna and Foxglove, and items the Soviet Union had itself imported until recently. The last included "crude opium in cakes" and "alkaloids of opium (codeine and its salts, morphine, ethylomorphine, diacetylomorphine, papaverine, etc.)." Additionally, 70 "medicinal preparations from the factories of VOCHIMPHARM [sic] (formerly Gosmedtorgprom)" were touted, especially "Soviet biologicals," such as "crude endocrins, cold-stored or dried...of the ovaries, hypophysis, testicles, and the thyroid, parathyroid, pancreatic, and suprarenal glands...Spermocrin, Ovaricrin, Mammocrin, Prephysocrin, Pituicrin, Insulincrin, etc." and "bacteriological serums and vaccines."[82]

According to Russian pharmaceutical journals (hence the difference in spelling), these biologicals had been developed in 1929 by the Institute of Experimental Endocrinology in Moscow, then under the jurisdiction of the Commissariat of Health. "[S]upplied with first class quality raw materials, foreign apparatus, animals on which to test products, and specialist professors," these "*lege artis* preparations" not only were "standardized...but clinically tested" and "by their quality" were "not surpassed by the preparations of the best European and American firms." They also were "significantly cheaper" than foreign preparations. Three dealt with sexual dysfunction. Ovarikrin, in flagons, ampules, tablets, and powders, was a female sex hormone to treat "hypoovarism." Spermikrin, in flagons and ampules, was a sperm extract to treat sexual neurasthenia, senility, weakness, and anemia. Okhikrin, in flagons, ampules, tablets and powders was intended to treat sexual insufficiency, sexual impotency, senility, and hypertension. Pituikrin "P" in flagons and ampules was intended to help women during childbirth and Mammokrin in tablets and powder was to help nursing mothers unable to produce enough milk. Pituikrin "A" in ampules, tablets, and powder was designed for growth problems. Other biologicals included Tireokrin and Antitireokrin, designated for hypothyroidism and hyperthyroidism, respectively; adrenalin in flagons and ampules, to treat falling blood pressure; and insulin in ampules for diabetics. Pankreon, "an improvement on Pancreatin" because, made from "the pancreas of horned cattle or swine," as was the latter, "combined with tannin" it "had less activity on digestive juices" had been patented and was being produced in the Semashko [former Keler] Factory.[83]

Foreign buyers were reminded that the Soviet Union sold time-honored remedies that could not be procured elsewhere, such as Naftalan ointment, "made from a concentrated naphtha oil possessing valuable curative properties and found only in Soviet Azerbaijan in the Transcaucasus"; "bulbs"; "spirits of hartshorn"; "Gum tragacanth"; "Laminaria Japonica and philiphora [sic]"; "Catgut"; and "Tibetan medicines such as musk, jen-sheng, and ospenis of the pinniped." [84]

Fig. 10.1 Left to right, "Drying in the Leningrad Export Base with Caloric Heater"; "Sorting Botanicals sent from Bunkers into Sacks";.F. Satsyperov & I. Murav'ev, *Za kachestvo eksportnogo, lekarstvenno-tekhnicheskogo syr'ia* (Moscow, 1933) pp. 38, 43.

Рис. 2. Сушилка на Ленинградской экспортной базе с калориферным обогревателем

Рис. 5. Отсортированное лектехсырье (зерновые товары) ссыпаются из бункеров в мешки

Fig. 10.2 Clockwise from top left, "Forms of Ukranian Bales"; "Lycopodium in a Paper Package"; "Sea Tonnage of Bark of Buckthorn, in Packages and Kilos," Satsyperov and Murav'ev, ibid, pp. 60,65,and 63.

Рис. 10. Образцы украинского тюка

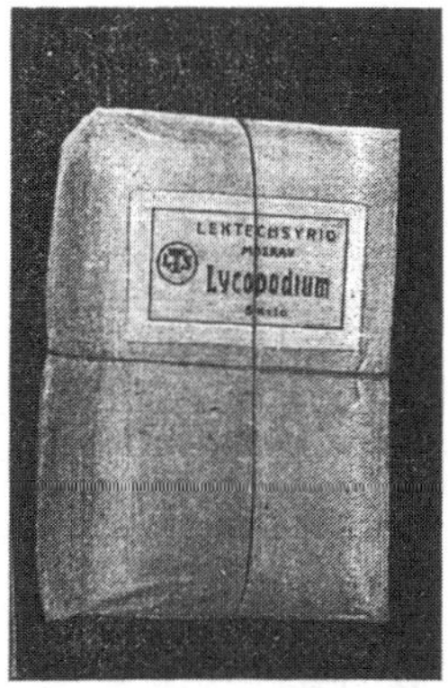

Рис. 16. Упакованный в бумажный пакет ликоподий

Рис. 13. Экономия в морском тоннаже при упаковке крушины в кипы

But, in contrast to the NEP period, during the First Five-Year Plan period, chemicals, prepared drugs, and surgical items also were listed for export. These included salicylic acid, terpin hydrate, barium for x-rays, Adonilen, Adrenalin, Gitalen, benzoic natron, and the antivenereal Novarsenol.[85] An English-language pamphlet supplied photographs of manufacturing and testimonials from physicians to persuade buyers that "every strand" of "Soviet Catgut," made from sheep casings was superlative and "guaranteed."[86] Another nine-page brochure, in English and handsomely illustrated, touted "Soviet Chemicals." Fourteen salts, acids and other "Basic Chemicals" were available for export, including sodium sulfide, bleaching powder, caustic potash, and calcium carbide. Coal tar products included pitch, naphthalene, benzene, solvent naphtha, and anthracene. Naval stores included gum spirits of turpentine, wood turpentine, "Wood Tar from Minsk and Arkhangel'sk," and acetic acid. Six products of the Aniline Dye Industry were listed. "Pitch Coke" for electrodes was noted.[87]

Fig. 10.3 Left to Right, *Russian Catgut; Every Strand Guaranteed* (Moscow, n.d.), p. 7; *Chemical Goods* (Moscow, n.d.), p. 4

Twisting the Strands mechanically

The following table shows the comparative strength of Russian catgut and foreign makes:

	000	00	0	1	2	3	4	5	6
Per Price-List of Brown & Co.	1.5	2.0	2.9	4.2	6.0	8.3	11.0	13.0	—
Tested sample of foreign make	1.4	2.2	2.1	3.6	4.9	6.0	8.9	—	—
Russian Catgut	1.5	2.1	2.6	3.9	5.9	6.5	9.8	13.2	—

Calcium carbide packed in iron drums enclosed in plywood drums

The naive reader would have been impressed by how far the Soviet pharmaceutical industry had come. Unfortunately, as we shall see, in the Soviet Union there were severe shortages of the items being pitched. The naive reader also would probably not have been aware that the foreign sales branches for pharmaceutical items—Arcos in London and Amtorg in New York, whose addresses were duly provided, along with that of the Plants Trust—were Communist-front organizations, designed to channel funds to Communist parties abroad, including the American Communist Party.[88]

For, although there were no diplomatic relations between the United States and the Soviet Union until 1933, as during the NEP, Americans bought Soviet pharmaceuticals. Imports of miscellaneous crude drugs from Russia to the United States, excluding licorice, amounted to $58,000 in 1931 and $51,000 in 1932.[89] The United States imported a whopping 85 percent of Soviet licorice in 1929, and also peppermint oil, oil of lime, oil of coriander, and ergot.[90] According to one source, Soviet exports of Santonin averaged 9,000 kilograms during 1929 and 1930, the United States importing annually 750 kilograms or 1,650 pounds.[91] According to another source the United States imported an average of 1,300 pounds of

Santonin annually during the 1920s and early 1930s. Carroll, County, Maryland wormseed, successfully grown around Quincy, Illinois, as noted in Chapter 5, and cultivation of "santonica (Levant wormseed)" in 1929, may have helped reduce American imports of Soviet Santonin to 261 pounds in 1932. However, in 1933, they leapt back to over 1,800 pounds in 1933.[92] In January 1931, the United States also purchased 806 pounds—and possibly more—of acetyl salicylic acid, the basis for aspirin, from the Soviet Union.[93] The Soviet Union purchased Methanol and Formaldehyde from the United States.[94] But that did not make up for exports that shorted the domestic industry.

The 1930s "Lektechsyrio" brochure for foreign consumption claimed that the botanicals and biologicals it promoted served the domestic as well as the foreign market. But behind the scenes, there was evidence of shortages of botanicals, biologicals, chemicals and prepared medicines for domestic use. In general, the availability of pharmaceuticals on the wholesale and retail market did not keep pace with the profusion of prototypes the industry unveiled. Despite advertising hype many items were not available for domestic purchase or were available in some markets but not in others. Reasons varied. Shortages of some botanicals were due to bad weather. Lack of raw materials from domestic suppliers and cuts in imports impeded production of pharmaceuticals in other cases. In still other cases, shortages of containers, capsules and glass held up distribution of pharmaceuticals that were produced in sufficiency. For example, lack of formalin impeded manufacture of urotropin.[95] "Fitin" was touted in February 1927 as an important new product of Gosmedtorgprom.[96] In 1928, however, "absence of gelatin capsules from abroad" held up the dispensing of phytin in capsules although the industry did distribute phytin in tablet form.[97]

But, for shortages of some items, no explanation was provided.[98] Thus, it is quite likely that just as exports of grain contributed to shortages of grain in the Soviet Union in the early 1930s so too exports of raw materials, chemicals, prepared medicines and biologicals diminished the amount of these items on the domestic market.

For example, in the Ukraine in 1928, supplies of adrenaline were sufficient but pharmacy administrations were urged to conserve for it was rumored that supplies would be "interrupted" in the near future. Moreover, "narcotic chloroform, cocaine, narcotic ether, benzoic acid natron, the anti-syphilitic Novosal'varsan, terpinhydrate, and a whole range of other items were *defitsitnye* (deficit)."[99] A 1927 report detailing production in the factories of Gosmedtorgprom had trumpeted production of 15,000 kilograms of terpin-hydrate and 30,000 kilograms of narcotic chloroform.[100] What had gone wrong in one year? Perhaps these items were being withheld from the Ukraine because of pique on the part of Moscow-based Gosmedtorgprom. After all, Moscow unleashed a purge of Communist Party elites in the Ukraine in the late 1920s and collectivization took a great toll in the Ukraine. Further support for the conspiracy theory was the fact that in the Russian Republic both pure and narcotic chloroform, which Semashko had begun to produce in conjunction with a factory in the Chemical Trust, were dispensed "without interruption" in 1928 "within the limits of the full requirement for them."[101]

But, additionally, "Terpin hydrate." [sic] as well as "Adrenalin" [sic] were being pushed for export to gain foreign currency. Thus, a likely hypothesis for the shortages of these items was that excessive exports were to blame.[102] Similarly, supplies of bromine and iodine, which had increased in the first half of the production year 1928/1929, were limited. The reason put forth was "saturation of the market." Yet, "bromine isovalerianyl carbomid" was pushed for export in 1930.[103]

Only eight preparations could be dispensed without limitation in 1929/1930. These included the hormone preparations Ovarin, Spermine, and Vasogen; acetic acid, camphor, and two new preparations: Bismoverol, a bismuth preparation to treat syphilis, and Laktan, a protein-based product (a colloidal of "milk para nuclei co albumin-VK").[104]

At the same time, more than sixty-three very basic medical products were in short supply or unavailable on the retail market. Aspirin was said to be in short supply because of increased demand and lack of imported febrifuges. Staples like oak bark, lycopodium, and thousand leaf (for stomach and intestinal ailments) were not dispensed in 1929/1930 due to poor harvests. But also limited in distribution in 1929 were barium sulfate for x-rays, bismuth, insulin, glucose, novosal'varsan, all opium preparations, mercury, valerian root, digitalis leaves, iron, caffeine, benzoic acid, castor oil, belladonna, and urotropin. These all were crucial health items and their scarceness was mysterious. Sulfuric acid barium for x-rays, mercury, and alkaloids of opium had been produced in large quantities. According to the 1927 report from Gosmedtorgprom, production of barium amounted to 18,000 kilograms annually, production of mercury preparations had amounted to 40,000 kilograms, and production of alkaloids of opium close to 4,000 kilograms.[105] Again, what had gone wrong in a scant two years? The only logical explanation is that aggressive exporting was the culprit. Novarsenol, sulfuric acid barium for x- rays, mercury preparations and alkaloids of opium—all were heavily advertised for export during the First Five-Year Plan. So too were *Follia belladonnae, Folia Digitalis, Semen likopodii,* and "crude opium in cakes."[106]

By the end of 1930, the pharmaceutical industry claimed that the number of preparations in sufficient supply had risen to twenty-nine, including some cardiac remedies, febrifuges, lecithin, and anti-venereals.[107] But eighteen very basic items, mainstays of the physician's arsenal in the 1920s and early 1930s, were still in short supply, including mercury, salicylic acid, opium, ammonia, silver nitrate, bismuth preparations, castor oil, and Urotropin. Once again, something was dreadfully amiss, for in the 1927 Gosmedtorgprom report, annual production of salicylic preparations had amounted to a stupendous 200,000 kilograms, nitrous oxide silver to 10,000 kilograms, and mercury and opium preparations to sizable amounts as noted above. There is the possibility that output had been exaggerated. Yet, in agreement with industry reports, Feodor Andreevich Ferrein maintained that most of the Soviet Union's need for salicylic preparations was covered by domestic production.[108] There was, however, the fact that the United States imported salicylic acid, noted above. And, curiously, although insulin was said to be in short supply in 1930, Gosmedtorgprom continued to advertise insulin produced by the Farmakon factory in Leningrad.[109]

The core pharmaceutical industry obvious faced serious challenges during the First Five-Year Plan. What were its coping mechanisms?

The Industry's Coping Strategies

Finances and Organization

As during the NEP the industry tried to buoy up its finances, overcome the fetters on it, and put out adequate amounts of pharmaceuticals through the use of traditional business strategies.

Like a conglomerate in a market-oriented economy, Gosmedtorgprom executives struggled to compensate for increased costs and diminished sales by "attracting more share capital," by "longer term credits"—bank debt, and by increasing sales. The last measure fizzled badly. Sales increased only 4.3 percent in 1928. This, coupled with the divestitures and increased outlays, meant that during the 1927/

1928 fiscal year Gosmedtorgprom suffered from "financial tension" (*finansovnoe napriazhenie*). [110]

By 1930 Gosmedtorgprom executives believed that the industry was too fragmented and needed more cohesiveness. They lobbied for acquisitions rather than divestitures for purposes of synergy. They proposed that the eighty or so large, medium, and small pharmaceutical enterprises and laboratories, under the management of local pharmacy administrations and workers coops, be knit with the six largest factories comprising Gosmedtorgprom. In particular, industry executives hoped to acquire the March 8 Bandaging Factory in Moscow, the Experimental Laboratory and Factory of Reagents in the Mining-Chemical Trust in Moscow, all factories producing iodine, bromine and nicotine, the Chimkent Chemical-Pharmaceutical Factory (the former Santonin Factory), located in the Kazakh Chemical Trust, and the Endocrinology Institute in Moscow, then housed in the Commissariat of Health.[111]

The trust acquired only one of these factories. In 1931 Gosmedtorgprom was rechristened Vokhimfarm—All Union Chemical-Pharmaceutical.[112] The Dzerzhinskii Santonin Factory was removed from the Kazakh Chemical Trust, which was "liquidated," and placed completely in the jurisdiction of Vokhimfarm.[113]

Old-Time Remedies and Botanicals

Specialists attempted to make up for shortfalls of raw materials and pharmaceuticals with a variety of measures, some bordering on the desperate. Pharmacologists dredged up old-time remedies and folk nostrums. For example, iodine shortages prompted pharmacologists to scrutinize the "home remedy Iodtannin," a mixture of a solution of tannin with a spiritous solution of iodine or a milk solution of iodine.[114] Another idea revolved around using sea cabbage, which contained iodine, as a food substance.[115] Pharmacologists re-investigated Periplotsin, derived in the 1890s from a plant *Periploca graeca L.*, as a potential substitute for digitalis and other unavailable heart medicines. In 1929, iodine shortages prompted the Ukrainian Commissariat of Health to resurrect the use of Brilliant Green, developed in 1907, as an antiseptic. Garmin, an alkaloid derived from a plant in Turkestan and known since 1848, received "wide application" in the early 1930s for treating diseases of the nervous system. It was said to be successful in combating Parkinson's disease, encephalitis, and "psychic" illnesses.[116] Thus the idea of using iodine residue to produce more of the product was resurrected. This was a complicated process that had first surfaced in 1915 during the desperate days of the Great War.[117] In the meantime, for consumers, Gosmedtorgprom urged use of a substitute product, "Bromferron," which could be acquired over the counter in "all pharmacies and *sanmagaziny* (drug stores)" as a replacement.[118]

Cultivation and collection of botanicals were not under the auspices of Gosmedtorgprom during the First Five-Year Plan. But industry pharmacologists frenetically researched plant alkaloids which could alleviate shortages of conventional pharmaceuticals. Several scientific teams set off for remote parts of the Soviet Union to locate new medicinal plants with alkaloids or active ingredients equivalent to crucial foreign varieties. The expeditions were sponsored by the Scientific-Chemical Institute and lent assistance by local institutes of plant production, such as that in Sukhum, Georgia. Researchers worked under arduous conditions, interviewing indigenous peoples and Russian migrants about medicinal uses of local plants. They gathered specimens and, back in Moscow, the plants were analyzed in the Alkaloid Department of the Scientific Chemical-Pharmaceutical Institute.[119]

Some of the plants eliciting the most excitement were *Anabasis aphylla, Leontice ewersmanii,* and *Lupinus luteus.* The last produced the alkaloid lutin and the first anabasine, which after oxidizing, gave nicotine acid. These plants had been discovered in Kazakhstan during a 1926 expedition but were being researched only in 1929. Three expeditions took place in the summer of 1930—to the Altai and Baikal regions of eastern Siberia, and to Tibet, to Issyk-kul (the famous archeological site in the Kirghiz Republic), and to the Caucasus. In 1930 fifteen plants from Central Asia were studied. Twelve contained alkaloids; two new alkaloids had been isolated. In 1931 and 1932 *Leonorus cardiaca L. (pustyrnik)* was studied. The plant had been used in seventeenth- and eighteenth-century pharmacy practice, but only for "simple" people. In 1932, at the end of the First Five-Year Plan and the beginning of the Second, there were more expeditions to the Caucasus and the Far East. The far eastern expedition traveled 1,200 kilometers and gathered eighty-two forms of raw materials, of which twenty-seven were thoroughly studied.[120]

Pharmacists and pharmacologists also pinned their hopes on more extensive cultivation of medicinal plants, asserting that cultivation of medical plants had not reached its fullest potential during the NEP.[121] In 1930, the newly established joint-stock company Lektekhsyr'e [this name being a currently favored transliteration of the Russian rather than the version chosen for the 1930s Soviet promotional brochure, cited above] investigated more systematic cultivation particularly of herbs like henbane (*belena*), stramonium or thorneapple (*durman*) and nettles (*krapiva*) with an eye for domestic use as well as export.[122] The company planned to train instructors and establish courses and even special departments focusing on medicinal botanicals in institutions of higher learning, especially pharmacy technicums.[123]

In the second half of 1930, a Russian-language publication for the industry, *Informatsionnyi biulleten'* (Information Bulletin), put out by the Corporation of Medicinal and Technical Raw Materials, Lektekhsyr'e, did confirm that cultivation of medicinal plants occurred on a large scale. State farms (*sovkhozy*) of 500 hectares in the Ukraine, 800 hectares in the middle Volga region, 3,000 hectares in the North Caucasus, and plantations in Tula and Zhitomir grew medicinal botanicals. In 1930-1931 a sovkhoz of 5,000 hectares and another of 2,000 hectares were established in the lower Volga region.[124]

The Results

Some research on botanicals yielded hoped-for results. Thirty-two new Soviet products in 1930, included Sekalen (analogous to the foreign preparation Sekakornin), a standardized preparation of *sporyn'ia* (made from parasites in roses); Frangulen (a standardized product made of buckthorn); pyrimidine, antipyrine, Phenacetin, veronal, strychnine, Hydrokhinon (a substitute for quinine) and vanillin.[125] It was claimed that some biologicals were produced in ample amounts. In 1930, for example, Gosmedtorgprom assured domestic buyers that Spermine, Mammin, "Tireoidin" [sic], Ovarin, Pituitrin, Adrenalin, and Insulin, put out by the Farmakon Factory in Leningrad, "could be asked for in all pharmacies in the USSR."[126]

A number of birth-control products, produced in the "Laboratory for the Preparation of Contraceptive Substances," located in the Department of Maternity and Minors in the Commissariat of Health were advertised in pharmacy journals in 1930: "Prekonsol'," a vaginal cream; Kontratseptin, vaginal beads made of cocoa oil; and a gelatin cylinder for "prevention of pregnancy."[127] For a "range of other products"—unspecified—developed in the Endocrine Institute, domestic buyers were informed that a "free detailed prospectus and *preis-kurant*" would be sent upon request.[128]

Nevertheless, in 1931, supplies of bromine, mercury, and bismuth were below what they had been in 1930. It was claimed that there had been "significant progress" in producing salts, ether, and chloroform; alkaloids of opium; Neosalvarsan, salicylates, digitalis, and "many other products."[129] But Phenacetin, antipyrine, pyrimidine, Veronal, and chloramine were put out in such small quantities that one analyst asserted they were "not produced in the USSR."[130]

In 1932, as officials proclaimed that the First Five-Year Plan was successfully being wound up, supplies of mercury were lower than in 1931—when only 30 percent of mercury needed was available. Supplies of camphor were inadequate. Only about 20 percent of the requirements of tartaric acid were fulfilled by the Odessa factory making this item. In 1932, thus, bromine, bismuth, barium, cocaine, quinine, and iodine still needed to be imported.[131]

Supplies of soap continued to be precarious. Earle Taylor, American Assistant Trade Commissioner in Paris reported to the Department of Commerce in Washington in 1932 that "[A]ccording to the French press, 115,653 metric tons of soap were produced in Soviet Russia during the first half of 1932." The French source commented that it was "doubtful whether" factories would "be able to carry out the program planned for the second half of 1932," because they had experienced difficulties in "obtaining supplies of raw materials. Last July, stock...were so low that most of the factories had to stop operation." On the other hand, the French account conceded that, if the data were accurate, soap production had increased 78.2 percent over the previous year's production.[132] This progress notwithstanding, the sobering fact remains that soap production was lower at the end of the First Five-Year Plan than during the NEP and below the 180,000 tons available on the eve of World War I.[133]

Conclusions

The main problem with which the industry had to reckon during the First Five-Year Plan was excessive exports of raw materials it needed. Otherwise, the environment in which the industry had to operate was pretty much the same as during the preceding NEP. During the First Five-Year Plan as earlier lack of autonomy was the main factor thwarting the industry.

Shortages of soap, disinfectants and antivenereals must have contributed to the spread of infectious diseases. Shortages of anesthetics, opiates, barium for x-rays might well have impacted the spike in mortality rates in the late twenties and early thirties. Certainly shortages of basics like aspirin increased the misery of the Soviet people. Of course, pharmaceutical firms in capitalist countries—Glaxo and Schering, for example—also were buffeted by external factors and made errors in policy decisions.[134] But because the Soviet pharmaceutical industry was so concentrated, its failures and policy errors on the part of government officials had much broader and deeper effect both on the industry and on Russia. Hopefully, matters would improve during the Second Five-Year Plan.

11
Keeping Up with the Competition During the Second Five-Year Plan

The Second Five-Year Plan (1932-1937) coincided with momentous developments in the pharmacy world at large. In the early 1930s, German scientists synthesized an antimalarial, Plasmochin. Malaria was one of the Soviet Union's chief communicable diseases. In 1935, the first bactericide sulfa drug appeared, the result of the discovery of Gerhard Domagk, director of research in the experimental pathology laboratory at the Bayer pharmaceutical firm in Germany, that Prontosil, "a red azo dye," prevented bacteria from using the *p*-aminobenzoic acid and was particularly effective against streptococcal and staphylococcal infections. Prontosil earned Domagk the Nobel Prize in 1939, a worthy award indeed, for sulfa drugs resulted in a precipitous drop in mortality, particularly among children, and remained important in underdeveloped countries despite newer antibiotics.[1] At about the same time, American scientists developed a method of mass-producing penicillin. The antibiotic properties of penicillin had been noted by Alexander Fleming in 1928. James Currie at the United States Department of Agriculture had been investigating molds since 1916, however. Key to mass producing penicillin were the discoveries he made at Charles Pfizer and Company "for mass-producing gluconic acid using mold fermentation."[2] In 1935, USDA scientists patented "a 'submerged' fermentation process in which a mold was grown throughout the medium." Rotary fermenters using aluminum aided the process. In 1936, the fermenters were installed at a USDA lab in Ames Iowa and two years later they were moved to a lab in Peoria, Illinois, "where they were used to test submerged growth of various *Penicillium* strains." In 1937, Andrew Moyer, a scientist in the Midwestern Department of Agriculture laboratories hit upon the use of corn steep liquor "as a component in the growth medium" of *Penicillium.* This medium "became the major component of all *Penicillium* growth media."[3] This achievement came about, according to Peter Neushul, as a result of cooperation between the American government, specifically the Department of Agriculture, and private industry, specifically Pfizer, Squibb and Merck—although there was some infighting.[4]

In the Soviet Union, meanwhile, the new 1936 Constitution proclaimed a generous social safety-net, including medical care for all "working people."[5] Soviet statistics trumpeted a threefold increase in medical personnel over the pre-revolutionary period; a tripling of general hospital beds; an almost fourfold increase in sanatoria and health resorts; campaigns against key infectious diseases; "instruction in nutrition and child hygiene" and "promotion of scientific interests." These developments "provided the basis," according to League of Nations demographer Frank Lorimer, "for notable advances in the health of the Soviet population."[6] But "basis" did not equal "fait accompli" and there was less cooperation between the Soviet government and pharmaceutical industry than the American government and industry. Thus, by the end of the Second Five-Year Plan and the second anniversary of the founding of the Soviet state, could the Soviet industry fulfill the promises of the new Constitution and match, even supersede, the pharmaceutical achievements of capitalist states?

Prognoses for the Industry from the Inside

Theoretically, the industry was favorably positioned to serve the Soviet people and compete with foreign houses. As a state-run conglomerate, supplying half the pharmaceuticals used in the Soviet Union, the core Soviet pharmaceutical industry possessed both economies of scale and the synergies needed to successfully bring drugs from the laboratory downstream. In 1931 the core industry, named Gosmedtorgprom since 1924, had been rechristened Vokhimfarm—the "All-Union Chemical-Pharmaceutical" conglomerate.[7] Despite the name change, the trust, consisting of some ten enterprises and three scientific institutes, remained a joint-stock conglomerate with government shareholders. In 1937, these included Prombank—the Industrial Bank and Vneshtorgbank—the Foreign Trade Bank.[8] The trust was a multimillion ruble business. Its "Statutory Fund" had grown from 6 or 7 million rubles in the 1920s to over 49 and a half million rubles in March 1936, in terms of 1926/1927 prices. Production for the period January 1 to March 1, 1936, was valued at about 11 and a half million rubles.[9]

At the outset of the Second Five-Year Plan, however, industry insiders gave mixed prognoses as to whether the industry was up to the job. Soap production continued to be parlous. However, the pharmaceutical industry was no longer responsible for this item.[10] S. I. Maimind was bullish on what the industry could produce. He admitted there had been a slump during the First Five-Year Plan. But he insisted the industry had begun to turn around in by 1932 and predicted further upsurge in 1933. The Karpov (former Ferrein) Factory had begun to produce oxalic acid and other reagents. The Phenacetin shop in the Farmakon Factory was grinding into action and the Semashko (former Keler) Factory was producing more sulfuric acid. Production of hydrastine (a hemostatic which Ferrein had tried to put out), darmine oil or Darminol (a salve made from plant seeds to treat rheumatism); betanaftol, lanolin, chloreton, pepton in ampules (to combat diarrhea and dysentery), saccharin (for diabetics), Folliculin (already used in the West to treat menstrual and conception problems), and several other products were "replacing heretofore imported" items.[11]

Other basics long used in the West, such as pyramidon, phenacetin, the barbiturate Liuminal, novocaine, and "a range of endocrine preparations," were only slated for production in 1933.[12] However, in that year the Scientific Research Chemical-Pharmaceutical Institute [NIKhFI] in Moscow proclaimed that it had synthesized about forty-one medicines and prepared sixty-five other products. Research and development projects included better forms of aspirin, new ways to get iodine, two new preparations to lower blood pressure; three urea preparations; an antiparasite preparation; better forms of caffeine; new anesthetics, better surgical glue, anti-diabetic preparations, Vitamin D, chemotherapy for cancer and tuberculosis, treatment of influenza, and laxatives. The NIKhFI also investigated medicinal plants and methods of improving the production of forty-one items including Adrenalin, synthesized the previous year, and antipyrine, codeine, Novarsenol, salvarsan, Santonin, opium alkaloids, and phenacetin.[13]

Other insiders were less sanguine than Maimind. Dr. I. S. Zelikin praised new items manufactured by the industry "at the end of the First Five-Year Plan," namely "Novarsenol—for treatment of syphilis," as well as "new galenicals (diginorm, gitalen, adonilen, etc.), preparations of bismuth for x-ray (metallic bismuth still being imported)" and "prepared forms (tablets, ampules, etc.) of factory character." But he was concerned about the quality of Soviet products as well as shortages of many important preparations. "[I]t cannot be said that here in Russia (*u nas*) all is positive (*blagopoluchno*)," Dr. Zelikin admitted. The "amount of pharmaceutical wares put out and their assortment does not fully satisfy the needs of the Soviet Union, and as for quality it is not always of the highest, since some medicaments are still somewhat surpassed by the quality of foreign ones." Zelikin criticized the "insufficiency of some preparations." These included bismuth and caffeine, noted above, as well as quinine, gum-Arabic and plants imported from "America, Africa and Asia."[14]

G. Tsander, who had praised American pharmacies, couched his reservations about the Soviet pharmaceutical industry obliquely—by lauding the American pharmaceutical industry. American houses had paralleled Russian before 1918. The pharmaceutical production of both countries had lagged behind German and Swiss houses. Now the United States had leapt ahead.

Amerikanizm, according to Hans Rogger, was the epitome of entrepreneurship and economic efficiency for many Soviet Russians.[15] In 1928 Ia. Kanevskii had marveled at how American pharmaceuticals had taken over the international market: "In Great Britain the United States sold 6 ½ times more prepared medicines than the United States received from great Britain...Germany appeared a significant provider of prepared medicines in the continental markets of Europe...but American prepared medicinal substances dominated in the Western half of the world."[16] German houses were still weak in the mid-1920s, Kanevskii's reference point. However, American achievements had continued, as Tsander emphasized.

He regarded American pharmaceutical production and dispensing as a benchmark. "The demands of the USA for medicines are nearly fully covered by domestic production," he informed readers of *Khimiko-farmatsevticheskaia promyshlennost'* (*Chemical-Pharmaceutical Industry*). "Only 1.5 to 2 percent of all products used are imported," while "6 percent of production is exported abroad." In 1930, imports of prepared medicines from Italy, Germany, England, France, Japan, Switzerland, and Hong Kong amounted to 2.55 million dollars whereas exports were nearly twice that—4.13 million. The American industry prepared dye products for pharmaceutical purposes, such as phenolphthalein, brilliant green, and methyl violet. Imports of ether, chloroform and urotropin were minuscule. Only barbiturates were imported, imports of diethylbarbituric acid (veronal) in 1930 amounting to 8,618 kilograms or 19 thousand English pounds. Of alkaloids, "except for quinine, nearly all were prepared within the country."

Tsander acknowledged the impact of the Great Depression on the American pharmaceutical industry. "The general value (*stoimost'*) of pharmaceutical production in 1931 equaled 276.6 million dollars," whereas in 1929 it had amounted to "336.8 million dollars, in 1927—

292.6 million dollars, and in the period 1923-1925—245 to 255 million dollars per year." The average amount of expenditure for medicines per person also had fallen with the Great Depression from 260 dollars in 1929 to 215 dollars in 1931. Moreover, "synthetic organic medicines made from coal tar" had contracted during the Depression from 4,327 tons in 1929 to 3,402 tons in 1930. But this was not entirely negative, for imports also had fallen during the Depression. This saved the industry money and "was the reason American needs for many years, with the exclusion of some specialized products, are covered by their own production." He praised the fact that the American industry produced for the masses. Of the three thousand plus tons of medicines the industry made from coal tar, more than two-thirds consisted of commonly used medicines like aspirin and salicylic acid. The industry produced crucial organic synthetic febrifuges and anesthetics, such as acetanalide, phenacetin, pyramidon, antipyrine, "anestizin," [sic] and novocaine. It addressed the problem of venereal disease; production of the antisyphilitic, neoarsphenamine (novosal'varsan), had increased one and a half times during the 1920s. [17]

Tsander particularly admired output of "patented substances" in the United States. These were packaged, dosed, standardized medicines—not snake-oil remedies—but rather "the specialities" of their houses, which amounted to "63 percent of all production." "Biological preparations," he noted "amounted to 5.5 percent and other prepared medicines to 28 percent." The other 70 percent of medicines produced consisted of "inorganic pure preparations, synthetic organic medicines and alkaloids. The basic mass of synthetic medicines" were "sold in the form of patented substances and labeled with corresponding rubric." Aggregate expenditure for medicines per year, "according to the American Pharmaceutical Association, was 715 million dollars in retail prices, of which about 50 percent were for patented substances ('specialities'), 27 percent for medicines dispensed upon a doctor's prescription, and 23 percent for the rest."[18] This was the product mix Soviet pharmaceutical executives had been striving for. So although Tsander's evaluation of the American pharmaceutical industry was low key, readers could infer that it was in an enviable position as compared to the core Soviet industry.

Several Soviet pharmacy specialists overtly criticized the performance of their own pharmaceutical industry in the second year of the plan. In 1934, a Soviet pharmacy journal lamented the "chronic shortage (*golod*) of medicaments," a term reminiscent of World War I. The author acknowledged that in the Soviet Union the "most important preparations" were "absent from pharmacies. A whole range of preparations" had "disappeared."[19] The old Bolshevik Izrail I. Levinshtein, a loyal Soviet citizen and tireless advocate for improving pharmacy education, lambasted "The Abnormal Situation in the Pharmaceutical Business" in 1934. Although the industry had "realized achievements," he asserted, "[In 1930] growth of production stopped and a whole range of important preparations necessary for life plummeted 5 to 20 percent in comparison with former years." Levinshtein put the onus on exogenous factors: "the health agencies significantly underestimated the actual needs of the country and satisfied them to a miserable degree... a range of preparations were deficit," such as diuretin (a cardiac remedy), cocaine, and sublimate. Levinshtein railed that "since the revolution not one new pharmaceutical factory has been built" and whereas "the pharmaceutical industry requires 400 specific raw materials...the great part of our requirements for raw materials are not filled." Capacity for mercury salts was filled only 35-40 percent; ingredients for urotropin, 50 percent; and inputs for technical salicylic acid, 50 percent. Because Russia did not produce caffeine, camphor, bismuth, theobromine, cocaine and some other items, cuts in imports affected the availability of these basic items. Levinshtein also alleged that government officials deliberately slighted the industry, so that "a range of raw materials, that were produced in the USSR, were not allocated to Vokhimfarm or were allocated in insufficient amounts, such as gelatin, catgut, endocrine raw materials, turpentine oil, glycerine, opium, phenol and others." Raw materials that were available were of poor quality and ancillary materials like paper were absent, limiting packaging and preventing labels from being placed on medicines.[20] A third article published in 1934 emphasized the difficulties involved in bringing a preparation from the experimental stage in the laboratory of the Karpov (former Ferrein) Factory to mass production.[21]

Impressive Research

Who were right—the optimists or the pessimists? Soviet pharmaceutical research and development appeared progressive. In Britain, during the interwar period, chemically synthesized medicines tended to be imported or produced through licenses with foreign firms.[22] The Soviet pharmaceutical industry, meanwhile, produced products analogous to Swiss and German ones—apparently without licensing.[23] The legality of this replication will be addressed again, later in the chapter. But it emphasized that, like American firms, which in the 1930s, began to establish in-house labs and hire university pharmacologists to staff them or partnered with university scientists,[24] the Soviet pharmaceutical industry had an active R and D program.

In the Soviet Union prototypes rolled off the assembly line at dizzying speed. In 1933 cardiac substances—Adonolin (a semi-patented substance of *Adonis vernalis*), Diginorm, and Gitalen—were being put out by the factories of Vokhimfarm. So were the hemostatics Hydrastine, "Stiptisin-hydrochloric acid kotarnin," and Sekalin, as well as antisyphilitic substances, Osarsol, Biokhinol, and Bismoverol. The new organo preparation Asmolizin combined "adrenalin with pituitrin, significantly raising and increasing the therapeutic effect of adrenalin in bronchial asthma." Other organo preparations or biologicals being produced included Lipotserebrin, a sterilized emulsion of protein and fats and Timofizin, used in obstetrical practice. Garmin, made from a plant grown in Turkestan and first used in 1848, was being produced to thwart Parkinson's disease; and Etilsalitsilikum (ethyl ether and salicylic acid) was being produced to "replace deficit methyl spirits."[25]

A major breakthrough in 1933 was synthesis of "Plazmotsid, an antimalarial replacing pure quinine." Plazmotsid was made in the Dzerzhinskii Factory in Kazakhstan, but, ironically, had not been prescribed by the plan.[26] It was, however, the outcome of a crash program inaugurated by the government in 1929, to develop a synthetic because "millions were sick with malaria," and the German synthetic Plazmochin, as well as quinine, needed to be imported.[27]

A further important step in the fight against malaria was the establishment of a factory outside of Moscow dedicated to producing a synthetic antimalarial, although originally the factory was under the jurisdiction of the chemical rather than the pharmaceutical industry. In 1930 German scientists had succeeded in synthesizing Atebrin. During the next three years, two teams of Russian scientists—Z. V. Benevolenskaia, I. L. Knuniants, on the one hand, and O. Iu. Magidson, A. M. Grigorovskii, and G. V. Chelintsev, on the other, deciphered and modified the molecular code of Atebrin. The resulting product, "Akrikhin," was given high priority by the Soviet government and the Commissariat of Heavy Industry. In the spring and fall of 1934 Sovnarkom issued *postanovleniia* (resolutions) decreeing the establishment of an "Akrikhin" factory in the village of Staraia Kupavna, located about 30 kilometers outside Moscow by railroad (and 39 kilometers by highway). The new factory actually was built on the site of an older chemical and dye factory, established in the first half of the nineteenth century. But no expense was spared to make it state of the art. Over 5.5 million rubles' worth of stainless steel and ceramic equipment was imported from "the best" foreign firms (that alone testifying to the lower state of Soviet equipment). Other Russian factories—Dorogomilovskii in Moscow, Farmakon in Leningrad—were raided for the best engineers and scientists. [28]

Ivan Grigor'evich Shuvalov, the director, was a civil war Red Army veteran, who had worked his way up the administrative ladder, serving as director of other chemical factories, an inspector of the Dye Trust, Aniltrest, director of an experimental chemical-technological factory, and finally, technical director of the Chemical Construction unit, "Anilstroi." Along the way he studied at the Mendeleev Chemical Technological Institute. Shuvalov had close connections with Iu. L. Piatakov, Trotsky supporter in the 1920's, but executive in the Commisariat of Heavy Industry in the 1930's. Shuvalov pushed production of narcotic ether, salicylate preparations, and other items. The factory was a sprawling compound of five or more shops. Construction of some lagged, however. Additionally, distance from Moscow necessitated building worker quarters and other infrastructure for the over 700 workers that appeared at the site in the inaugural year, 1935, for the original chemical factory had declined since its nationalization during the civil war [29] and the surrounding settlement was comprised of modest log houses with one main street and a handful of stores. Its only notable feature was a green and white church dating back to Catherine the Great. [30]

By 1936 NIKhFI had developed a sulfa drug named Pantotsid. It would be three more years before the drug could be produced on a factory basis, however, because of shortages of equipment. The Administration of the core industry, now called Khimfarmprom, into the jurisdiction of which Akrikhin had been moved, ordered the factory to produce the drug in 1939. Unfortunately, because of "undelivered apparatus," production was transferred to the Red Star Factory in Khar'kov.[31]

Thus, if on the surface, Soviet pharmaceutical research and development deserved applause, the failure to produce Pantotsid, strongly indicated breakdown at the production and distribution ends. We have seen that Ukrainian pharmacy specialists blamed over-centralization of production facilities under the jurisdiction of *Russian* authorities, niggardly funding of factories and pharmacy associations, and cuts in imports of products and apparatus for deficits of pharmaceuticals in Ukraine. Levinshtein, spokesman for the Russian industry, also blamed lack of investment and cuts in imports. How forthright were these criticisms? More importantly, could the Soviet pharmaceutical industry fix the problems by the end of the Second Five-Year Plan and the second anniversary of the Great October Revolution?

Impediments to Implementing Research

Military Production

Preparation for war might or might not have affected the pharmaceutical industry. The Soviet Union produced biological weapons in secret facilities from the mid 1920s.[32] Secret treaties with Germany involved chemical weapons production in the same decade. Russia was involved in skirmishes in the Far East in the late 1920s and early 1930s.[33] Preparation for war heated up in the mid-1930s, as Hitler rearmed openly and forged a pact with Poland. A 1935 article in the mouthpiece of the chemical-pharmaceutical industry, *Khimiko-farmatsevtichesaia promyshlennost'* suggested that Germany and Poland were conspiring against the USSR. Articles were reprinted from the 1934 German and Polish pharmaceutical press, which discussed "chemical defense," or the role pharmacists would have to play in a potential war using chemical weapons. Soviet pharmacists were reminded that Poland had twenty-one chemical-pharmaceutical factories which could turn out chemical weapons. Polish pharmacists, the article claimed, assumed that Soviet "intellectuals were not familiar with anti-air and anti-gas defense."[34]

In the fall of 1935, a leading Soviet pharmacy journal, *Sovetskaia farmatsiia,*reinforced fears of impending danger, warning that "[N]otwithstanding the prohibition on chemical weapons, the application of chemical weapons would suggest that, in the event of war, they would be used on a very wide scale." Pharmacists could not stand by, and to enable them to be prepared, the article described the contents of chief chemical weapons, gave the formulae of major poison gases, drops, and soil pollutants, and outlined the main chemical reagents to detect them.[35]

Although the pharmaceutical industry produced for the military, secret pharmaceutical production probably drained some resources.

However, medicines for civilians also were lost due to nothing more dramatic than workers' carelessness.

Brak and Workers

In 1931 and 1932, higher officials had criticized the pharmaceutical industry for employing too many workers, thus lowering productivity and increasing payroll costs. Individual factories responded to this criticism differently, indicating that Vokhimfarm and the separate factories comprising it had some amount of autonomy in day-to-day operations, even though they were subject to plans ordained from above. During the Second Five-Year Plan some factories decreased payroll (*zarplatnoi*) costs and increased productivity by shedding workers.[36] In other cases, pharmaceutical executives attempted to improve ratings without downsizing. In 1933, several factories, the Karpov and Farmakon factories tried to increase productivity through daily meetings between workers and on-site planners. The meetings were said to involve "lively exchange." The Karpov Factory, which employed one thousand in 1932, only 650 of whom were "workers" claimed to have produced more coal-tar by-products in 1933, "thanks to better use of labor." The Salicylate factory came "near to fulfilling its targets," and the Leningrad Farmakon Factory also achieved greater productivity."[37]

Still the work ethic remained less than stellar. Despite the earnest workers portrayed in Socialist-Realist novels and paintings, losses from ruined products (*brak*) "amounted to a significant sum and percentage of production—two hundred twenty thousand rubles or 35 percent of output."[38] Vokhimfarm explained that part of the spoilage was due to insufficient or poor quality raw materials but industry executives also admitted that sloppiness—"antisanitary conditions in the shops" and lack of proper warehouse space—ruined products. Vokhimfarm claimed that it was trying to rectify the situation by establishing more quality control.[39] In 1934, however, a number of Vokhimfarm products were rejected at the shipping stage because of poor color, dirtiness or instability.[40] In the same year not only did raw materials arrive at the Dzerzhinskii Factory in poor condition but storage facilities were dirty and bottles and boxes in which medicines were packaged for distribution were not clean, precipitating forty complaints about the ether produced by the factory.[41]

The Dorogomilovskii Factory in Moscow was in the Chemical

Industry and on a higher rung than the core pharmaceutical industry, although it manufactured pharmaceuticals. Thus, it had greater resources to boost productivity. At the end of 1934, six employees were awarded automobiles for advancing production. The recipients included the director, two technical directors, the chief mechanic, a shop head, and one worker.[42]

The Soviet government continued to press pharmaceutical enterprises to prove in their annual reports how much new procedures saved government monies. For example, Vokhimfarm's 1937 report assured the government that "128 worker proposals [for rationalization] gave 762 thousand rubles' economic effect and 24 large rationalization measures implemented in experimental laboratories in general lowered costs for raw materials in the sum of more than 2 million rubles." Six accompanying pages detailed the new, more economic procedures for making Novarsenol, sublimate, reagents, bromine and iodine combinations, aspirin, Plazmotsid, codeine, novocaine, and other products.[43]

Realizing economies in production was and is, of course, the goal of pharmaceutical enterprises in market economies, as well. And state investment did increase markedly up until 1936, as noted early in the chapter, although inflation may have diluted gains, as Christopher Davis postulated with regard to the Commissariat of Health. But the detailed reports which the Soviet pharmaceutical industry had to complete point to yet another factor that hampered the core pharmaceutical industry—too much government interference in day-to-day operations.

In his monumental study of Schering, Christopher Kobrak laments government interference in the German pharmaceutical house that began after 1933 with the ascent of the National Socialists to power. Kobrak admits that some government policies helped German industry: wages were driven down, worker mobility was reduced, the government helped delay foreign payments and reduce foreign debt. But other policies were pernicious: "Taxes remained high and other 'charges' were added....The Nazis tightened the export and foreign exchange allocation system....In 1934, the new regime passed several restrictive dividend and investment laws."[44] Additionally—aside from the more familiar, notorious curtailment of Jews in company positions and on the Board of Directors—the Nazis insisted on more careful reporting to the government, using uniform accounting practices; opposed overtime work (which reduced unemployment but forced Schering to hire more workers); and opposed testing on animals.[45] Admittedly, Schering and its affiliate Kokswerke had sought government assistance, to some extent. Moreover, not only did the Nazis begin to interfere only in 1933/1934, their micromanagement was far less than that which the Soviet pharmaceutical industry had to endure. Finally, because the Soviet pharmaceutical industry was so concentrated, decisions by exogenous officials impacted large quantities of pharmaceuticals and not only one product or one firm as in market economies—which Germany still was, despite its four-year plans and which the United States, on whose pharmaceutical industry Soviet pharmaceutical executives modeled theirs, certainly was.

Exogenous Interference

Only in 1938 did "Trust Busters," in the Roosevelt Administration attack the Eli Lilly Company's monopoly on insulin.[46] In the Soviet Union, meddling by government officials was a constant occurrence. A major blow to the industry was the government's downgrading its status in 1936. At the outset of the Second Five-Year Plan, Vokhimfarm was under the authority of Vesenkha (the Supreme Council of the National Economy). In 1933, Vesenkha was abolished over the protestations of Stalin's compatriot Sergo Ordzhonikidze, who had been made chairman in 1930. Vesenkha was replaced with the three economic ministries or commissariats—the Commissariat of Heavy Industry to which Ordzhonikidze was appointed as commissar; the Commissariat of Light Industry; and the Timber Commissariat. [47]

Vokhimfarm first was relegated to the jurisdiction of the Commissariat of Heavy Industry (Narkomtiazhprom). This potentially put the pharmaceuticals trust in a strong position since investments and resources flowed in that direction.[48] Nevertheless, within the Commissariat the metallurgical, fuel and chemical industries were more favored than the pharmaceutical industry.

Then in April 1936, a *postanovlenie* (resolution) of the Council of People's Commissars (Sovnarkom—the Soviet government) transferred Vokhimfarm out of the USSR Commissariat of Heavy Industry and into the Russian Republic Commissariat of Health (RSFSR Narkomzdrav). This put the industry into the category of a light, consumer-goods industry—a less favored status than it had heretofore enjoyed, even as a stepchild of heavy industry.

The industry did not gain from being located in the RSFSR Commissariat of Health. As noted, historians have remarked that "substantial resources were invested in the health services in the 1930s." But the Commissariat of Health was mainly interested in producing "more doctors, nurses and others working in the health services."[49] In other words, monies and resources would not necessarily go to the core pharmaceutical industry. Additionally, the Commissariat of Health was on the republican rather than the All-Union level. As such, it had less importance in the Council of People's Commissars and its commissar was at a disadvantage in jockeying for investment.

In fact, at the time the move was being debated, many old Bolshevik pharmacists strongly opposed it, primarily for financial and sourcing reasons. L. O. Nisenman attacked the move as "unacceptable," because the "monetary resources of Narkomzdrav are much less than those of Narkomtiazhprom, and therefore from such a transfer Vokhimfarm will unarguably lose." He further pointed out that Narkomzdrav did not have "sufficient personnel," that "raw materials for the preparation of medicaments" were "closely connected to the Commissariat of Heavy Industry" and that Vokhimfarm would more likely get sufficient amounts of these if it remained in the jurisdiction of that commissariat, and that "Narkomzdrav did not have the necessary equipment to expand the factories of Vokhimfarm." S. Maimind averred that to build a new factory higher government and party organs had to put the pharmaceutical industry on the first priority and not merely give it "seasonal" attention. He urged that Vokhimfarm be kept in the Commissariat of Heavy Industry, with a separate organization. Yu. Kuperman likewise affirmed that "Vokhimfarm did not need to be transferred to Narkomzdrav."[50]

Despite pharmacists' protestations, the industry was transferred. Government officials did due diligence, but ignored the larger issues about which pharmacists had complained. The Act of April 13, 1936, cementing the transfer of the enterprises and archive of Vokhimfarm was punctilious in the extreme. It emphasized that a three-person "Presenting" commission from the Commissariat of Heavy Industry and a six-person "Reception" commission formed by a *prikaz* (order) of Narkomzdrav RSFSR, had documented all assets and liabilities of the trust, including the multimillion ruble capital and operating funds, noted above; the thirty-four thousand plus ruble fund for administrative expenses; the fifty-eight thousand plus ruble payroll fund for some 3,173 personnel; the two million ruble amortization fund; the one million, eight-hundred thousand ruble fund left to the discretion of enterprise directors; the three-million ruble fund "for improving living and working conditions of workers and white collar personnel," and so on. The USSR Commissariat of Heavy Industry promised to turn over all raw materials, fuel, and construction materials to the RSFSR Commissariat of Health.[51]

Divestitures by exogenous officials. Following on the heels of this development, the government divested the pharmaceutical industry of its sales arm. Although the Transfer Act of April 13, 1936 specified that the pharmaceutical trust was "an independent economic entity, functioning on the basis of *khozraschet* (self-financing) and responsible for "hiring and firing workers, concluding collective agreements, and caring for the means and property of the trust," the act did include a caveat. The trust [was expected to] "implement *the planned and organized* operative-productive direction of enterprises in its composition" [italics mine]—albeit "independently." This legalese signaled that Vokhimfarm and its enterprises were cogs in a larger machine.[52] The trust's subordinate status was borne out by the government's summary divestiture of Vokhimfarm's sales apparatus.

As it had from its inception, Vokhimfarm was allocated monies directly from the state budget and received bank loans. But it also realized operating capital from selling products put out by its factories. Indeed, a merger of the trading and sales arms of the industry in 1924 had made the industry a powerhouse. In 1937, however, government officials lopped off the trust's trading facility. Thus the industry reverted back to its pre-1924 position. Pharmaceutical wares—except for those scheduled for export and for military usage— were to be sold through a separate sales agency, Khimfarmtorg (Chemical-Pharmaceutical Trading).[53] This set up had impacted pharmaceutical industry cash flow negatively in the early twenties and was to do so again.

Constant reorganization. Very destabilizing to the pharmaceutical industry during the Second Five-Year Plan were incessant realignments of its component enterprises. Ordained by higher officials, these divestitures also affected industry revenues.

In 1933 a "Resolution of Sovnarkom" divested Vokhimfarm of four enterprises. Three were iodine factories. One, the Far Eastern Iodine Factory and Office, was transferred to the Commissariat of Supply, specifically to its "Trust for Exploiting Sea Products." The Arkhangel'sk Iodine Factory and Office was transferred to the People's Commissariat of Light Industry. The Lapominskii Experimental Iodine Factory was transferred to the Northern Oblast' Soviet Executive Committee. Finally, the Sverdlovsk Reagent Factory and Institute of Pure Chemical Reagents was transferred to the Trust of Union Laboratory Reagents (Soiuzlaborreaktiv) under Glavkhimprom, the Chemical Industry.[54]

Some of these divestitures may have been beneficial in the long run, since iodine production, though improving, was difficult. Nevertheless, the decisions descended deus ex machina on the pharmaceutical industry. Additionally, transferring the Dzerzhinskii Santonin/Opiate Factory into the system required "significant attention from the *apparat* of the Administration [of Vokhimfarm] and its factories."[55] And, while higher authorities orchestrated, they did not deliver the wherewithall necessary to make the mergers successful. On the contrary, along with the addition of the Dzerzhinskii Factory, "the planned volume of capital was cut, leading to removal of objects of…capital work outlined in the plan and hold up of others."[56] [See Figure 11.1]

In 1935 Vokhimfarm lost the March 8 Bandaging Factory in Moscow, with production in 1934 valued at 11 million rubles (in 1926/1927 prices). This amounted to a hefty 20 percent of Vokhimfarm's total production.[57] Vokhimfarm also lost two "very large" iodine factories in the Caspian Sea, the Nefte-Chalinskii and the Chelekenskii factories, whose combined production was 3 million rubles in 1926/1927 prices. The first divestiture was ordained by Sovnarkom at the end of December 1934 and seconded by the Commissariat of Heavy Industry in January 1935. The Commissariat of Health of the Russian Republic was the recipient of the factory. In October 1935, the Commissariat of Heavy Industry and the State Chemical Industry (GoKhProm) managed the transfer of the iodine factories, with no mention of Sovnarkom, to the newly formed Administration of Caspian Iodine-Bromine Construction, (Kaspiiiodbromstroi). Once again, Vokhimfarm had no say-so in these divestitures and a couple were money-makers that Vokhimfarm could ill afford to lose.[58]

Vokhimfarm did retain twelve enterprises in 1935. Four were located in Moscow: the Salicylate Factory, the Karpov (former Ferrein) Factory, the Semashko (former Keler) Factory, and the Alkaloid Factory. Farmakon was located in Leningrad; the Dzerzhinskii factory in Chimkent had been loosely attached to the system in 1926 . There were two iodine factories in the Crimean ASSR—Sakskii Chemistry Factory and Perekop Bromine Factory; two iodine factories in Azerbaidzhan: Ramaninskii and Surakhanskii; an experimental iodine factory in the city of Derbent, Dagestan ASSR, and the Scientific Research Chemical-

Pharmaceutical-Institute in Moscow, known by its acronym, NIKhFI. Production of galenicals and other non-complex pharmaceuticals were transferred to local pharmacy administrations. More production of reagents was transferred to Union Laboratory Reagents (Soiuzlaborreaktiv).[59] [See Figures 11.2 and 11.3]

In 1937 an Administrative Board (*Upravlenie*) of some twenty individuals managed the factories that comprised Vokhimfarm.[60] Nevertheless, the Soviet government—Sovnarkom—through its resolutions, and the USSR Commissariat of Health (Narkomzdrav), through its directives (*prikazy*), rather than Vokhimfarm's administrative board, transferred factories in and out of the core industry with bewildering frequency, seemingly unmindful as to whether the changes helped or hurt the industry. In 1937, Vokhimfarm acquired six enterprises. Simultaneously the trust lost three factories.[61] To repeat, these changes must have been destabilizing. Unfortunately high officials' interference in the core pharmaceutical industry's strategic policies was a systemic problem and one that could not be eliminated given the centrally planned economy that existed in the Soviet Union. So too were flaws in the macroeconomic environment. [See Figure 11.4]

Fig. 11.1 Vokhimfarm, 1933

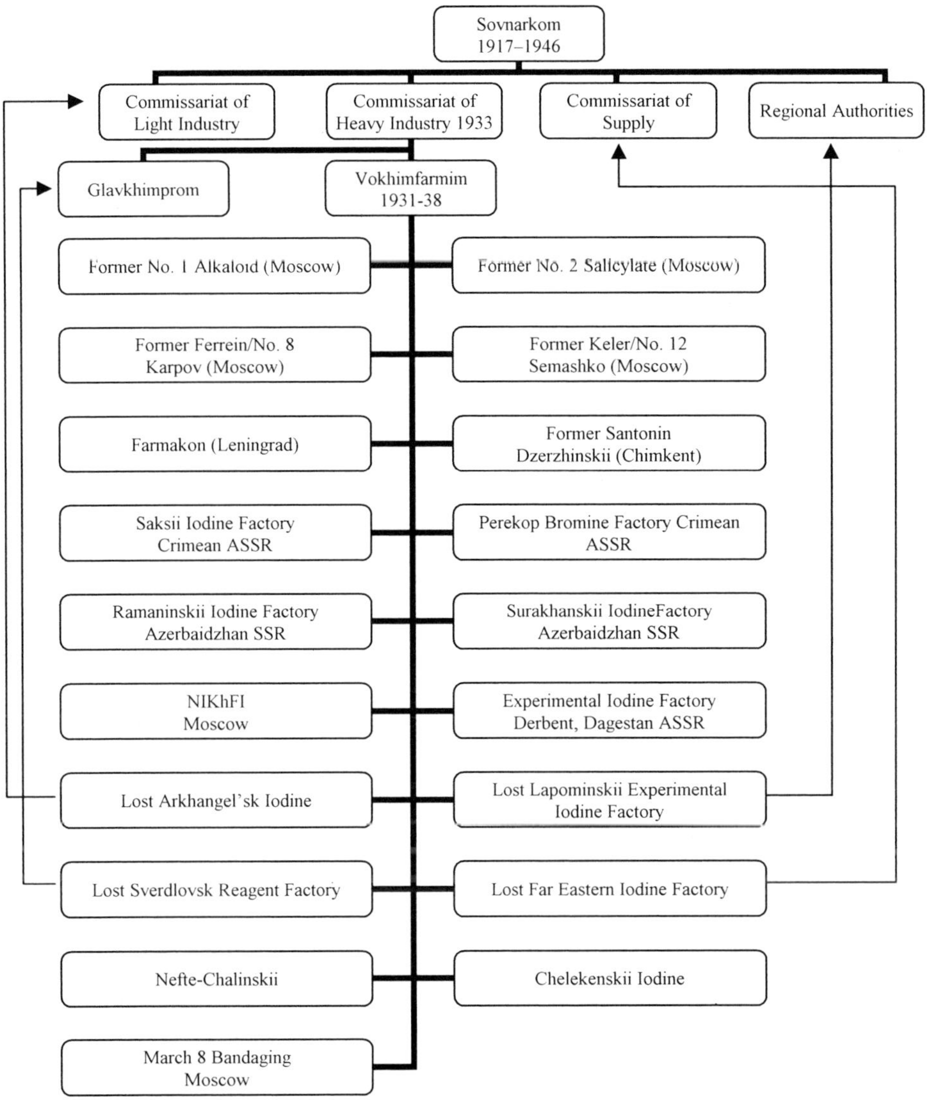

Fig. 11.2 Vokhimfarm, 1935

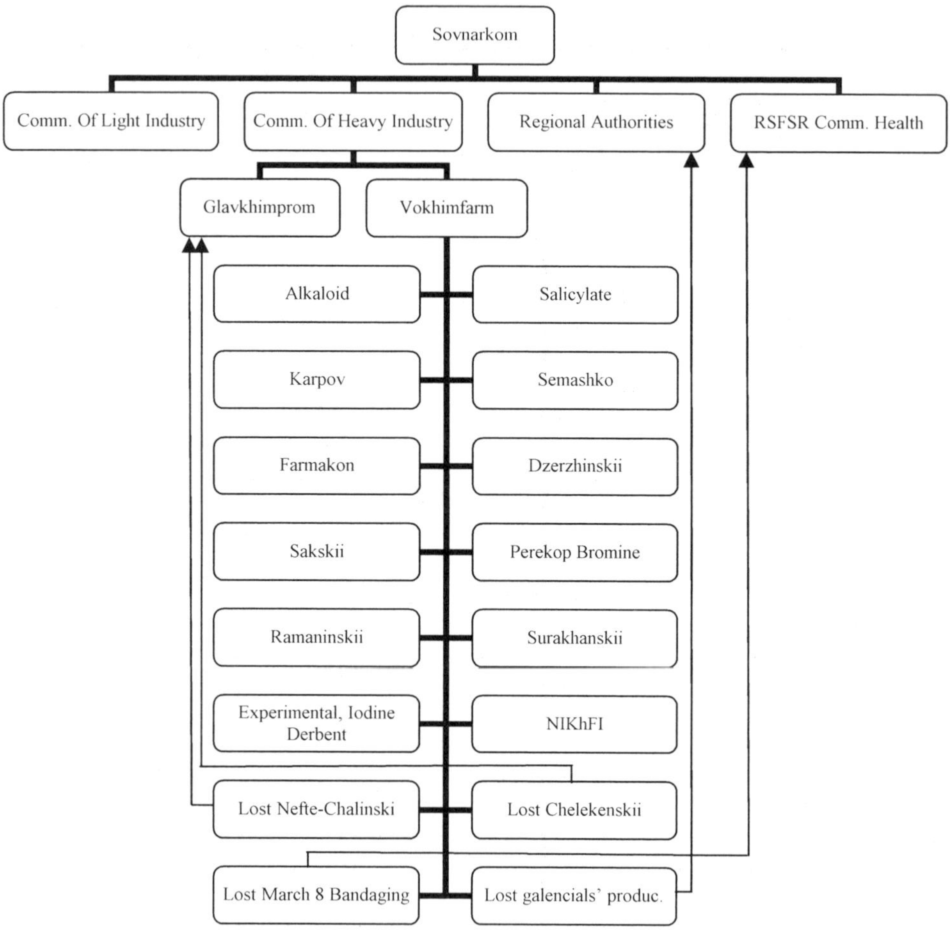

Fig. 11.3 Vokhimfarm 1936

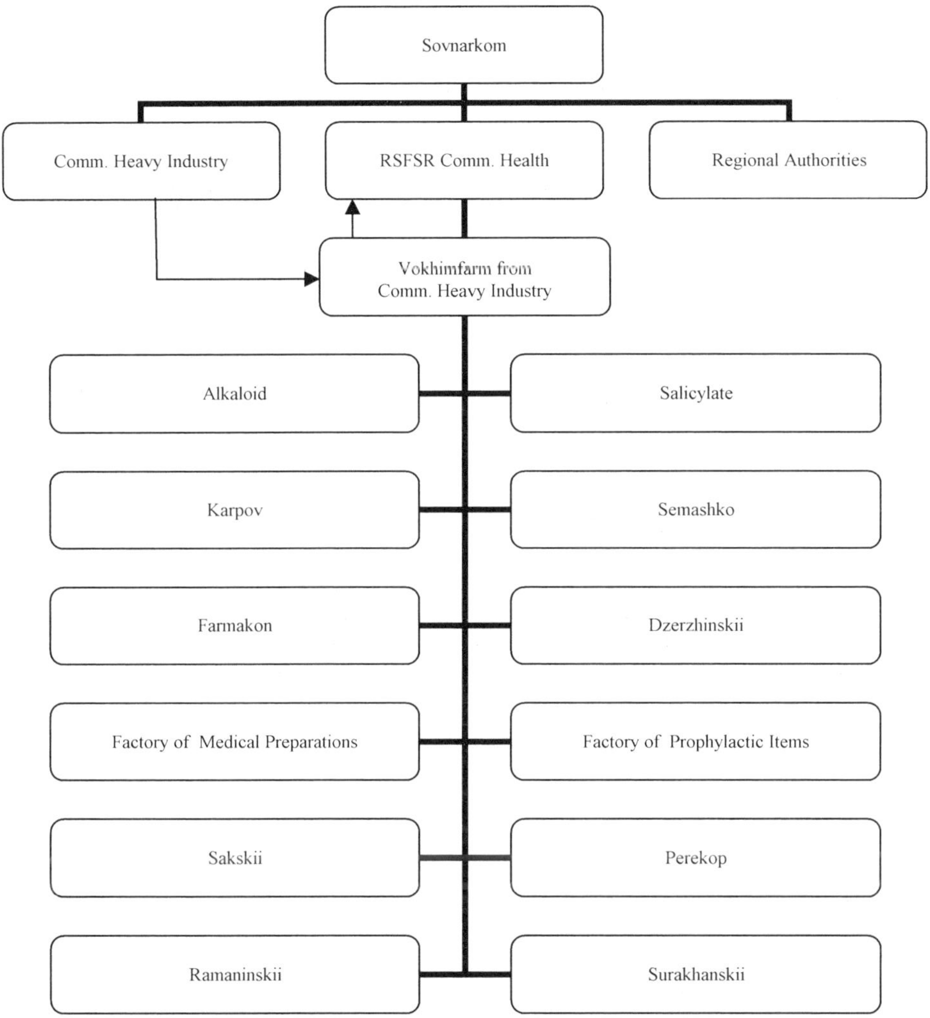

Fig. 11.4 Vokhimfarm 1937

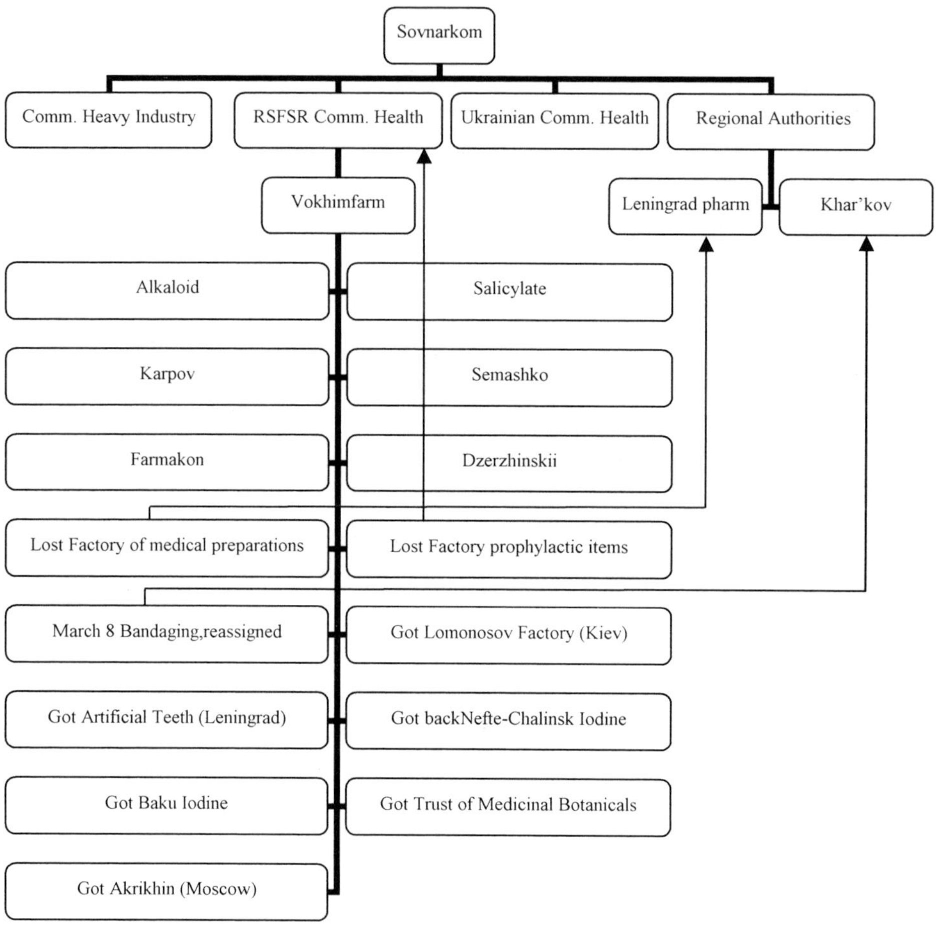

Macroeconomic Deficiencies

Although the economy appeared to be improving in general during the Second Five-Year Plan, for the pharmaceutical industry deliveries of raw materials were as unpredictable as during the First Five-Year Plan. The Act of April, 13 1936, which transferred the core industry out of the Commissariat of Heavy Industry and into the RSFSR Commissariat of Health, frankly acknowledged "severely deficit raw materials." "The most crucial" items and "the differences between actual requests" of them and "amounts received in 1936" were "recorded in...data appended." Six items were listed as "extremely deficit."[62]

The materials' problem may have resulted from lower priorities for the pharmaceutical industry as compared with fossil fuel and other heavy industrial sectors but, as before, it also stemmed from the compartmentalized organization of the macro economy and these demarcations became more severe during the Second Five-Year Plan. By the late 1930s, the commissariats of Heavy Industry, Light Industry and Timber had proliferated into many more commissariats, all handling specific sectors of the economy. This system multiplied the barriers between the pharmaceutical industry and the chemical industry, between the pharmaceutical industry and the medical equipment and apparatus industry, and between the pharmaceutical industry and makers of other inputs, complicating sourcing and distribution.

Factories producing mainly chemicals, even if they had pharmaceutical application, were housed, as before, in the Commissariat of Heavy Industry. The core chemical-pharmaceutical industry—Vokhimfarm/Khimfarmprom—which produced 50 percent or more of pharmaceuticals sold in the Soviet Union, was under the RSFSR Commissariat of Health after 1936. Other large-, medium- and small-scale enterprises that manufactured pharmaceuticals or medical apparatus and equipment were under the authority of various local authorities, including other republican (such as Ukrainian) commissariats of Health. Local pharmaceutical associations purchased for pharmacies in their jurisdictions. Marketing and sales not only were not connected with the core pharmaceutical industry within the commissariat but were located in separate commissariats. Fuel and electricity were supplied by agencies outside the pharmaceutical industry's control.

Industry executives lamented inadequate inputs in every one of their annual reports. In 1933 Vokhimfarm particularly complained about the shortage of iodine, as well as other crucial materials. Iodine production still caused the industry headaches for the same old reasons as in the 1920s—weather and geological conditions: "[U]nfortunate meteorological conditions" prevented more extraction of iodine and bromine and the industry was looking into new methods of producing these items. Other shortages were due to human error and malfunctioning of the planned economic order. "A range of raw materials were not available" in 1933, because suppliers "did not fulfill contracts." Specifically, Azneft did not supply iodine water to Nefte-Chalinskii iodine factory and the Alkaloid and Chimkent Dzerzhinskii factories did not receive supplies of opium. There were "interruptions in the supplies of fuel and energy, especially at the end of the year, cutting down the number of shifts." Production of Adalin was held up because supplies of semi-manufactured veronal were delayed, in turn, because of late installations. Similarly the apparatus for production of Khinozol and Iatren did not arrive.[63]

The report for 1935 noted that "supplies of raw materials were better in comparison with 1934. Nevertheless…for a range of specific items… there were severe insufficiencies leading to breaks in the program." Especially affected were production of Formalin, Dimetilsulfate (Dimethylsulfate), copper vitriol, chlorine, lanolin, and carbonic acid. Chemical inputs for these items came from various organizations outside the pharmaceutical industry: Khimplastmass, VKhTOP, Lakokraska, Glavkhimprom, and Soiuzkhimsbyt. Lanolin was supplied by the Commissariat of Light Industry (Narkomlegprom) and carbonic acid from the Food Industry (Narkompishcheprom).[64] Industry reports also complained about the "severe insufficiency of special forms of glass and other packaging materials" in 1935. [65] The industry had no leverage over these suppliers.

Insufficient electricity entirely prevented production of some items in 1935.[66] "Insufficiency of energy was especially severe." In the Perekop and Sakskii factories there were "interruptions in the supplies of fuel in the beginning of the year." The "strict limits for energy usage in Moscow and Leningrad" made "work of the factories exceptionally difficult." Breaks in electricity "led to accidents." The Farmakon Factory in Leningrad "had to shut down electricity two to three hours in one shop, to guarantee work in other shops. The artesian water could not be utilized because of absence of energy." Bromine factories worked round the clock but, while a few shops in pharmaceutical factories worked three shifts of six hours each, other shops were limited to two or even only one shift per day, because of lack of energy, and efforts to rectify matters were held up by lack of ancillary materials. "The transformer scheduled for the Farmakon Factory in December could not be installed because of lack of cable." [!] In the Sakskii and Perekopskii factories the holding tank for saltwater could not be finished on time because of lack of wood [!] and this, in turn, held up production of bromine.[67] It was obvious that the economy was not operating as the fine-tuned machine it was meant to be. The pharmaceutical industry reflected the fact that the gears—inter-factory and inter-agency supply—were not moving in unison.

Production and productivity in the core pharmaceutical industry were retarded by inadequate equipment. Levinshtein had decried this situation in 1934. In 1935 pharmaceutical industry administrators joined him, railing that "The equipment in the majority of factories in Vokhimfarm is old and outmoded, so that repair is not sufficient for maintaining it anymore. Corrosion quickly occurs in the production of acids, salt solutions, and so forth." [68] Government officials did begin to address this problem, allocating "significant sums" in 1934, "for ongoing repairs"—called in the jargon of the time—"planned, foreseen remodeling" or "P P R." [69]

But macroeconomic dysfunction continued. In 1937, for example, the pharmaceutical industry received only about two-thirds of the phenol it needed for aspirin; about one-half the accumulated acids it needed for milk sugar and the antivenereal Novarsol, only about two thirds of the technical chloroform needed for narcotic and pure chloroform, about one-half the carbonic acid needed for salicylic acid. And this was only a partial list of the "most important forms of chemicals…factories entered 1937 with only small reserves."[70] As a result, output declined in three of the seven core pharmaceutical factories in 1937 as compared with 1936. Production of salicylates in the Salicylate Factory in 1937 was only two-thirds that of 1936, production at the Farmakon Factory was some 14 percent lower in 1937 than in 1936, production at the Karpov Factory was lower, albeit by only a few percentage points. Production at the Endocrine Factory and the Chimkent Santonin Factory was one-half and one-third higher, respectively, than in 1936, production in the remaining two factories was just slightly higher.[71] Nevertheless, production of many important items in the seven core factories of the pharmaceutical industry in 1937 was far lower than capacity. And while factories met some quotas set for their products by the 1937 plan, they failed to meet targets on other key products.

Fig. 11.5 Discrepancies in Tons between Raw Materials Needed and Supplied, 1937

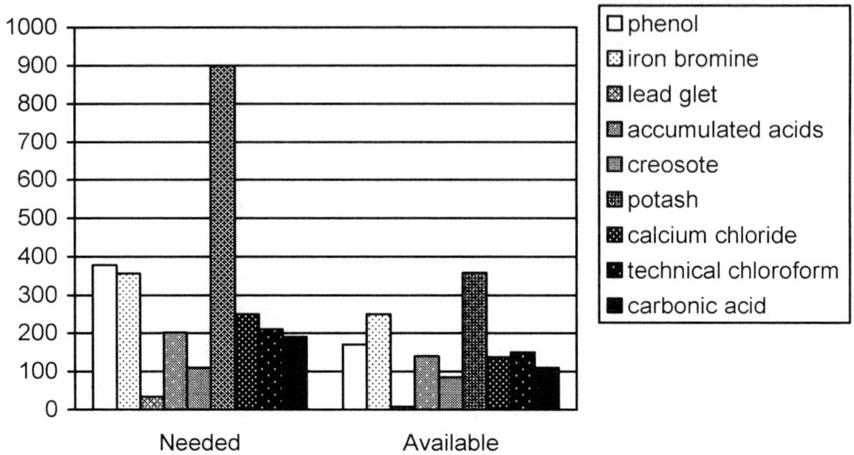

The linkage between enterprises in the core industry caused a domino effect. In 1937 lack of equipment held up output of the barbiturates Amital and Adurol and output of Khinon in the Semashko Factory. Moogrol, a new remedy for leprosy, was transferred from the Farmakon to the Salicylate Factory in order to guarantee that it would be produced on time. Dekholin in ampules was not distributed because of its unfavorable appearance. Now tablets of Liuminal and ampules of camphor oil and caffeine were being produced in the Semashko factory but users also rejected them because of poor quality. Production of Diethyl-aniline and another product were stopped by the Alkaloid Factory because of "parallel" production in the Union of Laboratory Reagents. In the Farmakon Factory production of antipyrine, benzoic acid, and Salipyrine were held up because of lack of methods and equipment. In the Endocrine Factory Pankreon was held up because the method of production was "inexact."[72] The concentration of Vitaminol was increased five times and its price was reduced, but it could only be dispensed with a prescription from a physician, which pointed to insufficient output.[73] The Alkaloid Factory surpassed its targets for Novocaine and codeine but limits on imports kept output of hydrochloric quinine at only half the amount set by the plan, using less than one-sixth of capacity.[74] After Liuminal was rejected by users the Semashko Factory stopped production of the barbiturate and entirely failed to produce Veronal. Production of Paraamidophenol was over plan but lower than capacity due to shortages of technical para-amidophenol.[75]

Such defects were said to be one of the reasons for the Great Purge of 1937-1938, as the attack on specialists during the First Five-Year Plan had been.

The Great Purge

The Great Purge of 1937-1938 was one of the defining moments in the Soviet Union. Arrests following the mysterious death of Sergei Kirov, First Party Secretary in Leningrad in December 1934 rose to a crescendo in 1937-1938. One million, three-hundred-thousand persons were arrested on spurious charges. Judges threw out some cases but about half those arrested were executed[76] and the rest were sent to labor camps in Siberia.[77] Many reasons have been adduced for the purges, which caused mayhem in local government, many branches of industry and in the military (though its impact on the last is said to have been exaggerated) and anxiety amongst ordinary folk. These include Stalin's paranoia, political vendettas, foreign-policy considerations, and the fact that the witch hunt took on a momentum of its own.[78] But high on the list of explanations for the Great Purge was its economic rationale. The purge provided forced laborers for enterprises in inhospitable climes.[79] It served up scapegoats for consumer shortages, demonstrating to the populace that their government was in charge.[80] And, although the purge disrupted production, some historians view it as a means of getting rid of low performers and bringing fresh blood into management. According to this interpretation, the purges were analogous to Boards of Directors and stockholders of corporations in capitalist countries firing chief executives for poor performance—albeit that Soviet punishment included banishment to labor camps and execution. Holland Hunter, for example, asserted that the railway sector improved after a 1935 shake up.[81] Roberta Manning acknowledges that industrial shortages resulted more from the inability of enterprises to pay for goods than absolute quantitative shortfalls, but she also documents cases in which there was justification for purging directors who had failed to meet plan quotas.[82]

The "Great Purge" was mild in the pharmaceutical industry, as had been the impact of purges during the First Five-Year Plan. In 1937, the directors of Vokhimfarm acknowledged that the industry had suffered "severe deficits of the most important and decisive kinds of raw materials... including those that in former years were not deficit, such as phenol, salicylic acid, bromine, caustic soda... and a range of others, and also interruptions in supplies of fuel and electroenergy." But they attributed these problems to "enemies of the people" and asserted that "the cleansing of enterprises made work significantly better in the second half of the year."[83]

Indeed, following a purge, "the new management" of Dzerzhinskii Factory, the executives at Vokhimfarm approvingly noted in their 1937 report, "took a range of measures—they retooled the morphine shop, increasing power from 600 kilograms a month to 800 kilograms, improved packaging, mechanized the anabasine shop, and especially "did great work, traveling together with the brigade of the Trust, to locate raw materials, opium and anabasis, which were uninterrupted."[84] The director of the Salicylate Factory in Moscow also managed to acquire "sometimes deficit raw materials," such as "salicylic acid," in 1937 but, instead of being congratulated, he was reproved for "overspending" his budget "to a significant degree."[85]

Other purges, tangential to the core pharmaceutical industry, were even more ambiguous. During 1937 and 1938 nine people were "repressed" in the Dorogomilovskii Factory in Moscow, including six directors, two engineers and the factory physician. Three of the purged had been awarded automobiles in 1934 for increasing the factory's performance.[86]

The Akrikhin Factory, which was joined to the core pharmaceutical industry in 1939, put out only 0.62 tons of the antimalarial for which it was named in 1936, but produced 35.3 tons by 1937. According to the factory's report to higher officials, "this allowed the possibility of treating the millions sick with malaria" and "severely cut imports of quinine."[87] Further, production costs declined, prompting officials to lower the distribution price—according to a second source (which gave amounts in kilograms instead of tons) from 2,180 rubles per kilogram in 1936 to 1,250 rubles per kilogram in 1937. [88]

Nevertheless, twelve engineers, mechanics, electricians and other specialists at the factory were arrested in 1937 and 1938. They were accused of spying, terrorist activity, and counter-revolutionary agitation. The fate of most is unknown but two were sent to labor camps, one for eight years, the other for ten. Director Shuvalov was ejected from the party in March of 1937. He was blamed for construction delays; being too closely associated with Iu. L. Piatakov, who was repressed as an enemy of the people in early 1937; and, finally, he was blamed for the fact that during Stalin's speech on the new Soviet Constitution, December 5, 1936, the electricity failed, thus allowing assembled workers to hear only a portion of the speech. Shuvalov was shot in April 1938 by order of a Collegium of the USSR Supreme Court.[89]

The attack on the old Bolshevik pharmacist Izrail I. Levinshtein appeared more an attempt to silence a whistle blower, than desire to grapple with real problems. Three years earlier Levinshtein had criticized government policies and macroeconomic dysfunction for holding back the industry. The attack on him seemed to be his punishment. It also reflected the anti-Semitism that permeated the "Great Purge."

In 1937, Levinshtein was Secretary of the Pharmacy Committee in the Medical Council of the Russian Republic Commissariat of Health. In February he was hauled on the carpet for references to Trotsky that had appeared in two of his articles published a decade before: "Fundamentals of Health Care and the Tasks of Pharmacy," which had appeared in 1926, and "Studies on the History of Pharmacy," published in 1927. Levinshtein resigned his position but he defended himself before the general meeting of the Medical Council in March 1937, stressing that the charges against him were unfounded and asking for a committee to review them. Professor Dr. I. A. Obergard, Chair of the Pharmacy Committee, supported his colleague—to a point. He agreed that "the activity of Trotsky and his servitors calls forth deep disgust in all honest toilers, not only among us but in countries of capitalist exploitation." Nevertheless, he argued that Levinshtein was "an honest specialist" who had "devoted more than thirty years of his life to creating and supporting socialized pharmacy." Further, Obergard pointed out, the references to Trotsky were incidental and "very little connected with the true content of Trotskyism" with which "the Jew Trotsky concealed the counterrevolutionary essence of his activity." Additionally, Obergard reminded the assemblage, "Levinshtein has not a few enemies. He created them from his unrelenting struggle in the field of pharmacy against imposters, against the blind following of foreigners, against the slighting of medical supply." Obergard admitted that he stood "in a difficult position." Twice the Scientific Research Institute in Leningrad and the Qualification Commission of the Commissariat of Health had expressed their "high regard for Levinshtein's works and their significance for Soviet pharmacy." At the end Obergard compromised and called for yet another commission of new specialists to review the matter. One of the specialists was the old revolutionary pharmacist Aluf.[90] Fortunately, Levinshtein's disgrace was not permanent. Like many military officers who were reinstated,[91] by 1940 he was again fully participating in the activities of the Moscow Pharmacy Society.

Ongoing Liabilities

In any case, if the intent of the purge had been to make the pharmaceutical industry more efficient, in general, the goal was only partially met. This was because systemic problems were not addressed. Macroeconomic inefficiencies continued. Officials issued plans late. For example, in1937 the Chief Pharmacy Department, which purchased for pharmacies, complained that "strict planning...was braked when the plan, approved August 28, 1937, in accordance with a resolution of the RSFSR Council of People's Commissars of the, was proposed to the Commissariat of Health only November 25, 1937."[92] And, as during the First Five-Year Plan, officials excessively exported. Undoubtedly these exports accounted for some of the shortages of raw materials with which the industry had to contend.

Expensive Imports and Aggressive Exports

The push for exports, as during the First Five-Year Plan, was tied to imports. Although the Soviet Union managed to create a large-scale machine-tool industry by the end of the Second Five-Year Plan in 1937,[93] some pharmaceuticals and much pharmaceutical-medical equipment still needed to be imported, the last, primarily from Germany.[94] A memorandum from the American Embassy in early 1938, "On the market in the Soviet Union for medical supplies and equipment of American manufacture," quoted Soviet statistics documenting imports of x-ray equipment that were four times greater than exports in 1935, fifteen times greater in 1936, and double the amount of exports for the first nine months of 1937. Imports of medical-surgical instruments were almost three times more than exports in 1936; imports were double the amount of exports for the first nine months of 1937.[95]

During the Second Five-Year Plan, the USSR imported huge amounts of quinine and its salts—over 100,000 kilograms in 1935 and almost 124,000 kilograms in 1936 (although the USSR also *exported* some quinine and quinine salts—17 tons in 1935 and 35 tons in 1936).[96] The exports of quinine were significant. And to pay for costly imports the Soviet government exported vast amounts of other raw materials.

Soviet exports of "pharmaceutical products" were three times more than imports in 1935 and five times more than imports in 1936. Unfortunately, the Soviet Union paid twice or over twice as much for the imports as it received as from the exports. For the first nine months of 1937 the Soviet Union exported some 202 tons of "pharmaceutical products" and imported only 37 tons, receiving over two million rubles for the exports but paying nearly one and a half million rubles for the much smaller amount of imports.[97]

The disparities between the cost of imports and revenues obtained from Soviet exports resulted from plummeting prices of Soviet exports on the international market. For example, the United States was still a major importer of Santonin in the 1930s, buying seven times more of the product in 1933 than in 1932. During the 1920s the price of Santonin had been as high as $175.00 per pound. But in 1932 increased output and marketing caused the price of Santonin to drop to $60.00 per pound. In 1933 Santonin dropped to $50.00 per pound.[98] The same phenomenon undoubtedly occurred with other products.

Economics propelled high Soviet officials to export ever greater amounts of botanicals, chemicals and prepared medicines. This is not to say that pharmaceutical executives did not also favor pushing exports—sensibly. In 1928 Ia. Kanevskii had noted that the world market for prepared medicines was not near to being filled, implying that Soviet pharmaceuticals might fill the gap. But, as he also decried "the continued *golod*" of some medicaments at home,[99] it is doubtful that he approved excessive exporting of pharmaceutical raw materials and products. This is what occurred, however, and, just as huge exports of grain contributed to famine in 1932 and 1933 and food shortages in succeeding years, huge exports of botanicals, chemicals and prepared medicines contributed to a *lekarstvennyi golod* or medicaments famine at the same time.

Dr. Zelikin bemoaned the poor quality of Soviet exports. He contended that they frequently were adulterated with dirt from machinery. Many did not fulfill the requirements of the Fourth German Pharmacopoeia. For example, Soviet aspirin was weak, smelled of vinegar, and contained mechanical dirt. Sodium salicylate had a rosy color and contained rope fibers from the filter. Urotropin had a strong smell and was sullied by mechanical dirt. Soviet Protargol, obtained from bloody albumin rather than eggs, contained admixtures of salts of silver, was too dark in color, and did not satisfy the German Pharmacopoeia. Soviet cartons and boxes were inferior to foreign, giving an amateurish (*kustar'*) appearance. Russian labels were tasteless (*bezvkusnyi),* inexact, did not give full description of the contents and often jumbled Cyrillic and Roman letters. Foreign labels, in contrast, were attractive because, Zelikin noted pointedly, competition forced them to be.[100] Satsyperov and Murav'ev also criticized Soviet exports: "mistakes had been observed in gathering"; the quality of licorice root, the chief export of the Ural Factory of Lektekhsyr'e, had gone down; Ukrainian chamomile had insufficiencies; cartons needed to be more flexible, lettering clearer, etc.[101]

Fig. 11.6 Soviet Packaging – aspirin – plain paper wrapping (Zelikin, *Za kachestvo,* p. 22)

Рис. 7. Упаковка в бумажные мешки—аспирин (завод № 2)

Fig. 11.7 Foreign labels – clear, concise, accurate doses, tight box (Zelikin, ibid, p. 26)

Рис. 12. Образец заграничной упаковки. Четкая этикетка, плотная коробка

Fig. 11.8 Foreign ampules – attractive packaging (Zelikin, loc. cit.)

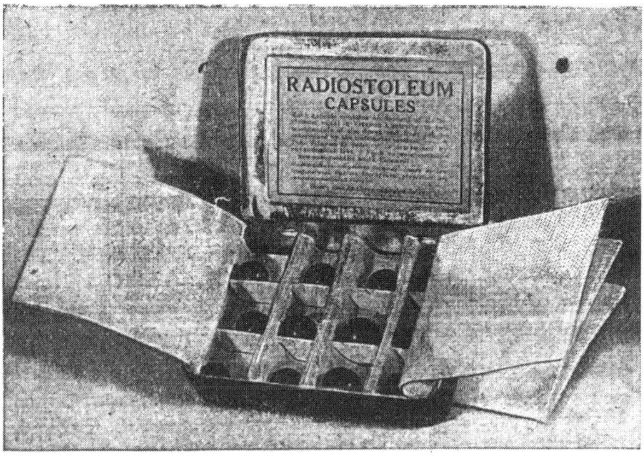

Рис. 13. Образец заграничной упаковки капсуль

Despite the criticisms of these pharmaceutical specialists, the Soviet Union exported large quantities of medicinal botanicals, minerals, chemicals and some prepared items during the Second Five-Year Plan.

Trading partners shifted. During the twenties NEP, the United States, Germany, England, and France had been chief buyers. During the First Five-Year Plan, Persia assumed first place. In 1931/1932, Poland became the Soviet Union's main export partner. Then, during 1932 exports to Poland halved, and exports to Germany and China rose to take second and third place, respectively.[102] France and Germany remained major buyers of botanicals.

Fig. 11.9 Medicinal Exports in Gold Rubles

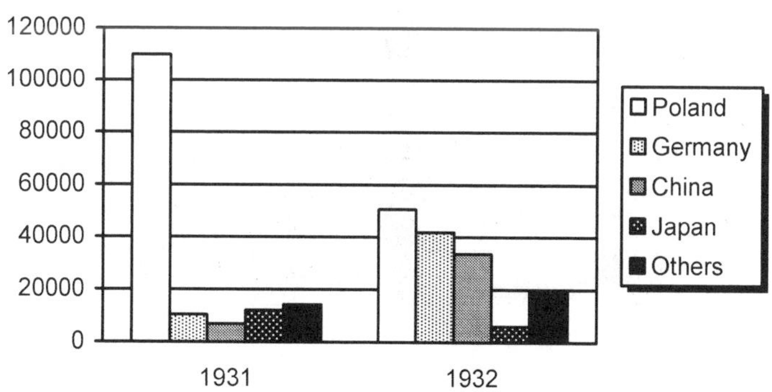

Sourcing from branches in the Urals, Gorkii, Vologda, Viazemskaia, Gomel, and Ukraine, in the three-year period from 1935 through 1937, Lektekhsyr'e exported 5,000 to 9 and 2 thousand tons of licorice root; 4,777 tons of Santonin in 1935 and 2, 431 tons in 1936. Exports of other botanicals ranged from 700 tons to 25 tons.[103] It was not so clear that exports of botanicals adversely affected Soviet consumers.

Exports of Chemicals and Medicines and Domestic Availability

But shortages of chemicals, minerals and prepared medicines on the domestic market during the Second Five-Year Plan, as during the First, may well have been the result of export rather than insufficient production. Zelikin's figures showed a huge leap in exports between 1930 and 1932. For example, in 1932 the Soviet Union exported a whopping 19,650 kilograms of salicylate preparations—over nine times more than two years previously; almost 2,000 kilograms of iodide salts—four times more than in 1930; 160 kilograms of metallic iodine (no figures were provided for 1930); 12, 285 ampules of the antivenereal Novarsenol (no figures provided for 1930); 5, 814 kilograms of chloroform—a fifty-fold increase over 1930 (!) ; 3,320 kilograms of bromide salts—a six-fold increase over 1930.[104]

Fig. 11.10 Pharmaceutical Exports in Kilograms and Ampules

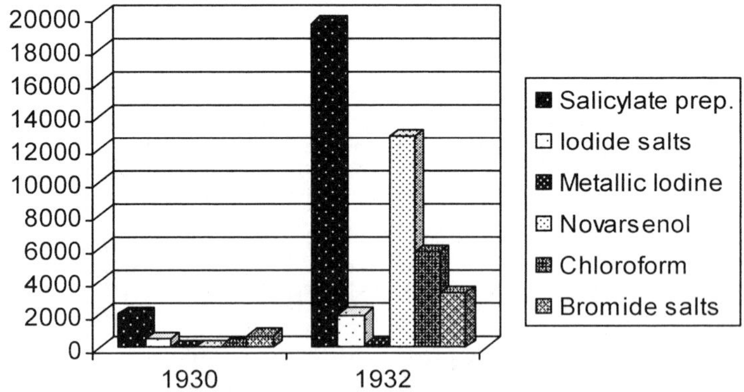

Zelikin claimed that production of Novarsenol from Factory Number 8 (Ferrein/Karpov) "fully replaced imports." But one wonders if exports were not responsible for the shortages lamented by Levinshtein and his colleagues throughout the Second Five-Year Plan. Surely efforts to export lanolin which Zelikin noted in 1933 dovetailed with the shortage of this item in 1935, noted above[105] Chlorine, also deficit in 1935, was touted in a Soviet export brochure.[106] And how did exports of salicylate preparations square with Levinshtein's distress over shortages of inputs for technical salicylic acid in 1934?

Nevertheless, despite apparent domestic deficits, officials relentlessly exported. In 1933, Vokhimfarm claimed to have overfulfilled its export plan 113 percent. Exports amounted to "a significant increase over 1932." They were averred to be "of better quality," constituting "8 percent of the value of production."[107] In the middle of the Second Five-Year Plan huge amounts of liquid ammonia were exported (some 3,700 plus tons in 1935 and 1936); sulfates (some 3,201 tons in 1935) and sulfides (2,880 tons in 1935); "hydrochlorides" (9,167 tons in 1935); and chromates (2,580 tons in 1935). Forty-three tons of phosphorus, bromine and iodine were exported in 1935 and 73 tons in 1936. The Soviet Union exported Dinitrochlorbenzene (61 tons and 66 tons in 1935 and 1936), over 200 tons of aniline salts and oils in 1935 and 1936, and of aspirin, 28 and 22 tons in 1935 and 1936. In 1937, figures reversed, the Soviet Union *importing* 2,788 tons of salicylic acid while exporting only 553 tons. Small amounts—3 and 4 tons—of Lysol were exported in 1935 and 1936.[108]

Fig. 11.11 Exports of chemicals & medicines may have shorted the domestic market (*Chemical Goods,* Moscow: Soyuzprom export, n.d. 1930-1933?, p. 3)

Potassium chlorate. Soyuspromexport warehouses in Odessa Port

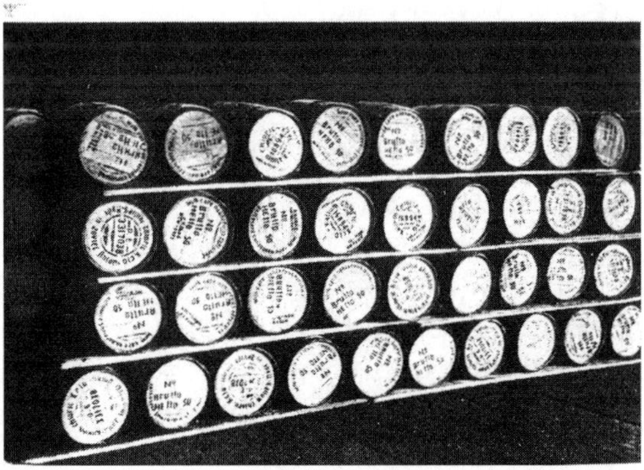

Fig. 11.12 Soviet Export Medicines & "patented" substances – mamochrine, gitaline, dionin, spermocrine (Zelikin, *Za kachestvo*, p. 25)

Рис. 10. Образцы упаковок наших экспортных медикаментов и патентованных средств

Fig. 11.13 Soviet Exports – phytin & biochinol (Zelikin, loc. cit.)

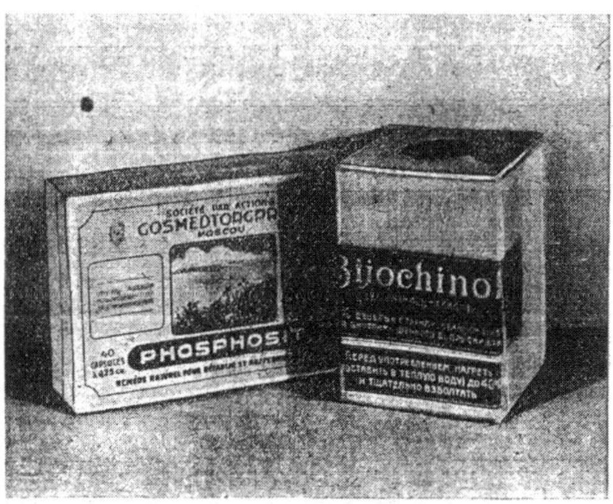

Рис. 11. Экспортная упаковка фитина и биохинола (Завод № 8 им. Карпова)

In 1935, Vokhimfarm announced that it "significantly overfulfilled the export plan." The industry also introduced new items of export—atropin, veronal, and raw iodine (*iod-syrets*), among others. It was claimed that output of veronal and iodide salts was robust, the latter because of good weather conditions.[109] The Soviet pharmaceutical industry also exported over 300,000 tons of caffeine and bromine salts in 1935.[110]

Fig. 11.14 Iodine Production in Tons

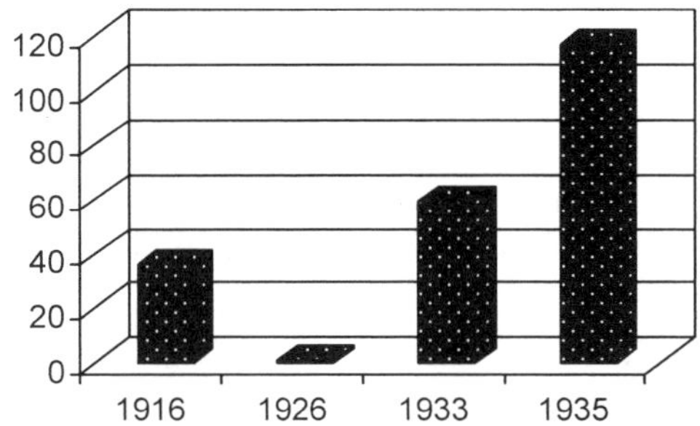

Massive exports of iodine, in particular, may have affected the amounts of this item, important for preventing thyroid problems and mental deficiency and as an antiseptic and disinfectant. Deficient at the outset of the Second Five-Year Plan, iodine production did increase slightly in 1933 from 46 tons to 59 tons, with production of bromine, which is found with iodine, increasing from 122 tons to 142 tons.[111] In 1935, iodine increased dramatically. As a result of remodeling and concerted efforts in the industry, in 1935 production of Plazmotsid rose four times in 1935, as compared with 1934; production of novocaine nearly doubled, production of the barbiturate Liuminal increased almost ten times, and Tripan-Blue increased thirty-fold.[112] Production of bromine leapt to 210.4 tons; iodine production nearly doubled between 1933 and 1935.[113]

But output of iodine still did not meet projected need in 1935, nor was it commensurate with amounts used in the United States or in Imperial Russia. The United States, as cited in a previous chapter used 270 to 300 tons in the early 1930s and Imperial Russia had used 100 to 120 tons before World War I. The glut of iodide salts was due not to oversupply, but rather to consumers' refusing to purchase the item because of steep price hikes.

How can we rate the core Soviet pharmaceutical industry at the end of the Second Five-Year Plan? We have seen that there were distribution problems but did positives balance out negatives on the production end? Put another way, did the centralized, state-run industry produce pharmaceuticals more effectively than its Tsarist predecessor or than contemporary industries in Western Europe and the United States? The answer was important not only for Soviet prestige but because by 1938 war loomed on both the Soviet Union's eastern and western fronts.

The Score Card for Pharmaceuticals in 1937

Pluses

The Akrikhin Factory, which was not brought into the core pharmaceutical industry until 1939, appeared to be a success story. In 1938 the factory put out 61.7 tons of Akrikhin. Costs were lower than ordained by the plan and the distribution price dropped from 1,200 thousand rubles per ton in 1937 to 600 thousand rubles per ton in 1938.[114] However, spoilage (*brak*) may have affected this product as it did others from the factory, as described below.

Industry executives considered the re-attachment of the three iodine factories to Vokhimfarm a plus. Additional government funding for raw materials arrived in the fourth quarter of 1937. Some remodeling and reconstruction in the Salicylate, Karpov, and Alkaloid factories took place. As a result, output of glucose in the Alkaloid Factory was said to have increased two and one half times as compared with 1936 and "fully satisfied requests." A method of obtaining synthetic Vitamin C was worked out in the Factory of Endocrine and Vitamin Preparations.[115] In 1937, the Karpov (former Ferrein) Factory produced the antisyphilitic Mioarsenol, for intramuscular application. However, the new leprosy treatment Moogrol was slow to appear and Dekholin, an iron substance, was rejected for impurities.[116]

The industry continued to surge forward in research and development, although in some cases there was double counting. In 1937, the industry publicized the advent of new barbiturates—Adurol and Medinal, similar to Veronal. New anesthetics included Uretan, designed for obstetrics and Vinetin; Omatropin, used in ophthalmic practice; and Pantokain. Antirheumatics and febrifuges included Atezal and Atofanil, which combined atofan (a clone of Schering's Atophan) and salicylic acid. Sergozin, claimed as a new contrast substance for x-rays, had been developed in 1933. Adkurekrin, for diabetes and "Preparation 118," designed to attack venereal disease in the infectious stage, were authentically new. But the industry also included Vitaminol and Folliculin in higher concentrations in its "new products" list.[117] The last, had been acclaimed as a new Soviet organo-preparation in 1933, as noted above, and was given a slightly new twist only in 1939, when, if large amounts did not stimulate ovarial function, Soviet pharmacologists combined Folliculin with Yohimbine, a poisonous alkaloid derived from the bark of a tree, that had long been produced by Merck and used as an aphrodisiac and local anesthetic.[118]

The industry did score a major breakthough in 1937 with the development of the sulfa drug, Streptotsid. This put the industry on par with Western Europe and the United States. Produced in the Semashko Factory, the drug targeted erysipelas—local inflamation of the skin and subcutaneous tissues caused by hemolytic streptococcus, which also caused puerperal or child-birth fever, a major factor in female mortality. Additionally, Streptotsid was said to be effective against "other" streptococcal infections. [119]

To put the Soviet achievement in perspective, about 5, 000 sulfa drugs have been developed world wide since the 1930s, although only 40 have been used, and only four or five are "best sellers."[120] In 1937 and 1938 the English pharmaceutical firm May and Baker also developed a new sulfa drug, Sulfapyridine or M&B 693. This drug, sold under the trade name Dagenan and licensed to Merck, was used in the United States to combat an outbreak of pneumonia in the winter of 1938 and 1939.[121]

Streptotsid was not sold on the world market. It did become the sulfa drug of choice domestically. White Streptotsid was particularly effective in treating gonorrhea in adults, according to a "Conference of Dermatologists and Venerealogists" that met in Kiev September 25-30, 1938. A "brigade of physicians" working throughout the Soviet Union during the year, under the supervision of Dr. R. M. Fronstein and Dr. Ovchinnikov, reported that white Streptotsid had been applied in 1,535 (out of 2,600) cases of severe gonorrhea with good results. Unfortunately, white Streptotsid did not work well in cases of juvenile gonorrhea. According to Dr. K. A. Karesheva, in Kiev, sulfanilamide was shown to be effective in five cases of girls over 15, but not with younger children. In any case, the specialists noted that white streptotsid had some undesirable side effects such as "weakened vision and dermatitis." Thus, they recommended that use of the sulfa drug in "children and pregnant women should be severely limited" and, further, that white Streptotsid should be "applied exclusively in clinics."[122]

Minuses

So the industry did make gains. But alongside them much production was under capacity and output of some basic and important items did not reach their quotas, which were based on estimated need. For example, the 1937 plan for salicylate products was "based on claims…for full satisfaction of need," but aspirin, salicylic acid, and sodium salicylate from the Salicylate Factory met only three-fourths, two-thirds, and one-half of their targets, respectively. Narcotic ether from the Karpov Factory met just over 80 percent of target and caustic soda from the same factory was way below par, as were bromide drops. Only half the quinine hydrochloric acid called for in the plan was produced in the Alkaloid Factory and the Semashko Factory produced only a little over a third of the Hydrokhinon called for. The same was true of the barbiturate Liuminal from the Semashko Factory, but it was claimed that a market was lacking. Phenacetin and Kollargol were underproduced in the Farmakon Factory in Leningrad. On the other hand, potassium iodide, iodine sublimate, mercury preparations, and iodoform from the Karpov Factory were right on target and Urotropin and the antivenereals Osarsol and Novarsenol from this factory were over their targets. The Alkaloid Factory put out Novocaine and Codeine on target. As noted paraamidophenol from the Semashko factory was well over target, although under capacity. Plazmotsid came in at just a fraction over.[123]

Only a little more than three-fourths of the "disinfecting substances" that were called for in the plan were produced in 1937, over 10 percent below the amount produced in 1936. Only 71 percent of "technical iodine," 62 percent of "technical bromine," and 83.5 percent of "various chemical products" called for in the 1937 plan were produced in 1937. Output of technical iodine in 1937 was below output in 1936.[124] In 1937 the Chief Pharmacy Administration decried "severe insufficiency of pharmacy vessels."[125]

A further issue was the poor quality of some pharmaceuticals. This continued to cause rejection (*reklamatsiia*) of products at the receiving end. Industry executives asserted that spoilage (*brak*) within the industry as a whole was a little lower in 1937 than in 1936. However, *brak* for Novarsenol (produced at the Akrikhin, Dzerzhinsky-Chimkent and Farmakon factories) was about two thirds higher. And *reklamatsiia* claims were higher in 1937 than in 1936—143 versus 133, the increases being connected with Aspirin, produced by the Salicylate Factory; technical morphine, produced by Dzerzhinsky; and Pepton, produced by Farmakon. Spoilage affected salol as well as Aspirin, technical morphine, and the color of Phenacetin, Pyramidon, and Lecithin put out by the Farmakon Factory.[126] In 1938, output of aspirin and other salicylate preparations did not meet production targets due to shortages of phenol and salicylic acid. Iodine, bromine, bismuth, and technical morphine also did not meet their production targets.[127]

Conclusion

The core Soviet pharmaceutical industry did not fulfill its challenge to consistently supply and distribute adequate amounts of pharmaceuticals so that universal, high-quality health care, promised by the 1936 Constitution, could become a reality. On the contrary, Soviet citizens periodically faced shortages of basic items such as aspirin, iodine, the barbiturate Liuminal, ether, disinfectants and sometimes sulfa drugs. Ukrainians were particularly hard hit during the 1930s. Ukrainian specialists implied that Russian specialists were largely responsible for their predicament. However, this was not the case because Russia also suffered deficits of pharmaceuticals. Levinshtein and Ukrainian specialists correctly pointed to some causal factors—inadequate investment and limited imports. But this chapter has shown that, in addition, excessive exports, a dysfunctional economy, and frequent exogenous reorganization straightjacketed the industry. The impediments to Soviet pharmaceutical production, in fact, were systemic. Levinshtein and Ukrainian pharmacists could not publicly admit this, nor could the problems be resolved without serious changes not only in the pharmaceutical sector but in the entire economy.

Industry managers appeared committed to supplying the populace despite some sloppiness within the industry. They achieved successes in production and distribution of pharmaceuticals, however, by bucking the Soviet economic and political system rather than because of it.

On first glance, the core Soviet pharmaceutical industry fulfilled the challenge of keeping pace with research and development in West European and American houses.[128] Yet cracks were visible in Soviet pharmaceutical R and D as well as the industry's quantitative output. Many of the products the core Soviet pharmaceutical industry developed in the 1930s were copies of foreign products, arrived at through reverse engineering without licensing. Soviet scientists modified and, in some cases, claimed to improve the products. They also resurrected old remedies studied in Imperial times and performed new research on botanicals. Nevertheless, legality aside, the intellectual piracy suggested a dependency on foreign R and D and, correspondingly, lack of originality in Soviet pharmaceutical R and D. Certainly, a crucial failure was the failure of the core Soviet pharmaceutical industry to develop a method of mass-producing penicillin before World War II.

The Second World War, in sum, in and of itself, was not responsible for the inadequacies in the core Soviet pharmaceutical industry for serious problems in production and distribution were noticeable well before the war. Micro management by exogenous officials, faulty political decisions and economic inefficiencies were the factors that blocked the Soviet pharmaceutical industry. Despite determination, energy and attempts to implement good business practices, industry managers and specialists could not overcome inherent obstacles. A complete overhaul of the Soviet pharmaceutical sector was necessary to make it function better.

Conclusion

The Imperial Russian government thwarted domestic pharmaceutical research and development by scrutinizing domestic products more zealously than foreign ones and at times applying tariffs that favored foreign prepared pharmaceuticals over imports of raw materials that were not available in the empire. However, these policies benefited consumers. Pharmaceutical enterprises were otherwise independent and there were no shortages of soap, disinfectants, medicines and other pharmaceutical products. Russia was an important exporter of medicinal botanicals. Dispensing was not sufficient in the countryside but was ample in the cities of the Empire, even in Siberia and Russian Turkestan, with drug stores supplementing pharmacies, which were limited by government regulations.

World War I loosened fetters on research and development, stimulating production of some items heretofore imported. Pharmaceutical production held its own during the three years Russia was in the Great War. In the main, the Imperial Russian pharmaceutical industry was on a par with British and American pharmaceutical industries and was poised for greater growth by 1916. Thus, the pre-Soviet status of the industry cannot be held responsible for shortages of pharmaceuticals in Soviet times.

The Soviet pharmaceutical industry and dispensing deteriorated during the civil war of 1917/1918- 1921. Sundered trade links and fighting were obvious problems. But, greatly to blame were overly theoretical Bolshevik officials who, ensconced in Moscow and fighting off political opponents, were taking over the Empire's assets, including pharmacies and pharmaceutical factories, and upsetting economic equilibrium by flouting economic laws. Nationalization of pharmacies and pharmaceutical enterprises was devastating. These entities lost the expertise of their founders and owners, they were not properly tended, and the new managers appointed by the government were party members first and pharmaceutical experts second. Pharmacies and drugs stores never fully recovered from the nationalization policies.

Key pharmaceutical factories in Moscow comprised the core pharmaceutical industry in the early NEP. Later other enterprises were added. Though the core industry included only a small percentage of the total pharmaceutical enterprises in Imperial Russia, its factories supplied over half the pharmaceuticals used in the Soviet Union. Managers of enterprises and the board that ran the industry gradually became proprietary and professional. But their job was an uphill battle during the first two decades of the Soviet Union's existence before the Great Patriotic War because they still had to contend with officials whose economic theories and desire to control the economy caused them to ignore objective economic forces, common sense and the public welfare. The extreme vertical organization of the Soviet economy was cumbersome and made domestic sourcing difficult. Separation of the chemical-pharmaceutical industry from the chemical industry was a liability from the outset. Periodic separation of the industry from the production of medicinal botanicals, glass and packaging and medical instruments operations also hampered production. The Soviet government was far more intrusive than the Imperial government and its policies exacerbated sourcing, financial, production and distribution of pharmaceuticals. Official control over imports and exports hampered the industry. Industry experts debated how much tariffs should protect the industry from foreign competition. Sensible industry executives realized that they would need imports of finished products and equipment for the foreseeable future. However, outside agencies limited imports, cramping not only the industry but the populace. Then, from the beginning of the first Five-Year plans in the late 1920s, excessive exports shorted materials pharmaceutical enterprises needed. Frequent reorganization was disruptive and hurt industry revenues. Lack of revenue hampered remodeling. Pricing policies and allocations to Pharmacy Organizations that purchased for pharmacies at times prevented sales of pharmaceutical products, accentuating cash-flow problems.

Production of prototypes was not always adequate. The output of pharmaceuticals increased during the NEP and again by the end of the Second Five-Year Plan but in spite of rather than because of the system set up for the industry. The amalgamation of enterprises and government coordination of inputs and outputs did not produce synergy. Rather output of pharmaceuticals increased through ongoing struggle by enterprise managers and the industry's administrative board to counter economic dysfunction and the government's policies, on the one hand, and to employ business methods traditional to market economies, on the other. Twenty years after the advent of Soviet power, shortages of basic pharmaceuticals, pharmacies and pharmacists persisted.

Perhaps an even greater problem was that the Soviet pharmaceutical industry competed with West European and American houses to a great extent by imitating their products. Soviet pharmacologists did do original research and did modify and improve foreign pharmaceuticals but there is a sense in industry records reposing in the archives and in comments from the pharmaceutical press that Soviet pharmacologists and industry executives regarded themselves in tutelage to West European and American houses.

The story of the Soviet pharmaceutical industry demonstrates that bigger is not always better. Small-scale *kustar'* entities often were able to perform better than the core industry. Pharmaceutical enterprises in market economies are affected by the world market and competition. But if their management makes strategic mistakes and they go under, remaining enterprises move into the vacuum. The concentration of the Soviet industry, on the other hand, magnified mistakes and made it difficult for Pharmacy Administrations and final consumers—the Soviet people—to look for other alternatives.

The Soviet pharmaceutical industry's saga proves that the shortages of medicines and other items noticed by visitors to the Soviet Union in the 1960s and 1970s were not merely the legacy of the Great Patriotic War. Shortages occurred before the war and were mainly due to systemic flaws. Although some historians claim that preventive medicine balanced out the problems in the pharmaceutical industry, the experiences of the Ufa Bacteriological Institute, though admittedly a small sample, suggest that macroeconomic inefficiency negatively affected production of vaccines and serums in the hinterlands where most of the Soviet population resided.

Industry specialists were aware of the problems and did not shrink from publicizing them. I. A. Obergard, the self same who had served as moderator at I. I. Levinshtein's in-house purge trial, for example, criticized pharmaceutical research in a speech he gave in 1937. Praising Stalin as a "leader in the world, guaranteeing to our people medical supplies, equal to the growth of culture and prosperity of the Stalinist epoch," he nonetheless asserted that the pharmaceutical press was poor, with only two journals dealing with pharmacology (one for the Ukraine and one for the entire USSR); that there were only three scientists in the Soviet Union with specialties in pharmacognosy; that pharmacy specialists needed more study on foreign production and more trips abroad; that health-care institutions were not sufficiently unified; that "planning did not always agree with reality."[1] A "state of the industry address," presented to the First All-Union Congress of Pharmacologists and Toxicologists in June 1937, asserted that the specialty of pharmacology was "severely backward, together with other physiological sciences" and "insufficiently answered to the needs of Soviet health care." Soviet pharmacology had been hampered, Congress delegates were informed, by an "insufficient amount of workers," as well as by an "insufficient connection with the chemical-pharmaceutical industry and with institutions managing the study and production of medicinal plants, not to mention…insufficiency of equipment…." [2] This does not appear formulaic *samokritika,* but rather an indictment of the Soviet economic system.

Deficits and problems in the pharmaceutical industry boded ill for war, which erupted in the far east in 1938 and in the west in 1939. It is difficult to tie disease and mortality rates to the availability or lack thereof of pharmaceuticals and thereby make definitive evaluation of Soviet health care during the first two decades. Certainly the irregular quantity and quality of pharmaceuticals posed just one more difficulty for the Soviet populace.

Without radical change in the Soviet macro economy and more autonomy for the industry the aforementioned obstacles could not be overcome. Fortunately these changes occurred in the 1990s when the centralized, government-dominated economic system was disbanded. Western and Japanese firms re-entered Russia. New Russian pharmaceutical enterprises sprouted. With autonomy and infusions of capital a number of old Soviet factories like Akrikhin and the Karpov (Ferrein) factories were retooled. A number of shops in the Akrikhin Factory, near Moscow, now sport state-of-the-art equipment and produce products that hold their own in the world market.[3] Domestic products from Akrikhin, Ferrein and other post-Soviet pharmaceutical companies now supplement foreign ones on pharmacy shelves. Post-Soviet researchers have entered into contracts with some foreign biotech and pharmaceutical firms. Soviet pharmaceutical and medical research now has more opportunity for realization.

Two caveats are necessary about the post-Soviet period. Because benefits have been cut and monetized, some segments of the population, particularly pensioners, have found it more difficult to purchase medicines. Additionally, Murray Feshbach, Judith Twigg, John (Jack) Kramer, Dan Goldberg, Harley Balzer, Mark Field—the pioneer of Soviet health studies—and other contemporary demographers, sociologists and health-care specialists have warned of a health crisis in post-Soviet Russia due to environmental problems, drug usage and sharing of needles and drug apparatus, poverty, poor diet, tobacco smoking, stress and lack of attention to AIDS, tuberculosis, smallpox, and other infectious diseases.[4] Ironically, the post-Soviet pharmaceutical industry has become healthier in the face of a decline in popular health.

Although a new era is emerging in post-Soviet Russia, the performance of the Soviet pharmaceutical industry need not be relegated to the dustbin. The core Soviet pharmaceutical industry provides a real, rather than hypothetical, model of pharmaceutical production and distribution dominated by exogenous forces. The experiences of the industry thus may have some relevance for current public-policy discourse on how much independence pharmaceutical industries of today should have. Of course the macro economy in the Soviet Union of the 1920s and 1930s and the mid-set of Soviet officials were sui generis. Nevertheless, the saga of the Soviet industry—what went wrong with centralized, government-controlled pharmaceutical production and distribution and why—offer some instructive lessons for health care and prescription debates at present.

Notes

Introduction

1. Talks with librarians and archivists; interviews with Lee Avrashov, Eugenia Pokrovskaya in Denver, 2002-2004; personal familiarity with a Russian colleague in Leningrad/St. Petersburg.
2. Conversations with Viktor Matveevich Salo, former director of the now defunct Pharmacy Museum in Moscow.
3. Sir Arthur Newsholme and John Kingsbury, *Red Medicine: Socialized Health in Soviet Russia* (New York: Doubleday, Doran &Company, 1934),p. 274.
4. Haden Guest, '"Medicine in the Soviet Union," *The Spectator,* October 2, 1936, p. 540.
5. Henry E. Sigerist, *Socialized Medicine in the Soviet Union* (New York: W. W. Norton & Company, 1934), p. 287-288.
6. "O nashikh nedochetakh," *Khimiko-farmatsevticheskaia promyshlennost',* vol. 3, no. 3, 1934, p. 57.
7. I. I. Levinshtein, "O nenormal'nom polozhenii farmatsevticheskogo dela," ibid., vol. 3, no. 4, 1934, pp. 5-7. See chapters 9 and 11 for more details. 32
8. Esfir Falkovich recounted that many young people constructing Komsomol'sk in Siberia in 1934 were debilitated by scurvy because of lack of vitamins, which were produced by factories in the core pharmaceutical industry. The young workers drank a decoction of boiled pine syrup to combat this serious medical condition, but boiling may have destroyed the potency of the vitamins in the decoction. Interview, May 21, 2004. Admittedly, the construction site was remote and the lack of vitamins may have been an oversight due to slipshod planning. However, Valentin Peschansky recalled that in European Russia at the outset of the war soap was in short supply. De-lousing stations set up at railway stations doled out only tiny slivers. Interview, May 21, 2004.
9. A. N. Sorokin, "Puty razvitiia farmatsevticheskoi promyshlennosti," *Farmatsiia,* vol. 3 , no. 7-8, 1940, pp. 9-11.
10. State Archive of the Russian Federation [hereafter cited GARF] fond A482, opis' 51, delo. 15, listy 11-13, 48-51 [hereafter cited " f.", "d.", "op.", "ll." or "l" in the singular .]
11. Russian State Archive of the Economy [hereafter cited RGAE], f. 8009, op. 2, d. 36, l. 42.
12. A. G. Natradze, "Zadachi khimiko-farmatsevticheskoi promyshlennosti v 1945 g.," *Farmatsiia,* vol. 8, no. 1, 1945, pp. 12-13. Though he repeatedly used the term chemical-pharmaceutical industry, this sentence reads,"*...pered voinoi meditsinskaia promyshlennost' ne udovletvoriala v polnoi mere potrebnosti nashei strany v medikamentakh."* (p. 13)
13. Henry Sigerist, *Medicine and Health in the Soviet Union* (New York: the Citadel Press, 1947), p. 105.

14. Mark Harrison, "Counting Soviet Deaths in the Great Patriotic War: Comment," *Europe-Asia Studies,* vol. 55, no. 6, 2003, pp. 939-944, estimates Soviet deaths "somewhere between 23.9 and 25.8 million, with the true figure likely to be somewhat above the mid-point. Those who prefer round numbers may go for 25 million plus or minus a million." (p. 943) See also Michael Haynes, "Clarifying Excess Deaths and Actual War Deaths in the Soviet Union During World War II: A Reply," ibid., pp. 945-947.
15. Newsholme and Kingsbury, *Red Medicine,* 271-274, 290-291.
16. Chart, Ibid., p. 203; Abortions without anesthesia, p. 184; X-ray diagnosis for TB, p. 248.
17. Guest, "Medicine," p. 540.
18. Frank Lorimer, *The Population of the Soviet Union: History and Prospects* (Geneva: League of Nations, 1946), p. 121.
19. Moscow, February 21, 1938, "The Market in the Soviet Union for Dental, Surgical, Medical, and Hospital Equipment, Apparatus, and Supplies," National Archives, United States of America [hereafter cited NAUSA], RG 489, Box 82, 11,100, Bureau of Foreign and Domestic Commerce, [hereafter cited BFDC], U.S. Department of Commerce.
20. Sigerist, *Socialized Medicine,* 208-222.
21. Christopher M. Davis, "Economics of Soviet Public Health," in Susan Gross Solomon and John F. Hutchinson, eds., *Health and Society in Revolutionary Russia* (Bloomington: Indiana University Press, 1990), p. 162. (Total chapter, pp. 146-172.)
22. Sally Ewing, "The Science and Politics of Soviet Insurance Medicine," ibid., pp. 69-96; Neil B. Weissman, "Origins of the Soviet Health Administration," ibid., pp. 97-120.
23. J. D. Barber and R. W. Davies, "Employment and Industrial Labour," in R. W. Davies, Mark Harrison and S. G. Wheatcroft, eds., *The Economic Transformation of the Soviet Union, 1913-1945* (Cambridge: Cambridge University Press, 1994), pp. 89-90.
24. George Borodin's *Red Surgeon* (London: Museum Press, Ltd, 1944) was an apology for Soviet medicine as were English-language articles published during the war. In any case they say virtually nothing about the pharmaceutical industry.

    In more recent works, the pharmaceutical industry also is an afterthought. See John F. Hutchinson, *Politics and Public Health in Revolutionary Russia, 1890-1918* (Baltimore: Johns Hopkins University Press, 1990) and Solomon and Hutchinson, *Health and Society in Revolutionary Russia.*

    Mark Field was a pioneer in describing Soviet health care after the Great Patriotic War. His *Soviet Socialized Medicine: An Introduction* (New York: The Free Press, 1967), discusses pharmaceuticals pp. 43, 63, 89-90. On p. 21, Field noted that although the USSR produced the bulk of pharmaceuticals for Comecon, only 9 percent of them were exported. Observing the Soviet medical system before the archives were open, Field acquired information through interviews with former Soviet citizens and extrapolated from Soviet medical journals and statistics. He cites sales of pharmaceuticals in terms of prices, rather than quantity, but notes that there were shortfalls. Mark G. Field, "Doctors and Patients" in Alex Inkeles and Kent Geiger, *Soviet Society: A Book of Readings* (Boston: Houghton Mifflin, 1961), pp. 510-520. (Reprinted from "Some Problems of Soviet Medical Practice: A Sociological Approach," *The New England Journal of Medicine* , vol. 248, 1953, pp. 919-926. Field discusses shortages of pharmaceuticals (from an article in *Meditsinskii rabotnik,* 1951) on p. 518.

Alec Nove echoed Field remarking that "the equipment of many Soviet hospitals is antiquated . . . drugs are often scarce, and the general level of health facilities is not up to the best Western standards. Nevertheless," he continued, "a great deal has certainly been done to spread hygiene, combat epidemics, and reduce infant mortality."Alec Nove, "Is the Soviet Union a Welfare State," in Inkeles and Geiger, *Soviet Society* (reprinted from "Social Welfare in the USSR," *Problems of Communism,* United States Information Agency, vol. 9, 1960, pp. 1-10), p. 501. Nove was a shrewd analyst of the Soviet economy, but his observations on the Soviet health system were somewhat off the mark, for archival evidence on the pharmaceutical industry reveals that, in addition to shortages of medicines, the Soviet Union was short of soap and disinfectants thus obviating the most dedicated efforts to promote good hygiene and combat epidemics.

Don Filtzer's recent book on workers in the post-war period, which uses archival evidence, takes into account this point, noting that shortages of basic medicines, following cuts of during the cold war, were complicated by lack of soap, resulting in appallingly filthy living and working quarters. Donald Filtzer, *Soviet Workers and Late Stalinism: Labour and the Restoration of the Stalinist System after World War II* (Cambridge: Cambridge University Press, 2002), pp. 105, 107, 108 and passim. Christopher Burton's comprehensive dissertation on physicians and medical care in the late Stalin period emphasizes the shortage of medicines in the post-war Soviet Union and citizens' complaints about this situation. (Chris Burton, "Medical Welfare during Late Stalinism: A Study of Doctors and the Soviet Health System, 1945-53." Ph. D. Dissertation, University of Chicago, 2000, pp. 309-324.)

See also Christopher Davis and Murray Feshbach, *Rising Infant Mortality in the U.S.S.R. in the 1970s* (U.S. Department of Commerce, September 1980), pp. 15, 16, 20, which notes shortages of disposable medical supplies and implies that poor hygiene and widespread bacterial infections resulting from influenza testify to defects in the pharmaceutical industry, although the industry is not their focus.

25. Communique from Michael Kaser November 29, 2004.
26. Along with charts indicating monies spent on pharmaceuticals Kaser noted that the Soviet Union accounted for 64 percent of Comecon's pharmaceutical production but only 9 percent of its exports, "most of which (38 percent)" were sold by Hungary (a statistic Mark Field also cited); that "the pill" and other contraceptives were rare; that although mass immunization had eliminated major infectious diseases, "the rates of acute intestinal disorders, measles, influenza, and leprospirosis" were "still high"; that outbreaks of cholera were still a danger in

certain areas because of poor hygiene as were staphylocci infections in hospitals because of lack of disposable instruments; that "closed-access shops...serving permit holders...usually have foreign pharmaceutical specialties and scarce Soviet preparations on sale"; and finally that free prescribing for inpatients amounted to "42 percent of ... pharmaceutical consumption." Michael Kaser, *Health Care in the Soviet Union and Eastern Europe* (London: Croom Helm, 1976), pp. 21, 47-48, 51-52, 63-64.

27. Kaser, ibid.(Boulder: Westview Press), pp. 172, 197.
28. Murray Feshbach and Alfred Friendly, *Ecoside in the USSR: Health and Nature Under Siege* (New York: Harper Collins/Basic Books, 1992), p. 197.
29. Bryan G. Reuben and Harold Wittcoff, *Pharmaceutical Chemicals in Perspective* (New York: John Wiley and Sons, 1989), pp. 11 and 19.
30. A. A. Utin, *Istoriia chimkentoskogo khimiko-farmatsevticheskogo zavoda im. F. E. Dzerzhinskogo* (Chimkent, 1958) and V. K. Afanas'ev, et. al, *Zhivi, "Akrikhin"!* (Staraia Kupavna, 1996).
31. E. I. Smirnov, chief editor, *Opyt sovetskoi meditsiny v velikoi otechestvennoi voine, 1941-1945 gg.* (Moscow: Medgiz, 1951-1955).
32. For the pre-Soviet Russian pharmaceutical industry see Mary Schaeffer Conroy, *In Health and In Sickness: Pharmacy, Pharmacists and the Pharmaceutical Industry in late Imperial, Early Soviet Russia* (Boulder, CO: East European Monographs, 1994), passim. For the American and British industries see Jonathan Libenau, *Medical Science and Medical Industry: The Formation of the American Pharmaceutical Industry* (Baltimore: The Johns Hopkins University Press, 1987), p. 110-11, 121, 126-134 and R. P. T. Davenport-Hines and Judy Slinn, *Glaxo: A History to 1962* (Cambridge: Cambridge University Press, 1992), pp. 86, 136, 143, and passim.
33. Mary Schaeffer Conroy, "Pharmacy in Soviet Russia before The Great Patriotic War (1941-45)," *Pharmacy in History,* vol. 40, no. 1, 1998, pp. 3-24.
34. Some of the best on the macro economy are Alec Nove, *An Economic History of the U.S.S.R.* (London: Penguin Press, First edition 1969, last reprint, 1990); James R. Millar and Susan J. Linz, ed. *The Soviet Economic Experiment* (Urbana and Chicago: University of Illinois Press, 1990); Holland Hunter and Janusz M. Szyrmer, *Faulty Foundations: Soviet Economic Policies, 1928-1940* (Princeton: Princeton University Press, 1992). On the macro and micro economy, in addition to Davies, Harrison, and Wheatcroft, *The Transformation of the Soviet Union,* see E. A. Rees, *Decision-Making in the Stalinist Command Economy, 1932-37* (Basingstoke: Macmillan Press, Ltd; New York, St. Martin's Press, Inc., 1997); Anthony Heywood, *Modernizing Lenin's Russia: Economic Reconstruction, Foreign Trade and the Railways* (Cambridge: Cambridge University Press, 1999); David R. Stone, *Hammer and Rifle: The Militarization of the Soviet Union, 1926-1933* (University Press of Kansas, 2000); and Julie Hessler, *A Social History of Soviet Trade* (Princeton: Princeton University Press, 2004). On agriculture and the similarities and the differences with regard to problems, solutions and real developments in late Imperial and Soviet Russia see George Yaney, *The Urge to Mobilize: Agrarian Reform in Russia, 1861-1930* (Urbana, Chicago, London: University of Illinois Press, 1982).

35. Archival materials after 1917 are from RGAE and GARF in Moscow and the Central State Historical Archive, Republic of Bashkortostan [hereafter cited TsGIA,RB]. Archival materials on the pre-Soviet period are from the Russian State Historical Archive [RGIA] in St. Petersburg.
36. John Haller emphasized that after 1939 only American eclectic physicians heavily relied on botanicals. Mainstream physicians increasingly prescribed the synthetics that the pharmaceutical industry was producing. John S. Haller, *Medical Protestants: The Eclectics in American Medicine, 1825-1939* (Carbondale: Southern Illinois University Press, 1994). Dennis Worthen, however, documents that botanicals were important in pharmacy practice during World War II. Worthen, *Pharmacy in World War II* (NY: Haworth Press, 2004), pp. 7, 16, 78, 80, 84-90, 94. In the post war-period, however, Americans relied on synthetics as well as antibiotics like penicillin, produced from mold, and streptomycin. It is only in the last decade that botanicals have become important to American consumers and are once again being recognized by American physicians.
37. Sarah Davies has the pioneering study on pre-war public opinion, *Popular Opinion in Stalin's Russia: Terror, Propaganda and Dissent, 1934-1941* (Cambridge: Cambridge University Press, 1997).

Chapter 1

1. For context, it can be noted that in Philadelphia alone in 1882 there were 144 concerns producing medicines and disinfectants. There were only a handful of really important pharmaceutical houses in the United States in the twentieth century, however. See Liebenau, *Medical Science and Medical Industry*, p. 24. See also John P. Swann, "The Evolution of the American Pharmaceutical Industry," *Pharmacy in History*, vol. 37, no. 2, 1995, pp. 76-86.
2. Conroy, *In Health and In Sickness*, pp. 137-161.
3. Louis Galambos with Jane Eliot Sewell, *Networks of Innovation: Vaccine Development at Merck, Sharp & Dohme, and Mulford, 1895-1995* (New York: Cambridge University Press, 1995), pp. x, 2-26.
4. See Joan Klobe Pratt, "The Free Economic Society and the Battle against Smallpox:" 'Public Sphere' in Action," *The Russian Review*, vol. 61, no. 4, 2002, pp. 560-578.
5. Introduction to TsGIA RB [Tsentralnyi Gosudarstvennyi Istoricheskii Arkhiv, Republic of Baskortostan] fond 1203, opis' 1, p. 1.
6. Conroy, *In Health and In Sickness*, pp. 137-161.
7. A number of the Warsaw factories dated to the first half of the nineteenth century and were major concerns. For example, the Tarchomin factory operated from 1823 to 1873 and the Dovichskoe Chemical Products Joint Stock Company had turnover of two million rubles a year. *Khimicheskoe delo v Rossii* (Odessa: Tipografiia "Poriadok," 1913), columns, 153-154, 180-184.
8. Among the enterprises in Latvia were Diubosk Brothers, annual production of which equaled two million rubles and Miul'grabenskii chemical factory with annual income of more than one million rubles. *Khimicheskoe delo v Rossii*, cols. 162-

164, 219-220.

9. Conroy, *In Health and In Sickness*, pp, 137-161
10. Four of the enterprises in Kherson were sizable, with annual incomes of a quarter of a million to over half a million rubles. Conroy, ibid., pp. 146-149 and *Khimicheskoe delo v Rossii*, passim.
11. *Khimicheskoe delo v Rossii* columns 169-170, 196-197. See also Conroy, *In Health and In Sickness*, pp. 137-161.
12. *Khimicheskoe delo v Rossii*, columns 165-167, 180, 191-194; also Conroy, *In Health and In Sickness*, pp. 149-150.
13. Conroy, ibid., pp. 40-41. V. K. Ferrein trained in the family's Staraia Nikolskaia pharmacy, then studied chemistry in Munich, and received a Master of Pharmacy degree from the University of Moscow in 1869. Ferrein expanded the pharmacy into a pharmaceutical empire and, in 1902, the Ferrein complex became a family held joint-stock company.
14. Ibid., pp. 40-41, 150-161.
15. Akts. O-vo "Gosmedtorgprom," *Gosudarstvennyi khimiko-farmatsevticheskii zavod imeni L. Ia. Karpova.* (Moscow, 1926), p 3. and Conroy, *In Health and In Sickness*, pp.137-161.
16. Utin, *Istoriia chimkentskogo khimiko-farmatsevticheskogo zavoda,* p.18. Three were located in Syr Dar'ia.
17. *Khimicheskoe delo v Rossii*, cols. 198, 199, 340.
18. "World Trade Notes on Chemical and Allied Products," No. 48, November 28, 1936, NAUSA, File RG 489, 10,700, in BFDC, U. S. Dept. of Commerce. On the importance of improved hygiene to public health see Reuben and Wittcoff, *Pharmaceutical Chemicals in Perspective*, pp. 8-9.
19. See M. Weatherall, *In Search of a Cure* (New York: Oxford University Press, 1990), pp. 83-93.
20. Renate A. Reidl (Head of Corporate Archives, Sandoz Ltd., Basel) has emphasized that the "quality of drugs produced in those days" was not "comparable with present-day formulations...The early patent remedies were either of low potency or, if stronger, caused serious side effects. Attention to purity was lax...Many years were to pass before industrial drug research attained a status equivalent to that enjoyed by university-level research." "A Brief History of the Pharmaceutical Industry in Basel," in Jonathan Libenau, Gregory J. Higby, and Elaine C. Stroud *Pill Peddlers: Essays on the History of the Pharmaceutical Industry* (Madison, WI; American Institute of the History of Pharmacy, 1990), pp. 54, 56.
21. The German professor converted benzene into nitrobenzene with nitrating acid, a mixture of saltpeter and sulfuric acid. Fritzsche also obtained indigo from the plant *Indigofera anil L.. The Story of the Chemical Industry in Basle* (Olten and Lausanne: Urs Graf Publishers, 1959), p. 97. On Russians and aniline see also L. F. Fokin, *Obzor khimicheskoi promyshlennosti v Rossii.* (Petrograd, 1921), p. 6.
22. The brothers Zhdanov pioneered the use of disinfectants made from bleach in Russia during the Crimean campaign of 1854. In 1862, A.A. Andreev founded a steam-powered laboratory in Moscow to produce pharmaceutical preparations and, in the late 1860s, one "Kilv'ein, Professor Kittary, and others" began to

produce disinfectants on a large scale from imported phenol, "for freshening the air in dwellings," that assumed a significant market. By the mid 1880s there were five enterprises in St. Petersburg producing about 100,000 rubles' worth of disinfecting and pharmaceutical preparations, four in Moscow producing 60,000 rubles' worth, and enterprises in Odessa, Iaroslavl', Ekaterinburg, and Mogilev provinces producing 20,000 to 25,000 rubles worth. Ivan Kozlov, "Khimicheskie produkty," in D. A Timiriazev, *Istoriko-statisticheskii obzor promyshlennosti Rossii* (St. Petersburg, 1886), vol. II, chapter VIII, pp.40, 43.

23. For Britain see, for example, the fate of Glaxo, which originated in New Zealand. Pharmaceutical firms in Britain remained small in the 1920s and Britain did not emancipate itself from German chemical products until World War II. Davenport-Hines and Slinn, *Glaxo*, pp. 1-138, esp. pp. 86, 136-138. America, like Russia, developed autonomy during World War I and matured during the 1920s. For the United States see, Liebenau, *Medical Science*, pp. 1-128.
24. *The Story of the Chemical Industry in Basle*, pp. 156-157, 160-161, 167, 169; 83-85. For the dry distillation process, see p. 97; for isonicotinic acid hydrazide, see p. 165. Also, Reidl, "A Brief History of the Pharmaceutical Industry in Basel," Libenau et al, *Pill Peddlers*, pp. 49-72.
25. Fokin, *Obzor khimicheskoi promyshlennosti*, p. 7.
26. Kozlov, "Khimicheskie produkty," in Timiriazev, *Istoriko-statisticheskii obzor promyshlennosti Rossii*, pp. 2-4.
27. Fokin, *Obzor khimicheskoi promyshlennosti* pp. 7-8.
28. *Khimicheskioe delo v Rossii*, Odessa, 1913, columns 152-340. Soviet pharmacy specialists tended to claim that most of these enterprises were "branches of German factories" established to divert Russian money to Germany. See, for example, A. E. Porai-Koshits, *K voprosu o sud'be krasochnoi promyshlennosti* (Petrograd, 1918), p. 10. In fact, this does not seem to have been the case. The majority of chemical factories listed in *Khimicheskoe delo v Rossii* had Russian owners. The ancillary chemical apparatus and equipment advertised in this compilation was partly of foreign and partly of Russian provenance. *Khimicheskoe delo v Rossii*, columns 151-286 and passim.
29. *Khimicheskoe delo v Rossii*, columns 245-258. *Magistr* of Pharmacy M. V. Tsypkin gives slightly different statistics for 1910 in his thirteen-page brochure, published during World War I. Namely, he cites 267 manufactories (*fabriki*) producing chemical and related products, 118 exclusively producing chemicals. *O fabrikakh, zavodakh i laboratoriiakh izgotovliaiushchikh khimicheskie produkty i khimiko-farmatsevticheskie preparaty v Rossii* (Moscow, 1915), pp. 4-5.
30. Christopher Kobrak, *National Cultures and International Competition: The Experience of Schering AG, 1851-1950.* (Cambridge University Press, 2002), pp. 45- 50, 74-75, 92-93.
31. *Khimicheskoe delo v Rossii*, passim and Fokin, *Obzor khimicheskoi promyshlennosti*, passim.
32. *Khimicheskoe delo v Rossii*, passim; Tsypkin, *O fabrikakh*, pp. 4-5. See also Fokin *Obzor khimicheskoi promyshlennosti* pp. 8-11, for information on *kustar'* and factory production of sulfuric acid, hydrochloric acid, vinegar acid, superphosphates, and

other items.

33. Fokin, *Obzor khimicheskoi promyshlennosti*, p. 42.
34. See chapter 4 of this work.
35. Tsypkin, *O fabrikakh*, pp. 5, 7.
36. Loc. Cit.
37. Fokin, *Obzor khimicheskoi promyshlennosti*, pp. 7-9. In 1906 duties on imported aniline were raised from 2 rubles, 25 kopeks to 4 rubles. In 1909 over 36,000 puds had been imported 1909.
38. Porai-Koshits, *K voprosu o sud'be krasochnoi promyshlennosti v Rossii* , pp. 2, 8.
39. See Galambos with Sewell, *Networks of Innovation*, pp. 1-35, as well as Liebenau, *Medical Science and Medical Industry*, pp. 1-113, esp, p. 110, and Davenport-Hines and Slinn, *Glaxo.*
40. F. Ferrein, "Tamozhennye tarify i ikh znachenie dlia khimiko-farmatsevticheskoi promyshlennosti," *Khimiko-farmatsevticheskii zhurnal*, no. 7, 1924, p. 10.
41. Porai-Koshits, *K voprosu o sud'be*, p. 3, on tariffs. For details on all these problems see Conroy, *In Health and In Sickness*, pp. 162-174.
42. For details on malaria and malaria research in nineteenth- and early twentieth-century Russia see Mary Schaeffer Conroy, "Malaria in Late Tsarist Russia," *Bulletin of the History of Medicine*, vol. 56, no. 1, 1982, pp. 41-55.
43. Conroy, *In Health and In Sickness*, pp. 164-165. For a few more details on iodine production in Tomsk before World War I, see Iantsenetskii (Director of the Tomsk Farmzavod), "Tomskii Farmzavod," in *Informatsionnyi biulleten'*, no. 3, 1940, p. 9. On discovery of iodine in the thyroid in 1895, its importance for growth and related research see Weatherall, *In Search of a Cure*, pp. 87-89. For basic information on iodine see *The World Book Encyclopedia*, Chicago: Field Enterprises, 1976, vol. 10, p. 292.
44. Conroy, *In Health and In Sickness*, pp. 164-165, 211-212. In 1903 the lower chamber of the Russian parliament, the Duma, was warned that contraband opium was coming into the Ussuri region of eastern Siberia from China. In 1909, the government was alerted to opium smoking in Central Asia. An opium pipe is on display in the museum in Tbilisi, Georgia.
45. Conroy, ibid., pp. 164-165. On hydrastine as a hemostatic, see N. Voroshilov, "Hydrastis canadensis L. Kanadskii zheltokoren', zolotaia pechat'," *Khimiko-farmatsevticheskii zhurnal*, vol. 2, no, 2 (5), 1924, p. 11.
46. A. Rabinovich, "Nasha Tribuna: Ob ispol'zovanii nekotorykh prirodnykh bogatstv Ukrainy," *Khimiko-farmatsevticheskii vestnik* (Odessa), no. 3-4, 1926, p. 20; E. Iu. Shass and F. A. Satsyperov, *Lekarstvennye i lekarstvenno-tekhnicheskie rasteniia SSSR: Sbor, kul'tura, pererabotka i eksport* (Moscow, 1927, passim).
47. Rabinovich, "Ob ispol'zovanii nekotorykh prirodnykh bogatstv Ukrainy," p. 20. Two thousand ounces of caraway-seed oil were derived annually, at a price of 60 to 70 kopeks per ounce.
48. Shass and Satsyperov, *Lekarstvennye i lekarstvenno-tekhnicheskie rasteniia SSSR*, pp. 9-10, 83-84.
49. Shass and Satsyperov, ibid., pp. 46-47.
50. Conroy, *In Health and In Sickness*, p. 142.

51. Utin, *Istoriia chimkentskogo khimiko-farmatsevticheskogo zavoda*, pp. 7-8. For more details on Russian Central Asia, see Seymour Becker, *Russia's Protectorates in Central Asia* (Cambridge, MA: Harvard University Press, 1968).
52. By the 1880s there were 15 match factories, 11 soap factories, 18 leather factories, and other factories in the Chimkent district. Utin, *Istoriia chimkentskogo khimiko-farmatsevticheskogo zavoda*, p. 6.
53. Ibid., pp. 5-22. The Savinkov factory in Chimkent had basic capital of 100,000 rubles. In 1913 the factory employed 60 workers and had annual production above 150,000 rubles. The manager was V. F. Gorshenin. *Khimicheskoe delo v Rossii*, col. 340.
54. Conroy, *In Health and In Sickness*, pp. 141-142
55. *The Dispensatory of the United States of America* (Philadelphia and London: J. B. Lippincott Company, 1918), pp. 1527, 1529. The dose subcutaneously was "sixteen minims (1 mil) of a two per cent solution," "by mouth, ten to thirty drops (0.6-1.8 mils.) of a four per cent solution."
56. Herbert Tabor, Celia W. Tabor, and Sanford M. Rosenthal, "The Biochemistry of the Polyamines: Spermidine and Spermine," *Annual Review of Biochemistry*, vol. 30, 1961, pp. 579-604)
57. Conroy, *In Health and In Sickness*, p. 142.
58. Ibid., pp. 175-199.
59. Shass and Satsyperov, *Lekarstvennye i lekarstvenno-tekhnicheskie rasteniia SSSR*, p. 10. The exact figure was 29,079 tons; only 1, 935 tons being used domestically. A later Soviet source gives an entirely different figure of 1,000 tons in 1913.
60. "Export of Herbs and Crude Drugs," *Economic Review of the Soviet Union*, November 1, 1931, pp. 493-494, NAUSA, File RG 489, Box 82, 10,300, BFDC, U.S. Dept. of Commerce.
61. First citation in Conroy, *In Health and In Sickness*, pp. 159-160. See also E. Iu. Shass, *Gosudarstvennyi standart eksportnogo lekarstvennogo i lekarstvenno-tekhnicheskogo syr'ia. Offitsialnyi tekst.* (Moscow: Narkomtorg USSR, 1927), pp. 28, 41-44. Licorice, Likopodium, and Sporyn'ia were still among the thirteen most marketable plant exports for Soviet Russia in 1927. Shass, ibid, p. 3. They were found in their natural state.
62. F. R. Eldridge, Jr., Chief Far Eastern Division, US Department of Commerce to Moorman Manufacturing Company, Quincy, Illinois, March 11, 1920, in NAUSA, File 231, RG 151, BFDC, U. S. Dept. of Commerce.
63. "Russia's Share in America's Crude-Drug Imports," *World Trade Notes on Chemicals*, January 8, 1934, NAUSA, File RG 489, 10,300, in BFDC, U.S. Dept of Commerce.
64. L. P. Cassidy, Secretary, Moorman Manufacturing Company (MoorMan's Stockman's Supplies and maker of MoorMan's Hog Remedy), Quincy, Illinois, to Bureau of Foreign and Domestic Commerce, Washington, DC, March 2, 1920; Commercial Attache in Charge of Russian Division, U.S. Dept of Commerce to Moorman Manufacturing Company, March 5, 1920; Director, Russian Division, BFDC, U.S. Dept of Commerce, to American Committee of Russian Cooperative Unions, New York City; to Mr. K. A. Kovalsky, Director, American Committee of

Siberian Agricultural Cooperative Unions, New York City; to Mr. E. C. Porter, Executive Secretary, American-Russian Chamber of Commerce, New York City; to R. Martens and Company, NYC; to Russian-American Committee for the Far East, Attention Mr. E. I. Omeltchenko; and to Youreveta Home and Foreign Trade Co, NYC, all March 5, 1920, in NAUSA, File 231, RG 151, BFDC, U.S. Dept. of Commerce.

65. For details see Conroy, *In Health and In Sickness*, especially pp. 12-13, 39-63. On pharmacists, including women pharmacists see ibid, pp. 26-38, 100-136.
66. Ibid., p. 123.
67. *.Illiustrirovannyi torgovo-promyshlennyi adresnyi al'bom g. Moskvy na 1909*. (Moscow, 1910), passim
68. In 1910, the Staraia Nikol'skaia Pharmacy of Vladimir Karlovich Ferrein, off Red Square employed 300 people, including 43 provizors, 121 assistant pharmacists and 22 women to type the signatury or labels for medicines. Like other pharmacies this pharmacy was open round the clock and some days dispensed 3,000 prescriptions for an annual total of 400,000 prescriptions. The pharmacy had state-of -the art equipment and also used an adjacent analytical laboratory. Employees were provided with a dining hall, a ventilation system and special chambers to protect staff dealing with poisonous materials, an outpatient clinic, and access to a profit-sharing plan. The pharmacy building was an enormous, Renaissance-style structure, with many storage and preparation rooms. A marble staircase with a wrought-iron art-nouveau railing led from the street level to the second floor. Ferrein's four drug stores also had beautiful cabinetry and bentwood chairs and tables where patrons could relax analogous in atmosphere though very different essentially from the American drugstore cum soda fountain. Conroy, *In Health and In Sickness*, pp. 40-41.
69. "Normal" pharmacies in small towns were often modest but as fully outfitted and equipped as those in larger cities. Such was the pharmacy in which one pharmacist who has left us his memoirs, Isaiah Ginzburg, apprenticed in 1894. The pharmacy, in a town some 150 miles from Moscow, was located in a frame building; it had rooms for drying herbs, cellars for preserving roots and special locked cabinets for storing poisons and strong-acting medicines. It dispensed traditional medicaments like beeswax, lily-of-the-valley and a powder made of dried beetles, purchased from local peasants. But it also included "plasters, cotton, ointments, quinine, sodium bromide, potassium iodide, and other drugs," made waxed paper, paper bags, filter papers, and boxes, and supplied oxygen to hospitals and home-bound patients. Conroy, *In Health and In Sickness*, p. 43.
70. Ibid., pp. 44-45; 39-46 passim, p. 13 for major cities cited..
71. Ibid., pp. 63-76.
72. See, for example, the popular manual by M. Platen, *Novyi sposob lecheniia: nastol'naia kniga dlia zdorovykh i bol'nikh*. (Translated from the German) (St. Petersburg: Tipo-litografiia Aktsionernago O-va "Samoobrazovanie", 1901).
73. Samuel C. Ramer, "Traditional Healers and Peasant Culture in Russia, 1861-1917," in Esther Kingston-Mann and Timothy Mixter, *Peasant Economy, Culture, and Politics of European Russia, 1800-1921* (Princeton: Princeton University Press, 1991),

pp. 207-235.

74. In the last decades of the nineteenth, century zemstvos began to buy up private pharmacies. In the first decades of the twentieth century, zemstvo activists lobbied government officials. They found a receptive ear in the Medical Council and amongst ministers of Internal Affairs, V. K. von Plehve [also spelled Pleve], P. N. Durnovo, and P. A. Stolypin. In 1906 Durnovo planned to establish 26 new pharmacies in St. Petersburg and 44 in Moscow, without waiting for the consent of nearby owners, as heretofore. Stolypin, whose support of private farms versus communal agriculture is well known, in the realm of pharmacy supported "public" pharmacy, albeit to fill in gaps rather than replace privately owned pharmacies altogether. On zemstvo "liberals" see Charles E. Timberlake, "The Tsarist Government's Preoccupation with the 'Liberal Party' in Tver' Province, 1890-1905," in Mary Schaeffer Conroy, ed., *Emerging Democracy in Late Imperial Russia.* (Niwot: University Press of Colorado, 1998), pp. 30-59 and Dittmar Dahlmann, "Liberals in the Provinces: The Kadets and the Duma Elections in Saratov, 1906-1912," ibid., 88-111. For details see Conroy, *In Health and In Sickness,* pp. 65-76, 296-301. For updated material on the issue see Mary Schaeffer Conroy, "P. A. Stolypin, Marxists and Liberals versus Owners of Private Pharmacies and Pharmaceutical Firms in Late Imperial Russia," in Conroy, *Emerging Democracy,* pp. 124-133.

Both the liberals and the government worked through the new parliament, once that body was instituted in 1906. In the spring of 1907, the press reported that the Medical Council had prepared a draft law, to be introduced by the Ministry of Internal Affairs for discussion in the State Duma, "which proposed to abolish the pharmacy monopoly," that is, to revise the existing pharmacy statute to allow public institutions, philanthropic entities, or private individuals to establish pharmacies "*iavochnym poriadkom,*" that is, without adhering to population figures and the consent of nearby pharmacists. ("Khronika," *Farmatsevticheskii trud,* vol.. 1, no. 14, 1907, p. 202. Also, "Farmatsevticheskii s"ezd," *Farmatsevticheskii trud,* vol. 1, no. 22, 1907, p. 308.) The Octobrist Party introduced a similar bill into the Second Duma. Both bills languished with the dissolution of that body after a few months, in the spring of 1907, but were reworked for submission to the Third Duma. (In September, 1907, *Farmatsevticheskii trud* approvingly noted that the draft law from the Stolypin's Ministry of Internal Affairs, which allowed wide latitude for public bodies to open pharmacies, was being sent out for comment to zemstvo and city administrations, although Saltykov did complain that the ministry was "revising the aptekarskii statute *gradually.*" "Reaktsiia," *Farmatsevticheskii trud,* vol. 1, no. 29, 1907, p. 392.) M. K. Safonov and thirty-three fellow Octobrists reintroduced their bill into the Third Duma in the spring of 1908. They were from very diverse backgrounds, their only commonality being that none were pharmacists. Supported by the Constitutional Democracts or Kadets, by 1911 the Safonov Bill metamorphosed into one stipulating that only public institutions could establish pharmacies freely, without prior consent. The Bill passed the Duma in 1911 and the upper chamber, the State Council, in 1912, to the detriment of owners of private pharmacies. Conroy, *In Health and In Sickness,* pp. 301-308.

75. After the Bolshevik takeover in the fall of 1917 and until his death in 1923, Sverdlov was Chair of the Central Executive Committee, the Soviet parliament of sorts which arose from lower soviets.
76. Saltykov helped administer nationalized pharmaceutical factories. In 1922, as assistant director of the Scientific Technical Department (NTO), located in the Soviet Supreme Council of the National Economy (Vesenkha), he would turn the Ferrein Laboratory, nationalized in 1919, into the Soviet "Scientific Chemical-Pharmaceutical Institute." Born in St. Petersburg in 1868, Saltykov's father was kapelmeistr in the Izmailovskii Guards' Regiment. He received his basic education at the 2nd Moscow Gimnaziia. In addition to pharmacy, he studied gardening in the Society of Lovers of Gardening and focused on medicinal plants in the "Shaniavskii University," a private institution that offered university-level courses. Saltykov apprenticed in the pharmacy of Ts. R. Khilinskii in Khar'kov. He began working at the Ferrein Laboratory in 1892. "Khronika: k 35-letnomu iubileiu B. N. Saltykova. Bibliograficheskii ocherk," *Khimiko-farmatsevticheskii vestnik* (Odessa), no. 3-4, 1926, pp. 24-25.
77. Gabrilovich's plan was termed "*samovykup.*" The pharmacy corporation (*soslovie*) or more probably the government would buy up (*kupit*) private pharmacies, thus gradually supplanting them with public ones. This was said to be modeled on a system in Sweden. Conroy, *In Health and In Sickness* , pp. 270-272. A G. O. Gabrilovich, not identified more thoroughly, delegate to the Pirogov Congress, was said to be a "liberal *aptekar'*," who "in October met with the universities." "Pirogovskii s"ezd: Sektsii farmatsii i farmakognozii," *Farmatsevticheskii trud*, vol. 1, no. 19, 1907, p. 363.
78. R. Idel'son, "O reformakh v aptechnom dele," *Farmatsevticheskii zhurnal*, vol. 47, no. 17, 1908, cols. 380-383 and Popov cited in "Reform aptek," ibid., no. 20, cols. 450-451.
79. "Poiasnitel'naia zapiska k proekty Ustava aptekarskago, razrabotannago Vysochaishe utverzhdennym S-Peterburgskim farmatsevticheskim obshchestvom po poruchenniiu s"ezda delegatov rossiiskikh farmatsevticheskikh obshchestv v S Peterburge v Ianvare 1906 goda," *Farmatsevticheskii trud* , vol. 1, no. 16, 1907, p. 220-221; ibid., no. 17., pp. 231-232; ibid., no. 18, pp. 246-248; ibid., no. 19, pp. 265-268.
80. Octobrists were left-of-center in their economic views, in contrast to their centrist or right-of center political orientation. Peter Gatrell has emphasized that not only Ministers of Internal Affairs and Agriculture, but also Ministers of Finance were anti-business. Peter Gatrell, *Government, Industry and Rearmament in Russia, 1900-1914* (Cambridge: Cambridge University Press, 1994), passim.
81. Conroy, *In Health and In Sickness*, pp. 168-170, 310-311.
82. Ibid., pp. 308-312.
83. Porai-Koshits, *K voprosu o sud'be*, p. 6
84. Fokin, *Obzor khimicheskoi promyshlennosti*, pp. 5, 17, 21, 27, 34-35, 40.
85. Ibid., pp. 22, 23, 24, 42.
86. For examples, see the *Syracuse Herald* (Syracuse, New York) for 1906.

Chapter 2

1. Gatrell also notes that horses were sequestered for the army but estimates that "[I]n 1915, livestock herds may have been slightly higher than before the war." Peter Gatrell, "The First World War and War Communism, 1914-1920," in Davis, Harrison and Wheatcroft, *The Economic Transformation of the Soviet Union*, pp. 224-228.

    Since the February Revolution was precipitated by individuals standing in bread lines in Petrograd, the capital, the notion that Russia was short of food assumed mythological proportions and has persisted amongst some historians. Rex A. Wade, *The Russian Revolution, 1917* (Cambridge: Cambridge University Press, 2000), pp. 23-27 and passim.

    In addition to Gatrell, however, contemporary observers and a growing number of latter day historians have countered this assumption. In 1919 Bernard Pares remarked on the huge shipments of food at Siberian railway stations. Cited in Jonathan D. Smele, *Civil War in Siberia: The Anti-Bolshevik Government of Admiral Kolchak, 1918-1920* (Cambridge: Cambridge University Press, 1996), p. 328. George Yaney's pioneering work, *The Urge to Mobilize*, emphasized that in 1915 and 1916, in certain provinces, people (including workers) were eating more than before the war "because they had more money to spend and, with the outlawing of vodka, less to spend it on." (p. 410) He also states that in January 1916, a "survey of grain reserves... found three times more than the government had hitherto believed to be available." (p. 412) Both Gatrell and Kimitaka Matsuzato, show that grain-producing regions enjoyed a surplus of grain. Tautness in grain supplies occurred in cities located in grain-consuming provinces. The shortages were artificial, though, brought on by competition between agents purchasing food for the army and civilian buyers; credits given to purchasers; price controls; grain embargoes imposed by food-producing provinces; and the central government's delegating control over railway shipments to local authorities, primarily zemstvos. See Matsuzato, "Interregional Conflicts and the Collapse of Tsarism: The Real Reason for the Food Crisis in Russia after the Autumn of 1916," in Conroy, *Emerging Democracy in Late Imperial Russia*, pp. 243-300. George Yaney, in *The Urge to Mobilize*, noted these same factors and further discussed the role that disorganization, requisitioning, and hysteria played. (pp. 404-433) He does conclude that "[B]y 1917...many people were facing starvation. Hysteria had created a fact." (p. 413)

    On the economic situation in Russia during World War I in general see R. W. Davies, *Soviet Economic Development from Lenin to Khrushchev*. Cambridge: (Cambridge University Press, 1998), pp. 15-16. He notes that the economy was quite good until 1916 but does not prove that it was intolerable afterward. Further, radical socialists contributed greatly to the economic decline. Prices for goods, including medicines, rose at the outset of the war. Workdays increased. See R. W. Davies, "Industry," in Davies, Harrison, and Wheatcroft, *The Economic Transformation of the Soviet Union*, p. 135. Peter Gatrell presents a nuanced picture of employment, investment and output during the war, with statements such as the following: "Employment in large-scale industry rose," whereas "[E]mployment in textiles registered no increase" and "small-scale industry registered a decline between 1913 and 1917." Ibid, p. 218. "Output per person rose slightly during 1915....Output per day" in "machinebuilding increased by 32 percent and in chemicals by 27 percent" between 1913 and 1916. Ibid., pp. 219-220. "The gross value of output in large-scale industry grew by about 17 percent between 1913 and 1916....The output of small-scale industry ...declined at the outbreak of the war, but then recovered between 1915 and 1916." Ibid., p. 233.

2. D. N. Prianishnikov, *Nedosevy, mineral'naia udobreniia i voennyia nuzhdy.* (Moscow: Tipografiia O. L. Somovoin, B. Nikitskaia, 1916), pp. 1-11.
3. Conroy, *In Health and In Sickness,* p. 321.
4. "Zasedanie Meditsinskago Soveta po voprosu o vzdorozhanii medikamentov," *Farmatsevticheskii zhurnal,*, vol. 53, no. 32, 1914, p. 367.
5. Between 1901 and 1903, typhus had affected only 3.9 to 5 per 10,000 of the population and remained the same during the war. Recurring fever had affected a minuscule 0.8 to 1.2 per 10,000 of the population, rising at the end of the 1905 to 1.8 per 10,000.

   Between 1902 and 1906 the incidence of cholera was low, ranging from 0.17 to 0.65 per 10,000 of the population . Typhoid fever, on the other hand, affected 18 to 24.4 per 10,000 of the population before the Russo-Japanese war, rising to 30.6 per 10,000 of the population at the end of the war. The army was little affected by typhus and recurring fever during the Russo-Japanese War. Typhus affected only 0.5 per 1,000 troops; recurring fever, 0.3 per 1,000.

   Typhoid fever, however, affected a whopping 32.6 per 1,000 of the military and dysentery, 12.9 per 1,000. E. I. Smirnov, ed. *Opyt sovetskoi meditsiny v velikoi otechestvennoi voine, 1941-1945 g.g.* [hereafter *Opyt sovetskoi meditsiny.*] (Moscow: Medgiz, series, 1951-1955) vol. 32, part 1, pp. 14-15.) In the years immediately following the war, communicable diseases rose among civilians as troops returned from the Far East and revolution flared up along the Trans-Siberian Railway, in the Volga region, and in major cities. Typhus affected up to 11.6 per 10,000 people; recurring fever, up to 8.4 per 10,000; typhoid fever affected 32.8 per 10,000 people; and cholera up to 14.08 per 10,000 people. (Ibid, vol. 32, part 1, p. 15.) A cholera epidemic erupted in St. Petersburg in 1908 and 1909. It did not, however, affect the army. In 1913, 26.8 or 10,000 (or 2.6 per 1,000) people were afflicted with typhoid. (*Opyt sovetskoi meditsiny,* vol. 32, part 1, p. 22.) Researchers studied the bacillus causing typhoid in 1906. *Opyt sovetskoi meditsiny,* vol. 32, part 2, p. 62.)
6. Ibid., vol. 32, part 2, pp. 64-65.
7. F. G. Krotkoe, "Vodosnabzhenie voisk," ibid., vol. 31, pp. 40, 43. The iodine-starch method was applied after World War I. In 1915, D. Kamenskii proposed purifying water with chlorine.
8. *Opyt sovetskoi meditsiny,* vol 23, p. 62.
9. Ibid., vol. 23, p. 151.
10. See Alan Clark, *The Eastern Front 1914-18* (Gloucestershire: Windrush Press, 1971),

for battle map, page 63. For the military see Bruce Menning, *Bayonets before Bullets: The Imperial Russia Army, 1861-1914.* (Bloomington: Indiana University Press, 2000). At the outset there were twenty-seven army corps in European Russia, three in the Caucasus, two in Turkestan and five in Siberia, funneled through seven military districts. See pp. 200-271, for mobilization patterns and general discussion of the Russian army in World War I. For German transplants and refugees, see Peter Gatrell, *A Whole Empire Walking: Refugees in Russia during World War I,* (Bloomington: Indiana University Press, 1999), pp. 3, 17-32 and passim. Some 7 million people—about 5 percent of the 125,000,000 to144,000,000 inhabitants of the Empire, consisting primarily of Jews, Ukrainians, Lithuanians, Latvians, and Poles—moved eastward in the wake of Russia's initial defeats and following the German take-over of Russian Poland in the summer of 1915, and some 200,000 German colonists from Volynia Province were shipped to the interior by the Russian government, who feared their collaboration with the enemy. Refugees swelled the population up to 30 percent in some cities.

11. *Opyt sovetskoi meditsiny,* vol. 6, p. 17.
12. Ibid., vol. 11, p. 18.
13. Ibid., vol. 6, pp. 23, 25. Those using it immediately were K. F. Tarasov, surgeon in the military hospital in Kiev; E. A. Efron and E. G. Lifshits in the Military Medical Hospital in Petrograd and D. A. Entin in the Red Cross hospital in Petrograd; and A. N. Pomerants in the hospital outfitted by the Union of Cities in Moscow.
14. Ibid., vol. 11, pp. 18-19. Zavadskii's report was delivered to a meeting of physicians from the Northwest front; Rokotilo's to the Fourteenth Congress of Russian Surgeons, held during the war.
15. Ibid., p. 401.
16. *Opyt sovetskoi meditsiny,* vol. 31, p. 196; Gatrell, *A Whole Empire Walking,* pp. 54, 135, 173.
17. *Opyt sovetskoi meditsiny,* vol. 31, p. 14.; mobibilization and numbers per 1,000 in Ibid., vol. 32, part 1, p. 15.
18. Ibid., vol. 32, part 1, p. 112.
19. Ibid., vol. 32, part 3, p. 72. The absolute number stricken with cholera was 30,810.
20. Ibid., vol. 32, part 1, p. 15.
21. Ibid., vol. 31, p. 196. This source claims incidence rose each year of the war but deaths from dysentery decreased, as stated below.
22. Ibid.,vol. 31, p.194.
23. Ibid., p. 198.
24. Ibid., p. 196.
25. Ibid., p., 195.
26. *Opyt sovetskoi meditsiny,* vol. 32, part 2, pp. 163, 165.
27. Ibid., vol. 30, p. 18.
28. Ibid., vol. 30, pp. 135, 145-146, 176, 180, 205-206.
29. *Opyt sovetskoi meditsiny,* vol. 24, p. 11.

30. Ibid., vol. 25, pp. 17, 19.
31. Paper presented by Michael Zdenek David, AAASS meeting, Denver, 2000.
32. Malaria had affected 10 percent of the army from 1887 to1891, on average 1,181.2 cases per 10,000. An epidemic of malaria occurred in Russia during the First World War, although the disease reached pandemic proportions only in 1923-1924. *Opyt sovetskoi meditsiny*, vol. 31, pp. 133,134.
33. Soviet medics claimed there were no exact statistics on skin diseases among the Russian army during the First World War. Ibid., vol. 27, p. 12
34. Ibid., p. 72.
35. Ibid., pp. 72-73.
36. Ibid., pp. 27, 48, 56, 80, 101, 123.
37. MS, "History of Dorogomilovskii Factory" ("Istoriia zavoda"), Moscow, (typescript located in the factory archives), p. 6.
38. Akts. O-vo "Gosmedtorgprom," *Gosudarstvennyi khimiko-farmatevticheskii zavod imeni L. Ia. Karpova*, (Moscow, 1926), p. 3.
39. K. S. Sarkisov, "Kratkii obzor polozheniia khimiko-farmatsevticheskikh promyshlennosti i rynka v Rossii," *Farmatsevticheskii zhurnal*, vol. 55, no. 6, 1916, p. 49.
40. V. Sadikov, "Voina i sostoianie," ibid., vol. 54, no. 35, 1915, p. 341.
41. *Ustroistvo gorodskogo khimiko-farmatsevticheskago zavoda. Doklad komissii akademika N. S. Kurnokova soveshcheniiu o zagotovlenii gorodom lekarstve* (Petrograd, 1916), pp. 90, 104.
42. Sadikov, "Voina i sostoianie," p. 342.
43. MS, "History of Dorogomilovskii Factory," pp. 6 -10
44. See chapter 11 of this work.
45. RGAE, f. 8140, op. 1, d. 19, l. 46 ob. Allen and Hansbury had pioneered the manufacture of cod liver oil, malted and infant foods in the nineteenth century. They also "enhanced the presentation of Pastilles and tablets." Davenport-Hines and Slinn, *Glaxo*, 1992, p. 196.
46. MS, History of Dorogomilovskii Factory, p. 6.
47. L. F. Fokin, *Obzor khimicheskoi promyshlennosti*. Petrograd: 1921, p. 48.
48. Conroy, *In Health and In Sickness*, p. 335.
49. Prianishnikov, *Nedosevy, mineral'nyia udobreniia*, p. 12.
50. MS, History of Dorogomilovskii Factory, pp. 6 and 7; Fokin, *Obzor khimicheskoi promyshlennosti*, pp. 48-51; also Conroy, *In Health and In Sickness*, pp. 340-341.
51. Fokin, *Obzor khimicheskoi promyshlennosti*, pp. 18, 20, 42, 52-53 (list of factories, p. 18)
52. MS, "History of Dorogomilovskii Factory," pp. 6 and 7; Fokin, *Obzor khimicheskoi promyshlennosti*, pp. 48-51; also Conroy, *In Health and In Sickness*, pp. 340-341.
53. Fokin, *Obzor khimicheskoi promyshlennosti*, p. 20.
54. Porai-Koshits, *K voprosu o sud'be*, pp. 6-7.
55. Fokin, *Obzor khimicheskoi promyshlennosti* , p. 17 .
56. Ibid., pp. 16-17.
57. Porai-Koshits, *K voprosu o sud'be*, p. 6.
58. Fokin, *Obzor khimicheskoi promyshlennosti*, pp. 18, 20, 42, 52-53 (list of factories, p.

18).
59. Smirnov, *Opyt sovetskoi meditsiny*, vol. 14, p. 274.
60. N. D. Averkiev, "Issledovanie iod-soderzhashchikh vodoroslei morei SSSR," *Khimiko-farmatsevticheskii vestnik* (Odessa), vol. 1, no. 3-4, 1926, p. 2.
61. Averkiev, ibid., pp. 2-3.
62. Conroy, *In Health and In Sickness*, pp. 341-342; also Conroy, "The Russian Pharmaceutical Industry in the Late Imperial-Early Soviet Period," in Kevin McDermott and John Morison, *Politics and society under the Bolsheviks* (Basingstoke: Macmillan Press, Ltd. and New York: St. Martin's Press, Inc., 1999), p. 26. See also, Fokin, *Obzor khimicheskoi promyshlennosti*, p. 41.
63. Orgkomitet vsesoiuznoi konferentsii po khimizatii narodnogo khozaistva S. S. S. R., *Materialy k vsesoiuznoi konferentsii po khimizatsii narodnogo khoziaistva s.s.s.r. vo 2-m piatiletii* (Leningrad: Goskhimtekizdat, 1932), p. 1. [hereafter cited *Materialy…*]
64. Conroy, *In Health and In Sickness*, p. 341.
65. "Vystavka otechestvennyoi promyshlennosti," *Farmatsevtucheskii zhurnal,*, vol. 55, no. 15, 1916, p. 132.
66. V. A. Izmail'skii, "O stovarsole i sal'varsanovykh preparatakh," *Khimiko—farmatsevticheskii zhurnal*, no. 2 (5), 1924, p. 14.
67. Conroy, *In Health and In Sickness*, pp. 331, 335, 340, 342, 345-348; also notes, pp. 605-609.
68. Conroy, ibid., p. 347.
69. Ibid., pp. 335-339.
70. Shass and Satsyperov, *Lekarstvennye i lekarstvenno-tekhnicheskie rasteniia SSSR*, p. 84.
71. The amount fell to 850 puds in 1918 and, significantly, plummeted to 80 puds at the high point of the civil war, rising back up to1,300 puds in 1920. G. Milovanov, "Turkestanskii opii," *Khimiko-farmatsevticheskii zhurnal*, no. 2 (5) 1924, p. 12.
72. I. A. Obergard, "O russkom bismute," *Khimiko-farmatsevticheskom vestnik (Odessa)*, vol. 1, no. 7-8, 1926, p. 4.
73. Conroy, *In Health and In Sickness*, p. 341; p. 607, note 192 for potassium.
74. Ibid., pp. 335—336.
75. Utin, *Istoriia chimkentskogo khimiko-farmatsevtskogo zavoda*, p. 21.
76. F. R. Eldridge, Jr., Chief, Far Eastern Division, U.S. Dept of Commerce to Moorman Manufacturing Company, Quincy, Illinois, March 11, 1920, NAUSA, File 231, BFDC, U.S. Dept. of Commerce. American firms estimated that Russia had produced 12,000 to 15,000 pounds of Santonin before the war. The product was used against roundworms in both hogs and humans.
77. U.S. Department of Commerce: Bureau of Foreign and Domestic Commerce: *Monthly Summary of Foreign Commerce of the United States, December, 1915*, Washington: Government Printing Office, 1916, pp. 56, 57; *Monthly Summary of Foreign Commerce, December 1917*, ibid., 1918, p. 6; *Monthly Summary of Foreign Commerce, December 1918*, ibid., 1919; pp. 6, 7.
78. Secretary of the Moorman Mfg., Co., Stockmen's Supplies, to Bureau of Foreign and Domestic Commerce, U.S. Dept of Commerce, March 2, 1920, NAUSA, File

231, BFDC, U.S. Dept of Commerce.

79. "Russian Soap Industry," in *World Trade Notes on Chemicals and Allied Products*, November 28, 1936, in NAUSA, File RG 489, Box 82, NN3—151—80—7, 10,700, BFDC, U. S. Department of Commerce.
80. *The American Perfumer and Essential Oil Review*, vol. 11, no. 6 (August), 1916, p. 184. Those investigating represented the Chemical Section of the Military Industrial Committee who were negotiating with private firms to make the soap.
81. David B. MacGowan, "Dearth of Soap and Fats in Russia," ibid., vol. 12, no. 8 (October), 1917, p. 251.
82. Galambos and Sewell, *Networks of Innovation: Vaccine Development at Merck, Sharp & Dohme, and Mulford*, pp. 26-27.
83. TsGIA RB, f. R 1203, op. 2, d. 1, ll. 1-12, 55-57, 64, 77-92 During the first 10 months of 1916 the Institute produced 13,519 doses of "antidiphtheria" serum, 214 flagons of 50 cubic centimeters each of streptococcus serum, 193 flagons at 20 cub. cent. each of antidysentery serum, 1,101 cubic centimeters of cholera vaccine, 13,260 cub. cent. of typhus vaccine, 200 cub. cent. of scarlatina vaccine, 554 flagons at 1 cub. cent. of gonococcus vaccine, and 42, 910 ampules (450,000 to 500,000 doses)of smallpox vaccine. (l. 3) After head physician Dr. A. N. Kryzhanovsky was called to war in November 1914, one Dr. Veraksa ran the Institute (l. 79).
84. "Zasedanie Meditsinskago Soveta po voprosu o vzdorozhanii medikamentov," *Farmatsevticheskii zhurnal,*, vol. 53, no. 32, 1914, p. 367.
85. "Zhurnal pervago zasedaniia Mezhduvedomstvennago Komiteta po delam farmatsevticheskoi promyshlennosti," Tsentral'nyi Gosudarstvennyi Istoricheskii Arkhiv in St. Petersburg (now RGIA), f. 1298, op. 1, d. 2066a, l. 2.
86. See Conroy, *In Health and In Sickness*, pp. 326-328.
87. Smirnov, *Opyt sovetskoi meditsiny*, vol 32, part 1, p. 112; part 2, pp. 65-66.
88. Conroy, *In Health and In Sickness*, pp. 331, 335, 340, 342, 345-348; also notes pp. 605-609.
89. Lorimer, *The Population of the Soviet Union*, pp. 40-41.
90. S. G. Wheatcroft and R. W. Davies, "Population," in Davies, Harrison, Wheatcroft, *The Economic Transformation of the Soviet Union*, p. 62 and note 16, p. 335.
91. Wheatcroft and Davies, ibid., p. 62. and note 17, p. 335.
92. F. A. Gaida, *Libera'lnaia oppozitsiia na putakh k vlasti (1914-vesna 1917 g.)* (Moscow: ROSSPEN, 2003), passim.
93. Michael Melancon, *The Socialist Revolutionaries and the Russian Anti-War Movement, 1914-1917* (Columbus: Ohio State University Press, 1990), passim.
94. Conroy, *In Health and In Sickness*, pp. 320-335.
95. Ibid., pp. 350-364.
96. Radical pharmacists and liberal journalists and politicians hostile to private companies claimed that pharmaceutical firms made fantastic fortunes during the war, thus justifying high pay and larger benefits to employees during the war with worker takeovers after it was over. Lack of financial records for Moscow companies hinders analysis. The Chimkent Santonin Factory of Savinkov and

Company, however, provides one gauge on the issue of profits and wartime productivity. The factory was located far from the theater of war but the main purchasers of its chief product were German firms. The amount of Santonin sold in 1914 was only half of that sold in 1913, namely 4.7 tons as compared with 9.9 tons in the last prewar year. However, sales rose to 6.1 tons in 1915, dipped to 5.6 tons in 1916, and then leapt up to 8.7 tons in 1917. Apparently sales from Merck continued someway or other during the war, since local archival materials record prices and profits in marks, as well as rubles. World prices did increase sizably during the war. Prices per kilogram in German marks rose from 31.94 in 1907 to 140 marks in 1914 to 177 marks per kilogram in 1917—a little over five times the price in 1907, when the company enjoyed a monopoly on Santonin. Santonin sold for 104 rubles per kilogram in 1913, bringing gross profits of 909,000 rubles. In 1914, prices on the world market rose to 116 rubles per kilogram. Since the amount sold halved, profits did also, to 504,000 rubles. In 1915 the price per kilogram in rubles rose to 140, to 160 in 1916 and to 180 in 1917, bringing profits of 1,350,000 rubles. Production costs rose also from 4.14 marks per kilogram in 1907 to 16.55 marks in 1917. The rise in costs, in other words, was over fourfold. The difference, therefore, between sales prices and costs of production—one indicator of net profits—was not astronomical in this very profitable sector of the pharmaceutical industry. Utin, *Istoriia chimkentskogo khimiko-farmatsevticheskogo zavoda,* pp. 20-21. Utin uses local archival materials for these computations.

97. Conroy, *In Health and In Sickness,* pp. 369-374.

98. "Women From the East Side, Crying 'We Want Bread,' Storm City hall in Vain Effort to See Mayor," *The New York Herald,* Wednesday, February 21, 1917, p. 3; "Women Riot Anew Here and In Philadelphia as Food Prices Mount; Confiscation of Stocks Threatened;" "State May Seize Edible Supplies and Distribute Them to Public," both headlines, ibid., February 23, 1917, p. 3. "Women Who try to Buy Food Are Attacked by Boycotters in Philadelphia," ibid., February 24, p. 4; "Food Mob Storms the Waldorf Here, While Prussians Torpedo Seven Dutch Steamships and American Senate Calls for Guns and Gunners to Break the Sea Blockade," ibid., Sunday, February 25, p. 13; "Screaming Women Rioters Invade Big Hotels, Cry for Bread, Defy Police and Demand Governor's Attention," ibid., February 25, 1917, p. 17; "Food Riots Are Denounced as Work of Agitators; Disturbers Pass Idle Day," ibid., February 26, p. 3.

99. See Conroy, *In Health and In Sickness,* pp. 379-391.

100. A. Fisher, "Nekrolog Professora K. V. Beninga," *Khimiko-farmatsevticheskii vestnik* (Odessa), vol. 1, no. 9-10, 1926, pp. 2-29. Bening also had worked on a new Russian Pharmacopoeia in 1916 and continued in this sphere, helping draft a Soviet Pharmacopoeia in 1923.

101. John F. Hutchinson, "'Who Killed Cock Robin?', An Inquiry into the death of Zemstvo Medicine," in Solomon and Hutchinson, eds., *Health and Society in Revolutionary Russia,* pp. 19-22. Likewise, Vera Tolz has documented the personal and professional reasons that motivated scientists in the Academy of Sciences, who were not predisposed to the Bolsheviks, to ultimately support them. *Russian*

Academicians and the Revolution: Combining Professionalism and Politics (Basingstoke: Macmillan Press, Ltd and New York: St. Martin's Press, 1997).

Chapter 3

1. See Wheatcroft and Davies, "Population," in Davies, Harrison, Wheatcroft, *The Economic Transformation of the Soviet Union,* pp. pp. 62-64.The two authors summarize very conflicting data and to make matters more complicated they sometimes lump together the world war and the civil war and sometimes separate the two wars. They emphasize, however, that the population fell most sharply between 1917 and 1922.
2. For examples see Geoffrey Swain, *Russia''s Civil War* (Charleston, SC: Tempus Publishing, 2000), p. 63, which describes Cossacks and followers of the "White" leader, Admiral Kolchak, slaughtering Socialist Revolutionaries in Omsk in November 1918, and A. L. Litvin, *Krasnyi i belyi terror v Rossii, 1918-1921* (Kazan', 1995), passim. In the genre of belles lettres see Isaac Babel, *The Collected Stories* (New York: Meridian Books , 1955) and Boris Pilnyak, *The Naked Year*. A. R. Tulloch, trans. (Ann Arbor: Ardis, 1975).
3. Wheatcroft and Davies, ibid., pp. 62-63.
4. As archives come open, particularly regional ones, historians have unearthed more details about the conflict and are hotly debating its origins. Geoffrey Swain, for example, has persuasively argued that Lenin and the Bolsheviks precipitated the civil war. They seized the government during the night of October 24/25, 1917 without waiting for scheduled elections. After losing the elections, which although not free and fair, gave plurality to the Socialist Revolutionary Party, Lenin refused to form a coalition government. He made it difficult for the Constituent Assembly, charged with writing a new constitution and forming a new government, to convene. And, adding insult to injury, Lenin closed the assembly in January 1918. He then signed a peace treaty with Germany, alienating not only monarchist army officers but the Left Socialist Revolutionaries which had allied themselves with the Bolsheviks during the preceding summer. Geoffrey Swain, *The Origins of the Russian Civil War* (London and New York: Longman, 1996).

   Peter Holquist, on the other hand, puts the onus of the war on more shoulders than the Bolsheviks. He postulates that in the area of the Don Cossacks, roughly the eastern Ukraine, the war resulted from long-standing social and political cleavages that intensified during 1917. Further, he documents how the opponents of the Bolsheviks used oppressive economic and political measures similar to theirs. Holquist, *Making War, Forging Revolution. Russia's Continuum of Crisis, 1914-1921* (Cambridge: Harvard University Press, 2002).
5. At least five armies and governments fought in Ukraine—White army officers and Cossacks in the southeast, Ukrainian nationalists in Kiev, Germans (who took over after signing a separate peace with Ukraine), Anarchist "Blacks," and Reds in the industrial city of Khar'kov. An abortive uprising in Iaroslavl', two hours by train

from Moscow, occurred in July 1918. The venerable socialist Chaikovskii, who had founded a commune in Kansas in the 1870s, was among those fighting the Bolsheviks in Arkhangel'sk. Admiral Kolchak and his followers clashed with Reds in the Urals and at cities along the Trans-Siberian rail line. During 1918 and 1919, American, British and French army units, the last two comprised largely of colonial peoples, entered the war, first at the invitation of the Bolsheviks, then against them, in Murmansk, Vladivostok, the Crimea and Caucasus. Cossacks and Japanese took over portions of eastern Siberia.

For the Iaroslavl' uprising of July see, in particular, "Listovki Iaroslavskogo vosstaniia 1918 goda (novye postupleniia v Iaroslavskii musei-zapovednik is arkhiva KGB," *Iaroslavskaia starina*, no. 1, 1994, pp. 51-58. On American troops see E. M. Halliday, *When Hell Froze Over* (New York: Simon and Schuster, ibooks, 2000). On Kolchak, see Jonathan D. Smele, *Civil War in Siberia: The Anti-Bolshevik Government of Admiral Kolchak, 1918-1920* (Cambridge: Cambridge University Press, 1996). Expropriated nobles and business people fled south to the Crimea; west to Austria, Czechoslovakia and Germany; east to Manchuria and China. Ordinary people went to the south for food. See Pilnyak's *The Naked Year;* Alexander Neweroff's *City of Bread* (original date of publication 1927; reprint Westport, CN: Hyperion Press, 1973); as well as factual accounts.

6. Conroy, *In Health and In Sickness*, pp. 391-393
7. Bolshevik-inspired sequestration of private property frightened businessmen and women and estate owners but Lenin also alienated workers through crushing their organizations in the spring of 1918. See Gennady Shkliarevsky, *Labor in the Russian Revolution: Factory Committees and Trade Unions, 1917-1918* (New York: St. Martin's Press, 1993). Meanwhile, the miners and workers of Iuzhovka in the Donbass were apathetic to the Bolsheviks. See Theodore H. Friedgut, *Iuzhovka and Revolution.* vol. II: *Politics and Revolution in Russia's Donbass, 1869-1924.* (Princeton: Princeton University Press, 1994), p. 285 and passim. On workers see Jonathan Aves, *Workers against Lenin: Labour Protest and the Bolshevik Dictatorship* (London, New York: Tauris Academic Studies, 1996). On Lenin's initial arousal of the peasantry in the spring of 1917, see Esther Kingston Mann, *Lenin and the Problem of Marxist Peasant Revolution* (New York: Oxford University Press, 1985).
8. *Opyt sovetskoi meditsiny,*, vol. 32, part 1, p. 15. Also ibid., vol. 31, p.31, pp. 15, 47-59. Typhus had affected only 0.5 per 1,000 of the Russian army in the Russo-Japanese War of 1904-1905. Ibid., vol. 32, part 1, p. 15.
9. Typhoid affected only 63 per 10,000 people in 1920 . Dysentery afflicted 17.5 per 1000 (175 per 10,000) of the Red Army in 1919. Civilians were less affected; in 1920, 65.7 of 10,000 people at large suffered from dysentery. Immunization ultimately lowered the incidence of typhoid. In 1921 only 51 of every 10,000 people were afflicted. In 1923, only a little more than one individual (1.15) out of every 1,000 were stricken. Ibid., vol. 32, part 1, pp. 15, 22, 112.
10. In 1918, only 389 soldiers were sick with cholera. The number nearly tripled to 929 in 1919, tripled again to 3,904 in 1920, and rose to 4,441 in 1921. However, this amounted to only a little more than one soldier (1.3) out of every 1,000 in 1918;

less than one (0.62) per 1,000 in 1919; again about one (0.99) per 1,000 in 1920; and 1.33 in 1921. V. M. Rozhdesvenskii, "Profilaktika kholery," Ibid., vol 32, part 3, p. 73.

11. Ibid., vol. 32, part 1, pp. 15, 22. The number of cholera sufferers cited in 1918 was 41, 247.
12. Ibid., vol. 32, part 1, p. 22.
13. Loc. Cit.
14. See George Leggett's monumental, *The Cheka: Lenin's Political Police* (Oxford: The Clarendon Press, 1981) and Litvin,'s *Krasnyi i bel'yi terror v Rossii.*
15. Mary Schaeffer Conroy, "Health Care in Prisons, Labour and Concentration Camps in Early Soviet Russia, 1918-1921," *Europe-Asia Studies,* vol. 52, no. 7, 2000, pp. 1257-1274, based on materials from GARF, f. 482 A, op. 12, various dela. For an account of the unsanitary conditions in the area of Siberia controlled by Kolchak, see Smele, *Civil War in Siberia,* p. 366.
16. For one example of Lenin's antipathy toward free trade see his Letter to N. A. Rozhkov, 29 January 1919, "Document 33," in Richard Pipes, ed. *The Unknown Lenin: From the Secret Archive* (New Haven: Yale University Press, 1996), p. 62.
17. The negative impact of nationalization, centralization, and bureaucratization on the economy as a whole, as well as the populace, has been increasingly revealed during the last decade as a result of greater access to Russian archival records. It used to be argued that the Bolsheviks saw War Communism solely as a wartime expedient. Revising that view is Thomas F. Remington's, *Building Socialism in Bolshevik Russia: Ideology and Industrial Organization, 1917-1921* (Pittsburgh: University of Pittsburgh Press, 1984). Additionally, Kendall Bailes has elaborated on how the Soviet economic system, with tiers of government agencies in charge of sequestered properties and directives flowing from the center, manifested the cult of engineering and technocratic management that emerged in the Western world, including the United States in the early twentieth century. See his *Technology and Society under Lenin and Stalin.* (Princeton: Princeton University Press, 1978), pp. 99-108.

    On problems in the housing sector due to lack of services and upkeep, see Mary McAuley, *Bread and Justice: State and Society in Petrograd, 1917-1922* (Oxford: The Clarendon Press, 1991). On the detrimental effect of Bolshevik commercial policies for consumers, see Arup Banerji, *Merchants and Markets in Revolutionary Russia, 1917-30* (Basingstoke: MacMillan; New York: St. Martin's Press, 1997), pp. 27-37. See also Alan M. Ball, *Russia's Last Capitalists: the NEPmen, 1921-1929* (Berkeley: University of California Press, 1987). For the decline of the metallurgical industry in Iuzovka during the civil war, following prosperity under the tsarist regime and the Austrian-German management in 1918 , see Friedgut, *Iuzovka and Revolution,* vol. I and vol. II, esp. pp. 360-433. For the negative effects of "War Communism" in the Urals metallurgical industry see Rustem Khaziev, *Gosudarstvennoe administrirovanie ekonomiki i rynok na Urale v 1917-1921 gg.* (Ufa, 2000), pp. 20-38 and passim. On the negative impact of war communism as a whole, see Nove, *An Economic History of the USSR,* pp. 37-72.

18. The White government of Ataman Krasnov and Anton Denikin in the Don region demanded sales of grain reserves at fixed prices and punished peasants who did not comply. Peter Holquist, "What's So Revolutionary About the Russian Revolution? State Practices and New-Style Politics, 1914-21," in David L. Hoffman and Yanni Kotsonis, *Russian Modernity: Politics, Knowledge, Practices* (Basingstoke: Macmillan Press Ltd. and New York: St. Martin's Press, 2000), pp. 98-103. Admiral Kolchak's government, which dominated Omsk from July to October 1918, kept control of factories confiscated by the Bolsheviks who had been there previously and, in the opinion of Jonathan Smele, one of his recent biographers, mismanaged food supply—but more by shrinking from force rather than by applying it. Smele, *Civil War in Siberia,* pp. 371-373, 391.
19. See Friedgut, *Iuzovka and Revolution,* vol. II, pp. 360-388 for the Donbass; for the pharmaceutical sector see Conroy, *In Health and In Sickness,* pp. 418-419.
20. Rustem Khaziev has demonstrated how officials in the Bashkir Republic, local Bolsheviks included, ignored Moscow's demands to requisition food and ship a percentage of manufactured products to the center, instead carrying on business as usual. Light and heavy industry and agriculture thrived and markets were well-stocked, luring outsiders. Khaziev, *Gosudarstvennoe administrirovanie ekonomiki,* passim. Anthony Heywood has detailed how Soviet officials negotiated with German firms, British banks and other foreigners for purchase of locomotives and railway equipment. Heywood, *Rebuilding Lenin's Russia,* pp. 63-159.
21. Conroy, *In Health and In Sickness,* pp. 394-399.
22. "IV Plenum TsB Aptsektsii," *Khimiko-farmatsevticheskii zhurnal,* vol. 7, no. 15 - 16 (87-88), 1929, pp. 17-18.
23. Conroy, *In Health and In Sickness,* pp. 399-404.
24. Conroy, ibid., 413-415.
25. RGAE, f. 8140, op.1, d. 6, l. 36.
26. Conroy, *In Health and In Sickness,* pp. 404-443; also Conroy, "The Russian Pharmaceutical Industry," in Kevin McDermott and John Morison, *Politics and Society Under the Bolsheviks*(Basingstoke: Macmillan Press, Ltd., 1999), p. 22. It ought to be noted that some workers and local officials shrank from nationalizing pharmacies and urged that former owners be compensated.
27. Sergei Sinenko, *Gorod nad beloi rekoi: Kratkaia istoriia Ufy v ocherkakh i zarisovkakh, 1574-2000* (Ufa: Gosudarstvennoe respublikanskoe izdatel'stvo "Bashkortostan," 2000), p. 114.
28. Sinenko describes the stores, businesses, schools, churches, mosques, parks and movies and other entertainment in Ufa, accompanied by photographs which confirm the city as a lively, normal provincial capital before 1917 in *Gorod nad beloi rekoi,* pp. 31-113.
29. TsGIA RB, R f. 443, op. 1, d. 258, l. 1.
30. TsGIA RB R f. 443, op. 1, d. 258, l. 1.
31. TsGIA RB, R f. 443, op. 1, d. 497, l. 1. (The listy are unnumbered in the file; I have counted each as I read them."
32. TsGIA RB, R f. 443, op. 1, d. 497, l. 6.
33. TsGIA RB, R f. 433, op. 1, d. 497, l. 8.

34. TsGIA RB R f. 433, op. 1, d. 497, l. 9.
35. TsGIA RB, R f. 443, op. 1, d. 474, l. 1.
36 TsGIA RB, R f. 443, op. 1, d. 474, l. 9.
37. TsGIA RB, R f. 443, op. 1, d. 497, no list number.
38. TsGIA RB, R f. 433, op. 1, d. 497, l. 11.
39. TsGIA RB, R f. 443, op. 1, d. 494, l. 17.
40. TsGIA RB, R f. 443, op. 1, d. 497, l. 21.
41. TsGIA RB, R f. 443, op. 1, d. 494, l. 26.
42. TsGIA RB, R f. 443, op. 1, d. 474, l. 19.
43. TsGIA RB, R f. 443, op. 1, d. 497, l. 29.
44. TsGIA RB, R f. 443, 0p. 1, d. 497, no list number.
45. TsGIA RB, R f. 443, op. 1, d. 474, l. 2.
46 TsGIA RB, R f. 443, op. 1, d. 497, l. 27.
47. TsGIA RB, R f. 443, op. 1, d. 474, l. 3.
48. TsGIA RB, R f. 443, op. 1, d. 474, l. 29.
49. TsGIA RB, R F. 443, op. 1, d. 478, ll. 1-4 ob.
50. See Pipes, ed., *The Unknown Lenin*, pp. 145-146.
51. See Conroy, *In Health and In Sickness*, pp. 217-218.
52. Conroy, *In Health and In Sickness* , pp. 411-412; Mary Schaeffer Conroy, "Abuse of Drugs other than Alcohol and Tobacco in the Soviet Union," *Soviet Studies*, now *Europe-Asia Studies*, vol. 42, no. 3, 1990, pp. 449-450.
53. Conroy, *In Health and In Sickness*, pp. 413-415.
54. TsGIA RB, R f. 443, op. 1, d. 493, l. 3.
55. TsGIA RB, R f. 443, op. 1, d. 493, l. 5.
56. TsGIA RB, R f. 443, op. 1, d. 493, l. 6.
57. TsGIA RB, R f. 443, op. 1, d. 493, ll. 8 and 9.
58. TsGIA RB, R f. 443, op. 1, do. 493, l. 13.
59. TsGIA RB, R f. 443, op. 1, d. 493, l. 12 and l. 11, respectively. The accounts of inspections are handwritten and difficult to read in their entirety.
60. See Khaziev, *Gosudarstvennoe administrirovanie ekonomiki.*
61. TsGIA RB, R f. 444, op. 1, d. 315, l. 5.
62. TsGIA RB, Rf. 443, op. 1, d. 478, l. 5.
63. TsGIA RB, R f. 444, op. 1. d. 315, l. 17.
64. Akty obsledovaniia: "Obsledovaniem ustanovleno. [sic] Doma starosti i khronikov," "Shkola Kommuny No. 1-i," "Shkola kommuny No. 2," and "Priiut detei doshkologo vozrasta," TsGIA RB, R f. 443, op. 1, d. 494, ll. 1 -2.
65. TsGIA RB, R f. 444, op. 1, d. 315, l. 21.
66. I. A. Obergard, "O russkom bismute," *Khimiko-farmatsevticheskii vestnik* (Odessa), vol. 1, no. 7-8, 1926, pp. 4-5.
67. Utin, *Istoriia chimkentskogo khimiko-farmatsevticheskogo zavoda*, pp. 26-28.
68. G. Milovanov, "Turkestanskii opii," *Khimiko-farmatsevticheskii zhurnal* , no. 2(5), 1924, p. 12.
69. Shass and Satsyperov, *Lekarstvennye i lekarstvenno-tekhnicheskie rasteniia SSSR*, p. 84.
70. L. Bassarskaia, "K voprosu sbora lekarstvennykh rastenii v raione g. Anan'eva,"

Khimiko-farmatsevticheskii vestnik (Odessa), vol. 1, no. 9-10, 1926, pp. 18-20.

71. RGAE, Moscow, f. 8140, op. 1, d. 30, ll. 140-140 ob.
72. A. Fisher, "Bibliografiia," *Khimiko-farmatsevticheskii vestnik* (Odessa), vol. 1, no. 9-10, 1926, pp. 22-23.
73. RGAE, f. 8140, op. 1, d. 19, l. 27.
74. Utin, *Istoriia chimkentskogo khimiko-farmatsevticheskogo zavoda*, p. 28. And only ruble amounts are cited further.
75. The Bolsheviks had begun overtures to Germany to end hostilities immediately after taking over the provisional government in October-November 1917, for Lenin realized that he could not maintain himself in power while fighting both the central powers and his internal foes.
76. Porai-Koshits, *K voprosu o sud' be krasochnoi promyshlennosti v Rossii*, p. 4.
77. Americans who favored trade with the Soviet Union included Raymond Robbins, erstwhile labor organizer and member of the United Mine Workers turned wealthy lawyer; Jacob Gumberg, a wealthy Russian immigrant; Dr. Frank Billings, noted Chicago physician and friend of Samuel Harper, University of Chicago history professor, who invited Paul Miliukov, leader of the Kadets and now an ardent anti-Bolshevik to lecture there in 1903; Chicagoan Charles Crane, scion of a plumbing-fixture fortune, founder of Westinghouse, friend of Harper and sponsor of Harper's trips to Russia and Miliukov's to Chicago; Senator Borah; Armand Hammer, whose Communist leanings are now well-documented; George Morris, manufacturer of Christmas stockings; the Baldwin Locomotive Works; the investment house Kuhn, Loeb and Company; General Electric, and International Harvester, "whose Russian holdings," along with those of Westinghouse, "had been saved from nationalization in 1917-18 through the efforts of Raymond Robbins." These pro-Soviet business, political and labor leaders lobbied hard for economic if not political connections with the Soviets through the Russian-American League, the Russian-American Chamber of Commerce (sponsored by the Morgan Banking House), and the American Federation of Labor.

    The anti-Bolshevik bloc included President Wilson; Herbert Hoover, Secretary of Commerce during the Russian civil war and later US president; David Francis, US Ambassador to Imperial Russia, who stayed on in the early years of the civil war; Frederick Corse, who had been manager of the Russian division of The New York Life Insurance Company for sixteen years and "considered Bolshevism no more than 'conscious, organized loot'," and most congressmen and senators. William Appleman Williams, *American Russian Relations, 1781-1947* (New York: Octagon Books, 1971), pp. 80-229, direct quotes: pp. 210, 148-149; On Crane, Harper and Miliukov, see Robert C. Williams, *Russian Art and American Money, 1900-1940.* (Cambridge, MA: Harvard University Press, 1980), pp. 89, 120. See also Melissa Kirschke Stockdale, *Paul Miliukov and the Quest for a Liberal Russia, 1880-1918* (Ithaca and London: Cornell University Press, 1996), pp. 99-100.
78. Heywood, *Modernizing Lenin's Russia*, pp. 86-92
79. Correspondence between Moorman Manufacturing Co, Quincy, Illinois (which used Santonin for killing roundworms in hogs) and the Bureau of Foreign and Domestic Commerce, U. S. Dept. of Commerce, March 2, 1920; BDFC with the

American Committee of Russian Cooperative Unions, March 5, 1920; Youreveta Home and Trade Co, March 5, 1920; E. I. Omeltchenko, American Representative, Russian Committee for the Far East, Vladivostok to Philip B. Kennedy, BFDC, March 8, 1920 in NAUSA, BDFC, U.S. Dept. of Commerce, File 231.

E. Somoff, Manager, All Russian Central Union of Consumers Societies, Inc. to Mr. Ph. D. Kennedy, BFDC, US Dept of Commerce, March 29, 1920, NAUSA, File 231, Box 1004, BFDC, U.S. Dept. of Commerce.

80. Letter from the Secretary of the Russo-British Chamber of Commerce, Incorporated, to E. I. Omeltchenko, Esq., The Russian-American Committee for the Far East, New York City, April 6, 1920, NAUSA, File 231, BFDC, U.S. Dept. of Commerce.
81. Utin, *Istoriia chimkentskogo khimiko-farmatsevticheskogo zavoda*, pp. 35-37
82. Omeltchenko to Kennedy, March 8, 1920, BFDC, U.S. Dept. Of Commerce.
83. R. S. MacElwee to Hon. Wilber J. Carr, Director of Consular Service, US Dept of State, May 7, 1920. MacElwee claimed that "3,618 poods of zedoary seeds, from which is extracted santonin, were exported from Windau, Courland,"during 1913. Also T. W. Delahanty, Acting Chief, Chemical Division, Dept of Agriculture, to Chicago District Office, Dept of Agriculture, September 19, 1923; C. C. Concannon, Chief, Chemical Division, U.S. Dept of Commerce, to Mr. John G. Wheelock, Illinois State Bank Bldg, Quincy, IL, September 14, 1923 in NAUSA, File 231.0 , BFDC, U.S. Dept of Commerce.
84. Agricultural Department, Youroveta Home and Foreign Trade, Co., Inc. to W. C. Huntington, BFDC, May 20, 1920, NAUSA, File 231, BFDC, U.S. Dept of Commerce.
85. E. R. Eldridge, Jr., Chief Far Eastern Division, U.S. Department of Commerce, to Moorman Manufacturing Company, March 11, 1920, and Omeltchenko to Kennedy, March 8, 1920.
86. Remington, *Building Socialism in Bolshevik Russia*, pp. 14, 20, and passim.
87. RGAE f. 8126, op. 1, d. 1, ll. 2, 2 ob.. The assembled members included V. M. Fisher, N. G. Patsukov, I. O. Piotrovskii, I. R. Kornblium, S. V. Maiat', and I. P. Ershov. At this initial time, Karpov was still expecting the nationalization of major factories and the board asked Vesenkha for an advance of 20,000 rubles. Ibid., l. 3. A few days later, on June 4, the board established its departments of Finance, Accounting, Materials, Commercial and so forth. Ibid., l. 8.
88. Utin, *Istoriia chimkentskogo khimiko-farmatsevticheskogo zavoda*, pp. 22-28.
89. Mar, "O reorganizatsii upravleniia farmatsevticheskoi promyshlennost'iu," *Vestnik farmatsiia*, 1930, no. 2, p. 58.
90. RGAE, f. 8126, op. 1, d. 1, ll. 2, 2ob., 3, 3ob. . Those present at the organizational meeting included L. Ia. Karpov, V.M. Fisher, N.G. Patsukov, I.O. Piotovskii, I. R. Kornblium, S. V. Maiat', and I. P. Ershov. Karpov was manager of the Department of Chemical Industry in Vesenkha.
91. RGAE, f. 8126, op. 1, d. 1, ll. 2-11.
92. RGAE, f. 8126, op. 1, d. 3, l. 52. Also due to be nationalized was the Red Cross Factory, renamed Factory No.1 and also called the Alkaloid factory.

    It is confusing because appellations and number changed during the civil war.

Subsequently the Allen and Hansbury factory, No. 13 was called the Alkaloid Factory. RGAE f. 8140, op. 1, d. 19, l. 4 ob. refers to the Schering Factory as No. 3. By 1922 the Schering Factory was known as No. 4.

Original names and numbers of other factories were as follows: the Factory of the Zemstvo Union, Factory No. 2; Schering Chemical Factory, Factory No. 3; "Russian Dye," Factory No. 4; the Ferrein Chemical and Pharmaceutical Factory in Mologa, Iaroslavl' Province, Factory No. 8; the Bliumental' Factory, Factory No. 9; the Ostromyslenskaia Laboratory, Factory No.11; the Keler Chemical and Pharmaceutical factory Factory No. 12; and the Allen and Hansbury Factory (Allen i Ganburis) Factory, Factory No.13. Factories No. 9 and No. 11 were subsequently combined into Factory No. 6.

93. RGAE, f. 8140, op. 1, d. 19, ll. 1, 1 ob., 2, 2 ob..
94. RGAE , f. 8126, op. 1, d. 1, ll. 16-17.
95. RGAE, f. 8126, op. 1, d. 3, ll. 52, 53, 55, 60.
96. RGAE, f. 8126, op. 1, d. 18, l. 29, 30, 89-95.
97. "IV Plenum Tsb Aptsektsii," *Khimiko-farmatesveticheskii zhurnal*, no. 15-16 (87-88), 1929, p. 17. See also Conroy, *In Health and In Sickness*, pp. 409-410.
98. "Woldemar Ferrein," *Sonderabdruck ans den Berichten der Deutschen Pharmazeutischen Gesellschaft*, 1923, Heft 5, p. 163. Ferrein's daughter, son-in-law, Joseph Wagner and their infant son Wenceslas, and perhaps other relatives, fled Russia through the Crimea in 1919. Conversations with Wence Wagner, Chicago, 1994, first cited in Conroy, "Health Care in Prisons, Labour and Concentration Camps in Early Soviet Russia," p. 1273, note 53.
99. Charles A. Ruud, *Russian Entrepreneur: Publisher Ivan Sytin of Moscow, 1851-1934* (Montreal and Kingston: McGill-Queen's University Press, 1990), pp. 170-189.
100. I. Levinshtein, compiler, V.S. N. Kh.: Gosudarstvennoe upravlenie ob"edinennymi moskovskimi khimiko-farmatsevtich. zavodami, *Farmatrest: Ukazatel' predpriiatii i tovarnyi katalog*, Moscow, 1922, pp 12-13. The catalog specifically noted that "in peacetime the factory produced about 3,000 kinds of chemical, galenical, and prepared dosed substances...extremely varied items for the pharmaceutical market. Following the growth of epidemics, the factory moved to large-scale production of disinfecting substances—naftalizol and lizol [Lysol] (up to 50,000 kilograms per month)." (p. 13)
101. RGAE, f. 8140, op. 1, d. 19, ll. 29-30.
102. RGAE f. 8140, op. 1, d. 19, l. 41; description of Neobenzarsan also in Levinshtein,V. S. N. Kh.: *Farmatrest: Ukazatel' predpriiatii i tovarnyi katalog*, p. 56.
103. RGAE, f. 8140, op. 1, d. 19, l. 43.
104. RGAE, f 8140, op. 1, d. 19, ll. 44, 45, 45ob., 46.
105. RGAE, f. 8126, op. 1, d. 26, ll. 15 ob, 18, 19, 22, 25, 26.
106. RGAE, f. 8126, op. 1, d. 1, ll. 2-17.
107. Levinshtein, V.S.N. Kh: *Farmatrest. Ukazatel' predpriatii i tovarnyi katalog* , p. 8.
108. *Kratkii otchet o rabote Gosmedtorgproma za oktiabr'-iiun' 1926-27 oper. god.*(Moscow: Izdanie gosmedtorgprom, 1927), pp. 34-35. To complicate matters further, in time the chemical factories came under the authority of the Commissariat of Heavy Industry.

109. RGAE, f. 8009, op. 2, d. 126, ll. 100-101.
110. RGAE, f. 871, op. 3, d. 4, ll. 13-25 and f. 8140, op. 1, d. 19, ll. 3, 3ob., 4 ob, 97, 200, 200 ob.. I. A. Pakovich was appointed assistant director of Factory No. 4. A. S. Pavlovskii was also appointed director of the former Ferrein warehouse., which also served as headquarters of the Pharmacy Administration.
111. *Ankety* and typed and handwritten autobiographies in RGAE, f. 871, op. 3, d. 4, l. 25.
112. RGAE, f. 8140, op. 1, d. 19, ll. 3, 200.
113. RGAE, f. 871, op. 3, d. 4, 11. 20-22. "Farmzavod No. 4"was said to be the former Schering Factory in Levinshtein, V. S. N. Kh.: *Farmatrest: Ukazatel' predpriatii i tovarnyi katalog*, p. 11.
114. RGAE, f. 8140, op. 1, d. 19, ll. 3, 200.
115. RGAE, f. 871, op 3. d. 4, l. 17; also f. 8140, op. 1, d. 19, l. 179.
116. RGAE, f. 871, op. 3, d. 4, l. 15; also f. 8140, op. 1, d. 19, l. 179.
117. RGAE, f. 8140, op. 1, d. 19, ll. 3 ob., 200 ob. .
118. RGAE, f. 8140, op. 1, d. 19, ll. 3 , 3 ob., 200, 200 ob. .
119. RGAE, f. 8140, op. 1, d. 19, l. 3.
120. RGAE, f.8140, op. 1, d. 19, l. 40.
121. RGAE, f. 871, op. 3, d. 4, l. 10.
122. RGAE, f. 871, op. 3, d. 4, l. 12.

Chapter 4

1. In 1921, the Bolsheviks ruled a partially reconstituted Russian Empire, the Ukraine and the Caucasus, having been conquered by 1921. Soviet government institutions were similar to tsarist, though without the democratic trends emerging in the late Imperial period and racked with power struggles following Lenin's death in January 1924. See Mikhail Pavlovich Iroshnikov, *Predsedatel' Soveta Narodnykh Komissarov* (Leningrad: Izdatel'stvo "Nauka," 1974) and T. H. Rigby, *Lenin's Government: Sovnarkom* (Cambridge: Cambridge University Press, 1979). For application of Tsarist pharmacy regulations in the Soviet pharmacy sector see Conroy, *In Health and In Sickness,* pp. 422-428. On Soviet power struggles see Dmitri Volkoganov, *Lenin: A New Biography* (New York: The Free Press,1994, pp. 233-407).
2. For American activities during the famine see Bertrand M. Patenaude, *The Big Show in Bololand*: *The American Relief Expedition to Soviet Russia in the Famine of 1921.* For the illness of 16 members of the ARA staff in Ufa with typhus in 1922, the death of one (Harold Blandy), and problems with TB, see pp. 236-243. For Lenin's manipulation of American relief efforts see Pipes, *The Unknown Lenin,* pp. 133-134.
3. Alan Ball, *And Now My Soul is Hardened: Abandoned Children in Soviet Russia, 1918-1930,* (Berkeley: University of California Press, 1994), passim, and Conroy, "Abuse of Drugs Other Than Alcohol and Tobacco in the Soviet Union," pp. 450-463.

4. Statistics in GARF, A 482, op.12, d. 7, l. 9. For more details see Conroy, "Health Care in Prisons, Labour and Concentration Camps in early Soviet Russia, 1918-1921," pp. 1257-1274.
5. "Bor'ba s maliariei i osnova ee profilaktiki," *Mediko-farmatsevticheskii zhurnal* , Odessa, no. 1, 1923, p. 10.
6. RGAE, f. 871, op. 3, d. 13, ll. 2, 3, 4.
7. "Russian Soap Industry," in *World Trade Notes on Chemicals and Allied Products,* November 28, 1936, in NAUSA, File RG 489, Box 82, NN3-151-80-7, 10,700, BFDC, U.S. Dept. of Commerce.
8. Levinshtein, V. S. N. Kh.. *Farmatrest: Ukazatel' predpriiatii i tovarnyi katalog,* pp. 12-13 and 52 with its "Spisok gotovykh sredstv v fabrichnoi upakovke (patentovannye) s ukazaniem sostava i primeneniia," ibid., p. 61. Photographs on pp. 15 (Optosklad); 17 and 21 (Fasovochnaia); and 23 and 25 (Peraviazochnaia laboratoriia) replicated photographs of Ferrein's home surrounded by laboratories, the packaging departments, and the bandaging laboratories (only a few of the many laboratories in the conglomerate) in Daniel Gourtschin, *Apercu historique du development de la Pharmacie en Russie et en particulier de la "Pharmacie Ferrein", fondee sous le regne de Pierre le Grand en 1701.* (Moscow, 1910), no pagination for photographs. Actual brochure, as well as copy of the Russian version, in author's possession.
9. *Ukazatel' predpriiatii i tovarnyi katalog,* pp. 62-90.
10. RGAE, f. 8140, op. 1, d. 24, l. 71.
11. RGAE, f.871, op. 3, d. 13, ll. 2, 3, 4.
12. RGAE, f. 8140, op. 1, d. 34, ll. 16-17 ob..
13. Rustem Khaziev avers that the Bolsheviks aimed to control the economy and populace from the beginning and never desisted. Khaziev, *Gosudarstvennoe administrirovanie ekonomiki i rynok na Urale,* passim. On consumer production and retail trade, see Ball, *Russia's Last Capitalists: The Nepmen;* on currency, see Yuri Goland, "Currency Regulation in the NEP Period," *Europe-Asia Studies,* vol. 46, no. 8, 1994, pp. 1251-1296; on economic discussion, see Vincent Barnett, "A Long Wave Goodbye: on Kondrat'ev and the Conjuncture Institute, 1920-28," ibid, vol. 47, no. 3, 1995, pp. 413-441; on films see Denise Youngblood, *Movies for the Masses* (Cambridge University Press, 1992). Films made in the twenties illustrate living and working conditions, as do the novels of the period.
14. RGAE, f. 8140, op. 1, d. 19, l. 12.
15. Factory No. 1, the former Moscow Alkaloid Factory, produced hyostsiamin (Hyocyamine) from thornapple seeds, codeine from technical morphine, theobromine from cocoa unfit to drink, and was attempting to produce anise oil and quinine, from cinchona bark. Factory No. 2, organized in 1916 by the Union of Zemstvos, produced predominantly salicylic preparations. The former Schering Joint Stock Company, established in 1905, its name now changed from Factory No. 3 to Factory No. 4, manufactured narcotic and sulfuric ether, tannin, muric acid, iron chloride, hydrogen peroxide, potassium, Glaubers salts, potassium iodide and soda, and other items. The factory boasted two diesel and steam-powered machines and boilers. Factory No. 6 combined the former Bliumental' Factory and Ostromyslenskaia Laboratory. The latter had been established to manufacture the

antivenereal Novarsol, a clone of the German Neosal'varsan. Factory No. 6 produced extracts, infusions, solutions, powders and oils, albunimate of iron, ferratin, and other iron salts. The former Ferrein factory remained Factory No. 8. Ferrein's laboratory, warehouse, and dwelling were located in the city of Moscow. His plantation of medicinal plants was on the outskirts of the city. The factory was located in Nizhnie Kotly, a village north of Moscow. The former Keler factory remained Factory No. 12. Factory No. 13, the former Allen and Hansbury Factory, established by the British in 1917, produced extracts, tinctures, powders, tablets, pills, capsules, salves, ampules, alkaloids and chemicals such as hydrocyanic or prussic acid, narcotic chloroform, peptone, benzoic and salicylic caffeine. Levinshtein, *Farmatrest: Ukazatel' predpriatii i tovarnyi katalog*, pp. 8-27. For details on production of "Arsol"("Russian Salvarsan") by I. I. Ostromyslenskii at his Moscow University clinic in 1916 see Conroy, *In Health and In Sickness*, p. 340.

16. RGAE, f. 871, op. 3, d. 3, l. 13.
17. RGAE, f. 8140, op. 1, d. 19, l. 3.
18. RGAE, f. 8140, op. 1, d. 19, ll. 4, 203.
19. RGAE, f. 8140, op. 1, d. 30, 325, 325 ob., 326, 326 ob., 327, 327 ob. .
20. RGAE, f. 8140, op. 1, d. 30, ll. 351, 288, 189, 183, 184 .
21. RGAE, f. 8140, op. 1, d. 19, ll. 73-74, 78, 94, 103-104, 169, 178, 179, 203- 208, 209, 210.
22. For quinine and football games see Samuel Cross to C. C. Concannon, October 10, 1926; and Concannon to Cross, October 18, 1926. For help in obtaining the flower heads of *Artemesia pauciflora* , the basis for Santonin, see L. Cassidy of Moorman Manufacturing Co, Quincy, IL to the Bureau of Foreign and Domestic Commerce, March 2, 1920, U.S. Dept. of Commerce, NAUSA, File no. 231, Box 1004, U.S. Dept. of Commerce.
23. *Kratkii ocherk deiatel' nosti " Gosmedtorgproma,"* (Moscow, February, 1927), p. 6 for chemical pharmaceutical factories and the medical trading arm. Pharmaceutical Administrations, which purchased many of Farmatrest's products, also were under the jurisdiction of the Commissariat of Health. For details and original citations see Mary Schaeffer Conroy, "Pharmacy in Soviet Russia before the Great Patriotic War (1941-45)," *Pharmacy in History*, vol. 40, no. 1, 1998, pp. 3-24
24. Mar, "O reorganizatsii upravleniia farmatsevticheskoi promyshlennost'iu," *Vestnik farmatsii*, no. 2, 1930, p. 58, for the last factories.
25. RGAE, f. 8140, op. 1, d. 19, ll. 110-116.
26. RGAE, f. 8140, op. 1, d. 30, l. 79.
27. For example, in 1924 Galin, representing fellow members of Farmapravlenie, Nisenman, Golubkov, Rotenburg, Zalkind, Gartsshtein, and Abramov, the "administrators of the Akts. O-Va (Joint Stock Company) Farmatrest, sent a report on the finances, output, (including chief products), productivity, and sales for 1923 of Factories No. 2, 4, 8 and 13 to Vesenkha. RGAE, f. 8140, op. 1, d. 29, ll. 168ob, 169.
28. RGAE, f. 8140, op. 1, d. 34, ll. 1-7ob..
29. RGAE, f. 871, op. 3, d. 37, ll. 21-24.
30. RGAE f. 8140, op. 1, d. 30, l. 325 ob., in "Protokol No. 12: soveshchaniia direktorov," 1 December 1923.

31. RGAE, f. 8140, op. 1, d. 19, p. 26 of the trust's financial report.
32. RGAE, f. 8140, op. 1, d. 19, l. 14 ob. and p. 24 of the trust's annual report.
33. RGAE, f. 8140, op. 1, d. 19, ll. 3, 4, 11-14 ob., 20, 21.
34. RGAE, f. 8140, op. 1, d. 19, ll. 12, 12 ob., 14, 14 ob., 15, 18, 19.
35. Stone, *Hammer and Rifle,* p. 20.
36. RGAE, f. 8140, op. 1, d. 19, l. 202.
37. RGAE, f. 8140, op. 1, d. 19, l. 53-55.
38. RGAE f. 871, op. 3, d, 3, l. 3.
39. RGAE, f. 871, op. 3, d. 3, l. 1, 3, 5, 9.
40. S. G. Wheatcroft and R. W. Davies, "Agriculture," pp. 111-112 and R. W. Davies, "Industry," in Davies, Harrison and Wheatcroft, eds., *The Economic Transformation of the Soviet Union,* pp. 111-112 and pp.132, 135-136, respectively. See also Nove, *An Economic History of the U.S.S.R.,* pp. 37-64.
41. Shass and Satsyperov, *Lekarstvennye i lekarstvenno-tekhnicheskie rasteniia SSSR,* pp. 12-13, 84-85.
42. RGAE, f. 8140, op. 1, d. 30, ll. 137, 140, 140 ob.; Shass and Satsyperov, ibid., p. 12; copy of decree, pp. 210-211.
43. Shass and Satsyperov, ibid., p. 11.
44. Ibid., pp.13, 14, 141.
45. R. W. Davies, "Changing Economic Systems: An Overview," in Davies, Harrison and Wheatcroft, eds., *The Economic Transformation of the Soviet Union,* pp. 9-10.
46. Discussion and citation in Conroy, "The Russian Pharmaceutical Industry in the Late Imperial-Early Soviet Period," in McDermott and Morison, ed., *Politics and Society Under the Bolsheviks,* p. 27.
47. S. I. Tilles, "K istorii belomorskogo ioda," *Khimiko-farmatsevticheskii zhurnal,* vol. 5, no. 7 (43), 1927, pp. 11-12.
48. Utin, *Istoriia chimkentskogo khimiko-farmatsevticheskogo zavoda,* pp. 28-30.
49. Original discussion and citation in Conroy, "The Russian Pharmaceutical Industry," *Politics and Society Under the Bolsheviks,* pp. 26, 27.
50. Utin, *Istoriia chimkentskogo,* p. 29.
51. M. El'kinson, "Razvedenie miaty i dobyvanie miatnogo masla na Poltavshchine," *Khimiko-farmatsevticheskii zhurnal* , vol. 5, no. 9 (45), 1927, p. 26 (original reference in Conroy, "The Russian Pharmaceutical Industry in the Late Imperial-Early Soviet Period," *Politics and Society under the Bolsheviks,* pp. 25, 32.)
52. RGAE, f. 871, op. 3, d. 17, l. 78.
53. RGAE, f. 8140, op. 1, d. 19, l. 49, 50, 50ob, 51.
54. RGAE, f. 8140, op. 1, d. 19, 1. 166. Neobenzarsan, described in Levinshtein, *Farmatrest: Ukazatel' predpriiatii i tovarnyi katalog,* p. 56.
55. RGAE, f. 8140, op. 1, d. 30, ll. 327, 327 ob., 326, 326 ob. .
56. RGAE, f. 8140, op. 1, d. 19, l. 44.
57. "Vypolnenie proizvodstvennoi programy za Iiul'-Sentiabr' 23 g., "(Fulfillment of the Production Program from July through September 1923), RGAE, f. 8140, op. 1, d. 30, ll. 79, 79 ob. . Factory No.1 (the former Alkaloid Factory) had fulfilled its plan only 23.8 percent during the quarter. Factory number 2, which had been established by the Union of Zemstvos in 1916, at the height of the Great War, had

fulfilled its plan only 46.9 percent. Factory No. 4, the former Schering Joint Stock Company, founded in 1905, had a somewhat better showing, having fulfilled its plan 88 percent. Factory No. 8, the former Ferrein factory, in the middle range, had fulfilled its plan 51.8 percent.

58. RGAE, f. 8140, op. 1, d. 30, ll. 165 ob., 166, 166 ob.
59. L. Gartsshtein, "Proizvodstvennaia rabota Gosmedtorgprom'a," *Khimiko-farmatsevticheskii zhurnal*, 1924, nos. 10-12 (13-15), p. 12.
60. RGAE, f. 8140, op. 1, d. 24, l. 18, 26; f. 871, op. 3, d. 20, l. 2; f. 871, op.3, d. 16, l. 9.
61. RGAE, f. 871, op. 3, d. 17, ll. 73, 75, 78.
62. RGAE, f. 871, op. 3, d. 17, ll. 73, 75.
63. RGAE, f. 871, op. 3, d. 17, ll. 76, 76 ob., 77.
64. RGAE, f. 871, op. 3, d. 37, ll. 23-30. For information on the Schering factory, built in 1906, see Chapter 1, pp. 16-17.
65. RGAE, f. 871, op. 3, d. 17, ll. 76, 78.
66. RGAE, f. 871. op. 3, d. 20. l. 2.
67. RGAE, f.871, op. 1, d. 28, l. 45. Theobromine, an alkaloid derived from the cacao bean was used as a diuretic and nerve stimulant.
68. RGAE, f.871, op. 3, d. 20, l. 62.
69. H. C. Wood et al, *The Dispensatory of the United States of America,* Twenty-Second Edition. Philadelphia: J. B. Lippencott, cited in Dennis B. Worthen, *Pharmacy in World War II,* p. 80.
70. Robert Lewis, "Foreign Economic Relations," in Davies, Harrison, and Wheatcroft, *The Economic Transformation of the Soviet Union,* p. 203.
71. RGAE, f. 871, op. 3, d. 3, l. 8.
72. RGAE, f. 8140, op. 1, d. 19, ll 40, 41.
73. RGAE, f. 871, op. 3, d. 17, l. 41 (London); ibid., f. 871, op. 1, d. 28, l. 6, 45 (Berlin).
74. *Kratkii otchet o robote Gosmedtorgproma za oktiabr'-iiun' 1926-27 operats. god.,* p. 4.
75. RGAE, f. 871, op. 3, d. 17, l. 43
76. RGAE, f. 871, op. 1, d. 11, no numbers on list, contract 1.
77. RGAE, f.871, op. 3, d. 17, l. 43.
78. RGAE, f. 871, op. 1, d. 28, l. 4, ll. 40, 29.
79. RGAE, f. 8140, op. 1, d. 24, ll. 18-28 (71-92).
80. RGAE, f. 871, op. 1, d. 28, l. 4.
81. RGAE, f. 871, op. 3, d. 17, l. 43.
82. RGAE, f.871, op. 3, d. 13, ll. 2 , 3, 4.
83. Holland Hunter and Janusz M. Szyrmer, *Faulty Foundations: Soviet Economic Policies, 1928-1940,* pp. 87-88. The authors note, however, that the Bolsheviks were fascinated by the large-scale factories in the United States.
84. Vice President, Dodge & Olcott Co, New York (their plant was at Bayonne, New Jersey) to C. C. Concannon, Chief Chemical Division, BFDC, U.S. Dept of Commerce, December 12, 1923, NAUSA, File 231.0, BFDC, U.S. Dept of Commerce.

    W. P. Elmslie (Former Vice President for Research, Moorman Manufacturing Company, Quincy Illinois), discusses oil of chenopodium or worm seed oil as a vermifuge; the attempts of the research pharmacist of the company to get the oil (here spelled wormseed), "which was produced in quantity only in Carroll

Country, Maryland"; and subsequent processing of the oil by Moorman in *Fifty Years of Livestock Research* (Hannibal, MO: Western Publishing Co. 1971), pp. 68-69, 120-121. (See also p. 99, below.) Elmslie does not mention Moorman's efforts to procure Santonin, for use as a vermifuge, from the Soviet Union, cited in the National Archives, USA, either because he did not have these records or possibly because the Cold War was on when he published his book.

85. T. W. Delahanty, Acting Chief, Chemical Division, BFDC, to Professor Alexander Lowry, University of Pittsburgh, September 25, 1923, in NAUSA, File 231.0, BFDC, U.S. Dept. of Commerce. Twenty one companies, making p-amidophenol, Iodoform, Anthraquinone, and saccharin were cited. Large, well-known companies included E. I. duPont, Monsanto and Eastman Kodak Company. Beaver Chemical Company, Damascus Virginia; the National Aniline Chemical Company, 40 Hector Street, New York City; and the Carus Chemical Co., Lasalle, Illinois appeared to be smaller.
86. A letter from Howard H. Tewksburg, Manager Detroit Office U.S. Dept of Commerce to the Chemical Division, thereof, May 8, 1926, mentions the Mixer Medicine Company, Chester Kent & Co., and the DePree Co. , NAUSA, File 231.0, BFDC, U.S. Dept of Commerce.
87. RGAE, f.8140, op. 1, d. 19, l. 41.
88. RGAE, f. 8140, op. 1, d. 19, l. 44.
89. RGAE, f. 8140, op. 1, d. 19, ll. 56-57 ob.. On Schering and camphor production see Kobrak, *National Cultures*, pp. 44-48, 124.
90. For the Medical Council and foreign "privileges" see Conroy, *In Health and In Sickness*, p. 171. For Lenin's paranoia regarding foreigners see, for example, his letter to Molotov of 23 August 1921 in Pipes, *The Unknown Lenin*, pp. 133-134.
91. See, for example, Stalin's letter to Molotov of 28 July 1925 regarding purchase of cotton for the Soviet textile industry. Lars T. Lih, Oleg V. Naumov, Oleg V. Khlevniuk, *Stalin's Letters to Molotov*, New Haven and London: Yale University Press, 1995, pp. 88-89.
92. RGAE, f. 871, op. 3, d. 15, ll. 1-6ob. .
93. "Farmatsevticheskaia promyshlennost' Iaponii," *Khimiko-farmatsevticheskaia promyshlennost'*, no. 1, 1935, pp. 66-67.
94. RGAE, f. 8140, op. 1, d. 30, ll. 87, 134.
95. RGAE, f. 871, op. 3, d. 19, ll. 1-3.
96. RGAE, f. 871, op. 3, d. 19, ll. 1-3.
97. RGAE, f. 871, op. 3, d. 19, ll. 7-8.
98. RGAE, f. 871, op. 3, d. 37, l. 4.
99. RGAE, f. 871, op. 3, d. 19, ll. 4, 6, 6ob. .
100. On details of technological transfers—for cash (p. 210), trade proposals to develop the Donets State Coal Trust in 1925, proposals and trade between the USSR and General Electric, Chase Manhattan Bank, Bethlehem Steel, Standard Oil, various engineering and other American firms during the 1920s see Williams, *American-Russian Relations, 1781-1947*, pp. 177-228.
101. See Harvey Klehr, John Earl Haynes, Fridrikh Igorevich Firsov, *The Secret World of American Communism* (New Haven and London: Yale University Press, 1995), pp.

26-29.

102. 1870 U. S. Census; 1880 U. S. Census, White Township, Benton County, Missouri.

103. *R. W. Robbins Central Business College Catalogue, 1888-1899*, p. 34; J. D. Smith, "Robbins's Central Business College, Sedalia," *Pettis County, Missouri*, September 1917, p. 15.; E. Virgil Neal and John H. Moore, *Modern Illustrative Banking*. (Williams and Rogers Series) New York, Cincinnati, Chicago: The American Book Company, 1904). Accounts of Neal's success and teaching positions in Mary Eleanor Filkin's interview with Neal's former Central College School chum Fred W. Tamblyn, "Missourian, Who Has Lost Many Fortunes, Now Millionaire Cosmetic Manufacturer in France," *Kansas-City Journal Post*, May 15, 1932, p. 18.

104. "Opera Stars at Deal Beach (N. J.)," special to *The New York Times*, August 30, 1903, p. 28; "E. V. Neal Sued for $50,000," *The New York Times*, January 3, 1904, p. 16.

105. On-line advertisement "To-Kalon Manufacturing Co., Syracuse New York, To-kalon (France/England)-1900," www.repronews.com/perfume.html; "The Perfume Tokalon," *The New York Times*, April 5, 1914, p. RPA 8; "Creme Tokalon—A Safeguard Against Sunburn," ibid., June 24, 1914, p. 4; "New Incorporations," *The New York Times*, April 1, 1915, p. 20. Tokalon was incorporated in New York State.

106. X. Lamotte Sage (A. M., Ph. D., L.L. D), *Hypnotism As It Is: A Book for Everybody*. (Rochester, NY: The National Publishing Company, 1899. Incidentally, this book was translated into Russian in 1931. X. Lamotte Sage's tenets are cited in Hudson Tuttle's *Mediumship and Its Laws* . (Berlin Heights, OH. 1900), pp. 62-63. Here he is referred to as "Dr." Neal also co-edited a book under his real name with Charles S. Clark, *Hypnotism and Hypnotic Suggestion* (Rochester: New York State Publishing Company, 1900). Neal's own illustrated contribution, amongst the other twenty-nine authors, was "How to Control People in Their Waking State," pp. 32-48. Here he appended the titles A. M. And LL. D. to his name. Neal also was affiliated with the Columbia Scientific Academy, 1135 Broadway, New York, NY.

107. Maria Carlson, *"No Religion Higher Than Truth": A History of the Theosophical Movement in Russia, 1875-1922* (Princeton: Princeton University Press, 1993). Also, Sylvia Cranston, *The Extraordinary Life and Influence of Helena Blavatsky: Founder of the Modern Theosophical Movement* (New York: G. P. Putnam's Sons, 1993), pp. 113-187 and passim.

108. "Warrants for Neal and Williams," *The Syracuse Herald*, January 13, 1906, p. 7; "Medical Miracle Workers Arrested," *The New York Times*, January 13, 1906, p. 1, "Two of Medical firm Miss the Police Net, "ibid., January 14, 1906, p. 3; "Can't Find E. Virgil Neal," ibid., January 15, 1906, p. 4; "Still Looking for Neal," *The Syracuse Herald*, January 18, 1906, p. 14; "Force-of-Lifers Up for Fraud Charge," *The New York Times*, January 20, 1906, p. 6; "Force-of-Lifers on Trial," ibid., February 6, 1906, p. 2; "Force-of-Lifers Sent Many Decoy Letters," ibid., February 7, 1906, p. 16; "Mail Ordered Held," *The Syracuse Herald*., February 17, 1906, p. 6.

109. *The Syracuse Herald*, 1899; 1905-1906; 1908.

110. "Neal Looks Well: Fig Biscuit Says Government Has Been Worth $25,000 to Company," *The Syracuse Herald*, April 30, 1906, p. 6; Neal's Fig Biscuits'

Advertisements, *The Syracuse Herald,* May 3, 1906, p. 10; ibid., May 6, 1906, p. 12; ibid., May 9, 1906, p. 6; ibid., June 8, 1906, p. 3; ibid., June 10, 1906, p. 8.

111. "'Force of Life' Must Pay," *The New York Times,* May 10, 1912, p. 20; "Court Calendars," ibid., January 27, 1913, p. 18; "Court Calendars," ibid., February 4, 1916, p. 18; ibid., March 30, 1916, p. 13.
112. Box 0081, folder 17, American Medical Association Historical Health Fraud and Alternative Medicine Collection, AMA Archive, Chicago, IL.
113. RGAE, f. 871, op. 3, d. 19, l. 9.
114. RGAE, f. 871, op. 3, d. 19, ll. 9-14.
115. See Cristie Mayer Lefkowith, *The Art of Perfume,* New York: Thames and Hudson, 1994, p. 204 and Ken Leach, *Perfume Presentation,* Toronto: Kres Publishing, 1997, pp.128, 321 for discussion and illustrations. See Dawn's Vanity Treasures and other sites for Internet sales.
116. "Dempsey is Named in Brevities Suit: Defense Says Pugilist Was Paid $10,000 to Endorse a preparation He Never Used," *The New York Times,* January 24, 1925, p. 28. See also Roger Kahn, *A Flame of Pure Fire: Jack Dempsey and the Roaring '20s* (New York: Harcourt Brace and Co., 1999), pp. 103-105.
117. RGAE, f. 871, op. 3, d. 19, ll. 17-20.
118. T. W. Delahanty, BFDC, U.S. Dept of Commerce, to Chief, Chemical Division, BFDC, February 15, 1924, NAUSA, File 231.0, BFDC, U.S. Dept. of Commerce.
119. "Proizvodstvo farmazavoda No. 8 za 1922 g.," RGAE, f. 871, op. 3, d. 16, l. 3
120. RGAE., f. 871, op. 3, d. 16, l. 4.
121. R. R. Keler, *Pravda po odnomu obshchestvennomu voprosu* (Moscow, 1898), pp. 4-32,and passim. Comparative figures on pp. 6, 15,16, 23; on zemstvos' duty to purchase medicines as cheaply as possible, pp. 7, 9, 11, 19; on his wares being cheaper than the Ferrein firm, p. 13; on danger of war, p. 25.
122. "Usloviia prodazhi," *Optovyi Preis-kurant tovarov firmennoi zadel'ki Moskovskogo tsentral'nago optovago sklada Fabrichno-torgovago Tovarishchestva "R. Keler i Ko. v Moskve."* (Moscow, 1914), Introductory pages, 1 and 2.
123. RGAE, f. 871, op. 1, d. 11, contracts 1, 2, 3, 4., 5, 6, 7, 8, 9, 11, 12, 14, 17, 18, 19, 22-no numbers on the listy.
124. Shass and Satsyperov, *Lekarstvennye i lekarstvenno-tekhnicheskie rasteniia SSSR* , pp. 13, 141.
125. Howard Adams , Acting Commercial Attache in the Hague, to the Bureau of Domestic and Foreign Commerce, U.S. Department of Commerce, Washington, June 2, 1922; Philip E. Mc Kenny to the Director of the BFDC, October 25, 1923; C. C. Concannon, Chief, Chemical Division, U.S. Dept of Commerce to Samuel H. Cross, Commercial Attache, the Hague, December 5, 1923; Samuel Cross to C. C. Concannon, October 10, 1926; Concannon to Cross, October 18, 1926; F. J. McDonough, President of the New York Quinine and Chemical Works to Mr. T. W. Delahanty, BDFC, August 19 1927; H. R. Neilson of Merck and Co to BFDC, September 21, 1927. NAUSA, File no. 231, BDFC , U.S. Dept. of Commerce.
126. The Amsterdam Company of one Mr. Schmidt, which was "the largest dealer in this chemical in Holland" was forced in 1923 to acquire the liquid sulfur dioxide from Czeckoslovakia and Belgium, as well as Germany, because of "the unsettled

condition of Germany." Letter of Philip E. McKenney, Office of Commercial Attache, the Hague, to the BFDC regarding liquid sulphur [as spelled in the original] dioxide for the Virginia Smelting Company, Boston, MA., August 28, 1923, NAUSA, File 231.0, BFDC, U. S. Dept. Of Commerce.

127. T. W. Delahanty to Chief. Chemical Division, BFDC, U.S. Dept of Commerce, February 15, 1924, File 231.0, BFDC, U.S. Dept of Commerce.
128. J. F. Butler, Assistant Commerical Attache in Paris, to Mr. Concannon, Chief Chemical Division, BFDC, March 21, 1924, NAUSA, File 231, BFDC, U.S. Dept of Commerce.
129. RGAE, f.871, op. 1, d. 28, ll. 5, 7, 40, 45.
130. S. Ia Shiutte and E Iu Shass, *Gosudarstvennyi Standart eksportnogo lekarstvennogo i lekarstvenno-tekhnicheshkogo syr'ia, offitisal'nyi tekst s prilozheniiami, sostavlennymi direktorom Khimicheskogo Direktora S. Ia. Shiutte i Gosudarvennym brakerom po leksyr'iu E. Iu. Shass* (Moscow: Narkomtorg SSSR, 1927). Addresses of London and Paris branches in above, p. 73.
131. For the last three agencies see E. Iu Shass, *Gosudarstvennyi standart eksportnogo lekarstvennogo i lekarstvenno-tekhnicheskogo syr'ia* (Moscow, Narkomtorg U.S.S.R., 1927), pp. 4-5.
132. RGAE, f. 871, op. 1, d. 11, no list number, between agreement 5 and agreement 8 in file.
133. Utin, *Istoriia chimkentskogo khimiko-farmatsevticheskogo zavoda*, p. 40.
134. C. C. Concannon , Chief, Chemical Division, BFDC, U. S. Dept of Commerce, to "Bureau of Chemistry," Washington, DC , May 13, 1924, and MacKinnon, Acting Chief, Bureau of Chemistry, United States Dept of Agriculture to C. C. Concannon, Chief, Chemical Division, BFDC, May 20, 1924 in NAUSA, File 231.0, BFDC, U.S. Dept of Commerce.
135. C. C. Concannon, Chief, Chemical Divisions, BFDC, US Department of Commerce, to Mr. John G. Wheelock, Illinois State Bank Bldg, Quincy, IL, September 14, 1923 and T. W. Delahanty, Acting Chief, Chemical Division, to Chicago District Office, BFDC, September 19, 1923 in NAUSA, File 231.0, BFDC, U.S. Dept. of Commerce.
136. Elmslie, *Fifty Years of Livestock Research*, pp. 63-65, 68-69.
137. Utin, *Istoriia chimkentskogo khimiko-farmatsevticheskogo zavoda*, p. 39.
138. RGAE, f. 8140, op. 1, d. 30, l. 326 ob. .
139. Both catalogues in my possession. First cited in Conroy, "Pharmacy in Soviet Russia before the Great Patriotic War," *Pharmacy in History*, pp. 5-6.
140. T. V. A. MacMurray , "Discovery of Borate Deposits in Soviet Russia," Riga, March 16, 1934, to the Honorable Secretary of State, Washington, D. C., pp. 1 and 3 (compiled from *Vneshnyaya togovlya soyuza sovetskikh sotsialisticheskikh respublikh za period 1918-1927/28*, Leningrad-Moscow, 1931, pp. 426-429) in NAUSA, File RG 489, Box 82, NN3-151-80-7, 10, 900, BFDC, U.S. Dept. of Commerce.
141. Gartsshtein, "Proizvodstvennaia rabota Gosmedtorgprom'a," pp. 12-13. First discussed in Conroy, The Russian Pharmaceutical Industry," McDermott and Morison, *Politics and Society under the Bolsheviks*, p. 25.

142. F. Ferrein, "Perspektivy farmatsvticheskoi promyshlennosti," *Vestnik farmatsii,* 1924, nos. 8-9, pp. 134-135. First discussed in ibid., p. 27.
143. V. A. Izmailskii, "O stovarsole i sal'varsanovykh preparatakh," *Khimiko-farmatsevticheskii zhurnal,* 2 (5), 1924, pp. 14-16.
144. Samuel H. Cross, Chief, European Division, to Mr. Wizeman, BFDC, U.S. Dept. of Commerce, February 28, 1925 and C. C. Concannon, Chief, Chemical Division to Mr. J. W. Lyons, Major C. W. S., (Room 3506, Munitions Bldg. Washington, D. C.), March 3, 1925. NAUSA, File 231, BFDC, U.S. Dept. of Commerce.
145. C. C. Concannon to Mr. Charles E. Harring, Commercial Attache, Berlin, September 15, 1924. NAUSA, File 231, BFDC, U.S. Dept. of Commerce.

Chapter 5

1. *Kratkii ocherk deiatel'nosti "Gosmedtorgproma,"* (1927), p. 6.
2. R. W. Davies, "Industry," *The Economic Transformation of the Soviet Union,* pp. 135-136. Davies questions the official statistic that outputs in heavy industry may have been 4 percent higher in 1926/1927 than in 1913 but concedes that "the rate of recovery was far more rapid than anyone had anticipated." (p. 135) On food production see S. G. Wheatcroft and Davies, "Agriculture," ibid., pp. 111-112. C
3. Reuben and Wittcoff, *Pharmaceutical Chemicals,* pp. 3-9.
4. Galambos with Sewell, *Networks of Innovation: Vaccine Development at Merck, Sharp & Dohme, and Mulford,* pp. 34-35.
5. *Kratkii otchet o rabote "Gosmedtorgproma" za 1924/25 god.,* p. 3.
6. RGAE], f. 8140, op.1, d.1, ll. 137, 137 ob., merger meeting of March 4, 1924.
7. RGAE, f. 8140, op. 1, d. 29, ll. 138, 139, 143. Meetings of March 7 and March 14.
8. Vesenkha's exact contribution was 3,430,000 rubles; the Commissariat of Health's, 2,561,000 rubles. *Kratkii otchet.... za 1924/25 god.,* p 15.
9. Ibid., p. 2.
10. RGAE, f. 8140, op. 1, d. 29, l. 139; March 14 meeting, l. 143.
11. Stephen F. Cohen, *Bukharin and the Bolshevik Revolution: A Political Biography, 1888-1938* (Oxford: Oxford University Press, 1980), p. 200 and passim.
12. *Kratkii Ocherk Deiatel'nosti Glavnoi Khimicheskoi i Farmatsevticheskoi Kontory Gostorga, "Khimfarmtorg"* (Moscow, 1926), pp. 1-3, 6, 8, 13.
13. *Kratkii otchet... za 1924/25 god.,* p. 3.
14. *Kratkii Ocherk Deiatel'nosti Glavnoi Khimicheskoi i Farmatsevticheskoi Kontory Gostorga "Khimfarmtorg,"* p. 11, 13-15.
15. *Kratkii otchet... 1924/25 god.,* p. 3.
16. *Kratkii otchet... za okt-iiun' 1926-27 oper god.,* pp. 3-4.
17. *Kratkii ocherk deiatel'nosti "Gosmedtorgproma"* (1927), p. 13.
18. In the 1924/1925 operating year 50 percent of the Trust's income came from banking operations; 23.8 percent came from sales (*prodazha* or *torgovyi oborot*). Income from these sources amounted to 27 million rubles. Ten percent of Gosmedtorgprom's income came from "imposed payments"; 8 percent from city trade enterprises; 4 percent from "out-of-city" departments; and the

remainder from promissory notes and "other." *Kratkii otchet... za 1924/25 god.*, pp. 12, 15.

19. *Kratkii otchet... za 1925/26 operats. god.*, pp. 4, 5, 15, 27-28.
20. "Perspektivy," *Kratkii otchet... za 1924/25 god.*, p. 16-17.
21. *Kratkii otchet . . . 1925/26 operats. god.*, p. 29.
22. These seemed to be "the equalizing collection" (*uravnitel'nyi sbor*) and the "superimposed" (*nakladnye*) expenditures which may have been part of the Trust's "immediate obligations" (*srochnym obiazatel'stvam*), which amounted to 42 percent of its outlay in 1925/1926, part of the payments for payroll deficiencies (*s nachetami*), amounting to 10 percent of its outlay in that operating year, or payments to factories for economic (*khozaistv.*) expenditures, which amounted to 7 percent of the Trust's outlay for 1925/1926. *Kratkii otchet.... za 1924/25 god.*, pp. 15-16 and *Kratkii otchet.... za 1925/26 operats. god.*, p. 25.
23. *Kratkii otchet... za 1924/25 god.*, p. 16.
24. In the mid 1920s, the government began to buy large amounts of peasant grain at rock-bottom prices, predictably generating resistance on the part of peasants. Taxes for small-scale producers were ratcheted up, choking off their businesses. Currency speculators, small traders, shopkeepers, and some officials in the Commissariat of Finance were arrested. See Goland, "Currency Regulation," pp. 1279-1282. See also Ball, *Russia's Last Capitalists*, passim.

    A fall in grain exports led to balance of payments problems, which, in turn, resulted in the ruble again becoming non-convertible in 1926. Robert Lewis, "Foreign Economic Relations," Davis, Harrison and Wheatcroft, *The Economic Transformation*, pp. 203-204.
25. RGAE, 871, op. 3, d. 92. See also p. 159 and note 1, of "The Second Decade," section of this book, below.
26. R. W. Davies and O. Khlevnyuk, "Gosplan," in E. A. Rees, *Decision-Making*, p. 34.
27. Nove, *Economic History*, pp. 137-138.
28. *Kratkii otchet... za oktiabr' – iiun' 1926-27 oper. god.*, p. 22.
29. Ibid., p. 20.
30. *Kratkii otchet . . . za 1924/25 god.*, p. 15.
31. Ibid., pp. 16-17.
32. *Kratkii otchet... za 1925/26 operats. god.*,pp. 26, 30-31. Of course the banks would be in trouble if the purchasers of Gosmedtorgprom's wares did not pay the bank, now that Gosmedtorgprom was relieved from collecting.
33. Ibid., pp. 13, 17-18. Apparently Vesenkha had given out too many licenses in the first quarter of the year and was forced to withhold permissions during the rest of the year.
34. RGAE, f. 871, op. 3, d. 37, ll. 1, 2, 4, 6, 7, 8, 11-12.
35. RGAE, f. 871, op. 3, d. 37, l. 13, 13 ob..
36. RGAE, f. 871, op. 3, d. 93, ll. 1, 2.
37. Cited in Conroy, *In Health and In Sickness*, p. 342 and note 192, p. 607.
38. Some important raw materials "absent" included tannin from nut-gall (*chernil'nykh*

oreshkakh), alkaloids from opium, sublimate and calomel from mercury, green soap made from vegetable oil, castor oil from the *kleshchevina* plant, and vinegar anhydride made from vinegar acid potassium. *Kratkii otchet . . . za 1925/26 operats. god.*, pp. 6-7, 9.

39. L. Gartsshtein, "Narkomvneshtorg i torgovlia medikamentami," *Khimiko-farmatsevticheskii zhurnal*, 2 (5), 1924, pp. 5-6.
40. S. Mar, "K voprosu o 'nozhnitsakh' v farmatsevticheskom dele," *Khimiko-farmatsevticheskii zhurnal*, no. 1 (4), 1924, pp. 4-6.
41. F. Ferrein, "Tamozhennye tarify i ikh znachenie dlia khimiko-farmatsevticheskoi promyshlennosti," *Khimiko-farnmatsevticheskii zhurnal*, no. 10-12 (8-9), 1924, pp. 9-11.
42. Davies and Khlevnyuk, "Gosplan," p. 34.
43. *Kratkii otchet... za oktiabr' – iiun' 1926-27 oper. god.*, pp. 22, 25, 27.
44. Duties on mercury preparations shot up 266 percent, those on bromine, iodine, and their compounds were raised 222 percent, duties on salts containing silver were raised 200 percent, duties for adrenaline were raised 147 percent, those for cocoa oil, ether oil and cocaine were raised 111 percent, 400 percent, and 490 percent, respectively. High duties were placed on alkaloids produced in the USSR, an improvement over the 1924 tariff which imposed high duties on alkaloids even if they were not produced in the USSR. Prohibitively high import duties were imposed on cosmetics and perfumes and also on medical instruments. The reason for the rise in import duties was "to protect domestic industry," but undoubtedly increasing state revenues also was a consideration. I. Bychkov, "Oblozhenie poshlinami importnykh medtovarov," *Khimiko-farmatsevticheskii zhurnal*, no. 7 (43), 1927, pp. 10-11.
45. "V Ukrmedtorg," *Farmatsevticheskii zhurnal*, 1, no. 10, 1928, p. 578.
46. RGAE, f. 8009, op. 2, d. 126, l. 100.
47. I. Ia. Bychkov, "Farmatsevticheskaia promyshlennost': Proizvodstvo meditsinskikh instrumentov i priborov v SSSR," *Khimiko-farmatsevticheskii zhurnal*, no. 12 (60), 1928, p. 7.
48. *Kratkii otchet... za 1925/26 operats. god.*, p. 26. A little over 5.5 million rubles was "liquid"; the rest was "non-liquid"—slated for securities, shares, and moveable property.
49. ("Nakladnye raskhody") ibid., p. 26.
50. Ibid., pp. 25, 28-29. Almost half the credit (47 percent) came from the Industrial Bank (*Prombank*). Over one-third (36 percent) came from the State Bank (*Gosbank*). About 10 percent came from the Moscow City Bank (*Mosgodbank*) and a little over 6 percent from the Russian Bank (*Roskombank*).
51. RGAE, f.8140, op. 1, d. 29, l. 143.
52. *Kratkii otchet . . . za 1925/26 operats. god.*, p. 17.
53. Ibid., p. 7.
54. Ibid., p. 26.
55. The number of ordinary workers declined from a high of 1,656 to 1,618; the number of white collar workers (*sluzhashchie)* declined from 390 to 319. Ibid., p. 10.
56. Examples of these contracts with Gosmedtorg, in the spring of 1924, before the

creation of Gosmedtorgprom can be found in RGAE, f. 871, op. 1, d. 11. The listy are unnumbered. Contracts are numbered: Soglashenie No. 2 with Voronezh; No. 8 with Vitebsk; No. 11 with Riazan'; No. 9 with Poltava; No. 4 with the Crimean Medtorg; No. 17 with the Saratov Gubmedtorg; No. 14 with Kursk; No. 12 with Bashmedtorg; No. 18 with the Samara Gubmedtorg; No. 22 with the Don Medtorg; No. 19 with the Nizhegorod Aptekoupravlenie. These agencies agreed to purchase wares exclusively from Gosmedtorg.

57. *Kratkii otchet.... za 1925/26 operats. god.*, pp. 14-15. Exact sales' amounts were 27,109,938 rubles in 1924/1925 and 32,460,504 rubles in 1926/1926.
58. Ibid., p. 27.
59. Professor V. F. Pasternatskaia, "Nasha tribuna: O neobkhodimosti ratsional'noi postanovki sbora lekarstvennykh rastenii na Ukraine," *Khimiko-farmatsevticheskii vestnik* (Odessa) 1, no. 5-6 ,1926, p. 20.
60. N. A. Vliashko and I. A. Krasuski, "K voprosu ob organizatsii khimiko-farmatsevticheskoi promyshlennosti na Ukraine," *Khimiko-farmatsevticheskii vestnik* (Odessa) 1, no. 7-8, 1926, pp.13-14. In addition to Iurotat and Snapir, which both produced galenicals, Ukrainian pharmaceutical enterprises included the Buchanskii Factory of salicylic preparations; the Chloroform Factory; Farmgalen, which produced manganate salts; Stella, another galenical factory; the Russian-Technical Society; the Factory of Vinegar Acid; the Ether Factory; the Sanitary-Bacteriologocal Institute; Galenika, which prepared "organo-therapeutic preparations," Phytin, and others; Vega, which produced mercury salts; eight factories that produced Mint Oil; a factory that produced high-quality turpentine; and factories in Kiev and Volynia that put out products of dry-distillation of wood.
61. Zomin and Dukhin, "Vtoroe Vseukrainskoe Soveshchanie po farmobrazovaniiu," *Khimiko-farmatsevticheskii vestnik* (Odessa), no. 7-8 ,1926, pp. 15-29.
62. "Issues about Trade and Supplying Medicines to the Ukraine," January 18, 1924, RGAE, f. 8140, op. 1. d. 28, l. 51.
63. March 7, 1924, meeting RGAE, f. 8140, op. 1, d. 29, l. 139. Even before the merger, Farmapravlenie had stated that "it was principally desirable to immediately connect Odessa and Kiev with Moscow . . . for the purpose of a swift struggle with competition in the Ukraine," although the "stated connection" would have to "be done after the union of Farmatrest with Gosmedtorg." RGAE, f. 8140, op. 1, d. 28, l. 24.
64. RGAE, f. 8140, op. 1, d. 34, ll. 10, 12, 14.
65. RGAE, f. 8140, op. 1, d. 28, l. 21. Other members of the Ukrainian delegation included a representative from the Ukrainian chemical industry and the Ukrainian representative of Farmatrest.
66. RGAE, f. 8140, op. 1, d. 28, l. 30. According to Landis "the chief objections to the work of Gosmedtorg in the Ukraine" had been recorded in a meeting of Ukrainians, held months earlier.
67. RGAE, f. 8140, op. 1, d. 28, l. 30 ob.
68. He noted "the defects, the abnormality of the supply of medicaments —partially filled orders—incomplete assortment and interruption of production from instance

to instance." His solution was to abolish Ukrmedtorg in Kiev while retaining the Pharmacy Administration in Khar'kov. RGAE, f. 8140, op. 1, d. 28, l. 52.

69. RGAE, f. 8140, op. 1. d. 28, ll. 30, 30 ob.. To buttress his contention, Kagan cited the "Dava-Bristol Firm," which had done this during 1923.
70. RGAE, f. 8140, op. 1, d. 28, ll. 8, 8 ob. Meeting of April 22, 1924.
71. *Kratkii otchet... za 1925/26 operats. god.*, p. 3.
72. Advertisement (Ob" iavlenie), "'Ukrmedtorg'," *Khimiko-farmatsevticheskii vestnik*, vol. 1, 1926, end pages of each number.
73. *Kratkii otchet....za oktiabr'-iiun' 1926-27 oper. god.*, p. 20.
74. *Kratkii otchet... za 1924/25 god.*, pp. 18-22.
75. L.Gartsshtein, "Proizvodstvennaia rabota gosmedtorgprom'a," *Khimiko-farmatsevticheskii zhurnal*, vol. 2, no. 10-12 (13-15), 1924, p. 13.
76. *Kratkii otchet.... za 1925/26 operats. god.*, p. 15.
77. L. Gartsshtein, "Proizvodstvennaia rabota Gosmedtorgprom'a," *Khimiko-farmatsevticheskii zhurnal*, no. 10-12 (13-15), 1924, p. 13. New production in that year also included Gitalen, Heroin, Dionin, and Pantopon. (p. 12)
78. Shass and Satsyperov, *Lekarstvennye rasteniia*, p. 12.
79. RGAE, f. 871, op. 1, d. 28, ll. 5, 7, 40, 45.
80. RGAE, f. 871, op. 1, d. 28, l. 45, 60 ob, 61, 64 ob.
81. *Kratkii Ocherk Deiatel'nosti Glavnoi Khimicheskoi i Farmatsevticheskoi Kontory Gostorga "Khimfarmtorg,"* pp. 11-13.
82. Shass and Satsyperov, *Lekarstvennye rasteniia*, p. 142.
83. Ibid., pp. 13, 76-82.
84. Ibid., p. 157.
85. *Kratkii Ocherk Deiatel'nosti Glavnoi Khimicheskoi i Farmatsevticheskoi Kontory Gostorga "Khimfarmtorg,"* p. 13.
86. *Kratkii otchet.... za 1925/26 operats. god*, p. 22. Germany's exact share was 42.6 percent, England's was 21.1 percent, and that of the United States, 28.1 percent.
87. Ibid., p. 22.
88. Ibid., pp. 21-22. The exact amount was 39.5 percent.
89. *Kratkii otchet . . . za oktiabr'-iiun' 1926-27 oper. god.*, p. 26.
90. Utin, *Istoriia chimkentskogo khimiko-farmatsevticheskogo zavoda*, pp. 35-37
91. Ibid., p. 37.
92. Ibid., pp. 37-38.
93. Lyman D. Wilbur, "Surveying Through Khoresm: A Journey Into Parts of Asiatic Russia Which Have been Closed to Western Travelers Since the World War," *The National Geographic Magazine*, 41, no. 6 ,1932, p. 757.
94. Described in Chapter 10.
95. Utin, *Istoriia chimkentskogo khimiko-farmatsevticheskogo zavoda*, pp. 38-42.
96. *Kratkii otchet . . . za 1927-28 op. god.*, p. 9.
97. Utin, *Istoriia chimkentskogo khimiko-farmatsevticheskogo zavoda*, p. 49.
98. It should be noted that Russia standardized rhubarb in the seventeenth and eighteenth centuries, exporting only the best quality. Clifford M. Foust. *Rhubarb: The Wondrous Drug* (Princeton: Princeton University Press, 1992).

99. "Predpriiatiia Gosmedtorgproma," *Kratkii ocherk deiatel'nosti "Gosmedtorgproma,"* Moscow, February, 1927, p. 13. Skublinskii was the plenipoteniary in charge of iodine production in Baku. Zemlinskii was in charge of medicinal plants in Leningrad, Chulkov occupied the post in Voronezh, Tsirlin in the Caucasus, Radilevskii in Kiev, Timchenko in Rostov-on-the-Don and Iakuner in Odessa.
100. R-r Rann, "Chto dolzhen znat' farmatsevt pri prigotovlenii lekarstvennykh form iz naperstianki" (translation of A. G. Fisher from Pharmatzeufiche Zeitung, 1926, no. 20, p. 312), *Khimiko-farmatsevticheskii vestnik*, 1, no. 5-6 (1926): pp 6-9.
101. Shiutte and Shass, *Gosudarstvennyi standart*, p. 4. Commission members included Professor D. M. Shcherbachev, Professor M. I. Golenkin, A. K. Podgorodetskii, E. Iu. Shass, I. I. Parkinson, G. S. Ogolevets, A. N. Obukhov, E. M. Solomonov, and I. R. Dubchinskii. Also participating were the Chair of the Russian Republic Commissariat of Agriculture (RSFSR Narkomzem), M. I. Kuprianov; Chair of Russian Republic Commissariat of Health (RSFSR Narkomzdrav), I. Ia. Bychkov; and Chair of the Bureau for Standardization in Narkomtorg USSR, E. Kh. Poliakov.
102. Shiutte and Shass, *Gosudarstvennyi standart*, p. 3
103. (1) *Rhizoma calami* (*Airnyi koren'*); (4) the botanical and Russian names for anise were *Fructus anisi vulgaris* or *Anisovoe semia*; (15) mustard — *Semina sinapsis albae* or *Gorchita belaia semena* and (16) *Semina sinapsis rossicae* or *Gorchitsa sareptskaia*; (28) *Flores verbasci* or Koroviak flowers; (29) *Fructrus coriandri* or *Koriandrovoe semia*; (32) *Cortex fragulae* or *krushina*; (34) Lycopodium — *Sporae lycopodii* or *licopodii*; (35) Lime blossom — *Flores tiliae* or *Lipovyi tsvet* ; (41) *Ova formicarum* or *Murav'inie iaitsa*; (52) Licorice — *Radix glycyrrhizae* or *Solodkovyi koren'*; (53) another form of licorice; and (55) *Secale cornutum* or Sporyn'ia, also called black rose, a rose parasite. E. Iu. Shass, *Gosudarstvennyi standart*, pp. 6, 8, 15, 16, 24, 26-28, 33, 41-44.
104. Shiutte and Shass, *Gosudarstvennyi standart*, passim.
105. Shass and Satsyperov, *Lekarstevnnye rasteniia.*
106. N. A. Monteverde, et al. Sev. zap. oblastnaia torgovaia palata: Biuro Lekarstvennii, *Lekarstvennoe promyshlennoe syr'e: Rukovodstvo po standartizatsii* (Leningrad, 1927).
107. E. Iu. Shass, *Orientirovochnaia kal'kulatsiia nakladnykh raskhodov na eksportnoe leksyr'e po severo-zapadnoi oblasti* (Leningrad: Publication of the author, 1927).
108. *Kratkii ocherk deiatel'nosti "Gosmedtorgproma"* (Moscow, 1927), p. 6.
109. On production of these items by Beechams and other British firms in the interwar period, see Davenport-Hines and Slinn, *Glaxo*, pp. 86.
110. RGAE, f. 871, op. 3, d. 104, ll. 5, 6, 9.
111. RGAE, f. 871, op. 3, d. 104.
112. RGAE, f. 871, op. 3, d. 30.
113. RGAE, f. 871, op. 3, d. 56, ll. 1-7.
114. RGAE, f. 871, op. 3, d. 107, ll. 53, 55.
115. RGAE, f. 971, op. 3, d. 96, ll. 20, 25.
116. Vl. Saposhnikov, "Limonnaia kislota i limonokisloe brozhenie," *Khimiko-farmatsevticheskii zhurnal*, no. 6-7, 1924, pp. 17-19.
117. *Kratkii otchet . . . za 1925/26 operats. god.*, p. 8. See Kobrak, *National Cultures*, pp. 56-

57, 364 for details on Schering's production of Urotropin and Atophan, 1913-1928. Of course Schering was nationalized in 1914 but it appears that Urotropin was not produced in Russia prior to 1925/1926. On Schering's trademark rights to Urotropin and Atophan see Kobrak, ibid., pp. 163, 181.

118. *Kratkii otchet o rabote Gosmedtorgproma za oktiabr'-iiun' 1926-27 oper.god.* (Moscow: izdanie gosmedtorgproma, 1927), p. 29.
119. *Kratkii ocherk deiatel'nosti " Gosmedtorgproma,"* (1927), p. 4. Tyreoidin was spelled this way in this publication, whereas in a 1930 Russian journal the product was spelled Tireoidin. (See Chapter 10, page 207.) For provenance of Pantopon and "Thryeoidin" in 1922 see Farmatrest, *Ukazatel' predpriiatii i tovarnii catalog* (Moscow, 1922), pp. 81, 88.
120. *Kratkii ochet o rabote Gosmedtorgproma za 1925/26 operats. god.*, p. 8 and *Kratkii ocherk deiatel'nosti "Gosmedtorgproma"* (1927), p. 8.
121. "Khronika: k 35-letnemy iubileiu B. N. Saltykova," *Khimiko-farmatsevticheskii vestnik* (Odessa), no. 3-4 ,1926, p. 24.
122. *Kratkii ochet o rabote Gosmedtorgproma za 1925/26 operats. god.*, p. 8.
123. *Kratkii ocherk deiatel'nosti "Gosmedtorgproma"* (1927, p. 9
124. Ibid., pp. 5, 10.
125. For example, D. Shcherbachev, "Obzor novykh sredstv," *Khimiko-farmatsevticheskii zhurnal,* no. 1(4) ,1924, pp. 13-14; V. Izmail'ski, "Khloraminy — novyi tip antiseptiki," ibid., p. 17; "Frantsuzskie sal'varsonye preparaty," loc. cit.; "Tonephosphan," loc. cit.; "Sintez letsitina," loc. cit. ; V. A. Izmail'skii, "O Stovarsole i sal'varsanovykh preparatakh," no.2 (5), 1924, pp. 14-16; A Mogil'skii, "Kolichestvennoe opredelenie khimicheskikh, Farmatsevticheskikh i galenovykh preparatov," *Khimiko-farmatsevticheskii zhurnal,* 2(5), 1924, p. 17
126. On production of camphor, see Kobrak, *National Cultures,*, p. 124; on Schering's sales of santonin, see ibid., p. 165. On production of camphor in the Soviet Union see p. 114 and note 51 above and Akts. O-va "Gosmedtorgprom", *Gosudarstvennyi khimiko-farmatsevticheskii zavod imeni L. Ia. Karpova* (Moscow, 1926), p. 5.
127. Weatherall, *In Search of a Cure,* pp. 84-89.
128. See chapter 1 and Conroy, *In Health and In Sickness,* pp. 133-134.
129. Weatherall, *In Search of a Cure,* pp. 89-93; Madison, *Eli Lilly,* pp. 55-64. For the Roosevelt Administration's attack on the Eli Lilly Company for its monopoly on insulin, pp. 102-103; for the making of ephedrine or adrenalin in the 1920s, p. 65.
130. "Retsenzii i referaty," *Khimiko-farmatsevticheskii vestnik* (Odessa), no. 3-4, 1926, pp, 23-24. The text reviewed was that by S. Loewl (Dorpat), *O novykh metodakh opredeleniia valorizatsii gormonykh preparatov.*
131. *The Story of the Chemical Industry in Basle,* pp. 184-187. For general work on hormones in the 1930s, see Weatherall, *In Search of a Cure,* pp. 94-95.
132. Akts.-O-vo. "Gosmedtorgprom," *Gosudarstvennyi khimiko-farmatsevticheskii zavod imeni L. Ia. Karpova,* Moscow, 1926, pp. 11-18.
133. *Kratkii otchet . . . za 1925/26 operats. god.*, p. 8.

134. *Kratkii ocherk deiatel'nosti " Gosmedtorgproma"* (1927), pp. 6-7.
135. *Kratkii otchet . . . za oktiabr'-iiun' 1926-1927 oper. god.*, p. 8.
136. Conroy, "The Russian Pharmaceutical Industry," p. 28.
137. *Kratkii ocherk deiatel'nosti "Gosmedtorgproma"* (1927), pp. 10-11.
138. *Kratkii otchet . . . za oktiabr'-iiun' 1926-27 oper. god.*, p. 12 .
139. Tilles, "K istorii belomorskogo ioda," p. 11.
140. F. A. Ferrein, "Uspekhi v snabzhenii khimiko-farmatsevticheskoi promyshlennosti syr'em i polufabrikantami," *Khimiko-farmatsevticheskii zhurnal*, 6, no. 22 (70), 1928, pp. 5-6; iodine, p. 6.
141. This appears to have been no longer a Hoffmann-La Roche product but a Soviet item, as were "Aspirin" and "Piramidon" in the mid-1920s. For the Soviet clones of the latter, formerly German-made products, see "Otlichie original'nykh 'Aspirin'a' i 'Piramidon'a' ot preparatov, ikh zameniaiushchikh," *Khimiko-farmatevticheskii vestnik* (Odessa), no. 7-8 ,1926, p. 5.
142. Kobrak, *National Cultures*, pp. 56-57, 364.
143. Conroy, "The Russian Pharmaceutical Industry," pp.27-28.
144. Ia. Mazover, "Gosudarstvennyi salitsilovyi zavod," *Khimiko-farmatsevticheskii zhurnal*, no. 12 (60) ,1928, p. 9.
145. *Kratkii otchet . . . za 1925/26 operats. god.*, pp. 8, 9, 16.
146. Davenport-Hines and Slinn, *Glaxo*, pp. 86, 136-137. Britain continued to import chemically synthesized drugs from Germany during the 1930s. When these were cut off at the start of World War II British firms had to scramble to catch up.
147. *Kratkii otchet . . . za oktiabr'-iiun, 1926-27*, pp. 17-18.
148. Ibid., p. 27.
149. Ibid., pp., 12-13, 28-29, 8-9, 26, 32, respectively.
150. There were discrepancies in reports. According to information in the 1927 report of the industry, "chemical preparations" produced in 1926-1927 amounted to 2,445,744 kilograms. The 2,133,000 kilograms of chemicals cited in the first report came close to this figure. The 1929 report claimed production of galenical items (*shtuk*) amounted to 984,852 kilograms in 1926-1927, while galenical items were said to be about 300,000 kilograms higher in the February 1927 report. In the 1929 report 1,316,822 kilograms of "patented" items (*shtuk*) were produced in 1926-1927. This may have referred to the hormone, castor oil, colloids, and antivenereal preparations cited in the 1927 report. They only amounted to 462,000 kilograms in that report, however. Finally, the 1929 report also cited 606,850 kilograms of "other" items, for a grand total of 4,047,446 kilograms of chemicals and pharmaceuticals produced in 1926-1927. "Non-pharmaceutical" products were said to amount to 3,323, 300 kilograms. *Kratkii otchet . . . za 1927-28 op. god.*, pp. 6–7.
151. Kobrak, *National Cultures*, pp. 105, 116, 118-121, 124, 148, 151-156, 160, 178, 183-200.
152. Kobrak, ibid., p. 151.
153. A. Aluf, "Ratsionalizatsiia lekarstvennykh form," *Khimiko-farmatsevticheskii zhurnal*, vol. 5, no. 2 (38), 1927, p. 2.

Chapter 6

1. Soviet citizens were especially enthralled with American movies For details see Youngblood, *Movies for the Masses*, passim.
2. See the Pharmacopoeia of the USSR, 1937, and that of Britain, 1932, in M. Kh. Bergol'ts, "Osnovnye puti razvitiia galenovogo proizvodstva SSSR," *Farmatsiia*, vol. 8, no. 4, 1945, p. 18 and the Pharmacopoeia of the United States, 1936, in M. Kh. Bergol'ts, "Galevovye preparaty v novykh izdaniia farmakopei (XII) i national'nogo formuliara (VII) SshA," *Farmatsiia*, vol. 8, no. 6, 1945, p. 36
3. S. Rachkovskii, "Obsluzhivanie zastrakhovannykh lekarstvennoi pomoshch'iu v RSFSR," *Farmatsevticheskii zhurnal*, vol. 1, no. 6, 1928 (Ukraine), p. 301 first cited in Conroy, "Pharmacy in Soviet Russia before the Great Patriotic War," p. 6.
4. For example, S. A. Vein, "Polozhenie uezdnoi apteki," *Khimiko-farmatsevticheskii zhurnal*, no. 1(4), 1924, pp. 19-20 and S. Maimind, "Ocherednye zadachi aptechnogo stroitel'tva," ibid., no. 2(5), pp. 2-3.
5. K-ch, "Aptechnoe delo v Kostromskoi gubernii," *Khimiko-farmatsevticheskii zhurnal*, no. 2(5), 1924, p. 20, first cited in Conroy, "The Russian Pharmaceutical Industry," in McDermott and Morison, *Politics and Society under the Bolsheviks, p. 29.*
6. "Tsifrovye dannye o sostoianii aptechnogo dela na Ukraine na I/X 1927 g.," *Farmatsevticheskii zhurnal* (Ukraine), vol. 1, no. 1-2, 1928, p. 67. First cited in Conroy, "Pharmacy in Soviet Russia before the Great Patriotic War," *Pharmacy in History*, vol. 40, no. 1, 1998, p. 6.
7. TsGIA RB, Introduction to fond, R 1911, p. 2.
8. "IV Plenum TsB Aptsektsii," *Khimiko-farmatsevticheskii zhurnal*, vol. 7, no. 15-16 (87-88), 1929, p. 17.
9. "Ot oboronyi k nastupleniiu (K prekrashcheniiu sdachi aptek v arendu)," *Khimiko-farmatsevticheskii zhurnal*, no. 7, 1924, p. 4.
10. For example, Advertisement, "K konkursu na luchshie apteki, ob'iavlennomu redaktsiei 'Khimiko-farmatsevticheskii zhurnala,'" *Khimiko-farmatsevticheskii zhurnal*, no. 7, 1924, p. 3. See also Conroy, "Pharmacy in Soviet Russia before the Great Patriotic War," p. 6.
11. Wheatcroft and Davies, "Agriculture," in Davies, Harrison and Wheatcroft, *The Economic Transformation of the Soviet Union*, pp. 111-112. The authors note that grain production nearly achieved 1913 levels by 1926 although, because of increased population there was less grain per head of population and peasants marketed less grain, diverting it to their cattle as fodder. Nevertheless, increased fodder resulted in increased marketings of meat and dairy products, and this, plus increased output of potatoes, fruit and vegetables, meant that Soviet citizens were eating as well, and in some cases, better than before the First World War. The *chervonets* ruble strengthened and was accepted as legal tender within the country. See Goland, "Currency Regulation in the NEP Period," pp. 1251-1296. For consumer goods, see Ball, *Russia's Last Capitalists.*

12. TsGIA RB, R 443, op. 1, d, 496, ll. 25-25 ob..
13. TsGIA RB, f. R 443, op. 1, d. 496, l. 14.
14. For example, "Ob"iavleniia," *Khimiko-farmatsevticheskii vestnik* (Odessa), vol. 1, no 3-4, 1926, 5 pages of advertisements following p. 27.
15. Advertisement, *Farmatsevticheskii zhurnal*, vol. 1, no. 11, 1928, following p. 653.
16. Advertisement, *Farmatsevticheskii zhurnal*, vol. 1, no. 11, 1928, following p. 653.
17. Advertisement, *Farmatsevticheskii zhurnal*, vol. 1, no. 7, 1928, following p. 386. The razorblade "Lora" also appears in the section of advertisements.
18. *Kratkii otchet o rabote Gosmedtorgproma za 1925/26 operats. god* (Moscow, April 1927), p. 14.
19. E. Iu. Shass, "Import farmatsevticheskikh tovarov," *Farmatsevticheskii zhurnal*, vol. 1, no. 3, 1928, pp. 12-13.
20. L Gartsshtein, "Farmatsevticheskaia promyshlennost'. Torgovaia politika Gosmedtorgproma," *Khimiko-farmatevticheskii zhurnal*, vol. 5, no. 3 (39), 1927, pp. 9-10.
21. M. I. Iaroslav, "Nuzhno li Ukraine svoe khimiko-farmatsevticheskoe proizvodstvo," *Farmatsevticheskii zhurnal*, vol. 1, no. 2, 1928, pp. 20-21.
22. Loc. Cit.
23. A. Babskii, "Rol' medsnabzheniia v deiatel'nosti lechuchrezhdeniia," *Farmatsevticheskii zhurnal*, vol. 1, no. 10, 1928, pp. 514-516.
24. Maimind, "Ocherednye zadachi," *Khimiko-farmatsevticheskii zhurnal*, no. 2(5), 1924, p. 2.
25. A. Aluf, "Likvidatsiia chastnogo aptekovladeniia," *Khimiko-farnatsevticheskii zhurnal*, no. 10-12 (13-15), 1924, p. 2.
26. "Tsirkulia N.K.Z.o prekrashchenii dal'neishchei sdachi aptek v arendu chastnym litsam ot 2 iiunia 1924 g., za No. 116," *Khimiko-farmatsevticheskii zhurnal*, no. 5-6, 1924, p. 30.
27. Ball, *Russia's Last Capitalists*, pp. 68-69, 100-107 and passim.
28. S. Rachkovskii, "Obsluzhivanie zastrakhovannykh lekarstvennoi pomoshch'iu v RSFSR," *Farmatsevticheskii zhurnal*, vol. 1, no. 6 , 1928, p. 301. First cited in Conroy, "Pharmacy in Soviet Russia before the Great Patriotic War," p. 6.
29. "Na mestakh: Deiatel'nost' Moskovskogo aptekoupravleniia za 1923/4 i 1924/5 g. g. i perspektivy na 1926/7g.," *Khimiko-farmatsevticheskii zhurnal*, vol. 5, no.1 (37), 1927, p. 25.
30. "Diatel'nost' Moskovskogo aptekoupravleniia za 1923/4 I 1924/5 g," p. 25.
31. A. Aluf, "15 let stroitel'stva sotsialisticheskioi apteki," *Sovetskaia farmatsiia*, vol. 4, no. 2-3, 1933, p. 1. First cited in Conroy, "Pharmacy in Soviet Russia before the Great Patriotic War," p. 6.
32. *Kratkii otchet o rabote Gosmedtorgproma za oktiabr'-iiun' 1926-27 operats. god.* (Moscow, 1927), pp. 3-4.
33. S. I. Pel'ts, "Nashi dostizheniia," *Farmatsevticheskii zhurnal*, vol. 1, no. 12, 1928, p.

673.

34. I. Minnovich, ibid., p. 674.
35. G. Gellerleib, ibid., p. 676.
36. A. Shass, ibid., p. 680.
37. D. I. Efimov, "Desiat' let Sovetskogo Zdravookhraneniia na Ukraine," *Farmatsevticheskii zhurnal* , vol. 1, no. 7, 1928, p. 60. Also Tsifrovye dannye o sostoianii aptechnogo dela na Ukraine na I/X 1927 g., ibid., no. 1-2, pp. 67-68. Detailed discussion in Conroy, "Pharmacy in Soviet Russia before the Great Patriotic War," p. 6.
38. N. Shamipron, "Dislokatsiia gorodskoi aptechnoi seti v Kieve," *Farmatsevticheskii zhurnal,* vol. 1, no. 4, 1928, pp. 165-166.
39. I. N. Tkalun, "O vykhodnykh dniakh vremeni zaveduiushchikh aptekami," *Farmatsevticheskii zhurnal*, vol. 1, no. 3, 1928, p. 47 and Nikolaevskii, "O rabochem vremeni zaveduiushchikh sel'aptekami," ibid., pp. 48-49.
40. "Tsifrovye dannye o sostoianii aptechnogo dela na Ukraine," p. 67.
41. "O postanovke medsnabzheniia v ob"edinennom MSU Iuzhnykh i Donetskikh zhel. dorog.," *Farmatsevticheskii zhurnal,* vol. 1, no. 1-2, 1928, p. 84.
42. TsGIA RB, f. R 444, d. 317a, ll. 1-70.
43. TsGIA RB, f. R. 444, op. 1, d. 317a, l. 22.
44. TsGIA RB, f. R 444, op. 1, d. 317a, l. 76.
45. TsGIA R B., f. R 444, op. 1, d. 317a, l. 32.
46. TsGIA RB, f. R 444, op. 1, d. 317a, l. 21 and l. 34 (23 kopeks), l. 32 (35.2 kopeks).
47. TsGIA RB, f. R444, op. 1, d. 317a, l. 2.
48. Conroy, *In Health and In Sickness,* pp. 26-35, 109-136, 364-369, 413-414.
49. I. Levinshtein, *Materialy po profess.-tekhnicheskomu obrazovaniiu* (Moscow: Gosudarstvenoe izdatel'stvo, 1921), p. 3.
50. I. Levinshtein, *Materialy po farmatsevticheskomu obrazovaniiu* (Moscow: Gosudarstvennoe izdatel'stvo, 1922), pp. 7, 8, 10 and passim. First cited in Conroy, *In Health and in Sickness,* 414-415. See Michael David-Fox for politicization of school curricula at higher levels, *Revolution of the Mind: Higher Learning among the Bolsheviks* (Ithaca: Cornell University Press, 1997).
51. TsGIA RB, f. R 444, op. 1, d. 317, l. 1 ob., 2.
52. See Chapter 10 of this work for references to Leningrad, Moscow, and some other areas in 1930. For Odessa see I. E., "O deiatel'nosti Odesskogo Khimfarina," *Farmatsevticheskii Zhurnal* vol. 1, no. 3, 1928, p. 51.
53. G. Shvartsman, "Likvidatsiia uchenichestva v aptekakh," *Farmatsevticheskii zhurnal,* vol. 1, no. 1-2, 1928, pp. 77-79; A. L., "Po povodu stat'i 'Likvidatsiia uchenichestva v aptekakh' tov. G. Shvartsmana," ibid., pp. 79-80; "O likvidatasii aptuchenichestva," ibid., p. 89.
54. G. Sh., "Vseukrainskie kursy dlia perekvalifikatsii aptechnykh praktikantov v g. Kieve," *Farmatsevticheskii zhurnal,* vol. 1, no. 3, 1928, pp. 52-53.
55. For American pharmacies see Glenn Sonnedecker, David L. Cowen & Gregory J. Higby, *Drugstore Memories: American Pharmacists Recall Life Behind the Counter, 1824-1933* (Madison, WI: American Institute of the History of Pharmacy, 2002).

Chapter 7

1. On Ufa through the 1920s, see Sinenko, *Gorod nad beloi rekoi,* pp. 38-124. Also Interview with Rustem Khaziev, historian, Ufa, July 7, 13, 2003. On medical care in Colorado see Robert H. Shikes, *Rocky Mountain Medicine: Doctors, Drugs, and Disease in Early Colorado* (Boulder: Johnson Books, 1986). For medical care in the 1920s see pp. 228-232.
2. Shikes, *Rocky Mountain Medicine,* pp. 228-229.
3. TsGIA RB, R f. 444, op. 1, d. 316, ll. 16, 26.
4. TsGIA RB, R f. 1203, op. 2, d. 1, l. 103.
5. TsGIA RB, R f. 1203, op. 2, d. 1, ll. 151, 151 ob., 152 ob. .
6. See "Vaccination," *World Book Encyclopedia* (Chicago: Field Enterprises, 1975), vol. 20, pp. 200-201.
7. See "Serum," *World Book Encyclopedia* (Chicago: Field Enterprises, 1975), vol. 17, pp. 248b-249.
8. TsGIA RB, R f. 1203, op. 2, d. 1, ll. 156 ob., 157.
9. TsGIA RB, R f. 1203, op. 2, d. 1, l. 147.
10. TsGIA RB, R f. 1203, op. 2, d. 1, l. 182 ob. .
11. TsGIA RB, R f. 1203, op. 2, d. 1, l. 183.
12. TsGIA RB, R f. 1203, op. 2, d. 1, l. 189 ob. .
13. TsGIA RB, R f. 1203, op. 2, d. 1, ll. 115, 115 ob., 151, quote about the ARA on l. 148.
14. TsGIA RB, R f. 1203, op. 2, d. 1, ll. 146, 149, quotes on l. 152 and on 1. 153.
15. TsGIA RB, R f. 1203, op. 2, d. 1, l. 155.
16. TsGIA RB, f. 1203, op. 2, l. 151.
17. TsGIA RB, R f. 1203, op. 2, d. 1, l. 152.
18. TsGIA RB, R f. 1203, op. 2, d. 1, ll. 183, 183 ob. .
19. See Joan Klobe Pratt, "The Free Economic Society and the Battle against Smallpox: A 'Public Sphere' in Action," *The Russian Review* , vol. 61, no. 4, 2002, pp. 568-569, 572-573 for the distinctions. Only six provinces in Imperial Russia lacked vaccination points in 1904. Pratt, ibid., p. 574.
20. TsGIA RB, R f. 1203, op. 2, d. 1, ll. 111ob. and 123 ob. .
21. TsGIA RB, R f. 1203, op. 2, d. 1, l. 151.
22. TsGIA RB, R f. 1203, op. 2, d. 1, l. 111 ob. .
23. TsGIA RB, R f. 1203, op. 2, d.1, ll.151, 151 ob., 152.
24. TsGIA RB, R f. 1203, op. 2, d. 1, l. 153 ob. .
25. TsGIA RB, R f. 1203, op. 2, d. 1, ll. 188 ob. and 189.
26. TsGIA RB, R f. 1203, op. 1, d. 2, l. 66.
27. TsGIA RB, R f. 1203, op. 1, d. 2, ll. 66, 67.
28. TsGIA RB, R f. 1203, op. 1, d. 2, l. 68. For Zoshchenko's story see Mikhail Zozhchenko, "*Kocherga* (The Poker)," *Scenes from the Bathhouse and Other Stories of Communist Russia* (Ann Arbor: University of Michigan Press, 1962), pp. 169-172.

29. TsGIA RB, R f. 1203, op. 1, d. 2, l. 68.
30. TsGIA RB, R f. 1203, op. 1, d. 2, ll. 43, 68 ob. .
31. TsGIA RB, R f. 1203, op. 1, d. 2, l. 66.
32. TsGIA RB, R f. 1203, op. 1, d. 2, ll. 73, 73 ob., 74, 74 ob., 75, 75 ob. .
33. TsGIA RB, R f. 1203, op. 1, d. 2, l. 76.
34. TsGIA RB, R f. 1203, op. 1, d. 2, ll. 76 ob, 77.
35. TsGIA RB, R f. 1203, op. 1, d. 2, l. 77 ob..
36. TsGIA RB, R f. 1203, op. 1, d. 2, l. 79 ob..
37. TsGIA RB, Rf. 1203, op. 1, d. 2, l. 83 ob..
38. TsGIA RB, R f. 1203, op. 1, d. 2, l. 84 ob..
39. TsGIA RB, R f. 1203, op. 1, d. 2, ll. 85, 85 ob., 86, 86 ob..
40. TsGIA RB, R f. 1203, op. 1, d. 2, l. 87.
41. TsGIA RB, R f. 1203, op. 1, d. 2, ll. 87 ob., 88.

The Second Decade

1. Gosplan (the State Planning agency), the Commissariat of Finance, the Workers' and Peasants' Inspectorate, and other government and Party bodies had been discussing and compiling statistics for an all-encompassing economic plan throughout the twenties. See R. W. Davies and O. Khlevnyuk, "Gosplan" in Rees, *Decision-Making in the Stalinist Command Economy*, pp. 32-38. In 1926, economists pulled pharmaceutical-chemical specialists into the process. Professor Porai-Koshits, A. E. Kagan and other chemical-pharmaceutical specialists helped draft a report entitled "Secret Materials…on Enlarging Basic Capital in the Aniline Dye Industry." This sector study was part of a series, *Five-Year Hypotheses for Branches of Industry (Piatiletnie gipotezy po otrasliam promyshenlennosti)*, sponsored by the Supreme Council of the National Economy, Vesenkha, under the general editorship G. I. Piatakov, one of the leading "left" or radical economists who favored concentrating investment in and rapid growth of heavy industry. RGAE, f. 871, op. 3, d. 92 .
2. Pharmaceutical journals enthused that "[T]he great task of socialist reconstruction…demands mobilization" of "all strata of workers, working peasants, white collar workers and working intelligentsia" as well as "material resources…to move forward the industrialization of the country and socialist reconstruction of agriculture." "O tret'em zaime industrializatsii," *Khimiko-farmatsevticheskii zhurnal*, vol. 7, no. 15-16, (87-88), 1929, p. 1.
3. "Privete tov. Stalinu" and "Ob uchasti aptekorabotnikov v kul'tpokhode, posevnoi kampanii i kollektivizatsii sel'skogo khoziastva," *Khimiko-farmatsevticheskii zhurnal*, vol. 7, no. 1 (97), 1930, p. 16.
4. See John Scott, *Beyond the Urals* (Cambridge: Houghton Mifflin Company, 1942), passim, and Valentin Kataev *Time! Forward!* (Bloomington: Indiana University Press, 1976), as well as other factual accounts.
5. E. A. Rees, "The People's Commissariat of Water Transport," p. 240, and Khlevnyuk, "The People's Commissariat of Heavy Industry," p. 106, in Rees,

Decision-Making in the Stalinist Command Economy. Galina Ivanova has documented how slave labor was less efficient than free labor. Galina Mikhailovna Ivanova, *Labor Camp Socialism: The Gulag in the Soviet Totalitarian System* (Armonk, NY: M. E. Sharpe, 1997), p. 118 . Upon completion, 72,000 slave laborers were amnestied but the rest were reassigned to the Moscow-Volga Canal and Baikal-Amur railway construction projects. See also primary accounts of forced labor like VladimirV. Tchernavin, *I Speak for the Silent*. (Boston, New York: Hale, Cushman and Flint, 1935).

6. Sheila Fitzpatrick, *Everyday Stalinism. Ordinary Life in Extraordinary Times*. (Oxford University Press, 1999), pp. 150-151.Children and teenaged vagrants that had roamed the Soviet Union during the NEP had begun to subside.
7. Sheila Fitzpatrick, *Stalin's Peasants: Resistance and Survival in the Russian Village After Collectivization* (Oxford, New York: Oxford University Press, 1994). pp. xvii, 38, and passim.
8. For details on communal housing, barracks, lack of sewerage and so forth, see Fitzpatrick, *Everyday Stalinism*, pp. 46-50.
9. E. Khanin-Dobraia, "Za chistotu i gigienu," *Vestnik farmatsiia*, vol. 8, no. 7-8, 1930, p. 310.
10. I. Zil'berg, "Obzor sredstv protiv prokazy," *Khimiko-farmarsevticheskii zhurnal*, vol. 7, no. 1(97), 1930, p. 12.
11. G. Chistiakov, "Zaraznye zabolevaniia i bor'ba s nimi," *Vestnik farmatsii*, vol. 8, no. 7-8, 1930, pp. 357-358.
12. Mark B.Tauger, chapter on Ukraine in Donald J. Raleigh, ed., *Provincial Landscapes: Local Dimensions of Soviet Power, 1917-1953* (Pittsburgh, Pa: University of Pittsburgh, 2001), cited in review, *The American Historical Review*, vol. 108, no. 5, 2003, p. 1561.
13. The progressive sectors of heavy industry were "complex machine tools, iron and steel-making equipment, tanks and many other products," R. W. Davies, *Soviet Economic Development from Lenin to Khrushchev* (Cambridge: Cambridge University Press, 1998), p. 38 and chapters 5 and 6, passim.
14. One accessible source for living conditions in the 1930s is Fitzpatrick, *Everyday Stalinism*, pp. 40-114.
15. Lorimer, *The Population of the Soviet Union*, p. 121.
16. The famine resulted from the excesses of collectivization and bad weather. For statistics of victims see Michael Ellman, "A Note on the Number of 1933 Famine Victims," *Soviet Studies* now *Europe-Asia Studies*, vol 43, no. 2, 1991, p. 375. For background see Robert Conquest, *Harvest of Sorrow* (New York: Oxford University Press, 1986), pp. 90-198 and passim. See also Fitzpatrick, *Stalin's Peasants*, pp. 54-59, 82-85.
17. Lorimer, *The Population of the Soviet Union* , p. 121.
18. See Fitzpatrick, *Everyday Stalinism*, pp. 55-56 and passim. For Stalin's role in lifting the rationing and the reasons for this, see Oleg Khlevnyuk and R. W. Davies, "The End of Rationing in the Soviet Union, 1933-1935," *Europe-Asia Studies*, vol. 51, no. 4, 1999, pp. 557-609. For difficulties caused by higher prices in Leningrad see Sarah Davies, *Popular Opinion in Stalin's Russia* (Cambridge: Cambridge University Press,

1997), pp. 27-31.
19. G. Chistiakov, "Zaraznye zabolevaniia i bor'ba s nimi," *Vestnik farmatsii*, vol. 8, no. 7-8, 1930, pp. 357-358.
20. Prof. D. Shcherbachev, "Vitaminy," *Vestnik farmatii*, vol. 8, no. 7-8, 1930, pp. 354-357.
21. Scherbachev, "Vitaminy," pp. 354-357. On production of vitamins and food supplements by the British firm Glaxo see Davenport-Hines and Slinn, *Glaxo*, pp. 70-85.

Chapter 8

1. V. K. Kirsenko, "O techenii dizenterii u vaktsinirovannykh protiv nee po bezredka," *Voenno-sanitarnoe delo*, no. 8, 1940, pp. 75-77.
2. A. I. Siroko, "Novoe v bor'be s dizenteriei," *Voenno-sanitarnoe delo*, no. 10, 1940, pp. 100-101.
3. TsGIA RB, R f. 1203, op. 1, d. 20, 1. 69.
4. TsGIA RB, R f. 1203, op. 1, d. 20, ll. 64, 60ob. .
5. TsGIA RB R f. 1203, op. 1, d. 20, pp. 6, 7.
6. TsGIA RB, R f. 1203, op. 2, d. 1, ll. 330, 331.
7. TsGIA RB, R f. 1203, op. 2, d. 1, l. 295.
8. TsGIA RB, R f. 1203, op. 2, d. 1, ll. 295, 295 ob., 296, 333.
9. TsGIA RB, R f. 1203, op. 2, d. 1, l. 305.
10. TsGIA RB, R f. 1203, op. 2, d. 1, ll. 306 and 307.
11. TsGIA RB, R f. 1203, op. 2, d. 1, l. 333.
12. TsGIA RB, R f. 1203, op. 2, d. 1, l. 331.
13. TsGIA RB, R f. 1203, op. 1, d. 15, l. 7.
14. TsGIA BR, R f. 1203, op. 1, d. 15, l. 7, 7 ob..
15. TsGIA RB, R f. 1203, op. 1, d. 15, l. 5 ob. .
16. TsGIA RB, R f. 1203, op. 1, d. 15, l. 6
17. TsGIA RB, Rf. 1203, op. 1, d. 15, ll. 8 and 9.
18. TsGIA RB, R f. 1203, op. 1, d. 15, l. 16.
19. TsGIA RB, R f. 1203, op. 1, d. 15, ll. 17-22 ob..
20. TsGIA RB, R f. 1203, op. 1, d. 15, l. 38.
21. TsGIA RB, R f. 1203, op. 1, d. 15, ll. 38, 38 ob..
22. TsGIA RB, R f. 1203, op. 1, d. 15, l. 38 ob..
23. TsGISA RB, R f. 1203, op. 1, d. 15, l. 38 ob..
24. TsGIA RB, R f. 1203, op. 1, d. 15, ll. 35, 35 ob., 36, 36 ob., 37.
25. TsGIA RB, R f. 1203, op. 1, d. 15, ll. 39, 39 ob., 40.
26. TsGIA RB, R f. 1203, op. 1, d. 20, p. 6.
27. TsGIA RB, R f. 1203, op. 1, d. 20, p. 9.
28. TsGIA RB, R f. 1203, op. 1, d. 20, pp. 11-12.
29. TsGIA, RB, R f. 1203, op. 1, d. 20, pp. 13-17.
30. TsGIA RB, R f. 1203, op. 1, d. 20, ll. 64, 65 ob. , 66 ob. , 67, 67 ob..
31. TsGIA RB, R f. 1203, op. 1, d. 20, ll. 764 ob and 68 ob. On the distinction between

rotnye and *shkol'nye fel'dshers* (the latter being trained, the former learning on the job) and their activities in the countryside in Imperial and Soviet Russia see Samuel C. Ramer, "Feldshers and Rural Health Care in the Early Soviet Period," in Solomon and Hutchinson, *Health and Society in Revolutionary Russia,* pp. 121-145.

32. TsGIA RB, R f. 1205, op. 1, d. 20, ll. 64ob., 65.
33. TsGIA RB, R f. 1205, op. 1, d. 20, ll. 68 ob, 69.
34. TsGIA RB, R f. 1205, op. 1, d. 20, l. 65 ob..
35. TsGIA RB, R f. 1205, op. 1, d. 20, ll. 68, 71 ob..
36. TsGIA RB, R f. 1205, op. 1, d. 20, l. 67 ob..
37. TsGIA RB, R f. 1205, op. 1, d. 20, ll. 65 ob, 66.
38. TsGIA RB, R f. 1205, op. 1, d. 20, l. 70.
39. TsGIA RB, R f. 1203, op. 1, d. 35, ll. 7, 7 ob..

Chapter 9

1. G. Tsander, "Amerikanskaia farmatsevticheskaia promyshlennost'," *Khimiko-farmatsevticheskaia promyshlennost'*, no. 1, 1933, p. 168.
2. See the accounts in Sonnedecker, Cowen, and Higby, eds., *Drugstore Memories: American Pharmacists Recall Life Behind the Counter,* passim.
3. "V plenum TsB Aptechnoi sektsii. Postanovlenie plenuma TsB aptechnoi sektsii o lekarstvennoi pomoshchi v promyshlennykh raionakh, sotssektore sel'skogo khoziastva i sel'skikh mestnostakh," *Khimiko-farmatsevticheskii zhurnal,* vol. 7, no. 2 (98), 1930, p. 15.

   Sally Ewing discusses the lower caliber of public health care as opposed to private during the NEP and the use of funds earmarked for health insurance for other purposes. "The Science and Politics of Soviet Insurance Medicine," in Solomon and Hutchinson, *Health and Society in Revolutionary Russia,* pp. 69-96, esp. pp. 80-81. Christopher Davis discusses how the goal of the Commissariat of Health, Narkomzdrav, to serve the entire population was forced to shift, because of funding constraints and pressure from Gosplan and other agencies, to focusing on serving mainly the insured, during the First Five Year Plan. "Economics of Soviet Public Health, 1928-1932," in ibid., pp. 146-172, esp. pp. 154-156.
4. Lupandin, "Aptechnoe khozaistvo Moskvy v tret'em, reshaiushchem godu piatiletki," *Sovetskaia farmatsiia,* vol. 3, no. 5, 1932, p. 34.
5. I. Chelidze, M. A. Berlovich, "Itogi obsledovaniia moskovskogo aptekoupravl eniia i leningradskogo medsnabtorga," ibid., vol. 2, no. 5-6, 1931, pp. 21-22.
6. Ia. Z., Severokavkazskoe kraevnoe aptekoupravlenie," ibid., p. 19.
7. "O meditsinkom obsluzhivanii rabochikh i krest'ian. Postanovlenie Ts K VKP (b)," *Vestnik farmatsii,* vol. 8, no. 2, 1930, p. 51. and *Khimiko-farmatsevticheskii zhurnal,* vol. 7, no. 1 (97), front page overleaf.
8. A. Aluf, "Osnovnye voprosy vtoroi piatiletki po medsnabzheniiu i aptechnomu stroitel'stvu," *Sovetskaia farmatsiia,* vol. 3, no. 5, 1932, p. 5.
9. Report of Khaimovich, "V Plenum TsB Aptechnoi sektsii. Postanovlenie plenuma

TsB aptechnoi sektsii," p. 15.

10. "Ob ispol'sovanii byvshei v upotreblenii posudy," *Khimiko-farmatsevticheskii zhurnal*, vol. 7, no. 12 (84), 1929, p. 20.
11. "Nepravil'nyi podkhod," *Khimiko-farmatsevticheskii zhurnal*, vol. 7, no. 12 (84), 1929, pp. 19-20. In Azerbaidzhan in 1929, nine pharmacies, under the authority of the Azerbaidzhan medical trade agency (Azmedtorg) were in the city of Baku and fifteen pharmacies were in outlying districts. Of the urban pharmacies nine were self-financed (*khozraschet*) and well-equipped but one had to be closed because of "deficits" and another was transferred to the Baku pharmacy administration to serve the insured.
12. "V Moskovskoi nauchno-farmatsevticheskoi assotsiataii," *Vestnik farmatsii*, vol. 8, no. 1, 1930, p. 35.
13. "Sredi moskovskikh aptechnikov," *Vestnik farmatsii*, vol. 8, no. 5-6, 1930, p. 287. The implication was that *kustar'* industry had performed well and ought to be allowed more scope instead of being oppressively taxed and curtailed other ways.
14. "O meditsinskom obsluzhivanii rabochikh i krest'ian," *Vestnik farmatsii*, vol. 8, no. 2, 1930, p. 51.
15. Efe, "Standarty i sel'skie apteki," *Vestnik farmatsii*, vol. 8, no. 2, 1930, p. 65.
16. I. Mironovich , "Priblizim lekarstvennuiu pomoshch' k kollektivizirovannomu selu," *Vestnik farmatsii*, vol. 8, no. 2, 1930, pp. 64-65.
17. Efe, "Standarty i sel'skie apteki," p. 65.
18. Mark Zelikman, "Naperekor traditsii," *Sovetskaia farmatsiia*, vol. 2, no. 5-6, 1931, pp. 26-27.
19. "Predstoit rost aptechnoi seti," *Khimiko-farmatsevticheskii zhurnal*, vol. 7, no. 1 (97), 1930, p. 4.
20. K. L., "Begstvo iz aptek, ego prichiny i mery bor'by," *Vestnik farmatsii*, vol. 8, no. 5-6, pp. 279-283.
21. M. Ginzburg, S. Rachkovskii, G. Tufel'd, "Finansovo-ekonomicheskoe polozhenie aptekoupravlenii RSFSR i kontrol'nye tsifry na 1929/30 god," *Vestnik farmatsii*, vol. 8, no. 1, 1930, p. 4.
22. I. Ia. Bychkov and A. Chelidze, "K itogam kursov po meditsinskomu instrumentariiu," *Sovetskaia farmatsiia*, vol. 2, no. 4, 1931, p. 25.
23. E. L-v, "B'em trevogu! (K voprosu o kadrakh dlia raionov," *Sovetskaia farmatsiia*, vol. 1, no. 2, 1930, p. 27. Original discussion and citation, Conroy, Soviet pharmacy before the Great Patriotic War, pp. 16, 24.
24. E. Kashkin, "Na shipke ne vse spokoino," *Sovetskaia farmatsiia*, vol. 2, no. 4, 1931, p. 27. Original discussion and citation, Conroy, loc. cit.
25. Levkin, "Vnimaniiu sektora kadrov narkomzdrava," *Sovetskaia farmatsiia*, , vol. 2, no. 4, 1931, p. 22. Original discussion and citation in Conroy, loc cit.
26. Advertisement, *Sovetskaia farmatsiia*, vol. 2. No. 5-6, 1931, p. 52.Original discussion and citation in Conroy, loc cit.
27. Ges, "Material'no-bytovoe polozhenie aptechnykh rabotnikov v RSFSR," *Sovetskaia farmatsiia*, vol. 4, no. 2-3, 1933, p. 39.
28. GARF, f. A482, op. 51, d. 1, l. 19 (1935).
29. I. A. Kliom, "Na soveshchanii po kachestvu lekarstv v aptekakh," *Farmatsiia*, no. 4,

1939, p. 5.

30. Fitzpatrick, *Everyday Stalinism*, p. 54.
31. Ginzburg, Rachkovskii, Tufel'd, "Finansovo-ekonomicheskoe polozhenie aptekoupravlenii RSFSR.," *Vestnik farmnatsii*, vol. 8, no. 1, 1930, p. 3.
32. "O priblizhenii lekpomoshchi k naseleniiu," *Khimiko-farmatsevticheskii zhurnal*, vol. 7, no. 15-16 (87-88), 1929, p. 26.
33. Davis, "Economics of Soviet Public Health, 1928-1932" in Solomon and Hutchinson, *Health and Society in Revolutionary Russia*, p. 154 and passim.
34. G. Il'ichenko, "Finansy v aptechnom dele," *Vestnik farmatsii*, vol. 8, no. 5-6, 1930, p. 229.
35. For other industries on this system see Nove, *An Economic History of the USSR*, p. 215.
36. Novyi poriadok otpuska tovarov v sviazi s kreditnoi reformoi," *Vestnik farmatsii*, vol. 8, no. 5-6, 1930, p. 279.
37. Ginzburg, Rachkovskii, Tufel'd, "Finansovo-ekonomicheskoe polozhenie aptekoupravlenii RSFSR i kontrol'ye tsifry na 1929/30 god," *Vestnik farmatsii*, vol. 8, no. 1, 1930, pp. 3-7. Citation also for preceding paragraph.
38. G. Il'ichenko, "Finansy v aptechnom dele," *Vestnik farmatsii*, vol. 8, no. 5-6, 1930, pp. 229-231.
39. N. Mirlin, "O khozraschete, samostoiatel'nosti i 'novykh slovakh'," *Vestnik farmatsii*, vol. 8, no. 4, 1930, pp. 175-178.
40. Iu. Kuperman, "Rekonstruktsiia aptechnogo dela i stroitel'stvo sotsialisticheskoi apteki : Pervye itogi—k voprosu ob efektivnosti fabrik lekarstv," *Sovetskaia farmatsiia*, vol. 4, no. 6, 1933, pp. 1-3; M. Korniz, "Rekonstruktsiia aptechnoi seti v gorodakh," ibid., pp. 4-7; G. Korenblat, "I Moskovskaia fabrika lekarstv: Analiz deiatel'nost za 1932 god," ibid., pp. 7-17, photo p. 9; Lupandin, "Planirovanie na moskovskikh fabrikhakh lekarstv," ibid., pp. 18-19; Kh. D. Oksman, "II Leningradskaia fabrika lekarstv," ibid., 20-21.
41. K., "Konkurs na luchshuiu razrabotku tem po ratsionalizatsii aptechnogo sklada," ibid., pp. 23-24.
42. "Apteka na kolesakh," *Sovetskaia farmatsiia*, vol. 3, no. 5, 1932, pp. 39-40. Original discussion and citations of both urban and rural innovations in Conroy, "Pharmacy in Soviet Russia before the Great Patriotic War," pp. 17, 24.
43. In the Uzbek Republic there had been only 24 pharmacies before 1917; in 1940 there were 63 urban pharmacies and 98 rural ones, supplemented by 77 stalls selling medicinal herbs and a small selection of packaged medicines, 17 sanitary stores, 163 pharmacy points, and four chemical-analytical laboratories. Nevertheless, in Central Asia, which included three other republics, one pharmacy still served 40,000 on average. The ratio in Ukraine and Georgia was more favorable; one pharmacy served 8,500 in Georgia and 16,300 in the Ukraine. V. M. Salo, "Deiatel'nost' aptechnykh upravlenii v predvoennyi period (1936-1940 gg.)," *Farmatsiia*, vol.8, 1979, pp. 16-17. Between 1925 and 1940 the number of pharmacies increased from 13 to 61 in the Armenian Republic, from 6 to 59 in the Kirghiz Republic, and from 30 to 300 in the Kazakh republic. Salo, "Razvitie aptechnoi seti v SSSR za period 1940-1954 gg.," ibid., vol. 11, 1982, p. 67.

44. GARF, f. A482, op. 51, d. 1, l. 5.
45. GARF, f. A482, op. 51, d. 3, ll. 7, 8.
46. GARF, f. A482, op. 51, d. 3, l. 19. First cited Conroy, "Pharmacy in Soviet Russia before the Great Patriotic War," pp. 17, 24.
47. In 1940, when the borders of the Soviet Union more approximated those of the Russian Empire, there were 4,598 pharmacies in urban areas and 6,111 in rural areas, supplemented by 13,715 "pharmacy points." V. M. Salo, "Iz istorii farmatsevticheskoi sluzhby v gody velikoi otechestvennoi voiny," *Farmatsiia,* vol. 34, no. 2, 1985, p. 7. In the RSFSR in January 1941 there were 2,175 pharmacies in urban areas and 2,981 in villages, supplemented by 99 branch pharmacies, 1,918 kiosks, 6, 643 "pharmacy points" in towns and cities and 2,307 "pharmacy points" in rural medical micro districts. GARF. F. A 482, op. 51, d. 15, l. 5. Original citations in Conroy, "Pharmacy in Soviet Russia before the Great Patriotic War, "pp. 14,23-24.
48. M. L. Siatinia, *Istoriia farmatsiia* (L'viv, 2002), pp. 206-207, 209-210,258, 299-354.
49. "Document No. 8: Pro obslugovuvanniia naselenniia medikamentami; dopovidna zapiska viddilu radians'koi torgivli TsK KP (b) U." (from Ukrainian archive, original typed copy) replicated in Siatinia, *Istoriia farmatsii* , p. 380.
50. L. Babich, "Ukrainskoe aptekoupravlenie v 1934 g.,"*Sovetskaia farmatsiia,* vol. 6, no. 8, 1935, pp. 11-14. Much of the information in this note and those above originally cited in Conroy, "Pharmacy in Soviet Russia before the Great Patriotic War," p. 16.
51. "Document No. 2: Dopovidna zapiska ukrkhimfarmbiuro do shchodo nagal'nikh potreb rozvitku respublikans'koi khimiko-farmatsevtichnoi promislovosti," 1932 (from Ukrainian archive, original typed copy) replicated in Siatinia, *Istoriia farmatsiia,* pp. 359-361.
52. These were sal'vekrezin, a remedy for tuberculosis that replaced imported sanokrezin; biiodmin that replaced biokhinol, which in turn, replaced imported quinine; salergan novazural, a diuretic; izofen a soporific; tribromfenaliuminii, a dermatology product; nipagin, a preservative; iodinin , iodine oil; and sharlak rot. Siatinia, *Istoriia farmatsiia,* p. 319.
53. "Document No. 3: Z lista narkomatu okhoroni zdorov'ia USRR do TsK KP(b)U ta RNK USRR shchodo nagal'nikh potreb NKOZ USRR zokrema, problem likars'kogo zabezpechennia naselennia respubliki," 1934 (from Ukrainian archive) replicated in Siatinia, *Istoriia farmatsii,* pp. 362-367.
54. I. Z.,"O kachestve preparatov Vokhimfarma," *Khimiko-farmatsevticheskaia promyshlennost',* vol. 3, no. 3, 1934, pp. 1-5.
55. I. Levinshtein, "Nuzhna li nam reklama," and G. Sh., "O propaganda i roli v nei narkomzdrava," *Khimiko-farmatsevticheskaia promyshlennost',* vol. 2, no. 6, 1933, pp. 311-314, 315-316.
56. I. Levinshtein, "Esche o roli lekarstva," *Khimiko-farmatsevticheskaia promyshlennost'* vol. 3, no. 2, 1934 and ibid., no. 3, "Otchety i korrespondentsii," pp. 55-58, first cited Conroy, "Pharmacy in Russia before the Great Patriotic War," pp. 17, 24.
57. G. I. Stolkind, "Otchety i korrespondentsii," *Khimiko-farmatsevticheskaia*

promyshlennost', vol. 3, no. 3, 1934, p. 58.

58. Levinshtein, "O nenormal'nom polozhenii farmatsevticheskogo dela," *Khimiko-farmatsevticheskaia promyshlennost'*, p. 7.
59. GARF, f. A482, op. 51, d. 1, l. 9 (1935).
60. "Otchety i korrespondentsii," *Khimiko-farmatsevticheskaia promyshlennost'*, vol . 3, no. 3, 1934, pp. 55-56.
61. GARF, f. A482, op. 51, d. 1, ll. 2, 3.
Abolition of free prescriptions in 1935 caused the number of prescriptions dispensed at out-patient clinics to plummet to 1.3 million. State revenues were assured by the return of the populace to the pharmacies.
62. RGAE, f. 871, op. 2, d. 11, ll.56, 58.
63. RGAE, f. 871, op. 2, d. 38, l. 11.
64. G. Smolkin, "K Planu aptechnogo dela na 3-iu piatiletku," *Farmatsiia i farmakologiia*, no. 5-6, 1937, pp. 34-37.
65. G. Smolkin, "Obsluzhivanie sela," *Farmatsiia i farmakologiia*, no. 1, 1938, pp. 35-36.

Chapter 10

1. Pharmacies, of course, did move from private to government hands during the preceding NEP, as the previous chapter illustrated. These changes paralleled the government's suppression of private retail establishments and attempts to control peasant grain production. The government crippled small-scale private producers and retail traders during the first years of the NEP but burdens increased in 1926 and 1927 when taxes, licensing fees, and rents were sharply raised. Concomitantly, credit and materials for small-scale producers were contracted. In 1927 private businesses and banks began to be closed and some proprietors were arrested. In 1928 taxes were ratcheted still higher. See Ball, *Russia's Last Capitalists*, pp. 68-74. In 1926 and 1927, the government began the process of squeezing out peasant producers by procuring peasant grain at lower than market prices. Robert Conquest, *Harvest of Sorrow* (New York: Oxford University Press, 1994), pp. 87-89; Paul Gregory, *Before Command* (Princeton: Princeton University Press, 1994), pp. 108-113.
2. Mar, "O reorganizatsii upravleniia farmatsevticheskoi promyshlennost'iu," *Vestnik Farmatsii*, vol. 8, no. 2, 1930, pp. 58-62. For *kustar'* production see Kagan, Iarko, Kuperman, "O 5- letnem plane Gosmedtorgproma i VSNKh SSSR o kontrol'nykh tsifrakh 5-letnego plana razvitiia farmatsevticheskoi promyshlennosti," *Khimiko-farmatsevticheskii zhurnal*, vol. 7, no. 15-16 (87-88), 1929, p. 23.
3. Mar, "O reorganizatsii upravleniia farmatsevticheskoi promyshlennost'iu," p. 58. At the outset of the First Five-Year Plan, Gosmedtorgprom included six factories: the Salicylate Factory (No. 2), Karpov Factory (No. 8, former Ferrein Factory), Semashko Factory (No. 12; former Keler Factory), and Alkaloid Factory (No. 13; former Allen & Hansbury Factory), all in Moscow; the Dzerzhinskii Santonin

Factory in Chimkent; and the Experimental Iodine Factory in Baku. The trust also included three warehouses in Moscow and six retail sanitary hygiene stores in Moscow. Two of these were former Ferrein drug stores.

4. Vesenkha's exact percent of shares was 56.20. They were worth 3,935,000 rubles. Narkomzrav's 40 percent amounted to 2,789,000 rubles. The Ukrainian medical agency held 2.13 percent of the shares, amounting to 150,000 rubles' worth. *Kratkii otchet o rabote Akts. O-va "Gosmedtorgprom" za 1927-28 op. god.* (Moscow, 1929), p. 3.
5. RGAE, f. 871, op. 3, d. 106, ll.2-5.
6. See Nove, *An Economic History of the U.S.S.R.*, p. 185. For Nove's analyses of the entire plan period see ibid., pp. 127-214. Nove, for example stated that this created "a mighty engineering industry," with "output of machine-tools, turbines, tractors, metallurgical equipment" rising "by genuinely impressive percentages," but agreed with other historians that consumer goods and housing were given shorter shrift. For more recent discussions, see J. D. Barber and R. W. Davies, "Employment and Industrial Labor," in Davies, Harrison and Wheatcroft, *The Economic Transformation of the Soviet Union*, pp.89-90, 103-104; also R. W. Davies, "Industry," ibid., pp. 136-157.
7. Barber and Davies, "Employment and Industrial Labor," ibid., pp. 89-90.
8. Davis, "Economics of Soviet Public Health, 1928-1932," in Solomon and Hutchinson, *Health and Society in Revolutionary Russia*, pp. 160-163.
9. RGAE, f. 8009, op. 20, d. 170, ll. 1-106.
10. "Tri chertverti milliarda na industrializatsiiu," *Khimiko-farmatsevtcheskii zhurnal*, vol. 7, no. 15-16 (87-88), 1929, p. 1. James Millar noted that during the NEP bond sales provided the Soviet government with 6 percent of its revenue; in 1931, during the First Five-Year Plan, bond sales reached a "peak of 13 percent in 1931." *The Soviet Economic Experiment*, p. 113; discussion about the policy, pp. 113-135.
11. B. N. Saltykov, "Nauchno-tekhnicheskii sovet khimiko-farmatsevticheskoi promyshlennosti," *Khimiko-farmatsevticheskii zhurnal*, vol. 7, no. 2 (98), 1930, p. 13.
12. GARF, f. 482A, op. 51, d. 1, l. 5 (1935). I. Kh. Fel'dman, "O dal'eishem razvitii khimiko-farmatsevticheskoi promyshlennosti," *Biulleten' Khimiko-farmatsevticheskogo instituta*, vol. 2, no. 9, 1931, pp. 201-203, first cited in Conroy, "Pharmacy in Soviet Russia before the Great Patriotic War," p. 8.
13. In 1931 growth of production was low but the labor force quota was "over-fulfilled" 102.9 percent. Work discipline was low, absenteeism, some due to sickness, was frequent. "Iogi i perspektivy," *Khimiko-farmasevticheskaia promyshlennost'*, vol. 1, no. 7, 1932, p. 262. I. Maimind admitted in "Khimiko-farmatsevticheskaia promyshlennost' na poroge vtoroi piatiletki," ibid., no. 1, pp. 6-10 that "The year 1931 was difficult for the chemical-pharmaceutical industry ... Vokhimfarm [sic]. The prom-fin plan was not fulfilled either according to quantity or quality...In all factories the indicators for work were not fulfilled. In the majority of factories not-fulfilling quotas, the amount of workers exceeded planned figures; therefore productivity lagged behind the plan." Another

account acknowledged that "All basic indicators worsened in the factories during the fourth quarter of 1931... there was a high increase of expenditures, increased pay (zarplata) without increase of productivity." "Otvety i korrespondentsii: V Vokhimfarme," ibid., nos. 2-3, pp. 102. Cited in Conroy, ibid., pp. 7-8.

14. *Kratkii otchet o rabote Akts. O-va "Gosmedtorgprom" za 1927-28 op. god.*, pp. 4-6.
15. Ibid., pp. 4-5.
16. Galambos with Sewell, *Networks of Innovation: Vaccine Development at Merck, Sharp & Dohme, and Mulford,* p. 33.
17. In Britain, for example, tuberculosis declined by about 3 percent per year between 1880 and 1945, even though the antituberculosis drug, streptomycin, was not available until 1945. Reuben and Wittcoff, *Pharmaceutical Chemicals in Perspective,* pp. 8-9.
18. See chapter 1.
19. *Kratkii otchet o rabote Akts. O-va "Gosmedtorgprom" za 1927-28 op. god.*, p. 6.
20. "V Gosmedtorgprome," *Khimiko-farmatsevticheskii zhurnal,* vol. 6, no. 2 (50), 1928, p. 25.
21. Lektechsyrio: *Arzneistoffe, Drugs and Medicines, Drogues* (Moscow, n. d. but from internal evidence 1930 or 1931), p. 16.
22. See below.
23. *Kratkii otchet o rabote Gosmedtorgproma za 1925/26 operats. god,* Moscow, 1927, p. 5.
24. RGAE, f. 8551, op. 1, d. 5, l. 1.
25. RGAE, f. 8551, op. 1, d.. ll, pp. (no listy) 4 and 5 .
26. Frank Messenger, Assistant U.S .Trade Commissioner, London, December 4, 1928, NAUSA, File RG 489, Box 82, NN3-151-80-7, 10, 700, BFDC, European Division, Soviet Bloc, U. S. Dept. of Commerce.
27. RGAE, f. 8551, op. 1, d. 5, ll. 4, 5 ob. . In actual amounts, 14,112 tons of household soap were produced, 1,213 tons of liquid soap, and only 8,104 "thousand dozens" of toilet soap. The trust also referred to "conjuncture of the market"—a la Kondrat'ev—as a cause for non-fulfillment of the program for several items.
28. Frank Messenger, Assistant U.S. Trade Commissioner, London, December 4, 1928, NAUSA, File RG 489, Box 82, NN3-151-80-7, 10, 700, BFDC, European Division, Soviet Bloc, U. S. Dept. of Commerce.
29. RGAE, f. 8551, op. 1, d. 4, p. 2.
30. Nord, "Novoe syr'e dlia proizvodstva myla," *Sovetskaia farmatsiia,* vol. 1, no. 1, October 1930, p. 33.
31. The trust anguished over its lowered credit rating due to falling sales and higher costs. RGAE, f. 8551, op. 1, d 4, pp. 4, 5, 5 ob.
32. "Outlook for the Soviet Soap Industry," *Russian Economic Notes,* NAUSA File RG 489, Box 82, MM3-151-80-7, 10,700, BFDC, U.S. Dept. of Commerce.
33. "A Cooperative Soap Works in Siberia, Russia," *Economic Life,* Moscow (Official), 1/1/28, page 3, NAUSA File RG 489, Box 82, 10,700, BFDC," U. S. Dept. of Commerce.

34. Frank Messenger, Assistant Trade Representative, London, October 12, 1928, NAUSA File RG 489, Box 82, NN3, 151-80-7, 10,700, BFDC, U. S. Dept. of Commerce.
35. E. Khanin-Dobraia, "Za chistotu i gigienu," *Vestnik farmatsii,* vol. 8, no. 7-8, 1930, pp. 310-311.
36. RGAE, f. 8551, op. 1, d. 4, pp. 4, 5.
37. "Outlook for the Soviet Soap Industry," *Russian Economic Notes,* NAUSA File RG 489, Box 82, MM3-151-80-7, 10,700, BFDC, U. S. Dept. of Commerce.
38. Khanin-Dobraia, "Za chistotu i gigienu," pp. 310-311.
39. Vincent Barnett, "The People's Commissariat of Supply and The People's Commissariat of Internal Trade," in Rees, *Decision-making in the Stalinist Command Economy,* p. 195.
40. Nord, "Novoe syr'e dlia proizvodstva myla," p. 33.
41. "Russian Economic Notes," July 31, 1931, reverse, NAUSA, File, 489, Box 82, NN3-151-80-7, 10,700, BFDC, U. S. Dept. of Commerce
42. "Factory for the Manufacturing of Resin Soap from Pine Tar" and "Petroleum Soap Factory Opened in Tuapse," *Economic Review of USSR,* March 1, 1931, NAUSA File RG 489, Box 82BNN3-151-80-7, 10,700, BFDC, U.S. Dept. of Commerce.
43. In discussing food deprivation in Malawi, "Food for Thought," *The Economist,* July 31-August 6, p. 68, describes the influence of iodine deficiency, particularly on children, emphasizing that currently "nearly 2 million people consume less of this mineral than they should," with resultant developmental problems of the brain in addition to goitre.
44. *Kratkii otchet o rabote Akts. O-va "Gosmedtorgprom" za 1927-28 op. god.,* pp. 4-5, 6-7; A. Bonshtedt, "Khimiko-farmatsevticheskaia promyshlennost' v 1 polugodnii 1928/29 g.," *Khimiko-farmatsevticheskii zhurnal,* vol. 7, no. 15-16 (87-88), 1929, pp. 3-4.
45. "Iodnaia problema," *Vestnik farmatsii,* vol. 8, no. 1, 1930, p. 44.
46. "Novye iodistye istochki," ibid., p. 44.
47. "Finansirovanie iodnogo proizvodstvo," *Vestnik farmatsii,* vol. 8, no. 1, 1930, p. 44.
48. *Materialy k vsesoiuznoi konferentsii po khimizatsii narodnago khozaistva s.s.s.r. 2-m piatilteii.* (Leningrad: Goskhimtekhizdat, 1932), p. 1.
49. Nord, "Iodnyi zavod v Baku," *Sovetskaia farmatsiia,* vol. 1, no. 1, October 1930, p. 33.
50. A. Umanskii, "Iod i bura iz bulganakskikh sopok," *Vestnik farmatsii,* vol. 8, no. 5-6, 1930, pp. 250-251.
51. *Materialy... po khimizatsii narodnago khoziaistva,* pp. 5-7; for Arkhangel'sk, "Novye iodistye istochniki," *Vestnik farmatsiia,* vol. 8, no. 1, 1930, p. 44
52. "Na severe RSFSR," *Vestnik farmatsii,* vol. 8, no. 1, 1930, p. 44.
53. *Materialy* , pp 2-4. On deriving iodine from Red Phylophora, in Imperial Russia and in the 1920s, see also N. A. Averkiev, "O dobyche ioda v USSR [Ukrainian SSR] iz vodoroslei Chernogo moria 'krasnaia fillofora,'" *Khimiko-*

farmatsevticheskii zhurnal, vol. 6, no. 8 (56) , 1928, pp. 10-12 and ibid., no. 10 (58), pp. pp. 9-12.

54. *Materialy,* p. 1.
55. *Kratkii otchet o rabote Akts. O-va " Gosmedtorgprom" za 1927-28 op. god.,* pp. 4-5, 6-7; Bonshtedt, "Khimiko-farmatsevticheskaia promyshlennost' v 1 polugodnii 1928/29 g.,"pp.3-4.
56. See Conroy, "Pharmacy in Soviet Russia before the Great Patriotic War," p. 9.
57. See Conroy, ibid., p. 11.
58. "Production of thermometers in Russia," *Izvestiia,* March 12, 1928, NAUSA ,File RG 489, Box 82, 11,100, BFDC, U. S. Dept. of Commerce.
59. "Trade and Industrial Gazette" (Moscow , Official), 3/23/28 , NAUSA ,File 489, Box 82, 11,100, BFDC, U.S. Dept. of Commerce.
60. I. Bychkov, "Meditsinskoe i laboratornoe oborudovanie," *Vestnik farmatsii,* vol. 8, no. 1, 1930, pp. 12-15.
61. See chapter 9 for reports from pharmacy administrations on severe shortages of these items during the First and Second Five-Year Plans.
62. "Gotovye lekarstvennye formy," *Sovetskaia farmatsiia,* vol. 2, no. 4, 1931, p. 40.
63. *Kratkii otchet o rabote Akts. O-va "Gosmedtorgprom" za 1927-28 op. god.,* pp. 19, 35-36.
64. Ibid., p. 35.
65. Ibid., pp. 19 . The absolute amount of raw materials was 24.61 percent; the exact monetary amount was 1,244, 847 rubles. The monetary amount of iodine was 1,832, 834 (gold) rubles.
66. James Somerville, Jr., Division of Regional Information to Frank Messenger, Assistant Trade Commissioner in London, November 1, 1928, NAUSA, File RG 489, Box 82, BFDC, U. S. Dept. of Commerce. Somerville also advised Messenger to broaden his "a's" and answer the telephone, "'are you there' instead of 'hello'."
67. "O vospreshchenii otpuska khinina v ruchnoi prodazhe," *Farmatsevticheskii zhurnal,* vol. 1, no. 7, 1928, p. 406.
68. Maimind, "Khimiko-faratsevticheskaia promyshlennost' na doroge vtoroi piatiletki," pp. 6-10. He opined that lack of raw materials was a major reason the industry could not fulfill its plans. See also "Nash aktiv k 14-i godoshchina Oktiabria" and "O dal'neishem razvitii khimiko-farmatsevticheskoi promyshlennosti," *Biulleten' Khimiko-farmatsevticheskogo Instituta,* vol. 2, nos. 10-11, 1931, pp. 258-277.
69. "Offitsial'nye postanovleniia: O zamene nekotorykh importnykh ingredientov drugimi ingredientami," *Vestnik farmatsii,* vol. 8, no. 1, 1930, pp. 48-50.
70. "V Gosmedtorgprome," *Khimiko-farmatsevticheskii zhurnal,* vol. 6, no. 2 (50), 1928, p. 25.
71. "V Ukrmedtorge," *Farmatsevticheskii zhurnal,* no. 10, 1928, pp. 577-578 .
72. *Kratkii otchet o rabote Akts. O-va "Gosmedtorgprom" za 1927-28 op. god.* Moscow, 1929, pp. 35-35, presented slightly different figures. Tables showed that "medinstruments" amounted to about 7 percent in terms of ruble value in 1926/1927 and 10.15 percent in terms of ruble value in 1927/1928.
73. Gregory, *Before Command,* pp. 60-61.

74. See chapter 1 of this work.
75. See chapters 1-5 of the present work.
76. Davenport-Hines and Slinn, *Glaxo*, pp. 98-132.
77. *Kratkii otchet o rabote Akts. O-va "Gosmedtorgprom" za 1927-28 op. god.*, p. 36. The exact amount for exports of botanicals was 689, 450 rubles; the exact amount for finished products was 123,146 rubles.
78. "Drug Markets," October 1928, NAUSA, File RG 489, Box 82, 10,300, BFDC, US Dept of Commerce.
79. "Development of the Pharmaceutical Industry in the USSR," *L'Industrie Chimique*, March 1930, cited by Earle C Taylor, Assistant Trade Commissioner, Paris April 4, 1930, NAUSA, File RG 489, Box 82, 10,300, BFDC, U.S. Dept of Commerce.
80. E. Shass, "Razvitie eksporta lektekhsyr'ia," *Vestnik farmatsii* ,vol. 8, no. 4, 1930, pp. 195-196.
81. Lektechsyrio: *Arzneistoffe, Drugs and Medicines, Drogues* (n. d., just after 1930 by internal evidence), [English section],pp. 6-8. The brochure proclaimed that "from 1925 to 1930" the USSR had exported "16, 075 metric tons" "of "goods of this class ...valued at 3,534,000 gold rubles." Ibid., p. 6. A rough translation of the name of the corporation was "Medical-Technical Raw Materials."
82. Ibid., p. 16 and pp.6-7. Lists of export items in Latin, German, English and French, pp. 12-16.
83. Advertisement, *Khimiko-farmatsevticheskii zhurnal*, vol. 7, no. 12 (84), 1929, p. 22. The ovarian hormone was derived by a method developed in the biochemical laboratory of the Scientific Research Chemical-Pharmaceutical Institute (NIKhFI) that improved on the American method. The Soviet method mixed the ovarian hormone with water and the urine of pregnant women, testing the solution on mice. K D. Sargin, "Ovarial'nyi gormon," *Biulleten' khimiko-farmatsevticheskogo instituta*, no. 1, 1930, p. 10. Information on Pankreon, K. D. Liubovtseva, "Poluchenie preparata pankreatin," and "Poluchenie preparata 'pankreon'," ibid., and M. L. Utkin, " Poluchenie tripsina," ibid., pp. 10-11.
84. *Arzneisttoffe, Drugs and Medicines, Drogues*, pp. 6-8.
85. Ibid., 12-16.
86. *Russian Catgut: Every Strand Guaranteed*, Sole Exporters Moscow: USSR Lektechsyrio Corporation (n. d.) 15 pages.
87. Aniline products included "Aniline oil and sal," Dinitrichlorbenzene, Chlorbenzene, and "pour Phenol. Lithopone." *Chemical Goods*, Moscow: Soyuspromexport (n. d.), 9 pages.
88. See Klehr, Haynes, Firson, *The Secret World of American Communism*, pp. 27-28 and Klehr, Haynes, and Kyrill M. Anderson, *The Soviet World of American Communism* (New Haven : Yale University Press, 1998), pp. 109-110.
89. "Russia's share in America's Crude-Drug Imports," *World Trade Notes on Chemicals*, January 8, 1934, NAUSA, File RG 489 , 10,300, BFDC, U.S .Dept of Commerce.
90. Earle C. Taylor, Assistant Trade Commissioner, Paris to Chemical Division, BFDC, U.S .Dept of Commerce, April 4, 1930, NAUSA, RG 489, Box 82, 10,300, BFDC, U.S .Dept of Commerce.

91. Anon., "Export of Herbs and Crude Drugs," *Economic Review of the Soviet Union,* November 1, 1931, p. 494, NAUSA, RG 489, Box 82, 10,3000, BFDC, U.S. Dept of Commerce.
92. "Imports of Santonin in 1933 Increase Sharply," Report in NAUSA, RG 489, Box 82, BFDC, U.S. Dept of Commerce, 10,300.
93. C. C. Concannon, Chief Chemical Division, U.S. Department of Commerce to District Office Division, Bureau of Foreign and Domestic Commerce, U.S. Dept of Commerce, March 10, 1932, NAUSA, File 231, BFDC, U.S. Dept of Commerce.
94. Roger R. Townsend, Trade Commissioner, U.S. Embassy in London to Director of Foreign and Domestic Commerce, U.S . Dept of Commerce, November 5, 1931 and Chief, Division of Statistics, U.S. Dept of Commerce to London Office, Foreign Service Division, November 19, 1931, NAUSA, File 231, BFDC, U.S. Dept of Commerce.
95. Bonshtedt, "Khimiko-farmatsevticheskaia promyshlennost' v 1 polugodii 1928/29 g.," p. 3; deals with costs.
96. See chapter 5 of this work.
97. " V Gosmedtorgprome," *Khimiko-farmatsevticheskii zhurnal,* vol. 6, no. 2 (50), 1928, p. 25.
98. "V Ukrmedtorge," *Farmatsevticheskii zhurnal,* no. 10, 1928, p. 577.
99. "V Ukrmedtorg," *Farmatsevticheskii zhurnal,* no. 10, 1928, p. 578. First cited in Conroy, "Pharmacy in Soviet Russia before the Great Patriotic War," *Pharmacy in History,* 1998, pp. 10-11.
100. See chapter 5 of this work.
101. "V Gosmedtorgprome," *Khimiko-farmatsevticheskii zhurnal,* no. 2 (50), 1928, p. 25.
102. *Arzneistoffe, Drugs and Medicines, Drogues,* p. 6; pp. 2-16 lists plant materials for export. Salicylic acid, alkaloids of opium, terpinhydrate, benzoic natron, sulfuric barium for x-rays, Adonilen , Gitalen, Adrenalin, Novarsenol also were in short supply and had been pushed for export..
103. *Arzneistoffe, Drugs and Medicines, Drogues,* p. 16.
104. "Novye preparaty" and "V Gosmedtorgprome," *Vestnik farmatsii,* vol. 8, no. 2, 1930, pp. 95-97.
105. Loc. cit. See chapter 5 of this work for earlier production figures.
106. *Arzneistoffe, Drugs and Medicines, Drogues,* pp. 12-16.
107. "V Gosmedtorgprome," *Vestnik farmatsii,* vol. 8, no. 7-8, 1930, p. 367. The cardiac remedies were Adrenalin, Adonilen, and Gitalen. Other basic medicines produced in sufficiency included Antifebrin, lecithin, pepsin; acetic acid, and belladonna extract. Also available in sufficient supply were four medicinal plants, the antivenereal Neosalvarsan, and Bismoverol. It is very possible that reduced export rather than increased production of certain items affected their presence in the pharmacy. Adonilen, Adrenalin, Gitalen, and Belladonna had been among the medicines advertised for export. Perhaps fewer of these items were being sold abroad, thus increasing their availability at home.
108. See chapter 5 in this work, production during the NEP.

109. "V Gosmedtorgprome," *Vestnik farmatsii*, vol. 8, no. 7-8, 1930, p. 367 ; Insulin Advertisement in *Khimiko-farmatsevticheskii zhurnal*, vol. 7, no. 2 (98), 1930, p. 22.
110. *Kratkii otchet o rabote Ats. O-va "Gosmedtorgprom" za 1927-28 op. god.*, pp. 4, 5, 6.
111. Mar, "O reorganizatsii upravleniia farmatsevticheskoi promyshlennost'iu," *Vestnik farmatsii*, vol. 8, no. 2, 1930, p. 60.
112. *Materialy...po khimizatsii narodnogo khozaistva*, p. 3.
113. Utin, *Istoriia chimkentskogo khimiko-farmatsevticheskogo zavoda*, p. 49.
114. V. Skvortsov, "Iodtannin," *Vestnik farmatsii* ,vol. 8, no. 2, 1930, pp. 16-17.
115. A. F. Smirnova, "O farmako-terapevticheskoi i pitatel'noi tsennosti dal'nevostochnoi morskoi kapusty," *Khimiko-farmatsevticheskii zhurnal*, vol. 7, no. 1 (97), 1930, pp. 10-12.
116. See Conroy, "Pharmacy in Soviet Russia before the Great Patriotic War,"pp. 10, 22.
117. M. Vol'pe, F. Katsenelenbogen, "Ob utilizatsii ioda iz iodnykh tamponov," *Sovetskaia farmatsiia*, vol. 3, no. 5, 1932, pp. 16-20.
118. *Vestnik farmatsii*, 1930, vol. 8, no. 9, p. 428.
119. Leading medical botanists included A. P. Orekhov, G. P. Men'shikov, N. A. L'vov, L. A. Utkin, M. N. Varlakov, P. S. Massagetov. and V.V. Zverev.
120. See Conroy, "Pharmacy in Soviet Russia before the Great Patriotic War,"*Pharmacy in History*, pp. 10, 22 for details.
121. *Informatsionnyi biulleten'*, Lektekhsyr'e, no. 2, 1930, p. 27.
122. "Lekarstvennye travy," *Vestnik farmatsii*, vol. 8, no. 4, 1930, p. 215.
123. V. Arapov, Samara, "Sleduet li v farmtekhnikumakh pepodavat' sbor, sushku i kulturu lekarstvennykh rastenii," *Vestnik farmatsii*, vol. 8, no. 3, 1930, pp. 136-138.
124. "Sovkhozy po lektekhsyr'iu," *Informatsionnyi biulleten'*, Narkomtorg, SSSR, no. 3, 1930, p. 25. See also "Po sovkhozam," ibid., no. 4, p. 39 and passim.
125. "Novye proizvodstva," *Vestnik farmatsii*, vol. 8, no. 5-6, 1930, p. 279; L. O. Nisenman, "Kontrol'nye tsyfry Gosmedtorgproma na 1930/31 g.," *Biulleten' Khimiko-farmatsevticheskogo instituta*, vol. 1, no. 2, 1930, pp. 17-18. "Secalen" and "Frangulen" were also pushed for export on 1930.
126. "Aktsionernoe obshchestvo Gosmedtorgprom," *Khimiko-farmatsevticheskii zhurnal*, vol. 7, no. 2 (98), 1930, p. 22.
127. Advertisement, *Vestnik farmatsii*, vol. 8, no. 9, 1930, p. 421.
128. Advertisement, *Khimiko-farmatsevticheskii zhurnal*, vol. 7, no. 12 (84), 1929, p. 21.
129. Since mercury preparations; foxglove leaves, the raw source for digitalis, as well as Gitalen and Diginorm, two Soviet clones of digitalis; pure chloroform, alkaloids of opium, and salicylates had all been pushed for export, it may be that, not only had production of these items increased, but exports had been cut.
130. See Conroy, "Pharmacy in Soviet Russia before the Great Patriotic War," p. 11.
131. See Conroy, "Pharmacy in Soviet Russia before the Great Patriotic War," p. 11.
132. Earle C. Taylor, Assistant Trade Commissioner, September 1932, forwarding an article in *Industrie Chimique*, September, 1932, to the Chemical Division and Division of Regional Information, US Department of Commerce, October 12, 1932, NAUSA, File 489, Box 82, NN3-151-80-7, 10,700, BFDC, U.S. Dept. of Commerce.
133. "Russian Soap Industry," November 28, 1936, NAUSA, File 489, Box 82, NN3-151-80-7, 10,700, BFDC, U.S. Dept. of Commerce.

134. See, for example, Davenport-Hines and Slinn, *Glaxo*, pp. 86-87.

Chapter 11

1. Weatherall, *In Search of a Cure*, p. 150. See also World Book Encyclopedia, vol 18, p. 772 and Reuben and Wittcoff, *Pharmaceutical Chemicals in Perspective*, pp. 11-12, 115-120.
2. Peter Neushul, "Science, Government, and the Mass Production of Penicillin," *The Journal of the History of Medicine and Allied Sciences, Inc.*, vol. 48, no. 4, 1993, pp. 372-376. "Currie's research and Pfizer's experience with large-scale fermentation, helped the company become the world's largest producer of penicillin during WWII." (p. 375)
3. Neushul, ibid., pp. 373-377.
4. Ibid., pp. 371-395.
5. Article 120 proffered citizens of the U.S.S.R: "the right to maintenance in old age and also in the event of sickness or disability. This right shall be ensured by the extensive development of social insurance of industrial, office and professional workers at state expense, by free medical service for working people, and by placing a large number of health resorts at the disposal of the working people." *Constitution (Fundamental Law) of the Union of Soviet Socialist Republics* (Moscow: Progress Publishers, 1972), pp. 96-97. The term "working people" leaps out at the reader, however, and Vic George and Nick Manning have opined that Soviet health care was never intended to benefit the entire population, but rather its goal was "reproduction of labour" from the 1930s. Vic George and Nick Manning, *Socialism, Social Welfare and the Soviet Union* (London, Boston and Henley: Routledge & Kegan Paul, 1980), p. 115. Thus, the authors elaborated that the government did not care to involve the masses in their planning.
6. Lorimer, *The Population of the Soviet Union*, pp. 120-121. The statistics span the first through the mid-Third Five Year Plans (1928-1941). They show increase of total personnel in health work rising from "365,000 in 1926/1927 to 1, 267,000 at the beginning of 1939." During these same years "general hospital beds" increased from "218 thousand to 661 thousand, psychiatric hospital beds from 30 thousand to 74 thousand, maternity beds from 27 thousand to 142 thousand... sanatoria and health resorts from 36 thousand in 1928 to 132 thousand in 1941." TB mortality was said to have been reduced from "40 per 10,000 per annum in 1911-1913 to a level only 40 percent as high" in 1941.
7. RGAE, f. 8009, op. 2, d. 3, l. 2.
8. RGAE, f. 871, op. 2, d. 39, ll. 57, 64.
9. The exact amount of the fund was over 49,600,000 rubles. Production was more exactly 11, 432, 800 rubles. RGAE, f. 8009, op. 20, d. 170, ll. 1, 1ob., 2. We will not go into the Gerschenkron effect. For discussion of that issue see S. G. Wheatcroft and R. W. Davies, "The Crooked Mirror of Soviet Economic Statistics" in Davies, Harrison and Wheatcroft, *The Economic Transformation of the Soviet Union*, pp. 24-37.

10. Ongoing shortages of fats during the Second Five-Year Plan prompted the addition of bolus alba (*belaia glina*—white clay or kaolin) in pure form to toilet soap or combined with hydrate aluminum (known as "boliusal") or formalin and phenol (referred to "bolufen") for "the treatment of wounds and also as an additive to surgical soap for washing hands"— indicating ingenuity but also shortages of surgical gloves. I. Zelikin, "O prirode i primenenii beloi glini v terapii," *Khimiko-farmatsevticheskaia promyshlennost'*, vol. 2, no. 3, 1933, pp. 159-160. Bolus alba was found to be effective internally. I. Zelikin recounted that he had "applied white sterilized clay (obtained in the pharmacy and also personally made up kaolin) in cases of gastro-enteritis with preliminary cleansing of the digestive-intestinal tract with a laxative, and had seen fully hopeful results." As an internal medicament, he noted that in 1921 a "difficult case of ptomaine fish poisoning with severe vomiting and diarrhea" had been alleviated "with white clay and coal." Zelikin cited German and American literature that sanctioned use of bolus alba internally against Asiatic cholera, gastroenteritis, and diphtheria; as a topical treatment for burns; and in gynecology.
11. S. I. Maimind, "Khimiko-farmatsevticheskaia promyshlennost' v pervom godu vtoroi piatiletki," *Sovetskaia farmatsiia*, vol. 4, no. 4, 1933, p. 8–9.
12. Liadovskii, "Referaty," *Sovetskaia farmatsiia*, vol. 4, no. 6, 1933, p. 42.
13. I. L., "Otchety i korrespondentsii, zakonchennye raboty NIKhFI," *Khimiko-farmatsevticheskaia promyshlennost'*, vol. 2, no. 3, 1933, pp. 178-181; "NIKhFI v 1932 i 1933 gg.," ibid., no. 4, pp. 243-244. Original discussion and citations, Conroy, "Pharmacy in Soviet Russia before the Great Patriotic War," pp. 11-12, p. 23.
14. I. S. Zelikin, *Za kachestvo eksportnykh medikamentov* (Moscow, Leningrad: Vneshtorgizdat, 1933), p. 5.
15. Hans Rogger, "*Amerikanizm* and the Economic Development of Russia," *Comparative Studies in Society and History*, vol. 23, no. 3, 1981, pp. 415-420.
16. Ia. Kanevskii, "O gotovykh lekarstvennykh formakh," *Khimiko-farmatsevticheskii zhurnal*, vol. 6, no. 8 (56), 1928, pp. 12-13. Kanevskii added that American exports had grown from "4 %" of all production in 1924 to "7%" in 1928. Put another way, American exports "were *twice* more than before the war" and "the United States produced as many medical items as all the other countries put together." (p. 13)
17. G. Tsander, "Amerikanskaia farmatsevticheskaia promyshlennost'," *Khimiko-farmatsevticheskaia promyshlennost'*, vol. 2, no. 3, 1933, pp. 167-170. Tsander specifically noted that production of neoarsphenamine rose from 1,360 kilograms (kg) (3 thousand English pounds) to 2,270 kilograms (5 thousand English pounds) during the 1920s, although production contracted 60 percent in 1930. He mistakenly cited per capita purchases in 1931 as 2.15 dollars (p. 168).
18. Tsander, "Amerikansaia farmatsevticheskaia promyshlennost'," loc. cit.
19. "O nashikh nedochetakh," *Khimiko-farmatsevticheskaia promyshlennost'*, vol. 3, no. 3, 1934, p. 57.
20. I. Levinshtein, "O nenormal'nom polozhenii farmatsevticheskogo dela," *Khimiko-farmatsevticheskaia promyshlennost'*, vol. 3, no. 4, 1934, pp. 5-7.
21. "Iz deiatel'nosti eksperimental'noi laboratorii zavoda im. karpopva (O

nepoladkakh na proizvodstve akritsida)," *Khimiko-farmatsevticheskaia promyshlennost'*, vol. 3, no. 2, 1934, p. 56.

22. The British firm Glaxo did expand production and sales worldwide in the 1930s, but income from food products exceeded income from pharmaceuticals and the firm licensed foreign companies' drug-making procedures. Glaxo executives attributed the small scale of the firm's research to much lower investment, as compared with firms in the United States. Davenport-Hines and Slinn, *Glaxo*, pp. 86-88, 136, 146, 162, 174. During the last four years of the 1930s, Glaxo's income from food products exceeded income from pharmaceuticals, on average, 5.5 percent per year. Britain did not free itself from German imports until World War II. (p. 138)
23. See chapter 5.
24. John P. Swann, *Academic Scientists and the Pharmaceutical Industry* (Baltimore and London: The Johns Hopkins University Press, 1988). Interestingly, Merck management believed fundamental research was on a higher level than developmental. In the thirties, the fundamental problems "the [Merck] Institute investigated were the influence of anesthetics on nerve currents, the mode of action of curare, the effect of pain on the circulatory system, and the influence of oxygen deficiency in arterial blood on the liver." (p. 47) These were topics similar to those investigated by Soviet scientists in the forties.
25. B. E. Votchal and G. I. Minkin, "Obzor vazneishikh preparatov proizvodstva Vokhimfarma, zameniaiushchikh importnye defitsitnye sredstv," in G. Liadovskii, "Referaty," *Sovetskaia farmatsiia*, vol. 4, no. 6, 1933, pp.40-42.
26. RGAE, f. 871, op. 2, d. 11, ll. 56, 62.
27. O. Magidson, I. Strukhov, N. Deletorskii, I. Lipovich, "Sintez khinolovykh antimaliariinykh preparatov," *Khimiko-farmatsevticheskaia promyshlennost'*, vol. 2, no. 1, 1933, pp. 9-10. See Conroy, "Pharmacy in Soviet Russia before the Great Patriotic War," p. 12.
28. RGAE f. 8009, op. 20, d. 211, ll. 1-3, 5 and "Rozhdenie zavoda 'Akrikhin,'" in V. K. Afanas'ev, K. A. Ermolina, V. N. Kadurina, L. I. Lavrent'eva, L. F. Matveeva, *Zhivi, "Akrikhin"!* (Staraia kupavna ,Russia, 1996), pp. 21-30.
29. Afans'ev et al, *Zhivi, "Akrikhin" !*, pp. 24-32.
30. Observation of the author, July 2003.
31. A. V. Savitskii, V. P. Pavlov, "Organizatsiia proizvodstva pantotsida," *Biulleten' po obmenu opytom: "Zavod Akrikhin,"* no. 1-2, (Narkomzdrav USSR, 1940), p. 10.
32. Anthony Rimmington, "The Soviet Union's Offensive Program," Susan Wright, ed., *Biological Warfare and Disarmament* (Lanham: Rowman and Littlefield, 2002), pp. 105-108, 116, 121-122.
33. In the fall of 1929 Soviet troops clashed with Manchurian officials and Nationalist Chinese troops in Manchuria. The Chinese were annoyed about the Soviet government's refusal to appoint new Russian administrators to the joint Soviet-Chinese board that managed the Chinese-Eastern railway. For details see Lars T. Lih, Oleg V. Naumov, and Oleg V. Khlevniuk, eds., *Stalin's Letters to Molotov* (New Haven: Yale University Press, 1995), pp. 147-150.) The Chinese-Eastern had been built by the Russians in the 1890s to shorten the distance between Chita and

Vladivostok. In the early 1930s, Japan, Russia's sometimes enemy, sometimes ally, moved into Manchuria, becoming a greater menace than local war lords or Chiang Kai Shek. Russia still exported pharmaceutical items to Japan, indicating the same lack of correlation between international relations and trade that had existed in the 1920s. The new fragility in political relations between the USSR and Japan, however, seems to have been reflected in the halving of Japanese purchases from the USSR in 1932, as compared with 1931, and the great increase in Soviet exports to China in 1932, as compared with the previous year.

34. "O," "Farmatsevticheskaia khimiia v budushchei voine," *Khimiko-farmatsevticheskaia promyshlenost'*, no. 1, 1935, pp.63 -65.
35. A. Sanin, "Obnaruzhenie otravliaiushchikh veshchestv," *Sovetskaia farmatsiia*, vol. 6, no. 8, 1935, pp. 47.
36. RGAE, f. 871, op. 2, d. 11, l. 56.
37. B. Gorbovitskii, "Vnutrizavodskoe planirovanie na zavodakh Vokhimfarma," *Khimiko-farmatsevticheskaia promyshlennost'*, vol. 2, no. 1, 1933, p. 6-7, originally cited in Conroy, "Pharmacy in Soviet Russia before the Great Patriotic War,"pp. 8, 10.
38. I. Zelikin, "O kachestve preparatov vokhimfarma," *Khimiko-farmatsevticheskaia promyshlennost'*, vol. 3, no. 3, 1934, p. 1.
39. RGAE, f. 871, op. 2, d. 11, l. 66.
40. Zelikin, "O kachestve preparatov Vokhimkarma," pp. 1-5.
41. Buntsel'man, "O kachestve produktsii i rabote OTK," pp. 13-15.
42. MS, History of the Dorogomilovskii Factory, "Fakty istorii predpriatiia," p. 2 (copy in possession of author).
43. RGAE, f. 871, op. 2, d. 39, ll. 27-30.
44. Kobrak, *National Cultures*, p. 220.
45. Ibid., pp. 228, 244, 248. Entire discussion of Nazi domination of Schering, 1933-1937, ibid. pp. 217-254. (It ought to be noted that the party's right wing cancelled out the socialist proclivities of its left wing. Comment of Dr. Reza Ghods, Spring, 2005.) Kobrak admits that, Schering also had to grapple with international factors in the 1930s as well as internal ones. But despite these and internal annoyances from the Nazis, he concludes that Schering remained prosperous. (p. 253 and passim.)
46. James H. Madison, *Eli Lilly: A Life, 1885-1977* (Indianapolis: Indiana Historical Society, 1989), pp. 101-103; on Communist influence in the Roosevelt administration see Klehr, Haynes, Firsov, *The Secret World of American Communism*, pp. 117-118 and passim.
47. Nove, *An Economic History of the USSR*, pp. 215-217.; Khlevnyuk, "The People's Commissariat of Heavy Industry," in Rees, *Decision-making in the Stalinist Command Economy*, p. 104. Vesenkha had first been divided into 25 associations in 1925.
48. For details see Fitzpatrick, *Everyday Stalinism*, pp. 67-114.
49. Wheatcroft and Davies, "Population," in Davies, Harrison and Wheatcroft, *The*

Economic Transformation of the Soviet Union, p. 77.

50. Ion, "O nashikh nedochetakh," *Khimiko-farmatsevticheskaia promyshlennost'*, vol. 3, no. 3, 1934, pp. 57-58.
51. RGAE, f. 8009, op. 20, d. 170, ll. 1, 1ob, 2, 3 ob..
52. RGAE, f. 8009op. 20, d. 170, ll. 6 and 7.
53. RGAE, f. 871, op. 2, d. 39, ll. 57, 64.
54. RGAE, f. 871, op. 2, d. 11, ll. 55-56; Report, Vokhimfarm, 1933.
55. RGAE, f. 871, op. 2, d. 11, l. 58.
56. RGAE, f. 871, op. 2, d. 11, l. 58.
57. RGAE, f. 871, op. 2, d. 38, l. 7.
58. RGAE f. 871, op. 2, d. 38, l. 1; Report ,Vokhimfarm for 1935.
59. RGAE, f. 871, op. 2, d. 38, l. 2.
60. In January 1939 the Board of the Industry, now called Khimfarmprom, consisted of twenty-three individuals. Factory managers were ad hoc members. RGAE, f. 8009, op. 2, d. 3, l. 228.
61. In 1937 in addition to the decree ordaining the transfer of the Akrikhin Factory, Sovnarkom ordered that the Lomonosov Chemical-Pharmaceutical Factory in Kiev be moved from the jurisdiction of the Commissariat of Health to Vokhimfarm and, third, that the Red Star Factory in Khar'kov be shifted from the authority of the Ukrainian Commissariat of Health to Vokhimfarm. The factory of Artificial Teeth, located in the Lomonosov Porcelain Factory in Leningrad, was shuffled to the Stomatological or Dental Institute in Leningrad, then to the Union of Medical Equipment in the Belorussian Commissariat of Health, and finally, by *prikaz* of Narkomzdrav, to Vokhimfarm. In 1936, the Nefte-Chalinskii Iodine Factory had been transferred from the Commissariat of Heavy Industry (where it had been put in 1935) to the Commissariat of Health. In July 1937, however, this factory plus the Baku Iodine Factory, by resolution of Sovnarkom, was put back in the jurisdiction of Vokhimfarm. At the end of 1937, also by resolution of Sovnarkom, Vokhimfarm acquired the Trust of Medicinal Plants. RGAE, f. 871, op. 2, d. 39, ll. 1-2.

    In August 1937 the Factory of Medical Preparations, which had been "united to Vokhimfarm," barely a year before, was transferred back to the Leningrad Department of the Chief Pharmacy Administration of the Russian Republican Commissariat of Health. In September 1937 the Factory of Prophylactic Items, which had been "joined to Vokhimfarm" only the year before, was also transferred, by *prikaz* of Narkomzdrav , to the Chief Pharmacy Administration of the RSFSR Commissariat of Health. Equipment and materials in the March 8 Bandaging factory in Moscow, which had been transferred out of the jurisdiction of Vokhimfarm, were transferred to the Ukrainian Commissariat of Health and then distributed to the Lomonosov Factory in the city of Kiev and to the Red Star Factory in the city of Khar'kov. Finally, "[F]or the purpose of strengthening the economy and productivity of management"— perhaps code words for purging— by a result of a *prikaz* of Narkomzdrav, the Baku Iodine Factory was divided into two independent factories, Surakhanskii and Ramaninskii iodine factories.
62. RGAE, f. 8009, op. 20, d. 170, l. 9. The deficit items were methanol, gelatin, carbon

dioxide, sodium bisulfate, technical salicylic acid, ethyl acetate.

63. RGAE, f. 871, op. 2, d. 11, ll. 58-60, 64, 65.
64. RGAE, f. 871, op. 2, d. 38, l. 10.
65. RGAE, f. 871, op. 2, d. 38, l. 10.
66. RGAE, f. 871, op. 2, d. 38, l. 31.
67. RGAE, f. 871, op. 2, d. 38, ll. 11-13, 39-40.
68. RGAE, f. 871, op. 2 , d. 38, ll. 15-16.
69. RGAE, f. 871, op. 2, d. 38, l. 16.
70. Report of the Trust Vokhimfarm for 1937: *Otchetnyi doklad upravliaiushchego trestom Vokhimfarm za 1937*, RGAE, f. 871. op. 2, d. 39, l.55. The absolute numbers were 378 tons of phenol needed—170 tons received; 202 tons of accumulated acids needed —140 available; 210 tons of technical chloroform needed —150 available, 190 tons of carbonic acid needed—110 available.

    Five other crucial raw materials also were short: of 356 tons of iron bromine needed only 250 were sent out; of 34 tons of lead *glet*, needed for lead salts, only 8 were put out; of 110 tons of creosote needed for Naftalizol, only 85 were available; of 900 tons of potash needed for production of bromine, iodine salts, and caustic soda, only 358 were available; of 250 tons of calcium chloride needed for chlorethyl, only 137 were available. Loc. cit.
71. RGAE, f. 871, op. 2, d. 39, l. 10.
72. RGAE, f. 871, op. 2, d. 39, ll. 18-20.
73. "Farmatsevticheskaia promyshlennost'," *Farmatsiia i farmakologiia*, no. 7, 1937, p. 42.
74. RGAE f. 871, op. 2, d. 39, l. 8.
75. RGAE, f. 871, op. 2, d. 39, l. 9.
76. Peter H. Solomon, Jr. *Soviet Criminal Justice Under Stalin* (Cambridge: Cambridge University Press, 1996), particularly pp. 230-266. Solomon states that in 1937-1938 alone 1.33 million were arrested for specious crimes and "more than half" of these were executed. p. 232.
77. Galina Mikhailovna Ivanova, *Labor Camp Socialism: The Gulag in the Soviet Totalitarian System*. (Armonk: M. E. Sharpe, 2000).
78. Purges of enterprise directors in the First Five-Year-Plan, which barely affected the pharmaceutical industry in any case, had tapered off in 1933, when Procurator of the USSR Andrei Vyshinskii inaugurated a return to "Socialist Legality." In December 1934, however, Sergei Kirov, Leningrad Party Secretary, was mysteriously assassinated. Amy Knight, *Who Killed Kirov?* (New York: Hill and Wang, 1999). This led to a bloodbath that did away with some fifty "Old Bolsheviks" like Zinoviev, Kamenev, Rykov, Radek, and Bukharin, who were convicted of economic sabotage and treason in public trials and leading army leaders like Marshal Tukhachevsky.

    For general studies of the "Great Purge" see Merle Fainsod, *Smolensk Under Soviet Rule* Cambridge: Harvard University Press), pp. 210-237; Evgenia Ginzburg, *Into the Whirlwind* (New York: Harcourt, Brace and World, 1967); Robert Conquest, *The Great Terror* (New York: Collier Books, 1968); Robert C Tucker and Stephen F. Cohen, eds, *The Great Purge Trial* (New York: Grosset & Dunlap, 1965); J. Arch

Getty and Roberta T. Manning, *Stalinist Terror: New Perspectives* (Cambridge: Cambridge University Press, 1993), and a host of other works that provide details and theories about the purges.

On collective nervousness and the impact on ordinary people, see Veronique Garros et al, *Intimacy and Terror* (New York: The New Press, 1995).

79. In 1940 approximately 3.5 million persons toiled in labor camps and colonies. See Ivanova, *Labor Camp Socialism.* See also S. G. Wheatcroft, "The Scale and Nature of Stalinist Repression and its Demographic Significance: On Comments by Keep and Conquest," *Europe-Asia Studies,* vol. 52, no. 6, 2000, pp. 1145, 1148. For older estimates see J. Arch Getty, Gabor T. Rittersporn, Viktor N. Zemskov, "Victims of the Soviet Penal System in the Pre-war Years: A First Approach on the Basis of Archival Evidence," *The American Historical Review,* vol. 98, no. 4, 1993, p. 1020. The statistical analysis is impressive but the chronology is mistaken, World War II having begun in 1939. On life in the camps see also Veronica Shapovalov, *Remembering the Darkness* (Lanham, Boulder: Rowman and Littlefield, 2001).

80. Some historians have emphasized that the regime needed to find scapegoats for failures to fulfill quotas ordained by the Plan. For example, S. Tsakunov emphasized that executives in the Commissariat of Finance were blamed for problems obviously beyond their control. S. Tsakunov, "The People's Commissariat of Finance" in Rees, *Decision-making in the Stalinist Command Economy*, 91-92. Rees noted that executives in the Commissariat of Transport defended themselves during the purges by citing defects in the planning process and blaming its main architects— Gosplan, and the Commissariat of Heavy Industry—for the problems for which railway executives were being held responsible. E. A. Rees, "The People's Commissariat of Transport (Railways)," in ibid., p. 232.

81. Cited in ibid., p. 225.

82. Roberta T. Manning, "The Soviet Economic Crisis of 1936-1940 and the Great Purges," in Getty and Manning, *Stalinist Terror: New Perspectives,* pp. 116-141.

83. RGAE, f. 871, op. 2, d. 39, l. 3 ob.

84. RGAE, f. 871, op. 2, d. 39, l. 13.

85. RGAE, f. 871, op 2, d. 39, l. 5 ob.

86. MS, History of Dorogomilovskii Factory, p.3.

87. RGAE, f. 8009, op. 20, d. 211, ll. 1-12.

88. See also the Akrikhin Website, www.akrikhin.ru. "Farmatsevticheskaia promyshlennost': v Vokhimfarme," *Farmatsiia i farmakologiia,* no. 7, 1937, p. 42, presented slightly different figures, claiming that Akrikhin increased from 3,663 kilograms to 9,600 kilograms in the first two years with a price in 1937 of 1,250 rubles per kilogram.

89. Afanas'ev et al, *Zhivi, "Akrikhin," !* pp. 30-32.

90. GARF, f. 8009. op. 2, d. 74, ll. 6-12

91. Roger R. Reese, *Stalin's Reluctant Soldiers* (Lawrence: University Press of Kansas, 1996), pp. 132-141, see especially chart on page 134.

92. GARF, f. 482, op. 51, d. 3, l. 4 (*Glavnoe aptechnoe upravlenie narkomzdrava RSFSR, otchet . . . 1937).*

93. Davies, "Industry," in Davies, Harrison and Wheatcroft, *The Economic Transformation of the Soviet Union,* p. 151.
94. Advertisements : Machine from Robert Liebau, Chemnitz, Germaniia for making salves and "Mikrorota"—New in 1937 for making ampules from Deutsche Rotawerke, Aachen, Germaniia. End paper *Farmatsiia i farmakologiia,* no. 2, 1937. It was noted that all imports were made through the monopoly on foreign trade—i.e., the Commissariat of Foreign Trade.
95. "Vneshnaya torgovlya SSSR, 1935"; "Statistika vneshnei torgovli SSSR, 1936"; "Statistika vneshnei torgovli SSSR 1937," NAUSA, RG 487, Box 82, 11, 100, BFDC, U.S . Dept. of Commerce. The Table follows:

	1935		1936		1937 (9 months)	
	Export Kg/Rubles	Import Kg/Rubles	Export Kg/Rubles	Import Kg/Rubles	Export Kg/Rubles	Import Kg/Rubles
X-ray Apparatus	676/1,000	16,340/86,000	1,422/15,000	15,773/835,000	633/7,300	11,585/303,000
Other Electro-Medical Equipment	—	666/8,000	1,085/2,000	3,618/106,000	—	3,805/125,000
Medical Surgical Instruments	8,727/26,000	4,672/45,000	8,167/57,000	21,316/267,000	4,762/56,000	8,531/173,000
Orthopedic Apparatus	—	11/500	—	—	—	41/4,000
Safety Apparatus	1,967/1,000	357/3,000	510/2,000	8,343/39,000	—	1,572/19,000
Pharmaceutical Products (Tons/Rubles)	395/773,000	133/2,236,000	501/4,107,000	187/5,967,000	202/2,817,000	37/1,488,000

96. "Soviet Exports and Imports of Pharmaceutical Products, Table IV," NAUSA, RG 489, Box 82, 10,300, BFDC, U.S. Dept. of Commerce.
97. See Table above.
98. "Imports of Santonin in 1933 Increase Sharply," p. 10, overleaf of "Chemical and Trade Notes: Development of the Pharmaceutical Industry in the USSR," NAUSA, RG 489, Box 82, 10,300, BFDC, U.S. Dept. of Commerce.
99. Kanevskii, " O gotovykh lekarstvennykh formakh," p. 13
100. Zelikin, *Za kachestvo eksportnykh medikamentov,* pp. 11-29, 36-48.
101. F. Satsyperov and I. Murav'ev, *Za kachestvo eksportnogo lekarstvenno-tekhnicheskogo syr'ia,* Moscow, Leningrad, Vneshtorgizdat, 1933, pp. 19-25, 47-48, 52-73.

102. Zelikin, *Za kachestvo,* p. 8.
103. For example, 405 tons of "medicinal roots and tubers" were exported in 1935 and 366 tons in 1936; 726 tons of "medicinal bark" were exported in 1935, 418 tons in 1936, and 797 tons in 1937; 100 tons of "nux vomica" were exported in 1935; 604 tons of "other medicinal seeds and fruit" were exported in 1935, dipping to 98 tons in 1936 and to 57 tons in 1937; 25 tons of ergot were exported in 1935 and 28 tons in 1936. Medicinal herbs, leaves and buds were counted separately. Leaves amounted to 158 tons in 1935 and 137 tons in 1936. Exports of medicinal herbs amounted to 77 tons in 1935, but fell to 26 tons in 1936 and to 9 tons in 1937. Exports of buds amounted to 25 tons in 1935 but to only 7 and 2 tons respectively in 1936 and 1937. "Soviet Exports and Imports of Pharmaceutical Products, Table III and Table IV," NAUSA, RG 489, Box 82, 10,300, BFDC, U.S. Dept. of Commerce.
104. Zelikin, *Za kachestvo,* p. 9. Absolute figures of these items were: salicylate preparations—2,065 kilograms in 1930 (to 19,650 in 1932); 562 kilograms of iodide salts in 1930 to 2,000 kilograms in 1932; a modest 100 kilograms of chloroform in 1930 to 5,814 kilograms in 1932; 740 kilograms of bromide salts in 1930 to 3,320 kilograms in 1932.
105. Zelikin, *Za kachestvo,* pp. 8-9, 46.
106. *Chemical Goods,* Soyuzpromexport, Moscow, n. d., p. 4, no. 13.
107. RGAE, f. 871, op. 2, d. 11, l. 57.
108. Fifteen and 19 tons of resoursin were imported, respectively, in 1935 and 1936. "Soviet Exports and Imports of chemical Products and Preparations, Table V," NAUSA, RG489, Box 82, 10,300, BFDC, U.S. Dept of Commerce.
109. RGAE, f. 871, op. 2, d. 38, ll. 9, 11.
110. "Soviet Exports and Imports of Pharmaceutical Products, Table III and Table IV," NAUSA, RG 489, Box 82, 10,300, BFDC, U.S. Dept. of Commerce.
111. RGAE, f. 871, op. 2, d. 11, l. 56.
112. RGAE, f. 871, op. 2, d. 38, l. 37.

	1934	**1935**
Plazmotsid	2,854 kilograms	8,087 kilograms
Novocaine	909 kilograms	1,784 kilograms
Liuminal	253 kilograms	2,287 kilograms
Tripan-Blue	10 kilograms	344 kilograms

113. RGAE, f. 871, op. 2, d. 38, l. 7.
114. RGAE, f. 8009, op. 20, d. 211, ll. 8 and 12. In 1937 costs for producing Akrikhin were lower than the plan by 18.4 million rubles. In 1938 costs per ton of producing Akrikhin were only 392 thousand rubles versus 426.1 ordained by the plan. Cost in 1938 were 22.3 million rubles lower than in 1937. (l. 12)
115. RGAE, f. 871, op. 2, d. 39, ll. 4ob, 5, 12.
116. "Farmatsevticheskaia promyshlennost': v Vokhimfarme," *Farmatsiia i farmakologiia,*

no. 7, 1937, p. 42.

117. Ibid., pp. 42-43. Sergozin, listed in the list of "new products" in *Farmatsiia i farmakologiia*, no. 2, 1937, p. 41, had been listed in "Otchety i korrespondetsii," *Khimiko-farmatsevticheskaia promyshlennost'*, 1933, p. 181.

118. A. A. Miazdrikova, "Vliianie iokhimbina na spetsificheskoe deistvie follikulina," *Farmakologii i toksikologiia*, vol. 2, no. 5, 1939, p. 98.

119. "Farmatsevticheskaia promyshlennost': v Vokhimfarme," *Farmatsiia i farmakologiia*, no.2, 1937, p. 41.

120. Reuben and Wittcoff, *Pharmaceutical Chemicals in Perspective*, p. 117.

121. John E. Lesch, "The Discovery of M & B 693 (Sulfapyridine)," in Gregory J. Higby and Elaine C. Stroud, eds., *The Inside story of Medicines: A Symposium* (Madison, WI: American Institute of the History of Pharmacy, 1997), pp. 101-110.

122. F. I. Berezantsev, "Khronika: I Ukrainiskii s" ezd dermato-venerologov, Kiev 25-30 sentiabria 1938 g.," *Farmakologiia i toksikologiia*, vol. 2, no. 1, 1939, pp. 109-111.

123. RGAE, f. 871, op. 2, d. 39, ll. 7,8,9. In absolute terms 543.1 tons of salicylic acid sublimate were called for and only 364.7 produced; 200 tons of aspirin were called for and only 156.7 produced, 135 tons of sodium salicylate were called for and only 90 produced. The capacities of each product, respectively, were 572.6, 326.2, 144 tons. The capacity of narcotic ether was based on projections of "increased capacity of packaging, which was not done." The Karpov factory's capacity was 163.8 tons, the 1937 plan called for 100 tons, only 84.4 were produced. The capacity for caustic soda at Karpov was 337.1 tons, the plan called for 175 tons, only 78.4 were produced. Quinine hydrochloric was "limited by raw materials (imported)." The 1937 plan for Phenacetin was "on the level of need."

124. RGAE, f. 871, op. 2, d. 39, l. 16. In absolute terms, the plan called for 319 tons of disinfecting substances; only 241.7 were produced in 1937 compared with 271.4 in 1936. The plan called for 160 tons of technical iodine, 303 tons of technical bromine, and 386.4 tons of "various chemical products"; 114.45, 187.9 and 323.1 tons were produced, respectively.

125. GARF, f. A482, op. 51, d. 3, ll. 17, 18

126. RGAE, f. 871, op. 2, d. 39, l. 36.

127. RGAE, f. 8009, op. 2, d. 3, ll. 5, 34, 35, 37, 38, 40, 41, 43, 89. In some cases the problem was inadequate raw materials. These were massive: 430 tons of phenol required and 308 tons received; 2,600 tons of bisulfate required and 1,843 tons received; 12,000 tons of sulfuric acid called for and only 9,680 received; 340 tons of salicylic acid expected and, mercifully, only slightly less--330 tons-- received. But transportation inefficiencies and other economic dysfunctions also caused problems.

128. In the Eleventh US Pharmacopoeia of 1936, for example, "natural products"—botanical raw materials—were covered by 15 and a half percent of the articles. In the Seventh Soviet Pharmacopoeia of 1937, on the other hand, "natural products" —botanical raw materials—were addressed by over 20 percent of the articles. Conversely, "preparations of organic chemistry" were accorded a little over 22 percent of the articles in the Soviet Pharmacopoeia of 1937, whereas these products

received 30 percent of coverage in the US Pharmacopoeia of 1936. Preparations of inorganic chemistry were accorded about the same percentage of articles in both pharmacopoeias—14 percent in the American Pharmacopoeia and about 16 percent for the Soviet Pharmacopoeia. Hormone (Organo) preparations and vitamins were covered in over two percent of the articles in the US Pharmacopoeia as were serums and vaccines. These same items, however, were addressed by only one-half a percent of the articles and one-third a percent of articles, respectively, in the Soviet Pharmacopoeia. Galenical and "prepared forms" of medicine were covered by over 34 percent of the articles in the Soviet Pharmacopoeia, whereas only 30 percent of the articles covered these items in the US Pharmacopoeia. M. Kh. Bergol'ts, "Galenovye preparaty v novykh izdaniiakh farmakopei (XII) i national'nogo fomuliara (VII) SShA," *Farmatsiia,* vol. 8, no. 6, 1945, p. 36 and Bergol'ts, "Osnovnye puti razvitiia galenovogo proizvodstva SSSR," *Farmatsiia,* vol. 8, no. 4, 1945, p. 18.

Products of European houses were noted in *Sovetskaia farmatsiia*--for example, B. Kulakovskii, "Obzor novykh sredstv za 1933 g.," ibid, vol. 4, no. 2, 1933, pp. 29-35, discussed and analyzed the makeup of new German products.

Conclusion

1. Speech of I. A. Obergard to the All Union Institute of Experimental Medicine "O planirovanii farmatseticheskoi nauki," *Farmatsiia i farmakologiia,* no. 3, 1937, pp. 27-31.
2. "Pervaia vsesoiuznaia konferentsiia farmakologov i toksikologov, 1-5 iunia 1937 g.," *Farmakologiia,* vol. 1, no. 1, 1938, pp. 84-85.
3. The author visited the revived Ferrein (Bryntsalov) Factory near Moscow in June 1993. A special thanks to its owner, V. Bryntsalov, who personally authorized our tour of the facilities, which were still in the process of restoration, and arranged for lunch in his private dining room. On July 4, 2003, the author and her husband toured the impressive new facilities of the Akrikhin Factory, replete with state-of-the- art Italian equipment, in the village of Staraia Kupavna near Moscow. Special thanks to Dr. Tatiana Robakidze, Chief of the Department of Foreign Relations at Akhrikhin; Historian V. K. Afanas'ev; and other members of the Akrihkin team who enlightened us on the history of the factory, graciously showed my husband and myself the facilities and the enterprise museum, and treated us to a lovely dinner. Of course our thanks go also to Akrihhin CEO Dr. Ivan I. Tyulyaev, who authorized our visit.
4. See, for example Murray Feshbach, et al, *Russia's Health and Demographic Crises: Policy implications and Consequence* (Chemical and Biological Arms Control Institute, 2003) and the recent conference of the Association for the study of Health and Demography in the Former Soviet Union, including biographies of participants. at www.wcfia.harvard.edu/conferences/demography/biographies.asp, accessed May 12, 2005.

Bibliography

Primary Sources

Archival Sources

Gosudarstvennyi Arkhiv Rossiiskoi Federatsii (GARF) (Moscow)
Fond A 482, opis' 5, dela: 3, 12, 13
Fond, 482, opis' 12, delo 7
Fond, 482, opis' 51, dela : 1, 3, 5, 15
Fond 8009, opis' 2, delo 74

Rossiiskii gosudarstvennyi arkhiv economiki (RGAE) (Moscow)
Fond 871, opis' 1, delo 28
Fond 871, opis' 2, dela: 11, 38, 39
Fond 871, opis' 3, dela: 3, 4, 11, 13, 15, 16, 17, 19, 20, 30, 37, 56, 92, 93, 96, 104, 106, 107
Fond 8009, opis' 2, dela: 3, 36, 39, 126
Fond 8009, opis' 20, dela: 170, 211
Fond 8126, opis' 1, dela: 1, 3, 18, 26,
Fond 8140, opis' 1, dela: 1, 6, 19, 24, 28, 29, 30, 34
Fond 8551, opis' 1, dela: 4, 5, 11

Tsentral'nyi gosudarstvennyi istoricheskii arkhiv, Respublika Bashkortostana (TsGIA RB) (Ufa)
Fond 1203, opis' 2 , dela : 1, 13, 14, 17
Fond 1203, opis' 1, dela: 1, 2, 15, 20, 35
Fond 1205, opis' 1, delo 20
Fond (R) 443, opis' 1, dela: 66, 258, 317, 474, 478, 493, 494, 496, 497
Fond (R) 444, opis' 1, dela: 315, 316, 317, 317a
Fond (R) 1911, opis' 1

Archives of the American Medical Association (Chicago)

National Archives, United States of America (NAUSA), U.S. Department of Commerce, Bureau of Foreign and Domestic Commerce
File 231, RG 151
File 231, Box 1004
File RG 489 Box 82 10, 300; 10,700; 10,900; 11, 100.

Manuscripts

"Istoriia Zavoda" (History of the Dorogomilovskii Factory) Typescript located in Dorogomilovskii Factory Archives)

Books and Pamphlets

Akts. O-vo "Gosmedtorgprom": *Gosudarstvennyi khimiko-farmatsevticheskii zavod imeni L. Ia. Karpova*. Moscow, 1926.

Gourtschin, Daniel. *Apercu istorique du development general de la pharmacie en Russie, et en particulier de la "Pharmacie Ferrein," fondee sous le regne de Pierre le Grande en 1701*. Moscow, 1910

Arzneistoffe, Drugs and Medicines, Drogues. Moscow, n. d. 1930-1933 ?

Borodin, George. *Red Surgeon*. London: Museum Press, Ltd., 1944.

Biulleten' po obmenu opytom: "Zavod Akrikhin," no. 1-2 , Narkomzdrav USSR, 1940.

Chemical Goods. Moscow: Soyuzpromexport, n. d. 1930–1933?

Constitution (Fundamental Law) of the Union of Soviet Socialist Republics. Moscow: Progress Publishers, 1972 (slightly changed from 1936)

Farmatsevticheskoe Aktsionernoe obshchestvo "Ferein/Ferane." Moscow, 1991.

Fokin, L. F. *Obzor khimicheskoi promyshlennosti v Rossii* Petrograd, 1921.

Illiustrirovannyi torgovo-promyshlennyi adresnyi al'bom g. Moskvy na 1909. Moscow, 1910.

Keller, R. R. *Pravda po odnomu obshchestvennomu voprosu*. Moscow, 1898.

Khimicheskoe delo v Rossii. Odessa: Tipografiia "Poriadok," 1913.

Kratkii ocherk deiatel'nosti glavnoi Khimicheskoi i farmatsevticheskoi kontory Gostorga "Khimfarmtorg." Moscow, 1926.

Kratkii ocherk deiatel'nosti "Gosmedtorgproma." Moscow, February, 1927.

Kratkii otchet o rabote Akts. O-va "Gosmedtorgprom" za 1927-28 op. god. Moscow, 1929.

Kratkii otchet o rabote "Gosmedtorgproma" za 1924/25 god. Moscow, 1926.

Kratkii otchet o rabote Gosmedtorgproma za 1925/26 operats. god. Moscow, 1927.

Kratkii otchet o rabote Gosmedtorgprom za oktiabr'–iiun' 1926–27 oper. god. Moscow: Izdanie gosmedtorgprom, 1927.

Levinshtein, I. *Materialy po farmatsevticheskomu obrazovaniiu*. Moscow: Gosudarstvennoe izdatel'stvo, 1922.

_____ *Materialy po profess.-tekhnicheskomu obrazovaniiu*. Moscow: Gosudarstvennoe izdatel'stvo, 1921.

_____, ed. V.S.N. Kh: *Gosudarstvennoe upravlenie ob"edinenymi moskovskimi khimiko-farmatsevtich. zavodami, Farmatrest. Ukazatel' predpriatii i tovarnyi katalog*. Moscow, 1922.

Materialy vsesoiuznoi konferentsii po khimizatsii narodnogo khozaistva S.S.S.R. vo 2-m piatiletii. Moscow: Goskhimizdat, leningradskoe otdelenie, 1932.

Monteverde, N. A.; Monteverde, N. N.; Obergard, A.; Shass E. Iu., et al. Sev. Zap. Oblastnaia torgovaia palata: Biuro lekarstvennii, *Lekarstvennoe promyshlennoe syr'e (Rukovodstvo po standartizatsii)* . Leningrad, 1927.

Narkomtorg SSSR "Lekteksyr'e": *Informationnyi biulleten'*, no. 1-5, 1930.

Neal, E. Virgil and Moore, John H. *Modern Illustrative Banking*. New York: American Book Company, 1902, 1904.

Newsholme, Arthur and Kingsbury, John Adams. *Red Medicine: Socialized Health in Soviet Russia*. New York: Doubleday Doran and Co., Inc., 1934.

Optovyi Preis-kurant tovarov firmennoi zadel'ki Moskovskago tsentral'nago optovago sklada fabrichno-torgovago Tovarishchestva "R. Keler i Ko. v Moskve. Moscow, 1914.

Platen, M. *Novyi sposob lecheniia: nastol'naia kniga dlia zdorovykh i bol'nikh*. (Trans. from the German). St. Petersburg: Tipo-litografiia Aktionernago O-va "Samoobrazovanie," 1901.

Preis-kurant, Oskar Getling, July 1914

Porai-Koshits, A.E. *K voprosu o sudbe krasochnoi promyshlennosti*. Petrograd: Tip.T-va "Pechatnoe Slovo," 1918.

Russian Catgut: Every Strand Guaranteed. Moscow: Lektechsyrio [sic] Corporation, n. d. 1930–1933?

Sage, X. Lamotte. *Hypnotism As It Is*. Rochester, NY: National Publishing Company, 1899.

Shass, E. Iu. *Gosudarstvennyi standart eksportnogo lekarstvennogo i lekarstvenno tekhnicheskogo syr'ia*. Offitsialnyi tekst. Moscow: Narkomtorg USSR, 1927.

Shass, E. Iu. and Satsyperov, F. A. *Lekarstvennye i lekarstvenno-tekhnicheskie rasteniia SSSR: Sbor, kul'tura, pererabotka i eksport*. Moscow, 1927.

Shiutte, S. Ia. and E. Iu. Shass, *Gosudarstvennyi Standart eksportnogo lekarstvennogo i lekarstvenno-tekhnicheskogo syr'ia offitsial'nyi tekst s prilozheniiami, sostavlennymi direktorom Khimicheskogo Direktora S. Ia. Shiutte i gosudarstvennym brakerom po leksyr'iu E. Iu. Shass*. Moscow: Narkomtorg SSSR, 1927.

Sigerist, Henry. *Socialized Medicine in the Soviet Union*. New York: W. W. Norton, 1937

_____ *Medicine and Health in the Soviet Union*. New York: The Citadel Press, 1947.

Scott, John. *Beyond the Urals*. Cambridge, MA.: The Riverside Press, 1942.

Tchernavin, Vladimir V. *I Speak for the Silent*. Boston, New York: Hale, Cushman and Flint, 1935.

The Dispensatory of the United States of America. Philadelphia and London: J. B. Lippencott Company, 1918

The Pharmacopoeia of the United States of America. Tenth Decennial Revision. Philadelphia: J. B. Lippincott Company, 1926.

Tsypkin. M. V. *O fabrikakh, zavodakh i laboratoriiakh izgotovliaiushchikh khimicheskie produkty i khimiko-farmatsevticheskie preparaty v Rossii*. Moscow, 1915.

Vneshnaya torgovlya SSSR, 1935; Statistika vneshnei torgovli SSSR, 1936; Statistika vneshnei torgovli SSSR 1937.

V.S.N.Kh., Farmatrest: *Khimiko-Farmatsevticheskii zavod imeni N. A. Semashko, byvsh. Fabr. Torg. T-vo "R. Keler I Ko v Moskve": Optovyi Preis-kurant*. Moscow, November, 1923.

Zelikin, I. S. *Za kachestvo eksportnykh medikamentov*. Moscow, Leningrad: Vneshtorgizdat, 1933.

Journals and Selected Articles

Imperial

Farmatevticheskii trud, 1907.
Farmatsevticheskii zhurnal, 1908,

Soviet

Biulleten' Khimiko-farmatsevticheskogo instituta, 1930, 1931.
Farmakologiia , 1938
Farmakologiia i toksikologiia, 1938-1947
Farmatsiia, 1938-1946, 1979-1985
Farmatsiia i farmakologiia, 1937, 1938
Farmatevticheskii zhurnal, (Kharkov, Ukrainian SSR) 1928
Khimiko-farmatsevticheskaia promyshlennost', 1932, 1933, 1934, 1935.
Khimiko-farmatsevticheskii zhurnal, 1924, 1927-1930
Khimiko-farmatsevticheskii vestnik (Odessa), 1926.
Sovetskaia farmatsiia, 1930-1935
Vestnik farmatsii, 1924, 1930
Vserosiiskii Farmatsevticheskii Vestnik, 1923

Foreign

New York Herald, January 1 –May 30, 1917

"Bor'ba s malariei i osnova ee profilaktiki," *Mediko-farmatevticheskii zhurnal* Odessa, 1923.

Natradze, A. G., "Zadachi khimiko-farmatsevticheskoi promyshlennoisti v 1945 g.," *Farmatsiia* , vol. 8, no. 1, 1945, pp. 12-13.

Rabinovich, A. "Nasha Tribuna: Ob ispol'zovanii nekotorykh prirodnykh bogatstv Ukrainy," Khimiko-farmatsevticheskii vestnik (Odessa), no. 3-4, 1926, pp.

Voroshilov, N. "Hydrastis candensis L. Kanadskii zheltokoren', zolotaia pechat'," *Khimiko-farmatsevticheskii zhurnal,* no. 2 (5), 1924, pp.

Wilbur, Lyman D. "Surveying Through Khoresm: A Journey Into Parts of Asiatic Russia Which Have Been Closed to Western Travelers Since the World War," *The National Geographic Magazine* , vol. XLI, no. 6, 1932.

Reference Works

Davies, R. W. *Soviet Economic Development from Lenin to Khrushchev.* Cambridge: Cambridge University Press, 1998.

Davies, R. W.; Harrison, Mark; and Wheatcroft. *The Transformation of the Soviet Union, 1913-1945.* Cambridge: Cambridge University press, 1994.

Davis, Christopher and Feshbach, Murray. *Rising InfantMortality in the U.S.S.R. in the 1970s.* U.S. Department of Commerce series P-95, no. 74, 1980.

Feshbach, Murray and Friendly, Alfred. *Ecoside in the USSR: Health and Nature Under Siege.* New York: basic Books—Harper-Collins, 1992.

_____ *Russia's Health and Demographic Crises: Policy Implications.* Chemical and Biological Arms Control Institute, 2003.

Field, Mark G. *Soviet Socialized Medicine*. New York: The Free Press. London: Collier-Macmillan, Ltd. 1967.

_____ "Some Problems of Soviet Medical Practice: A Sociological Approach," *The New England Journal of Medicine*, vol. 248, 1953, pp. 919-926.

George, Vic and Manning, Nick. Socialism, Social Welfare and the Soviet Union. London: Routledge & Kegan Paul, 1980.

Golovin, N. N. The Russian Army in World War I. New Haven: Yale University Press, 1931.

Kaser, Michael. *Health Care in the Soviet Union and Eastern Europe*. Boulder, CO: Westview Press and London: Croom Helm, 1976.

Khaziev, R. A. *"Poslednie iz mogikan: krasnye kuptsy epokhi NEPa": Materialy i dokumenty ob ural'skikh kommersantakh, 1921–1928 godov.* Ufa: Bashkirskii gosudarstvennyi universitet, 2003.

Lorimer, Frank. *The Population of the Soviet Union: History and Prospects*. Geneva: League of Nations, 1946.

Nove, Alec, "Social Welfare in the USSR," *Problems of Communism*. United States information agency, vol. 9, 1960, pp. 1-10.

_____ *An Economic History of the U.S.S.R*. London: Penguin Press, First Edition, 1960; last reprint, 1990.

Reuben, Bryan G. and Wittcoff, Harold A. *Pharmaceutical Chemicals in Perspective*. New York: John Wiley & Sons, 1989.

Seton-Watson, Hugh. *The Russian Empire, 1801-1917*. Oxford: The Clarendon Press, 1967.

Siatinia, M. L. *Istoriia farmatsii: Navchal'nii posibnik dlia vishchikh navchal'nikh zakladie*. L'viv, 2002.

Smirnov, E. I., Chief Editor. *Opyt sovetskoi meditsiny v velikoi otechestvennoi voine, 1941–1945 gg*. 35 volumes. Moscow: Medgiz, 1951–1955.

Interviews about Soviet Health Care

Avrashov, Lee. November 2003

Avrashov, Alexander. May 2005.

Binevich, Vladimir. June 2003.

Bryntsalov, V. June 1993.

Falkovich, Esfir. 2003.

Finkelstein, Lucy. June 2003.

Gershteyn, Liubov. 2003, 2004.

Peschansky, Valentin and Marina. Fall 2004.

Salo, Viktor Matveevich and Lydiia Petrovna. 1989-1996

Staff, Akrikhin Pharmaceutical Factory, Moscow, July 2003.

Wagner, Wence, grandson of Vladimir Karlovich Ferrein, Chicago, 1994.

Secondary Sources

Books

Afanas'ev, V. k., et al. eds, *Zhivi, Akrikhin!* Staraia Kupavna, Russia, 1996.

Amdan, Rolv Petter; Sogner, Kurt. *Wealth of Contrasts: Nyegaard & Co.: A Norwegian Pharmaceutical Company, 1874-1985*. (Ad Notam Gyldendal, 1994)

Aves, Jonathan. Workers Against Lenin: *Labour Protest and the Bolshevik Dictatorship*. London: New York: Tauris Academic Studies, 1996.

Bailes, Kendall. *Technology and Society under Lenin and Stalin*. Princeton: Princeton University Press, 1978.

Ball, Alan M. *And Now My Soul is Hardened: Abandoned Children in Soviet Russia, 1918-1930*. Berkeley, Los Angeles, London: University of California Press, 1994.

_____ *Russia's Last Capitalists: The NEPmen, 1921-1929*. Berkeley: University of California Press, 1987.

Banerji, Arup. *Merchants and Markets in Revolutionary Russia, 1917-30*. Basingstoke: Macmillan; New York: St. Martin's Press, 1997.

Becker, Seymour. *Russia's Protectorates in Central Asia*. Cambridge, MA: Harvard University Press, 1968.

Burgin, Diana Lewis. *Sophia Parnok: The Life and Work of Russia's Sappho*. New York: New York University Press, 1994.

Clark , Roscoe Collins. *Threescore Years and Ten: A Narrative of the First Seventy* Years *of Eli Lilly and Company, 1876-1946*. (Privately printed, 1946)

Conquest, Robert. *Harvest of Sorrow*. New York: Oxford University press, 1994.

Conroy, Mary Schaeffer. *In Health and In Sickness: Pharmacy, Pharmacists and the Pharmaceutical Industry in Late Imperial, Early Soviet Russia*. Boulder: East European Monographs, 1994.
This book contains many primary sources for the first three chapters of the current manuscript. They are not repeated in those chapters, because readers can consult this published work. Only new primary and secondary sources are included in these chapters and this bibliography.

Davenport-Hines, R. P. T. and Slinn, Judy. *Glaxo: A History to 1962*. Cambridge: Cambridge University Press, 1992.

Davies, Sarah. *Popular Opinion in Stalin's Russia: Terror, Propaganda and Dissent, 1934-1941*. Cambridge: Cambridge University Press, 1997.

Elmslie, W. P. *Fifty Years of Livestock Research. Illustrated By the growth of the research program of the Moorman Manufacturing Company*. Hannibal, Missouri: 1970.

Filtzer, Donald. *Soviet Workers and late Stalinism: Labour and the Restoration of the Stalinist System after World War II*. Cambridge: Cambridge University press, 2002.

Fitzpatrick, Sheila. *Everyday Stalinism*. Oxford: Oxford University Press, 1999.

_____ *Stalin's Peasants*. New York Oxford University Press, 1994.

Foust, Clifford M. *Rhubarb: The Wondrous Drug*. Princeton: Princeton University Press, 1992.

Friedgut, Theodore H. *Iuzhovka and Revolution*. Vol I and Vol. II. *Politics and Revolution in Russia's Donbass, 1869-1924*. Princeton: Princeton University Press, 1924.

Gatrell, Peter. *A Whole Empire Walking: Refugees in Russia during World War I*. Bloomington: Indiana University Press, 1999.

_____ *Government, Industry and Rearmament in Russia, 1900-1914*. Cambridge: Cambridge University Press, 1994.

Galambos, Louis with Jane Eliot Sewell. *Networks of Innovation: Vaccine Development at Merck, Sharp & Dohme, and Mulford, 1895-1995*. Cambridge: Cambridge University Press, 1995.

Getty, Arch J. and Manning, Roberta T., eds., *Stalinist Terror: New Perspectives*. Cambridge: Cambridge University press, 1993.

Gregory, Paul. *Before Command*. Princeton: Princeton University Press, 1994.

Haller, John S. Jr. *Medical Protestants: The Eclectics in American Medicine, 1825-1939*. Carbondale: Southern Illinois University Press, 1994.

Hefsler, Julie. *A Social History of Soviet Trade*. Princeton: Princeton University Press, 2004.

Heywood, Anthony. *Modernizing Lenin's Russia: Economic Reconstruction, Foreign Trade and the Railways*. Cambridge: Cambridge University Press, 1999.

Higby, Gregory H. and Stroud, Elaine C., eds. *The Inside Story of Medicines: A Symposium*. Madison, WI: American Institute of the History of Pharmacy, 1997.

Holquist, Peter. *Making War; Forging Revolution: Russia's Continuum of Crisis, 1914-1921*. Cambridge, MA: Harvard University Press. 2002.

Hunter, Holland and Szyrmer, Janusz M. *Faulty Foundations: Soviet Economic Policies, 1928-1940*. Princeton: Princeton University Press, 1992.

Hutchinson, John F.. *Politics and Public Health in Revolutionary Russia, 1890-1918*. Baltimore and London: The Johns Hopkins University Press, 1990.

Ivanova, Galina Mikhailovna. *Labor Camp Socialism: The Gulag in the Soviet Totalitarian System*. Armonk, NY: M. E. Sharpe, 2000.

Jahn, Hubertus. *Patriotic Culture in Russia during World War I*. Ithaca and London: Cornell University press, 1995.

Kahn, Roger. *A Flame of Pure Fire: Jack Dempsey and the Roaring '20s*. New York: Harcourt Brace & Company, 1999.

Khaziev, Rustem A. *Gosudarstvennoe administrirovanie ekonomiki i rynok v 1917-1921 gg*. Ufa: Ministerstvo Obrazovaniia Rossiiskoi Federatsii. Bashkirskii gosudarstvennyi universitet, 2000.

Kingston-Mann. *Lenin and the Problem of Marxist Peasant Revolution*. New York: Oxford University Press, 1985.

Klehr, Harvey; Haynes, John Earl; Anderson, Kyrill M. *The Soviet World of American Communism*. New Haven and London: Yale University Press, 1998.

Klehr, Harvey; Haynes, John Earl; Firson, Fridrikh Igorevich. *The Secret World of American Communism*. New Haven: Yale University Press, 1995.

Knight, Amy. *Who Killed Kirov?* New York: Hill and Wang, 1999.

Kobrak, Christopher. *National Cultures and International Competition: The Experience of Schering AG, 1851-1950*. Cambridge: Cambridge University Press, 2002.

Krementsov, Nikolai. *Stalinist Science*. Princeton: Princeton University press, 1997.

_____ *The Cure: the Story of Cancer and Politics from the Annals of the Cold War*. Chicago and London: University of Chicago Press, 2002.

Lefkowith, Christie Mayer. *The Art of Perfume: Discovering and Collecting Perfume Bottles*. New York: Thames and Hudson, Inc., 1994.

Leggett, George. *The Cheka: Lenin's Political Police*. Oxford: The Clarendon Press, 1981.

Libenau, Jonathan. *Medical Science and Medical Industry: The Formation of the American Pharmaceutical Industry*. Baltimore: The Johns Hopkins University Press, 1987.

Lih, Lars T.; Naumov, Oleg V; Khlevniuk, Oleg V. *Stalin's Letters to Molotov*. New Haven and London: Yale University Press, 1995

Litvin, A. L. *Krasnyi i belyi terror v Rossii, 1918-1922 gg*. Kazan', 1995.

Madison, James H. *Eli Lilly: A Life, 1885-1977*. Indianapolis: Indiana Historical Society, 1989.

Mann, Charles C. and Plummer, Mark L. *The Aspirin Wars: Money, Medicine and 100 Years of Rampant Competition*. New York: Alfred A. Knoff, 1991.

McAuley, Mary. *Bread and Justice: State and Society in Petrograd, 1917-1922*. Oxford: The Clarendon Press, 1991.

Menning, Bruce. *Bayonets Before Bullets: The Imperial Russian Army, 1861-1914.* Bloomington: Indiana University Press, 2000.

Millar, James R. and Linz, Susan J., eds. *The Soviet Economic Experiment*. Urbana and Chicago: University of Illinois Press, 1990.

Natradze, A. G., *Ocherk razvitiia khimiko-farmatsevticheskoi promyshlennosti SSSR*. Moscow: Izdatel'stvo "Meditsina," 1967.

Patenaude, Bertrand M. *The Big Show in Bololand: The American Relief Expedition to Soviet Russia in the Famine of 1921*. Stanford: Stanford University Press, 2002.

Pipes, Richard, ed. *The Unknown Lenin: From the Secret Archive*. New Haven and London: Yale University Press, 1996.

Rees, E. A., ed. *Decision-Making in the Stalinist Command Economy, 1932-37*. Basingstoke: Macmillan Press, Ltd.; New York: St. Martin's Press, Inc., 1997.

Remington, Thomas F. *Building Socialism in Bolshevik Russia: Ideology and Industrial Organization, 1917-1921*. Pittsburgh: University of Pittsburgh Press, 1984.

Ruud, Charles A. *Russian Entrepreneur: Publisher Ivan Sytin of Moscow, 1851-1934*. Montreal and Kingston: McGill-Queen's University press, 1990.

Shikes, Robert H. *Rocky Mountain Medicine: Doctors, Drugs and Disease in Early Colorado*. Boulder: Johnson books, 1986.

Shkliarevsky. Gennady. *Labor in the Russian Revolution: Factory Committees and Trade Unions, 1917-1918*. New York; St. Martins's Press, 1993.

Silent Witness: Russian Films since 1908-1919. British Film Institute, 1989.

Sinenko, Sergei. *Gorod nad beloi rekoi: kratkaia istoriia Ufy v ocherkakh i zarisovkakh, 1574-2000*. Ufa: gosudarstvennoe respublikanskoe izdatel'stvo "Bashkortostana," 2000.

Smele, Jonathan D. *Civil War in Siberia: The Anti-Bolshevik Government of Admiral Kolchak, 1918-1920*. Cambridge: Cambridge University press, 1996.

Solomon, Peter H. (Jr.) *Soviet Criminal Justice under Stalin*. Cambridge: Cambridge University press, 1996.

Solomon, Susan Gross and Hutchinson, John F., eds. *Health and Society in Revolutionary Russia*. Bloomington: Indiana University press, 1990.

Sonnadecker, Glenn; Cowen, David L. & Higby, Gregory, eds. *Drugstore Memories: American Pharmacists Recall Life Behind the Counter, 1824-1933*. Madison, WI:, 2002.

Stockdale, Melissa Kischke. *Paul Miliukov and the Quest for a Liberal Russia, 1880-1918*. Ithaca and London: Cornell University Press, 1996.

Stone, David R. *Hammer and Rifle: The Militarization of the Soviet Union, 1926-1933*. Lawrence: University press of Kansas, 2000.

Swain, Geoffrey. *The Origins of the Russian Civil War*. London and New York: Longman, 1996.

Swann, John P. *Academic Scientists and the Pharmaceutical Industry: Cooperative Research in Twentieth-Century America.* Baltimore and London: The Johns Hopkins University Press, 1988.

The Story of the Chemical Industry in Basle. CIBA Ltd., Olten and Lausanne: Urs Graf Publishers, 1959.

Tolz, Vera. *Russian Academicians and the Revolution: Combining Professionalism and Politics.* Basingstoke: Macmillan Press, Ltd., New York: St. Martin's Press, 1997.

Trudy Leningradskogo khimiko-farmatsevticheskogo institute, *Istoriia farmatsevticheskogo dela v Peterburge-Petrograde-leningrade.* Leningrad, 1960.

Utin, A. A. *Istoriia chimkentskogo khimiko-farmatsevticheskogo zavoda im. F. E. Dzerzhinskogo.* Chimkent: Biuro tekhnicheskoi informatsii, 1958.

Wade, Rex A. *The Russian Revolution, 1917.* Cambridge: Cambridge UniversityPress, 2000.

Weatherall, M. *In Search of a Cure.* Oxford: New York, Tokyo: Oxford University Press, 1990.

Williams, Robert C. *Russian Art and American Money, 1900-1940.* Cambridge, MA: Harvard University Press, 1980.

Williams, William Appleman. *American-Russian Relations, 1781-1947.* New York: Octogan Books, 1971.

Worthen, Dennis. *Pharmacy in World War II.* New York: Haworth press, Inc., 2004.

Yaney, George. *The Urge to Mobilize: Agrarian Reform in Russia, 1861-1930.* Urbana, Chicago, London: University of Illinois Press, 1982.

Youngblood, Denise. *Movies for the Masses.* Cambridge: Cambridge University Press, 1992.

Selected Articles and Chapters

Barnett, Vincent, "A Long Wave Goodbye: On Kondrat'ev and the Conjuncture Institute, 1920-28," *Europe-Asia Studies,* vol. 47, no. 3, pp. 413-441.

Cooper, Dale, "Adequate Controls for New Drugs," *Pharmacy in History,* vol. 44, no. 1, 2002, pp. 12-23.

Conroy, Mary Schaeffer, "Abuse of Drugs Other than Alcohol and Tobacco in the Soviet Union," *Soviet Studies* (now *Europe-Asia Studies*), vol. 42, no. 3, 1990, pp. 447-480.

_____ "Health Care in Prisons Labour and Concentration Camps in Early Soviet Russia, 1918-1921," *Europe-Asia Studies,* vol. 52, no. 7, 2000, pp. 1257-1274.

_____ "Malaria in Late Tsarist Russia," *Bulletin of the History of Medicine,* vol. 56, no. 1, 1982, pp. 41-55.

_____ "Pharmacy in Soviet Russia before the Great Patriotic War (1941-45)," *Pharmacy in History,* vol. 40, no. 1, 1998, pp. 3-24.

_____ "The Russian Pharmaceutical Industry in the Late Imperial-Early Soviet Period," in McDermott, Kevin and Morison, John, eds. *Politics and Society under the Bolsheviks.* Basingstoke: Macmillan press Ltd., 1999, pp. 13-36.

Dahlmann, Dittmar, "Liberals in the Provinces: The Kadets and the Duma Elections in Saratov, 1906-1912," in Conroy, Mary Schaeffer, ed. *Emerging Democracy in Late Imperial Russia.* Niwot, CO: University Press of Colorado, 1998

Davis, Christopher M., "Economics of Soviet Public Health, 1928-1932," in Solomon, Susan Gross and Hutchinson, John F., eds. *Health and Society in Revolutionary Russia.* Bloomington: Indiana University Press, 1990, pp. 146-172.

Ellman, Michael, "A Note on the Number of 1933 Famine Victims," *Soviet Studies,* vol. 43, no. 2, 1991, p. 375.

Ewing, Sally, "The Science and Politics of Soviet Insurance Medicine," in Solomon and Hutchinson, eds. *Health and Society in Revolutionary Russia,* cited above.

Gatrell, Peter, "The First World War and War Communism, 1914-1920," in Davies, Harrison, Wheatcroft, *TheEconomic Transformation of the Soviet Union, 1913-45* (cited above), pp. 216-237.

Goland, Yuri, "Curency Regulation in the NEP Period," *Europe-Asia Studies,* vol. 46, no. 8, 1994, pp. 1251-1296.

Harrison, "Counting Soviet Deaths in the Great Patriotic War: Comment,"*Europe-Asia Studies,* vol. 55, no. 6, 2003, pp. 939-944.

Holquist, Peter, What's so Revolutionary about the Russian Revolution? State Practices and New-Style Politics, 1914-21," in David L. Hoffman and Yanni Kotsonis, eds. *Russian Modernity: Politics, Knowledge, Practices.* Basingstoke: Macmillan Press, Ltd.; New York: St. Martin's Press, 2000, pp. 87-111.

Hutchinson, John F., "Dances with Commissars: Sigerist and Soviet Medicine," in Elizabeth Fee and Theodore M. Brown, eds, *Making Medical History: The Life and Times of Henry E. Sigerist.* Baltimore and London: The Johns Hopkins University Press, 1997, pp. 229-259.

Lesch, John E., The Discovery of M&B 693 (Sulfapyradine)," in Gregory H. Higby and Elaine C. Stroud, eds. *The Inside Story of Medicines.* Madison, WI.: American Instituteof the History of Pharmacy, 1997, pp. 101-110.

Matsuzato, Kimitaka, "Interregional Conflicts and the Collapse of Tsarism: the Real Reason for the Food Crisis in Russia After the Autumn of 1916," in Conroy, *Emerging* Democracy, pp. 243-300.

Neushul, Peter, "Science, Government, and Mass Production of Penicillin," *The* Journal *of the History of Medicine and Allied Sciences, Inc.* vol. 48, no. 4, 1993, pp. 371-395.

Parascandola, John, "From Germs to Genes: Trends in Drug Therapy, 1852-2002," *Pharmacy in History,* vol. 44, no. 1, 2002, pp. 3-11.

Porter, Thomas and Gleason, William, " The Zemstvo and the Transformation of Russian Society," in Conroy, *Emerging Democracy in Late Imperial Russia,* pp. 60-87 and "The Democratization of the Zemstvo During the First World War," ibid., pp. 228-242.

Pratt, Joan Klobe, "The Free Economic Society and the Battle Against Smallpox: A 'Public Sphere' in Action," *The Russian Review,* vol. 61, no. 4, 2002, pp. 560-578.

Ramer, Samuel C., "Traditional Healers and Peasant Culture in Russia, 1861-1917," in Esther Kingston-Mann and Timothy Mixter, eds. *Peasant Economy, Culture, and Politics of European Russia,* 1800-1921. Princeton: Princeton University press, 1991, pp. 207-235.

Reidl, Renate A. "A Brief History of the Pharmaceutical Industry in Basel," in Jonathan Libenau, Gregory J. Higby, and Elaine C. Stroud, eds. *Pill Peddlers: Essays on the History of the Pharmaceutical Industry.* Madison, WI: American Institute of the History of Pharmacy, 1990, pp. 49-72.

Rimmington, Anthony, "The Soviet Union's Offensive program: The Implications for Contemporary Arms Control," in Susan Wright, ed., *Biological Warfare and Disarmament: New Problems/New Perspectives*. Lanham, Boulder, New York, Oxford: Rowman and Littlefield, 2002, pp. 103-148.

Salo, Viktor Matveevich, "Diatel'nost' aptechnykh upravlenii v predvoennyi period (1936-1940 gg.," *Farmatsiia*, vol. 28, 1979, pp. 16-17.

_____ "Iz istorii farmatsevticheskoi sluzhby v gody velikoi otechestvennoi voiny," *Farmatsiia*, vol. 34, no. 2, 1985, pp. 7

_____ "Razvitie aptechnoi seti v SSSR za period 1940-1954 gg.," *Farmatsiia*, 1982.

Swann, John P. "The Evolution of the American Pharmaceutical Industry," *Pharmacy in History*, vol. 37, no. 2, 1995, pp. 76-86.

Tabor, Herbert; Tabor Celia W., and Rosenthal, Sanford M., "The Biochemistry of the Polymines: Spermidine and Spermine," *Annual Review of Biochemistry*, vol. 30, 1961, pp. 579-604.

Timberlake, Charles E. "The Tsarist Government's Preoccupation with the 'Liberal Party' in Tver' Province, 1890-1905," in Conroy, ed., *Emerging Democracy in Late Imperial Russia*, pp. 30-59.

Wheatcroft, S. G., "The Scale and Nature of Stalinist Repression and its Demographic Significance: On Comments by Keep and Conquest," *Europe-Asia Studies*, vol. 52, no. 6, 2000, pp. 1145, 1148 passim.

"Woldemar Ferrein," *Sonderabdruck ans den Berichten der Deutschen Pharmazeutischen Gesellschaft*, 1923, Heft 3, p. 163.

Electronic Sources

"Health and Demography in the States of the Former Soviet Union," Conference, Harvard, April 29-April 30, 2005,
http://www.wcfia.edu/conferences/demography/program.asp

"Phage Therapy," *Phage Biotech ltd.*, http://www.phage-biotech.com/links.html

Index

B

Q

R

V

W

X

Y

Z